SPORT PSYCHOLOGY

PSYCHOLOGICAL CONSIDERATIONS IN MAXIMIZING SPORT PERFORMANCE

EDITORS:
LINDA K. BUNKER
ROBERT J. ROTELLA
ANN S. REILLY

UNIVERSITY OF VIRGINIA
DEPARTMENT OF HEALTH AND
PHYSICAL EDUCATION

Copyright © 1985 by Linda K. Bunker, Ph.D.
Robert J. Rotella, Ph.D.
Ann Reilly, Ph.D.
Production by Sandy Sharpe
Typeset by Strehle's Computerized Typesetting, Ithaca, New York
Printed in the United States of America by McNaughton and Gunn Inc., Ann Arbor, Michigan

ISBN 0-932392-20-2

10/2/86

ACKNOWLEDGEMENTS

The authors wish to acknowledge each of the writers who have shared their papers in this text. These noted experts in the field of sport psychology have gladly donated their time and energies to help advance both the knowledge and practice of sport psychology. The structure and content of each article, as well as the accuracy of data and references were the exclusive responsibility of each author. Their contributions are gratefully acknowledged.

Manuscripts such as this are never easy to produce or edit. But with the able assistance of our secretarial staff, this task was made much easier. A special thank you to Mrs. Nina Seaman, Mrs. "Jack" Scruby, Miss. Sarah Odom, and Ms. Doris Loving who participated in the production of the final manuscript. They are the individuals who make all things possible.

And finally a special tribute to all of the athletes who have shared their triumphs and tribulations with us. They are indeed the unsung heroes. Through their openness and desire to improve, we have been able to stretch our knowledge to its ultimate place — the practice of athletics. May their lives continue to be enriched as they participate in the challenges which sport offers each of us.

Linda Bunker
Bob Rotella
Ann Reilly

"If you can imagine it
You can achieve it
If you can dream it
You can become it"
—William Arthur Ward

TABLE OF CONTENTS

SECTION I

A Direction for Sport Psychology

Julie Heyward, Charlottesville, Va.

1

Give Sport Psychology To Sport

Linda K. Bunker
University of Virginia

Richard T. McGuire
University of Missouri

Sport psychology is not for psychologists . . . Psychology is for sport and its participants. Sport psychology must be *given away* in order to enhance the value of sport participation for all individuals! Sport psychology must deliver or provide its knowledge and application regarding skilled performance to the on-line consumer because of two related issues:

1. the need to provide practical applications of psychology in order to improve the quality of performance and the meaningfulness of participation;
2. the need to compensate for the fact that there are simply not enough professionals to meet every need for psychological services related to sport.

The implications for sport psychology suggest that knowledge must be shared in order to make each performer capable of dealing with his or her own mind and body. Sport psychology must be "given away" to those who really need it. The "medical model" of treatment and return to normalcy must be combined with a focus on prevention and maximizing potential.

The problems of varsity athletics include not just the athletic and/or academic, but also the lessons learned (or not learned) by athletes about life in general. Each individual's needs for developing positive self-concepts and expanding his/her own self esteem can be facilitated by sport psychologists. Concepts of sport psychology should be shared or "given away" to normal, active athletes. Sport psychologists must however be able to distinguish between the problems of athletic performance and those which may signify a pathological condition. Sport psychologists must be prepared to work with most athletes' problems, but also know when to refer an athlete for clinical services.

While the challenges are great, it would seem that the major thrusts and efforts for those in sport psychology during the next decade must fall into three relevant areas:

1. developing strategies for delivering our message in the most efficient and effective manner to those for whom it will provide the greatest benefit — the coaches and athletes;
2. continuing with even greater determination, to promote *expansion of the body of knowledge* with which we work. The development of new and better understandings, techniques and treatments that will contribute not only to the improvement of performance, but more significantly to the quality of life in general for everyone in our athletic population must be sought;
3. the barrier must be broken in order to utilize the *value of positive public relations* and actively seek ways to sell our profession and the value of our product in the market place of athletics. It's a buyer's market and we must have a saleable product.

As idealists in the most extreme sense, the ultimate goal must be to eliminate the interventionist role of the sport psychologist. In so doing, it may be possible to develop a mass of healthy, happy and high performing athletes. Like any ideal, this is an almost impossible challenge, but still well worth our energies and our most enthusiastic efforts. Let's not put ourselves out of business. Instead, let us recognize our *place* of business.

EXPANDING THE BODY OF KNOWLEDGE

"Hard Side" of Sport Psychology. Sport psychology is founded on a body of knowledge from both the natural and social sciences of psychology. This scientific and research-based foundation for sport psychology must be acknowledged and expanded. Valuable psychological theories and techniques have been developed which now must be applied to the constant quest for the "winning edge."

There are firmly established concepts about the "body of knowledge" or competencies which provide the foundation for sport psychology. Professional guidelines for sport psychology are being actively pursued by at least three groups: (1) the Sport Psychology Academy of NASPE, (2) The North American Society for the Psychology of Sport and Physical Activity (NASPSPA), and (3) the Canadian Society for Psychomotor Learning and Sport Psychology (CSPLSP). Their efforts to identify competencies and the role of sport psychologists are of great interest to everyone involved in sport.

During 1980, NASPE undertook the development of a list of *sport* psychology competencies. The areas of identified competence may be used to reflect the nature of skills from sport psychology which are available to intercollegiate athletes and coaches, including expertise related to the ten major areas listed appropriate to intercollegiate sport.

NASPE Sport Psychology Competencies
(Straub, 1980)
1. Sport Personality
2. Altered States of Consciousness
3. Motivation
4. Anxiety and Arousal
5. Attention
6. Assertion and Aggression
7. Self Regulation of Psychological Processes
8. Sport Leadership and Cohesion
9. Humanism in Sport
10. Sexism and Racism in Sport

RESEARCH IN THE FIELD

Throughout the rather brief, twenty year or so history of activity generated specifically in sport psychology, the major forum and medium for intellectual questioning and theoretical research has been the laboratory. This method of approach is not to be belittled; in fact, it should be applauded, for the traditional paradigms and constructs have provided the stamps of validity and scientific acceptance to the many significant and useful theories, models, instruments, treatments, and understandings developed within our field. This effort should continue to be strongly encouraged.

"Soft Side" of Sport Psychology. At the same time, sport psychology should continue to answer the call of the 1970's and 80's and increase our efforts to bring research to the field. Although field research poses several problems of design, quantification and validation, this should not and must not blunt our efforts. New methods and approaches can and will be found. The science of sport psychology must be taken out into the fields, courts and tracks, and into the gyms, arenas and rinks, and there address the most pressing questions and concerns of the coaches and athletes. By doing so, *relevance* and *credibility* will be gained while expanding the opportunity for sport psychology to provide positive and useful effects on the everyday practice of sport.

The body of knowledge of sport psychology gains its significance only by its ability to be applied in real life, field settings. The application of theoretical aspects of sport psychology presents many challenges. Sport psychologists coming from physical education and coaching, as well as those emerging from clinical psychology, are now being asked to provide services to athletes and coaches (Nideffer, et al, 1980). These services require the ability to provide sound educational programs and preventive or coping skills, and to employ crises interventions, communication techniques, and a variety of therapeutic strategies.

BREAKING BARRIERS IN THE MARKETPLACE

For sport psychology and its professionals to have the greatest impact on the performance and lives of athletes the issue of marketing must be squarely addressed. Initially, a product is not sought or purchased merely because it is good or useful, but rather, only because it is *desired* by those in the market. Surely, if it proved to have value and utility later, all the better for future sales and expansion of the market. But make no mistake, the original sales comes when the public *wants* a product.

Sport psychology has a good line of products, continually being upgraded and expanded. These services possess great potential value and usefulness for athletes, coaches and their families. The challenge is to make the public *want* the product.

In this effort, there are two prevailing attitudes within the athletic community which can be observed, one working for and one against our cause. It is unfortunate in one sense, that our field carries with it the moniker of sport "psychology." Athletes in general, and intercollegiate athletes and coaches in particular, consider themselves to be rather conservative, hard working, independent, proud and healthy individuals, subscribing fervently to the sound body-sound mind ethic. Merely the mention of the words "psychology" or "psychologist" may conjure reactions of contempt and images of tragedy, "crazies," "weirdos," "nuts," and "kooks." There just does not exist a general comfortableness in enlisting the aid and services of a psychologist when you know you are not sick in the first place. Coaches and athletes may willingly and proudly proclaim that their sport is 10% physical and 90% mental! Yet let those lips be damned that would suggest there might be a place or need for a "psychologist." For us, the englightened, this is, of course, a difficult and threatening thought to accept or deal with. Nonetheless, it is a reality — a reality that can and must be changed.

At the same time, another pervasive attitude, a positive and potentially stronger attitude, also exists within the world of athletes and coaches. These men and women continually commit incredible amounts of time, energy and dedication in the effort to produce better performance and gain greater enjoyment and satisfaction in their chosen sport. The essence of their lives focuses on achievement and goal attainment. In their undying quest for the peak performance or experiences, athletes and coaches are anxiously willing to use any means that are good and that work. (Unfortunately in

some cases, willing to use *anything* that works, period — whether good, or bad, legal or illegal.)

This is the key — coaches and athletes *want* and will use new skills or approaches if they think these will help them to play better, run faster or on the bottom line for many, to *win*! We must build upon this desire to succeed, for what sport psychology has to offer athletes and coaches is good, useful, sound, and can and will offer very real possibilities for increased performance and personal satisfaction.

The time is right! The recent boom in popular books and articles dealing with mental aspects of sport participation has done much to break down the barriers. Although several of these books have come from within the ranks of our profession, many others are strictly lay productions, grounded in opinions, beliefs, "gut feelings" and unsupported by substantive research. Regardless, these writings are well received by the public and are now serving to lay a foundation for our contributions as they erase the alienation from that which is "psychological."

The opportunity at hand must be seized in order to deliver to the public meaningful materials and useful tools for dealing with the problems, questions or desires within their own sport experience. The discipline must continue to be brought out of the hallowed halls of academia, out of the laboratories and professional journals, and presented full square to the people to be served. It is here, with the athletes, coaches, and trainers, the practitioners of the athletic world, that we must firmly establish our relevance and credibility, and strive to develop an enthusiastic desire to seek and use that which sport psychology has to offer.

WHAT ARE THE PROBLEMS AND ISSUES OF INTERCOLLEGIATE ATHLETICS?

Sport and Academics. Legislating values toward quality education is virtually impossible. In fact, our legislative efforts may have undermined the very attributes we extol. For example, the NCAA stipulates that a C average qualifies a high school athlete for

6

a grant-in-aid. With grade inflation, perhaps all that does is make a poor student temporarily respectable.

If athletes, and sport psychologists in particular, value hard work, setting goals, and constructive effort, then young athletes must be helped to establish goals and pursue their attainment. If athletics is to be a part of collegiate life, young men and women must come to it with the fundamental skills to be competitive academically as well as athletically. And once in college, the system must be honest — if they must be student-athletes, they must make "normal progress" toward a degree, not merely collect courses off-grounds or through non-existent extension courses, but as students they must pursue a predefined goal, with measurable outcomes within a set time.

This is difficult because academic standards have been eroded to the point where more undereducated student athletes than ever are getting into college. Not just underprivileged young men and women who need a chance but even unqualified young people who have no chance, not even in the classroom.

Colleges have allowed their "money sports" to become farm systems for professional leagues, and have therefore allowed athletes to believe that attending "farm team" classes in college is compatible with an academic, collegiate environment. Scholastically handicapped athletes may be invited into college to pursue an impossible dream — to become one of less than two percent of the collegiate players who make it in the NFL or NBA. Most don't make it to a B.A., much less the NBA!

Whose responsibility is the athletic-academic dilemma? Probably the academic world of collegiate life. Faculty and university administrators must emphasize the goal of degree attainment — even if it means reconsidering such things as freshmen eligibility, and coach or grant-in-aid penalties for programs in which athletes do not graduate (even within five years). A subculture of ex-athletes such as in the NFL where only one of three players has a bachelor's degree, despite the fact that 97 percent attended college for at least four years has thus emerged. When an individual is cheated out of a chance for learning, the institution is also cheated out of its reason for being.

What can sport psychology do to help athletes and athletics realize that we are doing no one a favor when we make all the tough decisions for athletes? When an A.D. arranges for academic counselors who organize classes, arrange for make-up exams, type papers, and generally nurse feed athletes, who benefits? Are we doing athletes a favor by making all their decisions for them?

Athletes must learn to accept responsibility for their own behavior, both on and off court, field, slope, water, or floor. Sport psychologists can help these individuals learn the value of self direction and personal control. We can help coaches and A.D.'s protect athletes from undue stress, and also insist that athletes meet academic responsibilities and personal commitments.

Economic Influences on Sport. The economic influences of the 1980's to 1990's will provide a double edged economic sword with Title IX equality for men and women, and the influence of rampant inflation. Emphasis on the revenues and expenses of athletics rather than the institution's educational programs have caused continual problems. Scandals related to academic eligibility, point-shaving and social incentives for athletes are plentiful.

During a six-week period early in 1980, *Sports Illustrated* cited thirteen news items related to intercollegiate scandals, involving eleven universities and twenty-six athletes. The natural reaction to these items is to recommend that more restrictive, institutional rules be employed. But the danger of minimums becoming maximums or standards, is ever present.

The "everything for nothing" lure of athletics is plainly false, and is dangerous for both athletes and coaches. Some high school coaches may arrange for an eighth grader to move so he or she can switch schools. Some college coaches "run up the score" to create a super star for his or her own public relations use. Some parents "hold back" an eighth grader for another year of playing time before advancing to the higher levels.

MINOR SPORTS

The problems and issues of intercollegiate sport are not restricted to major, revenue-producing sports. Athletes who participate in gymnastics, swimming, crew, field hockey, soccer, wrestling, weightlifting, ice hockey, cross-country, etc. are also in need of our services. They suffer from anxiety, fear, academic and personal stress like most other athletes. In addition, they often suffer from lack of recognition and absence of personal glory.

Consider the conflict of minor vs. major sport! For example, during an early week in March, 1981 the University of Tennessee Women's Basketball Team won a national AIAW Tourney second place, while the men's team was defeated in the regionals of the NCAA. Similarly, at the University of Virginia, the women's track and field team won the national indoor AIAW championship, while the men's basketball team lost in the ACC post-season tournament. During that week, the Virginia Men's Basketball Team received 64 column inches of newsprint while the Women's National Champion Track and Field Team received 9.5 inches of print, including 4.5 inches of editorial columns critizing their lack of news coverage. Yet these same minor sport teams now enjoy many of the same problems and pleasures of intercollegiate athletics. Let's look at some of those issues.

RECRUITING IS A MAJOR PROBLEM

"Three breeds of recruiters exist: the piranha, the barracuda, and the great white whale." "Some take a nibble and some swallow you whole, but they all want a piece" (Sherrer, 1980). Some young recruits have suggested that the problem is so rampant that they have trouble distinguishing between honesty and lack of interest. Fortunately, sport psychologists can help athletes realize that if colleges cheat in recruiting they may also cheat the individual.

WOMEN'S ATHLETICS — SPECIAL CONCERNS

The increased involvement of women in high level intercollegiate athletics may result in the need for sport psychologists to attend to the special needs of women and of women in competition. For instance, the pressures of intense competition may be an everyday occurrence to males who have a long history of such competition, but these pressures are relatively new experiences for many women. Will the "shock wave" create different types of psychological problems in women than it has for men? We should be prepared for this possibility, and develop potential strategies for both "too far . . . too fast . . ." and the "blackboard jungle" syndrome.

The stress of competition for women may also have more observable impacts on sexuality (though probably not more dramatic) than male manifestations. For example, adolescent female athletes may suffer anxiety over athletic amenorrhea, or more properly athletic infertility. The perceived threat to femininity, though somewhat unfounded, may have dramatic effects on personal behaviors and feelings. The contribution of a sport psychologist may be crucial in this area.

The coaches of women's teams may also need to utilize the assistance of sport psychologists. Women coaches may be thrust into the limelight suddenly, and not know how to relate to the situation or to their players. What happens when the winning coach of the women's team which is ranked No. 1 in the country gets less publicity than does the men's team, even though they have a losing record?

Male coaches of women's teams might also appreciate the services of a sport psychologist for the previously mentioned reasons and/or for advice on dealing with any potential male-female differences.

COACH AND SPORT PSYCHOLOGIST CONFLICTS

If sport psychologists are to help athletes and coaches, they must recognize the potential for interpersonal conflicts. If athletes are helped to be independent and to have clear values and goals, they must also understand the potential for conflicts with their coaches and teammates.

Similarly, sport psychologists must be careful as they deal with coaches. There is a great potential for conflict when intervention techniques are not accepted, or even resisted, by coaches. Many coaches feel compelled to maintain complete control over their athletes. This feeling may cause them to be overprotective or fearful of potential undermining their interaction with athletes. Being able to work through or with coaches and athletes is perhaps the sport psychologist's most critical personal skill.

BURN-OUT: ATHLETES, COACHES AND OFFICIALS

Athletic endeavors require tremendous amounts of intense involvement. The pressures of high level performance are dramatic at all levels. Athletes today begin serious competition at very early ages, compete hard and long, and may experience a satiation of interest, especially when coupled with plateauing performance. Sport psychologists can help young people understand this phenomenon, anticipate it and develop strategies for either avoiding it or coping with it, if or when it happens.

Coaches and officials also experience tremendous burn-out problems. The "winning is the only thing" syndrome has been aggravated by the economic realities of financing athletics and the lack of job security for coaches. The prevailing realities are coupled with the lack of recognition conveyed by the old adage that teams "win with recruiting and lose with coaching" — a difficult environment for relaxed coaching.

DELIVERING OUR MESSAGE: EDUCATING THE MASSES

Sport psychology has something very good and valuable to offer to athletes and athletics. In regard to inter-collegiate athletics, the question is, "How can we produce the most positive effects and create the most significant impact on athletics?"

Certainly we can and will continue our efforts to have staff level positions for sport psychologists made available in the athletic programs of colleges and universities throughout the land. These positions may evolve in a variety of forms as coach, counselor, or administrator, and they entail a wide range of responsibilities:

1. *Coach* — Throughout our athletic programs today we are seeing specialized athletic coaching distinctions (i.e., strength coach, weight coach, conditioning coach, etc). Certainly there can be a strong case made for a sport psychologist or "motivational performance" coach;

2. *Counselor* — The sport psychologist could certainly make significant contributions to athletes and athletic departments if coupled with the position, or at least with the office of the academic advisor or counselor. With all the recent concerns arising out of recent allegations and scandals, the atmosphere is at least conducive to making the case for such an involvement. But sport psychologists must be careful not to allow themselves to fall under the complete control of athletics;

3. *Administrator* — It would be a great breakthrough for all of us if professionals from sport psychology were to assume administrative positions at the associate, assistant or even better, the director of athletics' level. From this leadership base, programs could be easily and effectively developed and implemented directly into athletic programs.

Our field and our profession could gain direct access to, and an avenue of influence with, our intercollegiate athletic programs through positions related to coaching, counseling, and directing athletics. These all sound exciting and wonderful! But just how realistic are they? And even if they are realistic, we question whether or not they could actually deliver much impact on intercollegiate athletics in general, or more importantly, on intercollegiate athletes in particular.

It is easy to think of intercollegiate athletics as primarily involving the major sports of football and basketball, especially at the major college, Division I level. But when taken in the total, there are significantly more athletes involved in wrestling, swimming, track, hockey, golf, soccer, racquetball, etc. More athletes in more sports mean more *people,* and that's really what's important. Because in sport psychology we're not in the "sport business," we're in the "people business." We talk about ways of maximizing performance, but really what we're all trying to do in the long run is to "maximize" people first, and in so doing, maximize the performance and satisfaction of their sport experience.

In a similar manner, sport psychologists and the field of sport psychology *may* have missed much of its calling by concentrating too heavily on the "major" actors within the field. Traditionally, sport psychologists have dealt primarily with two significant target populations — the talented and the troubled — and missed the middle group.

1. *The Talented* — Much effort is given to developing techniques and to preparing talented athletes with the psychological edge that may spell the difference between victory and defeat, success or failure, at the highest levels of competition, whether it be the Olympics, NCAA or NAIA Championships or the County High School Playoffs.

2. *The Troubled* — Significant time and effort are given to those athletes who appear to have considerable talent, but for various personal and/or motivational reasons are not able to perform or produce up to their capability, or who have broken the rules and regulations of sport and/or society.

The services provided to the talented and troubled are, without question, valid, useful, needed, and in scores and scores of documented cases have proven to be incredibly successful. But what of the majority? The talented and troubled are the most noticed and publicized, however they do not represent a majority of our competitive athletes. At the very best, only five to ten percent of our student-athletes posses superior national or world class ability level; and it is unlikely that more than another five to ten percent are suffering from such personal and motivational crises that they would need or be referred for psychological counseling.

This leaves us with fully 80 to 90% of our intercollegiate athletic population who are either not receiving the direct benefit of our services or are, at best, not getting their deserved share of the professional pie. Add to those the "special" athletes (wheelchair,

cerebral palsied, special olympians, etc.) and we find that these are the "people" in the intercollegiate athletics, and *they* are our business.

If our strategies work with the talented and the troubled, then shouldn't they also be effective with the others? Too often these athletes of the other 80% go unnoticed — not *unappreciated* but unnoticed! Every coach is proud of the good, honest, reliable, hardworking kids who never cause a problem and make coaching a joy. It is always assumed that these athletes are "getting everything" out of their ability and are experiencing total satisfaction in their sport experience. None of us are so naive as to believe that either is necessarily the case. But, we all must recognize that we have something very real, very useful, very beneficial and very exciting to offer these athletes. And we also must assume that these same athletes will be equally excited with the possibilities that the understandings of sport psychology can bring to their athletic performance and to their lives. What can we provide these athletes?

SELF CONTROL TECHNIQUES

The primary responsibility of sport psychologists is to provide athletes and coaches with strategies and skills to control their own thoughts and behaviors. These skills deal not with athletics, but also with academics and personal lives. These skills have been investigated and field tested by a variety of researchers. Helping athletes deal with stress is critical, stress which is physical, social or psychological. There are certainly socially acceptable as well as unacceptable ways to deal with stress. Such positive techniques as systematic desensitization (hypnosis, biofeedback) and participant modeling have been suggested as potential techniques for athletes (Bandura, 1969; Leitenberg, 1976; Kazdin and Wilson, 1978). However these techniques are all rather passive.

Active procedures on the other hand can be controlled or sequenced by the athlete and are therefore more desirable. Techniques such as coping skills or visual imagery require that individuals be actively involved in learning preventive strategies (Barrios and Shigetomi, 1980). For example, fear and anxiety are two common problems for athletes, whether it is fear of failure or fear of success. A number of strategies have been developed for any one of these problems:

Applied Relaxation (Deffenbacher, Mathis and Michaels, 1979)
Coping Skills (Mahoney, 1974; Barrios and Shigetomi, 1979 and 1980)
Cue Controlled Relaxation (Russell and Sipich, 1974)
Poser's Pre-exposure Procedure (Poser, 1976)
Rational Restructuring (Golfried, Decenteceo and Weinberg, 1974)
Self-control Desensitization (Golfried, 1971)
Stress Innoculation (Meichenbaum and Cameron, 1973)
Self-actualization Training
Visual Imagery

How can these ideas, approaches, and understandings be shared with coaches and athletes? Sport psychologists must help provide the knowledge and practical skills. Perhaps the most ready-made, completely accessible forum for this transference of ideas is through the universities, colleges and schools. Sport psychology has a message to bring to the masses. Let us take it directly to them on a wide scale, and let it be now!

I. *Sport Psychology Must be Made Available to Athletes*
Each college or university should offer or possibly even require, all of its student athletes to take at least an introductory course in sport psychology. This course should be undertaken as early in the student's college experience as possible and should be made totally relevant to the needs of the student-athlete. Its content could include, but not be limited to, experience in:

a. values clarification
b. goal setting
c. time management
d. attributional analysis
e. personal stress evaluation, including sources of distraction and peak experiences, as well as strategies for dealing with stress
f. development of concentration improvement programs
g. relaxation training and the use of mastery and coping rehearsal techniques

This base should be available to all athletes, with follow-up study and further course work available for those interested.

II. *Sport Psychology for Coaches*
Course work in sport psychology should also be available for coaches and teachers. It should be included in all physical education major programs, physical education certifications and for all athletic coaching preparation and certification programs. By and large, coaches are fanatically interested in using whatever means will benefit their team's or athletes' performance. At the same time, they are often very hesitant to let someone else "mess" with their athletes, whether it's ego involvement or genuine fear of the potential results. So let's take what we have to offer directly to the coaches and athletes, and instruct them in the proper implementation of our techniques and understandings into their own programs. Certainly, this would not include the clinical interventionist role of the trained counselor, but there is so much more that we have to offer, and the coach is our real key to getting it to the greatest number of athletes.

In a similar manner, let every college and university target the present coaches and take to them experiences in sport psychology, whether it be through workshops, conferences, in-service training programs, extension courses or continuing education. Whatever the means, sport psychology must be available to the practitioners in the field.

III. *Sport Psychology for Allied Personnel*
The problems of sport are not restricted only to coaches and athletes. They impact the lives and pro-

fessional effectiveness of referees, umpires and other officials or athletic directors, sport journalists and even parents. Sport psychology can help each of these individuals deal with the stresses and satisfaction of sport.

Throughout this discussion the pervasive theme is one of *PREVENTION!* Sport psychology must stop focusing or intervening where there are existing problems, and start to make a full scale effort to prevent those problems from ever occurring.

If there were no fires, there would be no need for firemen! If there were no sicknesses, likewise there would be no need for medical doctors. Similarly athletic trainers, skillfully trained in the techniques of injury rehabilitation or stabilization, still consider their most significant contribution to sport to be their solid efforts in injury prevention. These helping professions mount massive campaigns for the cause of prevention. Let us, in sport psychology, channel our collective efforts, coupled with the efforts of coaches and athletes in the field, to make our mark in this most positive way possible — through prevention.

What exactly can be prevented? On the one hand, psychological problems in athletes can be prevented from becoming so great that there ever is the need for professional counseling as an intervention tool. But much more significantly, thousands and thousands, even millions of anonymous athletes can be prevented from missing out on all the joys and satisfactions that sport has to offer them. Similarly, we may help coaches and athletes from joining the epidemic ranks of the "burned-out."

Unfortunately, these proposals offer very little in the way of short term dramatic effects on intercollegiate athletics in general. Nowhere in history has education ever been a "quick answer" for major questions or problems. But, it is a lasting answer, and an effort that will bring significant long term dividends for some very committed short term investments. For example, the proposal to educate coaches may find its first effects occurring with the athletes of the junior high and high school levels. These junior athletes of today are, obviously, the intercollegiate athletes of tomorrow.

KEEPING SPORT IN ITS PROPER PERSPECTIVE

Sport and athletics are tremendously demanding and exhilarating experiences for everyone involved — the athletes, parents, coaches, and spectators. As sport psychologists, we must help each of these groups keep the experience in perspective and optimize its value to each individual.

The demands for talent, hard work and dedication are great. Athletes must recognize the relative contribution of hard work and effort coupled with ability and luck. Similarly, the talented high school athletes who "can't make it" at major universities must be able to sort out the demands of sport from their personal choices to play, or ability to participate at a given level. Techniques of values clarification and attribution identification can be quite helpful to those athletes, parents and coaches.

Pre-intercollegiates. Helping young athletes learn to make choices about their participation and level of involvement may avoid a great many problems in the future. Intercollegiate athletics means one thing if you are talking about Big-10 Football or ACC Basketball, but quite another thing if you are referring to minor sports, or schools with less emphasis on super players and more emphasis on the individual value of sport. Similarly, athletes need to recognize the important interaction of a coach's style, personality and philosophy with their own. If a coach believes in individual initiative, hard work and a rather democratic style of leadership, the interaction with a player who thrives on being told what to do, and being disciplined severely may be quite different.

Pre-intercollegiate concerns deal with parents as well. Parents and teachers must be supportive and also encourage young athletes to read, to write and do arithmetic. Adults must be helped to constantly improve our educational systems and the values shared with children. We may all be in trouble when a high school transcript makes better reading than "The Grapes of Wrath."

All the way from the Little League or YBA, youngsters have been encouraged by well meaning adults who have said, "You'll be great . . . But you've got to forego . . . piano, all other sports, girls, etc." Or by the high school papers and local citizens who treat young athletes as special privileged individuals . . . protected from almost everything.

The abuse and devastation of athletes begins long before intercollegiates. Athletes must be helped to recognize these dilemmas and choose accordingly. The problems of young athletes are quite varied. Many children dedicate their adolescent years to competition. How can we help thirteen-year-old gymnasts such as Michelle Rabourne, Blue Spring, Missouri, who says, "I think about the Olympics, but I'm getting too old. I'm not 'over the hill' yet, but the next Olympics I'll be seventeen — and that'll be just too old!" (*Women's Sports*, April 1981).

Coaches. Sport psychology must also help coaches deal with adolescent athletes. The skills of communication and persuasion can be powerful tools, and must not be misused. Coaches as recruiters, must be honest and be encouraged to be realistic and honest with prospective athletes, and present athletes or both sides will lose.

Coaches may need help in resisting the same temptations to fame and fortune that lure our athletes. Horror stories of coaches using athletes to advance their own careers are fortunately rare, and treatable. High school coaches from such places as Camden, New Jersey High School where the 1980 basketball team averaged 103 points per game in routes such as 122-51, 115-57, or 122-59, reflect an unreal need to win or "beat the hell out of someone." Or the coach of Linda Page who scored 100 points for Philadelphia's Doblins Tech High School in a 131-38 win, who admitted building up Linda's scoring statistics to get himself "back in the limelight" (*Sports Illustrated*, February 1981).

Coaches who contribute to the development of athletes must be reinforced and helped to be most effective. The commitment to develop athletes has somehow been lost in some areas and some sports. But to the small college soccer or field hockey coach, the importance of sport, and continuing to develop young people through statewide clinics and conferences cannot be overemphasized. These professional contributions build young athletes and develops their interests and skills.

During and After Intercollegiates. Athletes must anticipate the impact of future participation in sport — either as professionals or amateurs. The adjustment from intercollegiate sport to either extreme may be a dramatic one. To prepare for the future is to prepare for self-control and self-actualization.

Helping athletes deal with post intercollegiates is also a challenge. How do you help a young man deal with the self-talk of headlines which read, "Smith nears silver lining . . . million dollar contract . . ." as contrasted to being drafted in the seventh or tenth round, or not at all! The pro myth thrives on an irresistible hype! For example according to the National Federation of State High School Associations, every year over one million boys play football. On varsities at NCAA institutions that drops to 41,000 and by the time the NFL drafts about 320 college athletes, only about 150 make teams. If we displayed those odds on a tote board . . . who would take them!?

A variety of issues can be identified as they relate to intercollegiate athletics. Issues which focus on the problems of athletes, including performance-related issues, academic-related careers, and depicts personal, self-actualization. Some of these variables are displayed in Table 1. Similar issues can be articulated for coaches and other allied personnel, including athletic trainers, athletic directors, parents, etc.

This list of issues related to intercollegiate sport is far from exhaustive. It does, however, describe the range of controversies, problems and challenges of athletes. The challenges to sport psychology are exciting and exhilarating, for they relate to the ability of each human being to learn to control his or her own feelings and actions.

FUTURISTIC SPORT PSYCHOLOGY

Lest we become complacent, and begin to rest on our laurels, we must begin to prepare for the twenty-first century. Our psychology technology may easily keep pace with the sophistication of our knowledge — a sport space shuttle program if you will! Imagine a coach, with a whole team of "wired up" players. The pre-game pep talk, replaced in 1981 by pre-game cognitive restructuring, could be replaced in 2001 by instantaneous, telemetered, biocleansing signals. The coach's clipboard may become the coach's electronic control panel. Basketball, for example, may have sonar sensors which detect incidental contact between opponents or "cylinder violations" for goal tending. Our team physicians and trainers will be joined by psychoelectronic technicians to monitor and repair transcendental mind control devices.

From the ridiculous to the inane? Perhaps — but if we use our skills and knowledge, sport will be a better experience for everyone. Giving sport psychology to sport should certainly be our focus for the 80's.

Sport psychology has the potential to make the difference. Our biomechanical, physiological and sports medicine counterparts will all contribute — but ultimately it will be the athlete's ability to control his or her own body and mind in action and in all areas of life that will determine the level of ultimate athletic performance. It will be our ability to give sport psychology to sport — to free our athletes to be the best that they can be.

Table 1
Issues In Intercollegiate Sport

Performance-Related	Academic-Related	Personal
Achievement Motivation	Achievement Motivation	Aggression
Aggression/Assertion	Anxiety	Altered States of
Anxiety	Arousal	Consciousness
Arousal	Attention	Anxiety
Assertion	Coping Skills	Arousal
Attention	Effort Attribution	Assertion
Attributions	Fear of Failure or	Burn-out
Burn-out	Success	Cohesiveness
Cohesiveness	Goal Setting	Coping Skills
Coping Skills	College/Progress/	Crisis Intevention
Effort Attribution	Graduation	Fear of Failure or
Fear of Failure or	Academic Scandals	Success
Success	Hawthorne Effect	Flow Experiences
Goal Setting	Leadership	(Peak Experiences)
Leadership	Mental Capacity	Motivation
Mental Rehearsal	Motivation	Personality Development
Motivation	Relaxation Training	Psychometric Test
Pain Tolerance	Self-regulation of	Religion
Performance Prediction	Psychological Process	Self-regulation
Relaxation (biofeedback,		Psychological Process
hypnosis, meditation,		Separation Anxiety
progressive relaxation,		Stress Management
autogenic training)		Substance Use and Abuse
Self-regulation of		Values Clarification
Psychological Process		
Stress Management		
Substance Use and Abuse		
Success Phobia		

14

REFERENCES

Bandura, A. *Principles of Behavior Modification.* New York: Holt, Rhinehart and Winston, 1969.

Barrios, B. A. and Shigetomi, C. C. Coping Skills Training for the Management of Anxiety: A Critical Review. *Behavior Therapy,* 1979, *10,* 491-522.

Barrios, B. A. and Shigetomi, C. C. Coping Skills Training: Potential for Prevention of Fears and Anxieties. *Behavior Therapy,* 1980, *11,* 431-439.

Deffenbacher, J. L., Mathis, H. and Michaels, A. C. The Self-Control Procedure in the Reduction of Targeted and Non-Targeted Anxieties. *Journal of Counseling Psychology,* 1979, *26,* 120-127.

Golfried, M. R. Systematic Desensitization as Training in Self Control. *Journal of Consulting and Clinical Psychology,* 1971, *37,* 228-234.

Golfried, M. R., Decenteceo, E. T. and Weinberg, L. Systematic Rational Restructuring as a Self-Control Technique. *Behavior Therapy,* 1974, *5,* 247-254.

Kazdin, A. E. and Wilson, G. T. *Education of Behavior Therapy: Issues Evidence and Research Strategies.* New York: Ballinger, 1978.

Leitenberg, H. *Handbook of Behavior Modification and Behavior Therapy.* New York: Prentice-Hall, 1976.

Mahoney, M. J. *Cognition and Behavior Modification.* Cambridge, MA: Ballinger, 1974.

Meichenbaum, D., and Cameron, R. Stress Innoculation: A Skills Training Approach to Anxiety Management. University of Waterloo, unpublished, 1973.

Miller, G. A. Psychology as a Means of Promoting Human Welfare. *American Psychologist,* 1969, *24,* 1063-1075.

Nideffer, R. M., Dufresne, P., Nesrig, D. and Selder, D. The Future of Applied Sport Psychology. *Journal of Sport Psychology,* 1980, *2,* 170-174.

Poser, E. G. Strategies for Prevention. In P. O. Davidson (Ed.) *The Behavioral Management of Anxiety, Depression and Pain.* New York: Bruner/Mazel, 1976.

Russell, R. K., and Sipich, J. R. Treatment of Test Anxiety by Care-controlled Relaxation. *Behavior Therapy,* 1974, *5,* 673-676.

Sheerer, C. *Newsweek,* (September, 22, 1980), p. 58.

Straub, R. Sport Psychology Competencies. *Sport Psychology Academy Newsletter,* AAHPERD, 1980.

SECTION II

Personality and Athletic Performance

2

The Natural Athlete: Does She / He Exist?

John Billing
University of North Carolina
at Chapel Hill

What makes a champion? How can one explain the phenomenal performances of superior athletes? Are World Champions really made or are they born? There appears to be a variety of opinions as to the answers to these questions. Over the years we have heard expressions that anyone has the potential to become a world class athlete who is willing to devote themselves totally to training. Conversely others observe that some champions appear to rise from the masses with little formal training, somehow genetically destined to be superior performers.

Any maximal sport performance involves the interplay of a number of qualities including: physique, personality, skill, fitness and intellect. The question then is "How much genetic influence is there on these qualities?"

Components of physique are primarily genetically determined. Height, weight, basic body structure, limb lengths, size of hands and feet, center of gravity, etc. are all affected by heredity. Some of us possess bodies which are better suited for one sport than another: height in basketball, volleyball, and high jumping, weight in football line play, shot putting, etc., short limb length in weight lifting and gymnastics. The examples are endless. In addition to these obvious structural advantages an augmented sensory acuity can be a significant benefit in particular sports. Clarity of sight and peripheral vision as well as kinesthetic acuity and speed of reaction time appear to differ among individuals and be impervious to training. In selected activities these qualities would provide a definite advantage.

There is controversy over the importance of intelligence in athletic activities. Popular opinion for years has held that many fine athletes are actually below average in intelligence. There does, however, appear to be a slight positive correlation between I.Q. and motor abilities which increases as one examines the lower ranges of I.Q. It would appear of benefit to possess good intellectual abilities if the contest involves significant complexity, strategy and alternative modes of play. The complexity present in modern football or basketball is evident of the necessity for reasonable intellectual ability. Additionally, during the acquisition phase of any new skill an intellectually superior individual would be able to analyze conditions and profit from mistakes, thus reducing learning time.

The genetic impact on personality factors is a much debated and poorly researched question. It is a difficult question to investigate since the control of environmental influences is virtually impossible with normal human subjects. However, it seems a definite possibility that there may be some genetic predisposition for particular personality traits. Some of these could be quite valuable or quite detrimental to the maximum sport performance.

These areas of physique, intellect and personality are quite likely influenced by one's genetic make-up. However, their exact contribution to sport will vary with the activity in question. The logical extension of these statements is that specific athletic qualities, especially physique, can be bred by selective mating of individuals possessing these qualities. Regardless of the social acceptability of this concept, there is little doubt of its validity. In fact there appears to be encouragement in some coun-

18

tries for championship level athletes to marry. Their offspring, although not assured of possessing advantageous athletic qualities surely have a greater than normal chance of this inheritance.

Having an advantageous genetic predisposition for specific athletic activities does not assure development of these qualities. The contribution of skill and fitness are of paramount importance in the development of athletic prowess. There is no evidence that humans are born with any specific athletic skills. Thus, the major portion of all skill learning is a function of practice and experience. The marvelously tuned coordination of the superior athlete is only possible through years of dedicated practice and experience trials. There are simply no genetic short cuts to skill development.

The importance of physiological fitness for a specific sport performance has received significant attention in the past several decades. We have greatly enhanced our knowledge of training principles for maximum development of strength, endurance and flexibility of athletes. Realizing the importance of these qualities to many sport activities, accelerated training programs have produced human beings capable of physical feats previously thought impossible. As with skill learning, the vast majority of physical capacity is determined by the training program engaged in by the athlete. This physical development is primarily a function of intensity, duration and frequency of training.

Recent evidence does, however, suggest that some genetic difference can effect the organism's response to training. The most impressive data to date comes from studies on muscle fiber typing. It is now widely accepted that individuals possess differing proportions of "slow-twitch" and "fast-twitch" muscle fibers and that these proportions resist any change due to training. Individuals born with a high percentage of "fast-twitch" muscle fibers will be capable of responding more completely to training which enhances speed and explosive muscular contractions. Those born with a high percentage of "slow-twitch" fibers are more trainable for endurance type activities. This means that they will be capable of reaching higher maximum capabilities in the area in which they have the predominant muscle fiber type. It does not infer that they possess these qualities without training for them.

The world champion athlete is likely both born and made. Born with the genetic potential of optimal physique, appropriate intelligence and desirable personality qualities. Made through years of dedicated practice of skills and fitness training. As coaches and teachers we must realize that we have little or no effect, other than selection, on the physique, intellectual or neurological makeup of our students, that we may be capable of influencing to some degree their psychological approach to sport but that our real contribution lies in designing programs which will maximize each athlete's physical conditioning and skill attainment.

3

Application Of Rotter's Social Learning Theory To Sport

Walter J. Rejeski, Jr.
Wake Forest University

Personality is a common referent within the world of sport. Television and radio announcers describe athletes as dominant, stable, aggressive, and self-confident. Coaches are quick to recognize and label deviants and possess implicit theories about the mental faculties required for various roles and positions. Even spectators remark on the characteristics of players, coaches, managers, and sportcasters. We are all personologists. That is, when observing human behavior we perceive characteristic patterns and thus come to expect particular behaviors. Such a process functions to bring meaning and order to our lives. Think for a moment about the following individuals: Jack Nicklaus, Billie Jean King, Howard Cosell, Dorothy Hamill, Reggie Jackson, or Joe Namath. These names trigger specific cognitions and/or emotions in each of us. Through direct observation and the media we have formulated beliefs about their individual styles. Associated with these beliefs are varying degrees of positive and negative effect which accentuate individual characteristics. In fact, we might pride ourselves in our ability to understand and accurately predict particular sport figures, emulating and identifying with their specific behaviors and attitudinal patterns. Yet, if we were to encounter these renowned personalities across more diverse situations our beliefs and fantasies might well be shattered. In effect, personality assessment can be quite baffling and has at times eluded even the most competent psychologist.

What then does one mean when speaking of personality? What are the constituents of a sound theoretical approach? And what are the implications of such a theory for sport?

APPROACHES TO THE STUDY OF PERSONALITY

The term personality connotes something about the nature of man with implications for explanation and prediction. Like trait psychologists and those intrigued by psychodynamic theories (for example, the Freudians), most observers focus on the individual. That is, athletes act violently because they are aggressive or coaches behave adamantly due to their authoritative characters.

At the other extreme have been those who espouse to the belief that behavior in sport can be explained by carefully studying the structure of the situation. In a sense, personality is an epiphenomenon and behavior is determined by positive and negative reinforcers (see for example, Rushall and Siedentop, 1972). In this view, there is little need for coaches and parents to consider individual differences in athletes. To explain behavior, you merely need to identify the appropriate reinforcers and to control behavior, you carefully manage behavior-reward contingencies.

In 1954, Julian Rotter developed a Social Learning Theory of Personality (SLT). He recognized that an analysis of human behavior was impossible without giving consideration to both the individual and the situation; thus for Rotter, personality existed somewhere between the two. To illustrate Rotter's point; consider for a moment the individual who may be competitive in sport, yet cooperative in his/her interactions with peers in other social contexts. Would it be legitimate to label such an individual as competitive due to observations made in sport? We have all witnessed or at least heard of the famous Dr. Jeckel-Mr. Hyde transformation. What then is the utility in employing cross-situational traits to explain behavior?

BASIC ELEMENTS OF ROTTER'S SOCIAL LEARNING THEORY APPLIED TO SPORT

According to Social Learning Theory (SLT) behavior is situationally specific; co-determined by expectancy and reinforcement value. Expectancy represents the personal cognitive construct within SLT, while reinforcement value characterizes the importance of the situation.

Expectancy. By expectancy Rotter meant ". . . the subjective probability held by the individual that a particular reinforcement would occur as a function of, or in relation to, a specific behavior in a given situation" (1954, p. 112). For instance, coaches employ training strategies and teach specific skills under ideal conditions so that athletes can gain confidence in their athletic prowess. In other words, coaches provide a series of behaviors which will lead to the desired goals of the sport. The athlete repeats the skills and strategies in order to develop the expectancy that the selected behaviors will lead to team and/or individual success. Over time, coaches build a trust with their athletes and expectancies are transmitted verbally. Parenthetically, verbal expectancies have been a source of injustice in sport. For example, coaches have provided athletes with long term expectancies which could never realistically be achieved ("Come to our University and we will mold you into a professional."). Individuals invest years of their lives, often sacrificing alternate experience, only to realize the inevitable, their career and/or goals in sport were only illusions.

Central to the concept of expectancy is situational specificity. Where expectancies are acquired athletes are interacting with a specific task in a particular environment. Thus, while one might believe that a particular sport-related behavior is functional in the structured practice setting, it does not necessarily follow that expectancies exist for the same behavior in a competitive game situation. Thus, an obvious task for coaches is to create as closely as possible opponent teams and environments. The degree of transfer for expectancies across different tasks and environmental contexts will be contingent on cross-situational similarities. Thus, the transfer of expectancies for behaviors within a sport will be greater than the transfer between two different sports. This brings up an interesting question, one which has been posed by educators for a number of years: Does learning through sport transfer to other life situations? It is readily apparent that there is no blanket yes or no answer; one would have to consider the exact nature of the behavior in question. Although data relevant to this issue are scarce, there is evidence which suggests that achievement in sport may have some impact on perceptions of achievement in academic settings; conversely, academic achievement appears to influence perceptions of achievement to sport (Crandall, 1951; Jessor, 1954).

Finally, Rotter (1966) reported on an interesting individual difference variable which influences expectancies and thus behaviors. That is, some people have a general tendency to perceive that they have personal control over their reinforcements, while others perceive that reinforcements are controlled by external factors. Thus, athletes who are externally oriented are less apt to try as hard as internals because they feel that their personal efforts are not instrumental to success. Outcomes are determined largely by external forces, forces which are not under their direct influence. Building expectancies into the cognitive repertoire of athletes necessitates considering focus of control. This may well become an important trend and innovation in the future of training methodology for sport.

Reinforcement Value. Reinforcement value is defined as ". . . the degree of preference for any reinforcement to occur if the possibility of all reinforcers occurring were equal" (Rotter, 1954, p. 112). This implies that reinforcements are arranged in a hierarchical fashion and that reinforcements interact with expectancies. For example, most athletes have a psychological need for recognition. Achievement in sport would be an acceptable means of satisfying this need. However, let us suppose that the athlete in question has a low expectancy for such behavior. Under such conditions the individual may revert to devious acts. In effect, the potential negative reinforcement one might incur from cheating or demeaning others is less punishing than risking the reality of never being recognized. The same dynamics are often operating in the misbehaved child — the "wise" behaviors which are constantly observed by teachers and coaches. Attention is crucial at any age and when normal behaviors fail, people will often revert to behaviors which deviate from the norm.

An additional class of behaviors which can emerge from a low expectancy high reinforcement conflict are of a vicarious nature. Thus, rather than experiencing competition directly, individuals may live out their fantasies through their children or other sport heroes. In extreme pathological cases, one's entire self-worth may hinge on another's achievements. The emotional involvement in such situations reaches extremely high levels of intensity.

A final issue which is relevant to Rotter's SLT, and reinforcement in particular, is the concept known as delay of gratification. The essence of this construct is that some individuals are unable to engage in behaviors which are not reinforced immediately. In effect, such people lack the ability to work toward goals which are in the distant future. This is most common among the middle and lower classes and is especially true with children and delinquent populations. This can pose a serious problem in sports because the development of skills and strategies requires extended periods of time. In fact, even within a game situation it is unrealistic to expect that tides can be turned in one or two plays or moves. Indeed, it is this sort of perception which leads to "gambling strategies," behaviors which have been shown to be destructive to both players and teams. The solution in sport is to employ goal setting techniques. Coaches and teachers must learn to create identifiable intermediate goals which will reinforce behaviors that are central to long term objectives. Within sport, goal setting can be easily quantified through the use of physiological and biomechanical techniques.

Minimal Goal Level. A concept developed by Rotter which has direct implications for sport is that of minimal goal level. As examples of this concept, we might think for a moment of the numerous coaches and athletes who never appear satisfied with their team or individual achievement. Likewise, fans and institutions will often view relatively successful seasons as inadequate. The list of situations where minimal goal levels have been inordinately high is exhaustive. As a result, individuals have been unable to reap the rewards of success and oftentimes interpersonal conflict has emerged. The athlete who has extremely high minimal goals will never develop expectancies for success. He or she will never be satisfied with performance outcomes. It is highly probable that such individuals will discontinue sport involvement. The coach who sets unrealistic minimal goals for his/her team inadvertently undermines individual and team achievement. This sets the stage for group unrest and the loss of team cohesiveness. Finally, fans who display high minimal goals are more inclined to become frustrated in the face of failure. There is little doubt that this frustration may serve as a catalyst for violence in sport.

The concept of minimal goal levels again stresses the need for goal setting techniques. Through group dynamic sessions it is possible to discuss realistic goals and appropriate strategies for reaching such goals. With respect to the spectator, it is entirely possible that an educated media could assuage rather than exacerbate conflict for fans who possess inordinately high minimal goal levels.

SUMMARY

Rotter's Social Learning Theory (SLT) has offered a new perspective to the study of personality. As a blend of the cognitive and behavioral approaches, SLT could assist in understanding and giving direction to both practical and therapeutic issues in sport.

REFERENCES

Crandall, V. J. Induced frustration and punishment-reward expectancy in thematic apperception stories. *Journal of Consulting and Clinical Psychology, 15,* 400-401, 1951.

Jessor, R. The generalization of expectancies. *Journal of Abnormal and Social Psychology, 49,* 196-200, 1954.

22

Rotter, J. B. *Social learning and clinical psychology.* Englewood Cliffs, N.J.: Prentice-Hall, 1954.

Rotter, J. B. Generalized expectancies for internal versus external control of reinforcement. *Psychological Monographs, 80,* 1966.

Rushall, B. S. and Siedentop, D. *The development and control of behavior in sport and physical education.* Philadelphia, PA: Lea and Febiger, 1972.

Julie Heyward, Charlottesville, Va.

4

Personality In Sport Participants

Dorothy V. Harris
Penn State University

Psychiatrists, physical educationalists, clinical psychologists, social psychologists, educational psychologists, and others involved with the total program of sport and sports medicine are working in the general area of sport psychology. Without exception, all are supporting the premise that maximal performance is affected not only by physical skills and physiological conditioning but also by the personality, psychological preparation and conditioning of the athlete. In the American society conditioning and training have focused on the physical aspects; only recently has attention been directed toward the psychological conditioning.

Consideration of the psychological aspects of sport performance has been generally limited to a consultant speaking at a clinic for coaches and/or athletes. The approach has been one of applying principles and techniques that clinicians have used in mental health clinics. These models have been presented to coaches in the hopes that they would make application of these new skills in sports settings since few athletic teams have the regular support of a sport psychologist.

It is essential that any psychological consultant establish credibility with the coach, to be able to understand the sport the athletes are participating in, and to be able to discuss psychological considerations in nontechnical language. The psychologist may initially be considered an outsider and must work in a nonthreatening manner, establishing trust with both the coach and the athletes.

Each coach, each team, each sport is unique. Many different approaches produce successful programs. Coaches will generally recruit athletes they think will "fit into

their system," this in turn may produce a behavioral profile or a behavior type that will experience more success than one who is less compatible with the goals and the strategies that are dominant within that program. Within those generalized behavioral profiles each athlete on a team is still an individual with different needs and experiences, therefore must be treated as an individual. Most coaches support the practice of treating all athletes alike, convinced that this will avoid problems. More problems occur with the failure to treat players as individuals than are prevented by treating them alike. Treating athletes as individuals involves an awareness and understanding of other aspects and involvements of the athletes. All of the experiences and concerns the athlete encounters beyond the athletic arena affect his performance. A coach and/or psychologist must be understanding of these other demands and provide support to the athlete when they interfere with performance.

Coaches must accept the fact that they have a great deal of influence on young athletes, they serve as a model and their interaction with the athletes goes beyond what happens in the athletic arena. Lack of flexibility and compatibility will prevent the development of a relationship that is essential to maximize talent and ability.

Even the most successful coaches do not understand all of the psychological aspects of athletic performance. At the same time, a psychologist who understands a great deal about behavior will not be able to make application of that knowledge to athletes until he/she understands the sport and the behavioral demands that are made on the athlete in that sport. Further, an understanding of the coach's role and approach to training and conditioning athletes is basic to making appropriate suggestions and providing guidance in psychological skills. The goals of the coaches and athletes have to be congruent; these in turn, must be congruent with the values and ethics of the psychologist.

Any program that is designed to assist the athlete should select and/or develop appropriate methods for assessing the athlete with respect to cognitive style, anxiety levels, and behavioral responses to training and to competition. Athletes should be taught skills that are useful in mastery and control of anxiety, stress management, and in anticipating and coping with experiences and problems commonly experienced in competition. Opportunity should be provided to work with individuals with special problems as well as those who have greater difficulty in learning the skills.

ASSESSING PERSONALITY

Personality is the study of individual differences; personology includes the theory and research and the broad area of personality. The focus of sport personology has been on the athlete with the goal of trying to select and predict who will become the better athletes. Coaches have been fascinated with this type of prediction. They do not want to waste time working with athletes who will choke or fail to produce in tough situations. Some coaches have put their faith in instruments reported (without statistical evidence) to be able to select and predict superior athletes. As a result many very good athletes have been eliminated, not on the basis of their lack of skill but on the basis of their answers on a paper-pencil personality assessment instrument. Sport personology is not advanced enough to provide that type of prediction. This is not to say that self-report measures are not helpful in maximizing performance but it does suggest that such assessment is only one part of assessing an athlete's ability.

Based on the research available some generalizations can be made about those individuals who find competitive sport compatible with their behavioral makeup. Physical education majors and especially those involved in team sports, have been described as "stimulus seeking extroverts." They seek action, noise, body contact, bright colors, etc. They need more stimulation to stay aroused; they become bored if they do not have enough stimulation. Frequently physical education majors are known as the "trouble-makers" because they are seeking stimulation if none is available! On the other end of the continuum of stimulation are the introverts who need very little stimulation to stay aroused and who appear to stick to a task and to become conditioned much more easily than extroverts. As an example, extroverts need variation and change. If the same drills are repeated over and over, athletes begin to lose interest and look to other pursuits. Introverts, on the other hand, will persist without the need to seek additional stimulation; many distance runners are classified as introverts. Sprinters are frequently extroverts.

Generally athletes are more confident, more tough-minded, more emotionally stable, and more achievement oriented than non-athletes. When looking at the behavioral profiles of female athletes, they are much like those of the males. This is not surprising since individuals must have behaviors that are compatible with the behavioral demands of sport. At the same time, female athletes differ more from their non-athletic female counterparts than male athletes do from their non-athletic male counterparts. There is less variance in the behavior of female athletes than there is among male athletes. This can be explained by the fact that females who make a serious commitment to sport have to turn their backs on the stereotyped female behavior; the behavioral demands in sport to enhance and emulate what the male is supposed to be in the stereotyped profile.

The conflict between being athletic and being feminine has created the perpetuated notion that female athletes are masculinized. As indicated earlier, to be successful in competitive athletics the female must have behaviors that are compatible with the behavioral demands of sport. Many of these behaviors are the ones that are associated with masculinity. That is why sport has been used as a laboratory for "making boys into men;" the real fear has been what will happen to girls!

A MORE CONTEMPORARY PERSPECTIVE

The position that has dominated the writings of social and behavioral scientists is that masculine and feminine attributes are essentially bipolar opposites. The presence of feminine characteristics tends to preclude the appearance of masculine ones. Indeed, the absence of a feminine attribute is by definition, equivalent to masculinity. Conversely, masculine characteristics are assumed to preclude feminine ones and their absence is to define femininity. In most societies, the appropriate goal of socialization is to inculcate some appropriate attributes in members of each sex so that they may be capable of executing successfully the sex-roles that society has assigned them by virtue of their biological role. In fact, the link between masculine and feminine characteristics and sex-roles has been assumed to be so strong that these psychological dimensions are frequently discussed under the general sex-role rubric.

Differentiation between the sex-roles is universal among human societies; males are assigned different tasks, rights, and privileges, and are generally subject to different rules of conduct than females. Males and females are typically assumed to possess different temperamental characteristics and abilities whose existence is used to justify the perpetuation of double standards of behavior. Definitive data are lacking about whether there are genetically determined differences in the temperamental make-up of males and females. However, there is abundant evidence to support the fact that human personality is highly malleable. Observed differences in the behaviors of the two sexes in a given society can be shown to be strongly influenced by the sex-specific child-rearing practices and by the nature and severity of the sex-role differentiation promoted by that society.

Psychologists have tended to accept, as given, the complex set of sex-related phenomena and to focus attention on the processes by which individuals come to correspond in their behaviors and attributes to the expected norm for their sex within their culture. Psychologists have also been interested in the variability among individuals and have attempted to identify the factors that promote or interfere with the development of expected and appropriate patterns of behavior. Psychological inquiries have been based on the notion that the categorical variable of biological gender is intimately associated with masculine and feminine role behaviors and presumed psychological differences between males and females. This bipolar conception of masculinity and femininity has historically been the one that has guided the research efforts of psychologists. The major psychometric instruments designed to measure masculinity and femininity have been set up as unidimensional scales.

While the bipolar approach to the psychological aspects of masculinity and femininity has been the major one, dualistic approaches have also been proposed. In the psychoanalytic tradition, Jung distinguished between masculine *animus* and feminine *anima* and proposed that both were significant aspects of the psychological make-up. More recently Bakan (1966) has offered agency and communion as coexisting male and female principles. Agency demonstrates self-awareness and is manifested in self-assertion, self-expansion, and self-protection. Communion implies selflessness and concern for others. Both modalities are essential if society or the individual is to survive. Bakan further associated agency with masculinity and communion with femininity. Thus, according to Bakan, masculinity and femininity, in the sense of agency and communion are two separate dimensions, however, the manifestation of one neither logically or psychologically precludes the possession of the other.

Helmreich and Spence (1977) contend that the relationship among the various components of masculinity and femininity such as biological gender, sex-roles, sexual orientation and especially psychological attributes of masculinity and femininity and the adoption of conventional sex-roles is not as strong as has been traditionally assumed. Their position reflects the more contemporary concept that masculinity and femininity represent two separate dimensions which vary independently. Helmreich and Spence have developed a new instrument, the Personal Attributes Questionnaire (PAQ), to assess masculine-feminine components of behavior. While they have maintained the psychological aspects of masculinity and femininity, they have discarded a strictly bipolar model and structured an essentially dualistic concept.

The PAQ is composed of a masculinity and a femininity scale. The items which comprise the masculinity scale refer to those attributes which are considered to be socially desirable in both sexes but were found to a greater degree among males during preliminary investigations. Conversely, those attributes considered to be socially desirable for both sexes but observed to a greater extent among females created the femininity scale. Two scores are generated, one for each scale and an individual is classified according to his or her position relative to the scale medians. Helmreich and Spence have devised a simple classification scheme as shown in Table 1. At the lower right quadrant are those individuals who have scored above the median on both masculinity and femininity; these are labeled *androgynous*. In the upper right quadrant are those individuals who socred high in masculinity and low in femininity. Males who corresponded to the typical male stereotype and females judged as cross-sex fell in this group and were labeled *masculine*. The lower left quadrant included those individuals who displayed the typical feminine attributes or those males who displayed cross-sex behaviors; these were labeled *feminine*. Those who did not fall in any of the previous three categories, that is, they fell below the median on both masculinity and femininity were placed in the upper left quadrant and categorized as *undifferentiated*.

Table 1
Sex-role Classification: Personal Attributes Questionnaire*

	MASCULINITY	
FEMININITY	Below Median	Above Median
Below Median	Undifferentiated	Masculine
Above Median	Feminine	Androgynous

*After Helmreich and Spence (1977)

Using several hundred subjects, Helmreich and Spence have studied the relationship between the two scales. They have found a tendency for high masculine scores to be associated with low scores on the other scale. A bipolar conception would

suggest that the sets of scores should be negatively related. If one has a high masculine score the feminine score would be low. As indicated, this was not the case with those individuals sampled by Helmreich and Spence.

In order to examine the relationship between sex-role identity and self-esteem, Spence, Helmreich, and Stapp (1975) have correlated the PAQ data with Scores on the Texas Social Behavior Inventory (Helmreich and Stapp, 1974), a measure of self-esteem. They found that the self-esteem of the undifferentiated was lowest, that of the femine category next lowest, followed by masculine. The highest self-esteem was observed in the androgynous group. The differences between the means were significantly large and the relationship of sex-role classification and self-esteem held true for both males and females. The college population had the same percentage of males and females classified as androgynous, more males as masculine and more females as feminine and approximately the same percent as undifferentiated.

In summary, the Helmreich and Spence data suggested that masculinity and androgyny were related to desirable behaviors and to positive self-esteem in both males and females. These desirable attributes provided the androgynous individual, either male or female, with behavioral advantages over those falling in other categories. In an attempt to validate their findings, Helmreich and Spence studied unique populations of females where the existence or nonexistence of differences in the distribution of masculinity and femininity might support their theoretical proposition. A group of female athletes was included. The data from these women suggested that high-achieving women are more likely to possess both masculine and feminine attributes than their male counterparts without suffering any deficit in their femininity. On the contrary, they displayed significantly higher self-esteem than those females who were classified as feminine.

APPLICATION OF THE CONCEPT TO ATHLETIC GROUPS

In a series of studies which began in 1976, Harris and Jennings (1977, 1978) have found no evidence to support the supposed, inevitable trade-off of the female athlete's self-esteem and femininity for making a serious commitment to sport participation. The data generally support those of Helmreich and Spence in suggesting that those females who succeed in areas of endeavor considered stereotypically masculine do not do this at the expense of their femininity. As a matter of fact, the data suggest that high-achieving women are more likely to possess both masculine and feminine attributes than their male counterparts without suffering any deficit in their femininity. Androgynous individuals, male or female, appear to have behavioral advantages over others.

In the first study of 68 female distance runners (Harris and Jennings, 1977) 33.8% were androgynous, 27.9% masculine, 17.6% feminine and 20.6% undifferentiated. Helmreich and Spence (1977) had reported 39% were androgynous, 31% masculine, 10% feminine, and 20% undifferentiated in their athletic sample.

A second study involved 96 female athletes participating in a wide variety of sports, Harris and Jennings (1978) reported 54% were androgynous, 21% masculine, 14% feminine, and 11% undifferentiated. Among the 72 non-athletic women 38% were androgynous, 24% masculine, 28% feminine, and 10% undifferentiated.

In a study of 125 males and 150 females 22% of the males were androgynous, 31% masculine, 12% feminine and 35% undifferentiated. Forty-five percent of the females were androgynous, 23% masculine, 21% feminine and 11% undifferentiated. Yet another study looking at 64 male and 92 female athletes found 51% of the female athletes androgynous, 23% masculine, 15% feminine and 11% undifferentiated while 25% of the male athletes were androgynous, 34% masculine, 11% feminine and 30% undifferentiated. It should be noted that both of these studies used college-age subjects. The high percentage of undifferentiated males may reflect the slower maturation rate of the male, indicating that he has not established an identifiable behavioral frame of reference as yet.

Throughout all of the studies reported here individuals who were classified as androgynous also had significantly higher self-esteem. Masculine individuals, both male and female, had the next highest self-esteems while those classified as feminine and/or undifferentiated had significantly lower self-esteems. These studies indicated that it is not being male or female per se or being an athlete, but the psychological attributes that provide the behavioral frame of reference which was related to self-esteem.

SUMMARY

Increasing levels of understanding and changing attitudes about human behavior have indicated that the stereotyped masculine and feminine roles for males and females respectively are no longer appropriate for socializing human beings to function effectively in today's society. As a result, many of the personality instruments which perpetuate these stereotyped expectancies for male and female behavior are no longer appropriate.

Males and females are very much alike psychologically in many respects. Some of the ways that they differ can be explained by how they have been socialized to meet the stereotyped expectancies rather than being explained by a biological basis. Athletes, some of whom are male and some who are female, appear to be more alike than different behaviorally. This suggests that one's behavioral frame of reference must be compatible with the behavioral demands of the environments that the individual seeks.

The behavioral demands of competitive sport are more dissonant with the stereotyped expectancies of feminine behavior. This explains why there has been more concern about the conflict that the female athlete may experience than that of the male athlete. With new ways of conceiving behavior, that is, as dualistic as opposed to a bipolar perspective, male and female athletes have been demonstrated to be more similar than different in their behaviors. Further, other behaviors are better explained when examined within this perspective. Behaviors such as self-esteem and components of achievement motivation appear to be more related to one's behavioral frame of reference than one's gender.

There is an obvious need for more research regarding the possible side effects of changing the definitions of "masculine" and "feminine" that are traditionally used as the standard for rearing boys and girls. The evidence available in no way supports the notion that attempts to foster sex-typed behavior as traditionally defined will produce more effectively functioning men and women.

Based on what has been learned about behavior to date, it appears that societies have the option of minimizing, rather than maximizing, sex differences through socialization practices. This is especially pertinent to have the kinds of opportunities that are presented to males and females for sport competition as well as the reinforcements and rewards that are inherent in these competitive situations. Social institutions and social practices are not merely reflections of the biologically inevitable, according to Maccoby and Jacklin (1974). The social institution of sport needs to change many of its practices to insure that all who seek competitive sport experiences to maximize their potential have the same rewards and reinforcements, regardless of sex. For much too long the female has had her "femininity" questioned when she makes a serious commitment to competitive sport; conversely, the male has had his "masculinity" questioned when he chooses not to pursue such efforts.

It is up to human beings to determine what behaviors are needed to be learned by all human beings to foster the life styles they most value. Educators and coaches, likewise, must decide the attributes that are needed for the athlete to be effective behaviorally in competitive sport situations. One's biological sex does not appear to have very much to do with these behavioral dispositions.

BIBLIOGRAPHY

Bakan, D. *The Duality of Human Existence.* Chicago, IL: Rand McNally, 1966.

Broverman, J. K., Vogel, S. R., Broverman, D. M., Clarkson, F. E., and Rosenkrantz, P. S. Sex-role stereotypes: A current appraisal. *Journal of Social Issues,* 1972, 7, 146-152.

Harris, D. V. *Involvement in Sport: A Somatopsychic Rationale for Physical Activity.* Philadelphia: Lea and Febiger, 1973.

Harris, D. V. Physical Sex Differences: A Matter of Degree. *The Counseling Psychologist, Counseling Women II,* 1976, 6, 9-11.

Harris, D. V. Research studies on the female athlete: Psychological considerations. *Journal of Physical Education and Recreation,* 1975, 46, 32-36.

Harris, D. V. and Jennings, S. E. Achievement Motivation: There is no fear-of-success in female athletes. Paper presented at the Fall Conference of Eastern Association of Physical Education of College Women, Hershey, PA, October, 1978.

Harris, D. V. and Jennings, S. E. Self-perception of female distance runners. In Paul Milvy (Ed.), *The Marathon: Physiological, Medical, Epidemiological, and Psychological Studies.* New York: The New York Academic of Sciences, 1977.

Helmreich, R., and Spence, J. T. Sex-roles and achievement. In R. W. Christina and D. M. Landers (Eds.), *Psychology of Motor Behavior and Sport* (Vol. 2). Champaign, IL: Human Kinetics Publishers, 1977.

Helmreich, R. W., and Stapp, J. (1975). Life history questionnaire (short form): Instrument, norms, and intercorrelations. *JSAS Catalog of Selected Documents in Psychology,* 5, 327. (Ms. No. 1098).

Jones, W. H., Chernovetz, M. E., and Hansoon, R. O. The enigma of androgyny: Differential implications for males and females? *Journal of Consulting and Clinical Psychology,* 1978, 46, 298-313.

Maccoby, E. E. and Jacklin, C. N. *The Psychology of Sex Differences.* Stanford: Stanford University Press, 1974.

Rosenkrantz, P., Bee, H., Vogel, S., Broverman, I. and Broverman, D. Sex-role stereotypes and self-concepts in college students. *Journal of Consulting and Clinical Psychology,* 1968, 43, 287-295.

Spence, J. T., and Helmreich, R. L. *Masculinity and Femininity: Their Psychological Dimensions, Correlates, and Antecedents.* Austin, TX: University of Texas Press, 1978.

Spence, J. T., Helmreich, R. and Stapp, J. Ratings of self and peers on sex-role attributes and their relation to self-esteem and conceptions of masculinity and femininity. *Journal of Personality and Social Psychology,* 1975, 32, 29-39.

5

The Self-Esteem Of Winners and Losers

MiMi Murray
Springfield College

This discussion will briefly involve: the concept of self-esteem as an attitude, the difficulties of attribute study, sport and self-esteem, and conclusions.

CONCEPT OF SELF-ESTEEM

Self-esteem is the possession of a favorable opinion or evaluation of oneself, or self-worth. Occasionally, self-esteem is used synonomously with self-concept. There are many facets to one's self-esteem or self-evaluation, i.e. one's ability: as an athlete, in social relationships, as a student, in social virtue, and so on. All of these evaluations of one's self combine to form one's self-esteem.

SELF-ESTEEM AS AN ATTITUDE

Evaluations of self are based upon our values and attitudes. Values are deep-seated feelings and thoughts which form a basis or criteria for our evaluations or assessments. Values are culturally determined and socially taught. Our attitudes provide us with a means of expressing our values. Attitudes are ideas charged with emotion (positive or negative) which predispose us to certain behaviors (Triandis, 1971). As an example, value in our society might be, "men must be strong, women weak;" the attitude related to this value might be, "boys can't cry, girls can't throw a ball."

DIFFICULTIES OF ATTITUDE STUDY

One of the major concerns and questions in the attitude change area is if, in fact, atti-

tudes do predict behavior. One school of thought has produced many studies (Triandis, 1971) in which behavior was changed by changing attitudes. A conflicting approach is that by changing attitudes behavior does not necessarily change, therefore we should change or modify behavior (Bandura, 1969).

A possible answer to this is that humans appear to have two sets of attitudes and/or values: conceived and operant. Conceived attitudes are those ideas we espouse. Operant values or attitudes are the way in which we demonstrate behaviorally our attitudes and values. Our conceived and operant values and attitudes may be concomitant or antithetical. Sportsmanship is a conceived attitude which the majority of those of us in sport hold dearly. Yet, operantly we often teach athletes how to take "cheap shots" in football and ice hockey, to foul near the end of the game in basketball, to "brush back" a batter in baseball and so on. It is this speaker's opinion that one of our major problems in coaching is dealing with our own as well as our athletes' differences between conceived and operant values and attitudes. Possibly there would be fewer coach/athlete conflicts if our conceived and operant values were similar. This discussion of attitude and attitude change is relevant, for again self-esteem can be cosidered as one's attitude about his or her own being. Self-esteem, as an attitude, might be enhanced through Sheehan's (1965 and 1976) attitude change model.

SPORT AND SELF-ESTEEM

A common hypothesis regarding self-esteem is that accumulated successful experiences lead to positive self-esteem. Obviously, there are positive and negative outcomes for individuals in sport. Coakley (1978) has observed that for every child who has a good experience in sport there is one who has a bad experience. A bad experience does not increase an individual's confidence and self-esteem. He further indicates that parents who withold positive feedback and affection from their children because of poor athletic performance damage their parent-child relationship as well as their child's self-concept. Since sport can lead to a series of failures i.e. being "cut," "bench-sitting," losing more games than winning, how does this affect an individual's self-esteem or self-worth?

It can be assumed and has been empirically tested that since participation in sport is voluntary, individuals who meet with failure will "drop-out." Yet, sport is so pervasive and important in our society that there is extreme pressure on the individual to continue even though failing — for to be called a "quitter" is akin to calling a male athlete "a girl." Therefore, for some, sport may provide an environment of continued failure rather than success, which may affect self-esteem. Although, Sherif (1976) indicates that occasional failures are not usually destructive to self-esteem if cushioned by previous success.

In America sport leaders continue to proclaim that one who is successful in sport will be successful in life, for the outstanding quarterback or shortstop will always be satisfied and confident. Contradictorily, Beisser (1978) concludes that self-esteem of successful athletes can be damaged by sport-related problems, for they feel their personal relationships are based upon their sport accomplishments rather than their personal qualities. Also, the responsibilities associated with success can be difficult to handle. Sage (1974) further concludes that highly competitive sport is not a preparation for contemporary adult life in America for sport competition requires hard physical struggle, superiority, and dominance over others. In contrast, the present demands for success in life are personal initiative and cooperation in relationships.

One needs successes in many situations for self-esteem to be enhanced and one may perceive their "self as athlete" quite differently from "self as student" (Dowell et.al., 1968).

Our pool of research regarding the female is very limited. However, it might be of interest to note that in a study comparing female athletes and non-athletes on measures of psychological well-being and body image, athletes showed more positive self-attitudes (Snyder and Kivlin, 1975). The results of this study might be explained in that body structure is important in ego-identity of females (Marcia and Friedman, 1970) and body image has a positive correlation with self-esteem (Berscheid et.al., 1973).

In a recent pilot study Thimas (1978) compared members of winning and losing (team status based upon a four year record) womens' high school basketball teams on a measure of self-esteem. She concluded there were no differences in level of self-esteem between winners and losers. Does this relate to sport achievement not being perceived as important to high school women?

CONCLUSIONS

1. Self-esteem is not enhanced in sport, other than "self as an athlete" — one factor in total self-esteem.
2. Because sport is so pervasive in our society there is a possibility that children who meet with failure in sport are pressured to continue in sport rather than "drop-out." For these individuals sport can have a negative effect on "self as an athlete." If this individual has met with failure in many other areas of importance in his or her life the sum of these experiences can have a negative effect on one's total self-esteem or self-concept.
3. The importance of an area of self to the individual will determine the effect on self-esteem. In a study (Sears and Sherman, 1964) of fifth and sixth grade boys; physical ability or in the boys' words "being built for sports" was of prime importance. Thus failure in sport at this level could be damaging to one's self-esteem.
4. If we in sport wish to enhance self-esteem, we must provide for positive and success-filled experiences for all of our participants. We need more

winners, especially youngsters! To provide for more winners, sport should be designed for expressive rather than instrumental results. Solutions might involve: indirect competition (Billings, 1978), educational sport (Sheehan, 1978), new games (Shasby, 1978).

BIBLIOGRAPHY

Bandura, A. *Principles of behavior modification.* New York: Holt, Rinehart and Winston, Inc., 1969.

Beisser, A. *The madness in sports.* New York: Appleton-Century-Crofts, 2ed. 1978.

Berschmeid, E.; Walster, E.; and Bohrsted, G. Body image, physical appearance, and self-esteem. Presented to American Sociological Association, 1973.

Billings, J. *Direct and indirect competition.* Psychology of Sport Conference, University of Virginia, Charlottesville, June, 1978.

Blatnik, A. *An experimental study in selected required college physical education courses to determine the effect of a teaching model structured to produce positive attitudes toward participation in lifetime sports and conditioning activities for physiological and psychological well-being throughout life.* Unpublished doctoral dissertation. West Virginia University, Morgantown, 1968.

Bovyer, G. Children's concepts of sportsmanship in the fourth, fifth, and sixth grades. *Research Quarterly*, 1962, 34, 282-87.

Coakley, J. *Sport in society.* St. Louis: C. V. Mosby Company, 1978.

Corbin, C. A study of spectator attitudes about sportsmanship. *Texas AHPER Journal*, October 1971, 40, 6.

Davidson, I. *The effect of a structured teaching model upon cooperative behavior in a sport environment.* Unpublished doctoral dissertation, West Virginia University, 1972.

Deci, E. Work: Who does not like it and why. *Psychology Today*, August, 1972, 6, 57-58, 92.

Dowell, L., Badgett, J., and Landis, C. A study of the relationship between selected physical attributes and self-concept. In G. Kenyon, ed. *Contemporary psychology of sport.* Fla.: The Athletic Institute, 1968.

Heider, F. *The psychology of inter-personal relations.* New York: John Wiley & Sons, 1958.

Hart, M. (Ed.). *Sport in the socio-cultural process.* Dubuque, Iowa: Wm. C. Brown Company, Publishers, 2ed., 1978.

Hamachek, D. *Encounters with self.* New York: Holt, Rinehart and Winston, 1971.

Kistler, J. Attitudes expressed about behavior demonstrated in certain specific situations occurring in sports. In *60th Proceedings of the National College Physical Education Association for Men,* Washington, D.C., 1957.

Lewin, K. Group decision and social change. In T. M. Newcomb and E. L. Hartley (Eds.), *Readings in social psychology.* New York: Holt, 1947.

Loy, J. The nature of sport: a definitional effort. *Quest*, 1968, X, 1-15.

Loy, J. & Kenyon, G. *Sport, culture, and society.* The MacMillan Company, 1969.

Luschen, G. *The sociology of sport.* The Hague Paris: Mouton E. Co., 1968.

Marcia, J. and Friedman, M. Ego identity status in college women. *Journal of Personality*, 38:249-63, June, 1970.

McAfee, R. Sportsmanship attitudes of sixth, seventh and eighth grade boys. *Research Quarterly*, 1955, 26, 120-121.

McGuire, W. The nature of attitudes and attitude change. In G. Lindzey and E. Aronson (Eds.), *The handbook of social psychology.* Cambridge, MA: Addison-Wesley, 1969, pp. 136-314.

Metcalf, R. A. *An analysis of the components of a philosophical definition of sport and their relationship to the modification of social attitudes.* Unpublished doctoral dissertation. West Virginia University, 1973.

Murray, M. *The relationship of attitudes toward achievement of elementary school girls and participation in educational sport.* Unpublished doctoral dissertation, University of Connecticut, Storrs, 1976.

Ogilvie, B. and Tutko, T. Sport: if you want to build character, try something else. *Psychology Today*, 1971, 5, 61-63.

Orlick, T. and Botterill, C. *Every kid can win.* Chicago: Nelson-Hall Co., 1975.

Polgar, S. The social context of games: or when is play not play. *Sociology Education*, 1976, 49, 265-271.

Richardson, D. Ethical conduct in sport situations. In *66th Proceedings of the National College Physical Education Association for Men,* Washington, D.C., 1962.

Sage, G. Psychological implications of age group sports programs. Paper presented at the *AAHPER Convention,* Anaheim, California, 1974.

Sage, G. *Sport and American society.* Mass.: Addison-Wesley Publishing Co., Inc., 1974.

Sears, P. and Sherman, V. *In pursuit of self-esteem.* California: Wadsworth Publishing Company, 1964.

Seymour, E. Comparative study of certain behavior characteristics of participant and non-participant boys in little league baseball. *Research Quarterly,* 1956, *27,* 338-46.

Shaw, M. E. and Wright, J. M. *Scales for measurement attitudes.* New York: McGraw-Hill, 1967.

Shasby, G. "New Games." Presented at the Psychology of Sport Conference, University of Virginia, Charlottesville, June, 1978.

Sheehan, T. *The construction and testing of a teaching-model for attitude formation and change through physical education.* Unpublished doctoral dissertation. Ohio State University, Columbus, 1965.

Sheehan, T. *Educational sport.* Psychology of Sport Conference, University of Virginia, Charlottsville, 1978.

UNIVERSITY OF VIRGINIA FOOTBALL

Julie Heyward,
Charlottesville, Virginia

6

Risk Taking
For Sport

Chris Malone
University of Virginia

INTRODUCTION

Originally man had to face dangers and threats associated with daily life in order to survive. Those who learned to meet and control these challenges of life and death survived. In this manner man has played his role in Darwin's theory of survival of the fittest. A technological society has altered man's life style considerably so that the physical dangers associated with survival have been greatly reduced. Yet, risk continues to play a role in everyone's life. The manner in which people cope with risk varies according to each one's approach to life.

According to *Webster's New Collegiate Dictionary* (1977) risk is defined as a dangerous element or factor, possibility of loss or injury, hazardous speculation, danger or peril. The term itself brings to mind oppositional words such as safety-danger, success-failure, gain-loss, eustress-distress, and life-death. An individual seems to be in an either/or situation when contemplating risk.

Risk can be observed or identified in many forms. There seem to be four major types of situations where risk can be identified. First there is monetary risk where financial gains and losses are risked. Second, there are physical risks where bodily harm and even death can occur. Third, there are situations of ethical risk where normative ethical values are questioned. And fourth, there are social risks where an individual's self-esteem is at stake.

It must be kept in mind when considering risk as a concept that how an individual perceives a specific situation may vary with another person's perception of the same situation as to the degree of risk involved. This factor alone contributes to the complexity surrounding any study concerned with risk.

Risk has often been associated with sport due to the inherent physical harm that participants risk while engaging in sport activities. The sport activity is situational and does demand of its participants a certain amount of risk. Yet individuals bring to the sports situation various skills and abilities which determine the extent of risk to some degree. For example, the strategy one athlete selects over another may demand a higher level of risk than the activity inherently holds.

While many argue that the risks of sport participation are acceptable relative to the health benefits gained, some authors disagree. Hayes (1974) believes that many of the risks taken related to sports participation are unnecessary and should be reduced without changing the nature of the activity. He sees the problem as threefold: identification of the risks inherent in sport, differentiation between acceptable risks and undue risk taking, and implementation of preventive measures to reduce the incidence and severity of injuries to participants. Most likely it is impossible to identify the universal benefits of a sport, and at the same time it is highly speculative to think that one could identify what is undue risk for one athlete and not for another. Even if one could identify the person most susceptible to high risk-taking behavior, what could be done to reduce the risk factor and minimize injury?

With the growth of sport psychology, researchers have focused their attention on anxiety, stress, motivation, and personality structure of athletes. One area of interest has been the study of motivations for stress-seeking in sports where potential risks are very high. Many psychologists have studied risk-taking behavior quite extensively in order to determine personality variables which may be associated with the so-called high and low risk taker. However, there has been a great amount of inconsistency in their findings. Again it must be made clear that the concept of risk is multidimensional, and as yet no one has been able to test or measure risk consistently. A survey of the literature concerning risk as a concept is very sporadic, but does give evidence of considerable interest in the study of risk-taking behavior.

Assuming the inherent nature of sport as risk taking, the focus of this paper is a review of the literature from other disciplines in hope of deriving some conclusions concerning the motivations involved in risk-taking in sport.

MOTIVATIONS FOR RISK TAKERS

David McClelland (1958) noted in his study of children's behavior in a ring toss game that children high in need for achievement tended to stand at intermediate distances from the peg when tossing the ring. Yet, children with low need for achievement were more likely to stand quite close to or quite distant from the peg. McClelland (1958) proposed that this achievement motive had cultural or family origins in that standards of excellence are imposed which the child is expected to meet. Therefore this achievement motive is learned as a result of experience.

Atkinson (1960) proposes a theory of achievement motivation applicable to an individual when he knows his performance will be evaluated (by himself or others) in terms of success or failure. According to this theory, individuals have a need for achievement (nAch) and a concurrent motive to avoid failure. Atkinson has extended this theory in explaining decision-making processes. He has formulated a risk-taking paradigm which he uses to explain an individual's decisions in an achievement-oriented task situation. He states:

When there are alternatives which differ in difficulty, the choice of level of aspiration by persons more disposed

to avoid failure is diametrically opposite to that of persons more disposed to seek success. The person more motivated to achieve should prefer a moderate risk. His level of aspiration will fall at the point where his positive motivation is strongest, at the point where the odds seem to be 50-50. The fearful person, on the other hand, must select a task even though all the alternatives are threatening to him. He prefers the least threatening of the available alternatives; either the task which is so easy he cannot fail or the task which is so difficult that failure would be no cause for self-blame and embarrassment.

Atkinson's risk-taking paradigm is almost identical to McClelland's earlier investigation of children's behavior in a ring toss game. These two researchers are not alone in their findings. Experimental investigators have shown that individuals for whom the motive to succeed is greater than the motive to avoid failure will, preferring a moderate risk, select a task of intermediate difficulty, while individuals for whom the motive to avoid failure is dominant will, preferring an extreme risk, select either an easy or a difficult task.

One of the first relevant studies completed that supported Atkinson's theory was done by Atkinson, Bastian, Earl, and Litwin (1960). In this experiment, high and low need achievers were compared on the distance they stood from the target in a modified shuffleboard game. As proposed by the theory formulated by Atkinson, high need achievers chose intermediate distances or moderate risks to a significantly greater extent than did the low need achievers. In the choices of the low need achievers the very difficult was preferred over the very easy. In a later experiment by Atkinson and Litwin (1960), both a need-achievement and a test-anxiety measure was tested. This made it possible for four subgroups of subjects, those high in both the motive to achieve success and the motive to avoid failure, those low in both, and those high in one and low in the other. It was hypothesized that the high-low or low-high subgroups would yield the most interesting data. As expected, the group with the high need-achievement, high test-anxiety group preferred the extreme risk or no risk distances.

A more contemporary experiment performed by Shaban and Jelker (1968) further supports the Atkinson theory. This study extended Atkinson's model of achievement motivation and risk-taking paradigm to produce a hypothesis about risk preference in a situation where an individual did not select the difficulty of the task, but he could select among several levels of risk by having his performance negatively or positively evaluated. The motive to succeed was aroused by obtaining a positive evaluation, whereas the motive to avoid failure was identified by obtaining a negative evaluation. The motive to avoid failure and the motive to succeed was manipulated in this study by instilling in the subjects a high or low self-esteem. Subjects were given the California Psychological Inventory self-esteem scale and the results changed in order to instill low or high self-esteem in individual subjects. The expectations were that high self-esteem subjects would select an intermediate risk of a negative evaluation. The results supported these expectations. Yet the expectation that low self-esteem subjects would equally prefer a low risk of negative evaluation was not confirmed. This study is the second that has failed to show that low need achievers will select the easy risk as well as the high risk choice in alternatives for accomplishing a task. Therefore it would seem logical that there is a need for further research in this area.

In addition to the research generated by the Atkinson-McClelland theory, another team of psychologists has also been the source of interest in risk-taking behavior. Kogan and Wallach (1964; 1967) in their studies of risk-taking used a conceptual approach to the study of behavior. They saw a distinct difference between motivational risk-taking and cognitively determined risk-taking in decision situations. Furthermore they stressed the importance of test anxiety and defensiveness as moderators of one's views toward risk-taking. Based upon these hypotheses, they identified two types of risk-takers whose actions are rationally (cognitive) or irrationally (motivational) determined.

Risk involves uncertainty in various problem solving or decision-making situations. Kogan and Wallach (1967) designed for their purpose of study the Choice Dilemma

Questionnaire. This instrument presents several unique situations, each containing a central person who is faced with a choice between two courses of action. One of these choices entails a greater risk of failure, but also a higher reward if successful. The subjects' task is to advise the person in each of the twelve situations by selecting the probability of success considered sufficient to warrant choosing the risky alternative. Below is an example from this questionnaire:

Mr. D is the captain of College X's football team. College X is playing its traditional rival, College Y, in the final game of the season. The game is in its final seconds, and Mr. D's team, College X, is behind in the score. College X has time to run one more play. Mr. D, the captain, must decide whether it would be best to settle for a tie score with a play which would be almost certain to work or, on the other hand, should he try a more complicated and risky play which would bring victory if it succeeded, but defeat if not.

Imagine that you are advising Mr. D. Listed below are several probabilities or odds that the risky play will work.

Please select the lowest probability that you would consider acceptable for the risky play to be attempted.

_____ Place a check here if you think Mr. D should not attempt the risky play no matter what the probabilities.

_____ The chances are 9 in 10 that the risky play will work.

_____ The chances are 7 in 10 that the risky play will work.

_____ The chances are 5 in 10 that the risky play will work.

_____ The chances are 3 in 10 that the risky play will work.

In selecting a probability value the individual essentially is telling the extent to which possible failure will cause him to seek or not seek desirable outcomes. In general, then, it appears that the costs of possible failure do affect the risk that will be tolerated by the subjects. Thus, highly important determinants of the riskiness of a decision are the gain or success of a decision in relationship to the loss or failure caused by a decision. The question arises, does the cost of failure exceed the attraction value of gains from success in risk-taking behavior?

Evidence for the importance of gains and costs in risk taking comes from a study of unethical behavior by Rettig and Rawson (1963). These investigators hypothesized that unethical behavior is a function of perceived risk. They gave subjects an imaginary situation much like the Choice Dilemma Questionnaire developed by Kogan and Wallach. However, the situations concerned on unethical behavior conflict with ethical behavior. Below is an example.

The student treasurer of a social fraternity, who urgently needed a substantial sum of money for a crucial operation, was considering stealing money from the fraternity since he did not have any money of his own. The surgeon could not at all guarantee the student that the operation would cure his illness, but the student knew that sooner or later his theft would be detected. However, he was certain that he would be able to settle the matter privately with the president of the fraternity.

The results from the Rettig-Rawson investigation shows that costs are of great importance in the realm of ethical judgment, but beyond that fact, it has shown that some costs act as a greater deterrent to risk than do others. Evidently, costs must be assessed relative to the goals and values of the decision-making individual. What one person perceives as costly may not be costly to another, likewise gains.

Other theories of risk as related to motivation are proposed by Festinger and Deutsch. Festinger (1957) proposed a motivational theory which examined the conflict between cognitive elements and efforts of the individual to reduce the dissonance or inconsistency in order to obtain consonance or consistency. This theory is essentially an equilibrium model and the risk involved pertains to the amount of dissonance which can be tolerated. In other words, if one realizes that he does not want to die, yet he participates in a death defying activity like skydiving, he takes certain precautions that reduce the conflict between these two cognitive elements. For example, he might train on the ground in preparation for a dive, fold his own chute several times,

fly in certain planes, or dive with only certain jump masters. By taking these precautions he is perhaps reducing the dissonance between the two cognitive elements, life and death.

Deutsch (1960) distinguishes between a trusting and a risk-taking (gambling) choice in his discussion of the effect of motivation on trust and suspicion. Essentially he sees one who trusts as one who risks losing a large amount relative to what one can gain, thus one will not take much risk of losing. When one gambles, one risks losing a small amount relative to what one can gain, therefore one is willing to take a large risk of losing. His investigation supports the idea that cooperatively motivated behavior results in suspicion of others and untrustworthy behavior. This hypothesis certainly has great meaning for sport in the area of competition versus cooperation.

Achievement need in sports has been identified with winning and the motivation to succeed. Athletes have been found to be higher in achievement need than non-athletes and seek sport as a situation in which to resolve their need according to Singer (1968). Although Singer's views may not necessarily be predominant in today's research on this subject, closely associated with this idea that athletes engage in sports as a means of satisfying their high need achievement is the topic of stress seeking. Stress seeking as it pertains to sport refers to the rational approach of individuals to a challenge. Man has manipulated risk or danger in order to increase stress. This is accomplished by seeking faster speeds, gaining new heights, jumping further — in other words, narrowing the margin of safety. In most cases the stress is clearly apparent, but freely sought. The goal is sharp and visible. There is no doubt when one has succeeded or failed (Klausner, 1968).

Klausner (1966) in his study on the transformation of fear describes fear and enthusiasm as negative and positive components of a continuum of excitement. He proposes that fear is transformed as the level of excitement increases. Thus, the greater the degree of fear which the individual succeeds in generating within himself, the greater the enthusiasm he may experience.

Other writers refer to this stress seeking in terms of mastery and control. For example, Fenichel (1939) proposes a counterphobic attitude whereby the very source of fear and anxiety is sought in order to master the effective reaction to it. Specifically he refers to people for whom dangerous sports are highly participated in as true counterphobics. The transformation of passive helplessness into active mastery is seen as a defense against fear and anxiety. When faced with a challenge where injury and death are possible consequences, mastery or control of death and injury is a form of emotional self-control learned through experience. This has been observed in several sport activities.

The control or mastery of risk after careful calculation and estimation is perhaps an intense source of pleasure for those athletes engaging in sports. A distinction between danger as opposed to risk should be understood in this context. Danger is considered beyond control and is usually avoided by the rational risk taker according to Wenkart (1963). Abnormal or foolhardy behavior should not be confused with risk-taking behavior in sport.

Another source of motivation for risk taking may be in the need for realization of potential. Maslow (1968) in his heirarchy of human needs, perceives man as striving to develop two sets of needs, one of which inhibits due to fear and need for safety and the other which strives toward growth and realization of potential. Perhaps, self-fulfillment may be satisfied by undertaking mountain climbing, sky-diving, or car racing.

Whatever motivates one to take risks may never be fully understood, however there is a need for further research in attempting to clarify the risk-takers' behavior. As Kretchmar and Harper (1969) succinctly stated, "Man plays for many reasons, yet he plays for no reason at all . . . Man will act with spontaneity, irrationality, and abandon. The livid reality of this union between man and play defies all attempts to reduce it to a rationally explicable understanding."

CONCLUSION

When one thinks about the risk involved in sport the usual thoughts center upon physical danger. As mentioned previously, risk of physical harm is thought by many to be inherent in sport and is a calculated risk any performer must take if he wishes to participate and be successful. Various measures have been used in sport to reduce the risk involved in most activities. For example, equipment has been improved in order to avoid serious injuries; coaches use scientifically developed training methods; rules and safety regulations have been approved and implemented for eliminating possible dangerous results of a particular activity; and physicians are working with teams of all levels of participation. However, there are other forms of risk involved with sport that are not as evident to both the performer and the observer. Mainly this is due to the fact that performance is not usually interrupted as is the case in injury or death by these other forms of risk. Yet, social, monetary, or psychological losses or failures are all forms of risk involved in sport participation. Some of these forms of risk may be far more devastating in the long run than a physical injury. For this reason, forms of risk should be identified and recognized.

There have not been many research investigations concerned with risk and risk-taking behavior in sport. Yet many of the studies completed have great implications for coaches and athletes. For example, the effects of audiences on risk choices in performing a task; risk choices of high need achievers versus low need achievers; birth order and participation in risky sports; and most importantly, stress management and coping with stress of risky sports.

Vaughan (1971) proposes a construct for identifying the elements of risk in sport. Her construct is built around three components; the performance, the situational activity, and the environmental setting. The elements of risk inherent in sport (danger and uncertainty) are examined in relationship to the above construct. With this construct, Vaughan hopes that eventually someone will be able to understand what constitutes risk for participants in sport.

The identification of the risk involved in a particular sport might provide a basis which will help individuals select or avoid specific sport activities. By the same token, if the elements of risk could be determined it might be of value in further understanding risk-taking behavior and the motivational basis for it. Thus, someone who would like to participate in a risk-taking sport activity, but cannot due to psychological and motivational reasons, could be given cognitive therapy that may eventually allow them to participate.

Furthermore, identification of elements of risk in sport might provide a basis for classifying, rating and comparing sports. Comparisons of what constitutes risk might be obtained through a collection of dichotomous samples. For example, the responses of athletes could be compared to the responses of non-athletes. There are several other possibilities for making these comparisons, such as sex, age, level of competition, etc.

As coaches, what we perceive as risk in sport may or may not be risk for the athlete. This has important implications in coaching athletes. If an athlete's perception of risk could be determined for the sport he is a participant in, then a greater understanding of how to effectively coach that individual might be gained.

REFERENCES

Atkinson, J. W., Bastian, J. R., Earl, R. W., and Letivin, G. H. The achievement motive, goal setting, and probability preferences. *Journal of Abnormal Social Psychology*, 1960, *60*, 27-36.

Atkinson, J. W., and Feather, N. (Eds.). *A Theory of Achievement Motivation*. New York: John Wiley and Sons, 1966.

Deutsch, M. The effect of motivational orientation upon trust and suspicion. *Human Relations*, 1960, 123-139.

Fenichel, Otto. The counterphobic attitude. *International Journal of Psychoanalysis*, 1939, *20*, 263-274.

Festinger, L. A. *A Theory of Cognitive Dissonance*. Stanford, California: Stanford University Press, 1957.

Hayes, Don. Risk factors in sport. *Human Factors*, 1974, *16*, 454-458.

Klausner, Samuel, Ed. *Why Man Takes Chances: Studies in Stress Seeking*. Garden City, New York: Anchor Books, 1968.

Klausner, Samuel. *The Transformation of Fear*. Bureau of Social Sciences Research, Inc., Washington, D.C., 1966.

Kogan, N., and Wallach, M. A. Risk Taking as a Function of the Situation, the Person, and the Group. In *New Directions in Psychology, III*. New York: Holt, Rinehart, Winston, 1964.

Kogan, N., and Wallach, M. A. *Risk Taking: A Study in Cognition and Personality*. New York: Holt, Rinehart, Winston, 1967.

Kretchmar, R. S., and Harper, W. A. Why does man play? *Journal of Health, Physical Education and Recreation*, 1969, *40*, 57-58.

Maslow, Abraham. *Toward a Psychology of Being*. Princeton, New Jersey: D. Van Nostrand, 1968.

McClelland, David C. Risk Taking in Children with High and Low Need for Achievement. In *Motives in Fantasy, Action and Society*. Ed., John Atkinson. Princeton, New Jersey: D. Van Nostrand Co., 1958, 306-321.

McClelland, David C. et al. *The Achievement Motive*. New York: Appleton-Century and Crofts, 1953.

Rettig, S. and Rawson, H. E. The risk hypothesis in predictive judgments of unethical behavior. *Journal of Abnormal Social Psychology*, 1963, *66*, 243-248.

Shaban, Janet, and Jelker, J. Risk Preference in choosing an evaluator: an extension of Atkinson's achievement-motivation model. *Journal of Experimental Social Psychology*, 1968, *4*, 35-45.

Singer, Robert. *Motor Learning and Human Performance: An Application to Physical Education Skills*. New York: The McMillan Company, 1968.

Vaughan, Linda Kent. An Exploratory Study of Risk for the Identification of the Elements of Risk in Sport. *Dissertation Abstracts International*, 1971.

Webster's New Collegiate Dictionary (Springfield, Mass.: G. and C. Merriam Company, 1977), p. 1000.

Wenkart, Simon. The meaning of sports for contemporary man. *Journal of Existential Psychiatry III*, 1963, 397-404.

7

Using Psychological Tests To Help Athletic Performance

Dorothy V. Harris
Pennsylvania State University

Those of us in physical education and sport have traditionally operated under the assumption that the healthy, physically fit body is associated with a stable personality and good mental health. If literature that was published early in this area is reviewed, many studies supported the basic premise that somehow superior athletes are better put together people behaviorally. There are studies comparing athletes versus nonathletes; fit versus unfit; varsity players versus intramurals, etc. Inherent in many other studies is the assumption that those who choose athletics and vigorous physical activity exhibit better and more positive personalities. Personalities have been assessed before an exercise or sport intervention then again following the intervention. When changes were observed in the positive direction it as assumed that exercise was the causal factor.

Unfortunately, the chicken-egg problem is still a factor in much of this type of research. Much of the earlier research has been criticized for lack of a theoretical basis, for poor methodology, for poor design, and for lack of control groups. The lack of instruments designed to assess populations that were being studied was no small problem. Not to mention the fact that most coaches lack the training and experience of giving the tests, of scoring them, and of interpreting the results and making application to the athlete in an ethical, beneficial manner.

In the seventies numerous self-report instruments were developed specifically for athletic populations. These instruments ranged from general to specific sport assessment of such areas of personality as anxiety and arousal, attentional focus, and others. Several of the instruments that have been used frequently in the assess-

ment of athletes are discussed briefly in the following section. Additional information regarding these and other assessment instruments may be obtained in the Buros Mental Measurement Yearbook.

The first sport specific personality instrument, the *Athletic Motivation Inventory* was developed by Ogilvie in 1968. This instrument was widely used in its early development, however, lack of statistical support for validity and reliability has restricted its present use. Another problem was that the scoring was done by the Institute for Athletic Motivation in San Jose, CA and a computerized evaluation of each athlete was sent to that coach. Most coaches did not know how to interpret or to make application of this information, resulting in the dismissal of some skilled athletes who did not conform to the expected profile of a successful athlete. Individual differences were lost for the most part. In spite of the difficulties that Ogilvie and Tutko experienced and the criticism they received from many of their colleagues they did make a contribution by developing the first personality instrument for athletes.

The Sport Competition Anxiety Test (SCAT), developed by Martens (1977), is an assessment instrument to determine the general competitive anxiety of athletes. The Speilberger State-Trait Anxiety Test (1970) was used as a model in developing the SCAT, which presents statements that are sport specific rather than general in nature.

The State-Trait Anxiety Inventory (STAI) (Speilberger, 1970) has been applied to sport groups with good results. This test is widely used in psychological research and additional information is readily available in psychological publications concerning the reliability, validity, use, etc.

Nideffer (1976) developed a *Test of Atten-*

42

tional and Interpersonal Style (TAIS). The TAIS purposes to assess attentional strengths and weaknesses or the ability to concentrate and focus on the task at hand and the relevant cues necessary to perform that task most effectively.

Currently Dr. Mike Mahoney is developing a *Psychological Skills Inventory for Sport* (PSIS) which is designed to assess five areas: arousal level of the athlete, how the athlete concentrates, the confidence of the athlete, the social interaction, and the use of imagery. The PSIS shows some promise of being useful for assessing athletic groups, however, it is still in the developmental stage.

The future promises more instruments designed to assess athletic populations. As research increases in sport psychology and as more graduate students pursue this area of specialization and learn more about psychological theories and concepts, more interest and knowledge will be generated.

Regardless of the test selected for use, ethics and guidelines for use of human subjects should be followed. Any assessment should be used to help the athlete maximize his/her performance. Individuals conducting research and collecting data from athletes must respect the dignity and worth of the individual and honor the preservation 'and production of fundamental rights of human beings. They should be committed to increasing the knowledge of human behavior and the the athlete's understanding of themselves and others in sports environments. The utilization of knowledge gained should be for the promotion of human welfare.

Those who consider themselves special-ists or consultants in sport psychology require an atmosphere of free inquiry and communication without misrepresentation of their knowledge and methods by others. They have an obligation to prevent misuse of psychological techniques in sport through their personal influence, public statements, and professional sanction. Further, they have an obligation to make the results of their research available to other colleagues, to related scientists, and to others in allied professions. Future growth and development in sport psychology testing and research must abide by ethics and standards endorsed by organizations promoting sport psychology and/or by standards of psychological organizations.

REFERENCES

Buros Mental Measurement Yearbook. Highland Park, NJ: V Gryphon Press.

Mahoney, M. Psychological skills inventory for sport. The Pennsylvania State University, In press.

Martens, R. (1977). *Sport competition anxiety test.* Champaign, IL: Human Kinetics Publishers.

Nideffer, R. M. (1976). Test of attentional and interpersonal style. *Journal of Personality and Social Psychology, 34,* 394.

Ogilvie, B. C. (1968). Psychological consistencies within the personality of high-level competitors. *Journal of the American Medical Association, 205,* 156-162.

Speilberger, C. D., Gorusch, R. L., & Lushene, R. E. (1970). *Manual for the state-trait anxiety inventory.* Palo Alto, CA: Consulting Psychologists Press.

SECTION III

Individual Motivation

8

The Family
As An Influence
On Motivation
And Participation

Linda K. Bunker
University of Virginia

It is a well known fact that parents, brothers, and sisters have a very direct and emphatic effect on the development of children. The inherited characteristics which children receive from both of their parents form an important phylogenetic base, but the early years of life are also greatly affected and modified by the experiences and socialization imparted by parents. These years are most important to an individual's future success in sport. It is during these years that attitudes and interests, as well as intellectual and physical abilities, are developed. It is at this time that the foundation for motivation and personality characteristics related to sport success and happiness is laid down.

FAMILY INFLUENCES ON SPORT PARTICIPATION

Recent research supports the claim that early and lifelong sports participation is greatly affected by the influence of significant others, particularly the family environment (Orlick, 1972) (see Figure 1). It is obvious that *parents* function as *models* of behavior with which their children can identify. The traditional psychological viewpoint that assumed that girls identify with their mothers and boys with their father is no longer acceptable. Contemporary thought supports the notion that even though the functional role of mother and father differ, children normally identify with both parents rather than just one. Both mother and father serve an important function as attractive sport participants and role models. Mothers

must be certain that they do not transmit their fears and anxieties of sport participation to their offspring, especially their sons. Fathers must be careful not to discourage their daughters from sport participation because of their fear of masculinizing their daughter or discourage males from "female" sports. It is perfectly acceptable and even desirable in today's world for girls to be competitive, assertive, and achievement oriented athletes. In fact, today's male may favor females who are healthy and "athletic." Self-acceptance of these changing roles on the part of parents is of vital importance (Mussen and Rutherford, 1963).

Social categories such as ethnicity, race and religion also influence the sport development of children. Members of certain sub-groups may be given different opportunities and are influenced by the prevailing behaviors, values, attitudes and norms which are found within specific subcultures. That is, if children are members of a particular ethnic, religious or racial group they may be faced with norms and values which differ significantly from the mainstream of society. For example, Blacks have been found to be underrepresented at certain playing positions, thereby suggesting different opportunities or encouragements to occupy those roles (Loy and McElvogue, 1970).

There are however other variables in the family environment which can be readily modified during the developmental years to encourage sport participation by children. All children should be encouraged to participate in active rather than quiet or pas-

46

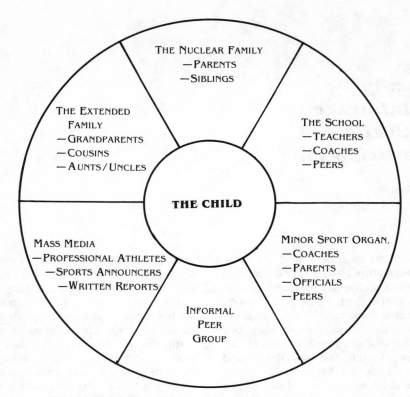

**Significant Others in the Social System of Children
(Adapted From McPherson, 1978)**

sive play. For example, girls should be taught to be less passive and more competitive in their play. Studies continue to show that girls display interest in "masculine" activities longer than boys do in "feminine" activities, inasmuch as the male role in our society still tends to be associated with greater freedom, privileges, and in some respects, status (Mussen, Conger, and Kagan, 1969). In other words, girls enjoy sports participation just as much as boys and will experience little if any role-conflict as they mature, provided that they are taught that sport participation is an appropriate behavior for both boys and girls (Barry, Bacon and Child, 1957) — that is, social reinforcement and evaluation are key factors.

In order to encourage sport participation, parents should frequently attend live sport contests as well as watch sports on television with their children. When children express interest in taking part in sports they should be enthusiastically encouraged. This is the time to give children that extra attention and affection. Finally, as the child

learns to read, make certain that sport literature is easily accessible in the home.

BIRTH ORDER, FAMILY SIZE, AND SIBLING-SEX

The actual composition of the family has an important influence on development. Birth order, family size, and sex of siblings all have an important impact on children as they develop. In large families the pressures and expectations of siblings eventually may outweigh those of parents. For example, the influence of siblings can be seen in White urban families in which boys with older sisters, within four years of age, typically display more "sissy" type behaviors than boys without older sisters. Similarly, girls with brothers more than two years older have a tendency to be relatively tomboyish (Koch, 1956). In addition, males with older sisters have been found to participate in a greater number of sports than do males with brothers or with no siblings.

Apparently there is a close association between birth order and participation in dangerous sports. It has been found that first born sons are taught to be less aggressive, more prone to guilt feelings, more conforming to their peers, more likely to fear physical harm, and more apt to avoid dangerous or high-risk sports (soccer, football, rugby) than are later borns. In large families, however, first borns are more likely to participate in dangerous sports as frequently as other family members. It appears that the first born child receives much more emotional involvement and anxiety transmitted from parents, especially the mother. The over-concern for the welfare of the first child leads to extra safe treatment, especially in the case of a small family or an only child (Nisbett, 1968).

Child rearing practices have a great deal to do with the desire of children to participate in sport. The ways in which parents deal with children vary from the free and supportive to the very restrictive. For example, sex differences in the way parents treat children have been observed as early as six months. A mother is more likely to pick up an infant daughter and thus restrict the range and area over which the daughter may explore (Goldberg and Lewis, 1969). Boys on the other hand are given more freedom to display aggressive behaviors and to engage in more vigorous activities with toys (Lewis, 1972).

The stereotyped male is self-reliant, achievement oriented, in control of his feelings and slow to express them, and has a concern for rule conformity. The stereotyped female on the other hand, is nurturant, socially oriented, emotional and quite expressive (Lewko and Greendorfer, 1977). Even·children recognize these differences, such that elementary aged girls identify "to be nice" and "to be smart" as the most essential desirable behaviors, while boys identify "to be good in sports" and "to be a leader" as most important (Caplan and Kinsbourne, 1974).

Parents also demonstrate different levels of expectation for some children than for others. Certain types of motor abilities are shared differentially with sons than with daughters, i.e. fathers wrestle more with sons, and teach them gross motor skills. In addition, the expectations and interests seem to change from child to child depending on their birth order (Greendorfer and Lewko, 1978).

Various theories have been proposed to explain the observed ordinal position and sibling-sex differences in regard to sport behavior. Of particular interest are the explanations derived from modeling theory which suggest that second born children model much of the behavior of the first born sibling, regardless of the sex or age difference. It might therefore be expected that males and females with brothers, as opposed to children with sisters as first born role models, would develop different interests and participation patterns. For example, Koch's (1956) study of two-child families showed that boys with an older sister (FM2)[1] were more often rated sissy than boys with an older brother (MM2). Similarly, girls with an older brother (MF2) were more often rated as tomboys than girls with an older sister. In general these findings hold over various studies and suggest that cross-sex siblings tend to assimilate traits of the opposite sex, and that this effect is most pronounced in the younger of the two siblings (Brim, 1958; Portz, 1972). Similarly, males and females with older brothers have reported significantly more past sport participation in games of physical skill and strategy than males and females with sisters (Sutton-Smith and Rosenberg, 1961).

Studies dealing with the composition of certain sport groups also show some interesting results. For example, in the traditionally masculine-conceived sports of basketball and track and field, the MF2 was over-presented while the F1F was under-represented. In a feminine-conceived sport such as gymnastics, the F1F was significantly over represented and the MF2 was under-represented (Portz, 1972).

According to these types of studies, the modeling effect is quite pronounced. Unfortunately, the explanations are not always that simplistic, and there is often an en-

---

[1]Rosenberg and Sutton-Smith's (1964) system of notation designates the possible combinations of sibling-sex and ordinal positions. The number indicates ordinal position and always follows the subject's sex. The F or M not followed by a number indicates the sex and position of the sibling, (i.e. F1M is a first born female with a younger brother, while MM2 is a second born male with an older brother).

tirely different influence exhibited by some children, a siblings-opposite hypothesis (Portz, 1972). That is, an older sibling may serve as a negative role model, or someone whose traits should not be acquired. For example, a young boy may find disapproval expressed by parents and peers if he acquires his older sister's response patterns or interests. This phenomenon can also occur with same-sex siblings, in the case where sibling rivalry exists and leads him to avoid modeling and therefore competing with an older brother.

Several authors have reported findings which would support this siblings-opposite theory. For example, the college aged FM2 has been found to be more interested in masculine-type activities than MM2 males (Leventhal, 1966). Similarly the FM2 have been found to compete in a significantly greater number of sports than M1 and M1M.

In review, each of the explanations dealing with family influences stems from a different conceptualization of family and peer relationships. The sibling-similarity and sibling-opposite hypotheses are based primarily upon the power relationships fostered by socialization. Parental influence is not directly linked to this modeling theory. Sibling association effects are matters of social learning and not simple facts of nature. These effects will demonstrate systematic relationships to cultural functions on the adult level. It will therefore be particularly interesting in the next ten years to see how the equalization of the positive aspects of sport skill and sport participation to both sexes may impact on these socialized sibling relationships.

PARENTS AS SPORT PARTICIPANTS

Parents, coaches, and sport psychologists are all extremely interested in identifying factors which stimulate children to a lifelong interest in sports. This is indeed a challenging task, and there is an abundance of information which can be quite helpful to parents wishing to interest and encourage their children in sport.

Probably the single most important thing that parents can do to interest their children in sports is to be active sport participants themselves. Children who frequently view their parents engaging in sport can identify with them and use them as effective role models, especially when the parent's behavior while playing emphasizes fun, enjoyment, and enthusiasm. Because kids are very desirous of moving and having fun these are behaviors that will motivate children to get interested in sports.

These qualities are much more important to children than their parent's level of performance. Children less than 6 or 7 years of age are not interested in, nor capable of, differentiating between skilled and non-skilled performance by others. Children are continually attempting to please and gain the affection of their parents. Kids will therefore be attracted to activities which appear to capture the interest and enthusiasm of their parents. Often they will directly imitate their partners. For this reason, children will soon show an interest in playing. When this desire to participate is perceived by parents the opportunity for children to play should be enthusiastically encouraged and allowed. It is at this point that parents should be certain to place the enjoyment of children ahead of themselves. Parents must make certain that the early experiences with sport are filled with fun and success. An open display of pleasure and affection toward children is definitely appropriate at this time.

Unless children express an unusual interest, highly specialized and mandatory practice sessions should not be started before the age of 10. Of course, some children will be ready at an earlier time and some not until later in life. The key is to be sure that the child is not forced into lessons and practice. Too often forcing kids into sports leads them to "burn out" and lose interest at an early age. Once they express an interest, be sure to keep practices motivating and interesting to the children. Similarly if they want to play — do it; if not, don't, or create a situation in which they want to play.

Sports are sometimes viewed as a mechanism which creates more losers than winners. Ultimately, advanced sports will produce only a few fortunate winners. The majority will be losers. Often children will drop out of sports at very young ages because of repeated failure experiences, being ridiculed by other players and/or coaches, receiving little playing time, or favoritism on the part of coaches. Parents can just as effectively discourage children by not showing interest in their participation or not observing their performance, unless, of course, they are winning. Parents and coaches should be sure to reinforce their kids for trying no matter what the outcome.

Young children need to learn to enjoy competing. If children are encouraged to compare their performance against their own past performance rather than against others, their chances of viewing themselves as successful and increasing their role-concept will be greatly enhanced. If this happens, children will be much more likely to continue to desire to participate in sports.

ENCOURAGING CHILDREN TO BE ASSERTIVE

Success in the world of sports, or for that matter, the world of school and work, depends upon an individual's ability to display a healthy level of assertiveness. People who are over worried about pleasing others, rather than themselves, tend to be overly sensitive to other people's thoughts and expectations. Certainly, all children should be raised to feel comfortable about expressing their feelings and expecting others to treat them with respect, listen to them, and take them seriously. People should never have to feel guilty about expressing their feelings, desires, and opinions. Individuals have a right to have their own priorities. These are basic human rights. Of course, in the process of teaching children to stand up for these rights we must be sure to teach them that others have these very same rights which must not be violated.

The goal of assertive behavior is to communicate honestly and directly. Assertive individuals make choices for themselves without harming or being harmed by others. Our clinical work with athletes tells us that far too often the frustrated, self-defeating, overly sensitive athletes are those who will not allow themselves to be assertive. Fortunately, assertiveness is learned and can be developed in the early years of life. Teaching children to be assertive can help them to learn to take responsibility for their own lives and in the process raise their self-esteem.

Children can learn to be assertive by having assertive behavior rewarded when it is appropriately displayed. We must encourage children to be independent and self-reliant, and avoid praising children for being passive and submissive. Children should be encouraged to deal with stress and not be encouraged to avoid conflict. When conflicts occur, especially between brother-sister, brother-brother, sister-sister, or playmates, children should be taught the importance of standing up for their own rights.

This is not to suggest that children must carry assertiveness to the point of being obnoxious to be a success in sport. Feelings of sensitivity for the rights of others must not be subdued or eliminated. Under some circumstances, being obnoxious while participating in sport may to some degree help a child, especially when competing against very sensitive athletes. But there are also many negative consequences for children who are obnoxious. Usually obnoxious children do not have many friends, for they are not perceived as caring much about others and consequently may be ostracized by others. However, in the few cases where obnoxious athletes make it to the very top, they may still manage to have friends. Of course, these friends may only be there as long as the athlete is a success.

We do not believe that parents should be encouraged to raise children to be obnoxious. Children should be raised to be assertive, for it is important to success and happiness in sport. Assertiveness does not eliminate sensitivity for the feelings of others. Rather it emphasizes that there are situations in which individuals need to be assertive and place themselves first, and there are other times to be sensitive and place the needs of others first. All athletes should be brought up capable of deciding when to display both of these behaviors.

DEVELOPING ACHIEVEMENT MOTIVATION AND COMPETITIVE DESIRE

Achievement motivation and the desire for competition on a theoretical level may be viewed as two slightly different constructs. However, for the purpose of the present discussion they will not be differentiated. Competitive desire and/or achievement motivation will be considered the desire to compare one's performance against a standard of excellence which will be evaluated by another person or persons.

For years scholars have tried to settle the most important issue as to whether man's competitive desire is largely innate or learned. It is quite obvious that there is no clear-cut answer, but rather it is a question of degree. Clearly, there are individual, religious, racial and cultural differences in competitiveness. For these reasons it is widely accepted today that competitiveness has its base in the genetic endowment of each individual. However, it is predominately determined by a variety of learning experiences. Parents, siblings, relatives, coaches, teammates, and an assortment of cultural and early social experiences will largely determine the degree of competitiveness that your children will display.

How is achievement motivation developed? What are the behaviors that teachers and parents can use to encourage high levels of achievement motivation in children?

The past 20 years have seen many developmental psychologists attempt to discover the parent-child interaction which will most likely lead to high achievement motivation. Achievement motivation can begin to be influenced as early as the age of two years. The theory of social learning argues that achievement motivation is largely a product of social learning and reinforcement by social sanctions. Undoubtedly, these sanctions are effective reinforcement and have a pronounced effect of achievement motivation. However, they do not constitute the only possible kind of reinforcement. As detailed, earlier, the experience of competence has in itself a reinforcing value even in the small child (White, 1959). Usually, however, the approval of a relevant person involved is not an end in itself but rather an important measure of success which greatly benefits the onset of achievement motivation (Heckhausen, 1967).

Mothers who expect their sons to be independent and do well at an early age tend to have sons with higher achievement motivation scores. That is, mothers who expect and require that their sons be self-reliant early in life, to find their own way around their part of town, will do well in competitive sports. Thus, there is a relationship between independence training and the desire to do well. Additionally, mothers of highly motivated boys, in comparison with mothers of less motivated boys, reward self-reliant mastery with more affection, and also insist on earlier observance of rules which, however, are not as numerous as they are for the boys with low motivation.

Parents' general attitudes and own personal needs have been found to be predictive of their child-rearing practices. A parent's orientation toward their own achievement may influence their behaviors with their children in everyday achievement experiences. Parents who begin early are apt also to be the ones for whom achievement is the most important and who reward their children for successful achievement and punish them for failure. The earlier such rewards and punishments are applied, the greater the effective arousal and the larger the number of undifferentiated achievement cues from which effect is associated (Winterbottom, 1953; McClelland, Atkinson, Clark, and Lowell, 1953).

Other studies have shown that the achievement behavior of 3 to 5 year-old kindergarten children correlated with the degree of positive reinforcement and recognition which they receive from their mothers and fathers for their achievement efforts. Typically parents apply the same expectations and evaluation attitudes toward achievement in their children as they do toward their own achievement. Unfortunately this may mean that low achieving parents will have negative attitudes toward achievement and low expectations, and must be taught to value achievement and to raise the expectations that they set for their children. Parents must consistently communicate positive attitudes toward achievement-related behaviors to their children.

A wide variety of child-training practices can be identified which would seem to be the most effective for developing children with high achievement motivation. The family should be characterized by high achievement oriented levels of aspiration and by warmth and harmonious personal relations. That is, in order to develop high achievement motivation the mother should assume a direct teaching role (especially for boys) making use of the classic principles of learning, i.e. reinforcing desirable behavior with rewards, and eliminating undesirable behavior with punishment or negative reinforcement. It is she who calls forth an effective change. The importance of the mother, or the surrogate mother, particularly in childhood, is very great.

The father is most effective in developing high achievement motivation in his sons when he takes the role of a benevolent and attractive model. The son must be allowed to imitate his father and yet develop independently. The classic learning theory of Bandura (1962) must be understood to completely comprehend this imitation and modeling process. It appears that children modify their individual delay of reward pattern after they have observed an adult model who exhibited delay behavior that was counter to the children's pattern of delay behavior. In this way children learn to put off immediate rewards for future rewards, a characteristic which differentiates high achievers from lower achievers (Bandura and Mischel, 1965).

The presence of a father figure has been shown to be a very significant factor in child development. Boys who were raised without a father during the first five years have been found to be significantly less aggressive, had more feminine preferences, and preferred non-competitive games (Biller, 1970; Stanrock, 1970). This may be due in part to the fact that fathers differentiate on sex roles more strictly, and may be the crucial agent in channeling sex-typed activities of both boys and girls (Block, 1973).

The identification of the father as the crucial factor in the sex-role socialization process does not discount the importance of the mother or the parent combination (Lewko and Greendorfer, 1977). Both parents have been found to react more strongly to sons who demonstrate sex-inappropriate behavior — that is, more social pressure is brought to bear to produce sex-appropriate behavior by boys and girls (Lansky, 1967; Fling and Manosevitz, 1972).

Parents should be encouraged to set goals which are challenging but not too difficult to master, offer general encouragement rather than detailed instruction, and give approval when a difficult task is accomplished creditably. Parents must learn to distinguish between pushing and pulling and learn to pull children from in front (emphasizing frequently desirable goals and

how good it would be to attain such goals) rather than to push children from behind (forcing them to attempt tasks) (Cratty, 1967). The most critical factor however is to display interest and involvement in children's achievement endeavors (Smith, 1969).

The judicious use of praise and criticism cannot be overestimated. It is well known that praise tends to raise levels of task performance while criticism tends to lower performance. Such evaluations also tend to affect the performer's expectancy of success. The child who has been praised — expects praise — a good example of self-fulfilling prophecy. When silence is encountered the child lowers expectancy of success much as if having been criticized (Hill and Shelton, 1971).

Much of the literature on achievement motivation development has seemed at times to place an emphasis on boys. It appears that the same practices are just as effective for girls but unfortunately there is much less research available, due to the traditionally held sex differences in achievement motivation training and some possible directions as they relate to girls, parents, coaches, and sport participation.

ACHIEVEMENT MOTIVATION AND SPORT PARTICIPATION

The American society, quite like other societies, has devised a system of controls by which children and adults pursue behaviors that are sex appropriate. The development of sex-related differences in behavior are due largely to the child-rearing reward system. It is obvious that the distinctions between male and female personalities are a result of factors other than biological ones (Mischel, 1966; Reese and Lipsit, 1970), and that those dissimilarities may therefore be susceptible to change.

The traditionally observed differences in the socialization of boys and girls are consistent with certain universal tendencies in the differentiation of the adult sex role. In the economic sphere, men are more frequently allotted tasks that involve leaving home and engaging in activities where a high level of skills yields important returns. An emphasis on training in self-reliance and achievement would function as preparation for such an economic role as well as sport participation.

The increase in our society of conditions favoring less sex discrimination has led some people to advocate a virtual elimination of sex differences in socializations. In recent years it has come to be accepted and valued for females to achieve in sport as well as in work and family life. Because the value placed on achievement for females has changed, parents must change the emphasis typically placed on achievement for girls.

Far too often over the years boys have been encouraged to be instrumentally competent and achievement oriented while girls were taught to acquire greater expressive abilities and affiliative needs. For example, if a preadolescent or adolescent girl cries after losing a game, this reaction is likely to be accepted as appropriate for the "weaker sex," but a boy who shows tears is likely to be reminded that "little men don't cry" (Mussen, Conger and Kagan, 1969). These sex differences are well established by age five when most children are keenly aware of sex-appropriate interest and behaviors in terms of achieving.

Historically, playing games has been a masculine phenomenon in American culture. However during the past sixty years the sex preferences have become increasingly similar, due primarily to shifts in the female preferences (Sutton-Smith and Rosenberg, 1961). For example, girls have been found to be more restricted in their body movement because they play indoors, and play in smaller, more homogeneous aged groups (Lever, 1976).

Society has taught many women that it is impossible to be both female and achievement-oriented. This dichotomy of values has caused many women to avoid striving for success, or to fear success, due to the potential sacrifice of feminine identity, or in accompanying social rejection. For girls, mastery motivation is more likely to decrease with age, because their anxiety over losing femininity causes inhibition of the drive to excel, unless strong cultural pressures are overcome. Therefore, parents must teach girls that it is desirable for females to achieve. They must be taught to value achieving. Mothers can greatly affect this process by participating in sports and other achievement situations. When this is not possible, attractive female models who are high achievers should be made available for young girls to imitate.

In essence, girls and boys should receive the same child training emphasis on achievement. Girls have as much right to be able to achieve in sport and still be considered female as men have to achieve in sport and still be considered masculine.

RAISING CHILDREN TO DISPLAY HEALTHY AGGRESSIVENESS

The importance of a healthy level of both assertiveness and aggressiveness to success in sport is universally accepted. It is also generally agreed that aggression is natural to human behavior. At birth the aggressive drive is present and has an instinctive nature. But there are most assuredly individual differences in the amounts of aggressive behavior displayed. Obviously then, aggressive behavior is shaped to a great extent by the environment.

Parents wishing to teach their children to be aggressive in sports must completely understand the issue. Children must be taught that aggressive behavior in society is not generally encouraged or accepted, and may be negatively reinforced or punished. In essence, children should be taught the specific situations in which aggressive behavior is accepted and rewarded. Children should also be taught that the purpose of aggressive behavior should be to attain some specific goal (win the contest). Children must never be taught to intentionally harm others, even when it is the most efficient way of achieving the desired goal, or when they are mad or frustrated by an individual.

Parents play the dominant role in teaching aggressiveness. Without always intending to do so, parents administer a series of rewards and punishments to their children for aggressive behaviors. When aggressive behavior is rewarded it will tend to occur more frequently. Reinforcement is most effective when it is partial and intermittent. (Be sure not to confuse violence with aggression.)

Of course, children also learn to be aggressive from reinforcements received during their interaction with siblings and peers. For instance, a child may hit a playmate (intentionally or accidentally) and the playmate relinquishes a toy. The hitting is thus reinforced. When faced with a similar situation the child is likely to hit again. The more frequently this behavior elicits the same results the more often the child will be aggressive. It is very difficult for parents to control these situations other than through the children they are allowed to play with.

Another way that children can learn to be aggressive is through the process of imitation or modeling. When children observe their parents being aggressive they copy them. Research has found that aggressive parents set an aggressive model for their children and as a result have aggressive children. Interestingly, very permissive parents also tend to have more aggressive children. It appears that even though the permissive parent neither rewards aggressive behavior nor acts as an aggressive model, children will be allowed to get away with aggressive behavior. Children may interpret the fact that their parents view and do not punish their aggressive behavior as a sign that aggressiveness is appropriate.

Children may also imitate the aggressive behaviors of others, such as friends, relatives, and/or attractive and dominant individuals viewed on television (including athletes). When children are attracted by others and wish to identify with them they will most likely imitate their behavior. If children view aggressive behavior and can justify its occurrence, most likely they will imitate it. Overt behavior by a model is not necessary. An attractive model merely saying that aggressive behavior is appropriate can increase the level of aggression in children.

There are in addition a variety of other factors for parents to consider when attempting to teach children to be appropriately aggressive. The more often that children are placed in environments in which aggressive behavior is desirable the more likely it will be that children will be aggressive. So the more often children partake in sports suitable to the display of aggression the more likely children will be aggressive in sports. Of course, if children expect to be successful as a result of aggressive behavior this behavior will be emitted more frequent-

ly. Parents would be wise in the early years to provide situations in which children can be successful as a result of aggressive behavior as often as possible. Parents as well as youth sport coaches must stress experiencing success based on specific skills and competitive or aggressive behavior rather than only winning the contest (Scanlan, 1973). If this is not done, do not expect young children who have played a hard, aggressive game to place any value on their performance if they lose. Too often winning is considered the only thing and when teams lose, coaches and parents wonder why motivation and aggressive levels deteriorate. The ridiculousness of this approach is even more evident when it is realized that in any contest there will be one winner and one loser.

Additionally, the more highly children value success in sports and the more highly aggression is associated with success, the more aggressive children will be. Any technique which will increase children's motivation to succeed in sports (achievement motivation) will by virtue of our direct forms of competition lead to increased levels of aggression.

Finally, parents and coaches must be encouraged to only allow and reward aggressiveness which is within the rules and socially acceptable. This is particularly true as the career of active sport participants comes to an end. They must receive help adjusting to the reduction of opportunities available for displaying aggression. We must be sure that we are not developing potential problems for sport participants and/or society.

PARENTAL GUIDANCE IN SPORT DECISION MAKING

Parents will likely have an important influence on many sport related decisions that their children will have to make. Careful thought should go into each and every decision made about sport participation.

For example, when asked which sports should my children participate in, the best suggestion we can give is that children should be influenced to participate in a variety of team, individual, and lifetime sports. This means that parents should plan for both short term participation as well as long term sport participation.

Through team sports children can learn to work with others to attain a goal (if we carefully use sport to teach such behaviors). Team experiences are similar to many work experiences encountered later in life. In the team sport experience children do not have to have all of the pressure of winning or losing on their shoulders alone. There are great benefits to having others with whom to share victory and defeat. Also, in team sports there is often room for individuals with very specific skills. Thus, there may be a place for individuals with one highly refined skill who are not as strong in all other aspects of the game. This is not true in individual sports. Of course, a weakness is that in adult life at the end of the school years, it may be difficult to get enough players together to play a large team sport.

Individual sports teach children to take responsibility for their own successes or failures. It can be a very positive experience but it can also be a very demoralizing and lonely experience to individuals who continually lose. However, individual sports can be practiced and played alone or with one other. The highly motivated children will not be frustrated by the lack of motivation on the part of others. They also may be played throughout life. Therefore, enjoyment will be received all through life as will the possible physical and psychological health benefits. Clearly, the physiological benefits greatly differ from sport to sport.

SUMMARY

Sport participants who eventually become highly proficient (i.e., Olympic stars) appear to have certain common experiences in their backgrounds. For example, a study of Olympic Track and Field Athletes showed that successful sport involvement began early in life (Kenyon and McPherson, 1973):

96% participated in elementary school athletics (football, baseball or basketball)

65% reported that they were winners the first time out

75% indicated their interest was aroused at school (other sports the parents were most important)

80% said teachers and peers valued

track and field (in other sport areas, i.e. basketball, the parents were considerably more important than teachers or school personnel)

If we were to attempt to identify a series of generalizations to help children develop in sport, we could learn a lesson from previously successful athletes.

—Encourage children to become involved in sports early in life (by age 8-9)

—Encourage participation in several different sports to establish a broad base before specializing

—Provide early successful experiences for children

—Encourage competition by positive social sanctions and reinforcements

—Set good role models of continuous participation

A variety of factors must also be considered. Size and ability level of the child as well as susceptibility to injury will be discussed in other chapters. For the present the importance of parental encouragement cannot be over emphasized. That is not to say that parents should get carried away by the glamour and attention associated with high level sport success, but that they should provide opportunities and reinforcement for the development of skill. Parents generally wish to have their children involved in sports for the success and happiness it may bring to their children. Parents must never allow their own desire for sport success or their own frustrations over lack of success in sports to control the treatment of their children. Most children will only be able to reap the joys of sport if allowed to develop at their own rate. The most important point for truly loving parents is to be able to look back as their children mature and know that they did everything possible for their children to have a chance to be happy and successful in sport.

REFERENCES

Bandura, A. Social learning through imitation. In M. R. Jones (Ed.) *Nebraska Symposium on Motivation*. Lincoln, Nebraska: University of Nebraska Press, 1962, pp. 211-269.

Bandura, A. and Mischel, W. Modification on self-imposed delay of reward through exposure to live and symbolic models. *Journal of Personality and Social Psychology*, 1965, *2*, pp. 698-705.

Barry, H. III, Bacon, M. K. and Child, I. L. A cross-cultural survey of some sex differences in socialization. *Journal of Abnormal and Social Psychology*, 1957, *55*, pp. 327-332.

Biller, H. B. Father absence and the personality development of the male child. *Developmental Psychology*, 1970, *2*, 181-201.

Block, J. H. Conceptions of sex role: Some cross-cultural and longitudinal perspectives. *American Psychologist*, 1973, *28*, 512-526.

Brim, O. G. Family structure and sex-role learning in children: A further analysis of Helen Koch's data. *Sociometry*, 1958, *21*, 1-16.

Caplan, P. J. and Kinsbourne, M. Sex differences in response to school failure. *Journal of Learning Disabilities*, 1974, *7*, (4), 232-235.

Cratty, B. J. *Social Dimensions of Physical Activity*. Englewood Cliffs, New Jersey: Prentice-Hall, Inc., 1967.

Fling, S. and Manosevitz, M. Sex typing in nursery school children's play interests. *Developmental Psychology*, 1972, *7*, (2), 146-152.

Goldberg, S. and Lewis, M. Play behavior in the year-old infant: Early sex differences. *Child Development*, 1969, *40*, 21-31.

Greendorfer, S. L. and Lewko, J. H. Role of family members in sport socialization. *Research Quarterly*, 1978, *49*, (2), 146-152.

Heckhausen, H. *The Anatomy of Achievement Motivation* (Traws, Butler, Birney and McClelland). New York: Academic Press, 1967.

Hill, J. P. and Shelton, J. *Readings in Adolescent Development and Behavior*. Englewood Cliffs, New Jersey: Prentice-Hall, Inc., 1971.

Kenyon, G. S. and McPherson, B. D. Becoming involved in physical activity and sport: A process of socialization. In G. L. Rarick (Ed.) *Physical Activity: Human Growth and Development*. New York: Academic Press, 1973.

Koch, H. Sissiness and tomboyishness in relation to sibling characteristics. *Journal of Genetic Psychology*, 1956, *88*, 321-244.

Lansky, L. M. The family structure also affects the model: Sex-role attitudes in parents of preschool children. *Merrill-Palmer Quarterly*, 1967, *13*, 139-150.

Leventhal, G. S. Sex of sibling, birth order and behavior of male college students from two-child families. Manuscript, Psychology Department, North Carolina State University, 1966.

Lever, J. Sex differences in the games children play. *Social Problems*, 1976, *23*(4) 478-487.

Lewis, N. Culture and gender roles: There is no unisex in the nursery. *Psychology Today*, 1972, *5*, (12), 54-57.

Lewko, J. H. and Greendorfer, S. L. Family influence and sex differences in children's socialization into sport: A review. Champaign, Illinois, Human Kinetic Press, 1977.

Loy, J. W. and McElvogue, J. F. Racial segregation in American sport. *Intenational Review of Sport Sociology*, 1970, *5*, 5-25.

McClelland, D. C., Atkinson, J. W., Clark, R. A. and Lowell, E. L. *The Achievement Motive*. New York: Appleton-Century-Crofts, 1953.

McPherson, B. D. The child in competitive sport: influence of the social milieu, in Magill, Ash and Smoll (Eds.) *Children in sport: A contemporary anthology*. Champaign, Ill.: Human Kinetics Press, 1978.

Mischel, W. A social learning view of sex differences in behavior. In E. E. Maccoby (Ed.) *The Development of Sex Differences*. Stanford, Cal.: Stanford University Press, 1966.

Mussen, P. H., Conger, J., and Kagan, J. *Child Development and Personality*. New York: Harper and Row Publishers, 1969.

Mussen, P. H., and Rutherford, E. Parent-child relations and parental personality in relation to young children's sex-role performances. *Child Development*, 1963, *34*, 589-607.

Nisbett, R. E. Birth order and participation in dangerous sports. *Journal of Personality and Social Psychology*, 1968, *8* (4), 351-353.

Orlick, T. D. *Family sports environment and early sports participation*. Paper presented at the Fourth Canadian Psychomotor Learning and Sports Symposium, University of Waterloo, Waterloo, Canada, 1972.

Portz, E. Influence of birth order, sibling sex on sports participation. In Harris, D. V. (Ed.) *Women and Sport: A National Research*

56

Conference. Penn State HPER Series No. 2, Pennsylvania State University, 1972.

Reese, H. W. and Lipsiff, L. P. *Experimental Child Psychology.* New York: Academic Press, 1970.

Rosenberg, B. G. and Sutton-Smith, B. Ordinal position and sex role identification. *Genetic Psychology Monographs,* 1964, *70,* 297-328.

Scanlan, T. K. Antecedents of Competitiveness. In M. G. Wade and R. Martens (Eds.) *Psychology of Motor Behavior and Sport.* Illinois: Human Kinetics Publishers, 1973.

Smith, L. E. (Ed.) *Psychology of Motor Learning.* Proceedings of C.I.C. Symposium on Psychology of Motor Learning. University of Iowa, Chicago: Athletic Institute, 1969.

Stanrock, J. W. Parental absence, sex-typing and identification. *Developmental Psychology,* 1970, *2,* 265-272.

Sutton-Smith, B., and Rosenberg, B. G. Sixty years of historical change in game preferences of American children. *Journal of American Folklore,* 1961, *74,* 17-46.

White, R. W. Motivation reconsidered: The concept of competence. *Psychological Review,* 1959, *66,* 297-333.

Winterbottom, M. R. The relation of childhood training in independence to achievement motivation. Unpublished doctoral dissertation. Ann Arbor: University of Michigan, 1953.

9

Coaching And Motivating The Superior Athlete

MiMi Murray
Springfield College

The successful athlete could be defined as one who produces close to his or her potential. The role of the coach is that of a faciliator. Thus, in terms of motivating the superior athlete, the coach should attempt to provide the best circumstances possible so that the athlete can fulfill his/her potential. At the expert level of motor learning, motivation can be maintained through: intense love of the sport, ambition or desire to achieve, and certain amounts of success. The learning curve for motor skills never shows smooth progress and the more skilled the athlete, the more plateaus he/she will experience in learning. The successful athlete will be most frustrated by these plateaus and the coach should educate the athlete about these, as well as demonstrate empathy for the frustration the athlete is experiencing.

As you are aware, some athletes motivate themselves well (internal motivation) while others need help from their peers, family, significant others, and the coach (external motivation). The coach's role is quite an easy one when involved with an athlete who is internally motivated. The athlete who needs external motivation poses other problems. Prior to effecting motivation in an athlete, he/she must feel unique or special, need to be dealt with on a personal level, and understand and agree with the team goals.

External motivation includes praise, compliments, correction, and at times anger from the coach. The superior athlete is usually quite capable of accurately evaluating his/her performance level. Therefore, the coach should be extremely honest and frank in discussing the strengths (primary emphasis with beginners) and weaknesses (can be a more "heavy-handed" approach with outstanding performers). Superior athletes need accurate feedback, whether it is from the coach, video-taping, film, or further mechanical analysis from other experts (refer to Rotella (1978) for more detail in this respect).

Successful athletes have certain personality traits or characteristics which can be divided into two major categories: desire factors or the individual's willingness to achieve; and emotional factors including attributes regarding self and the coach. Tutko and Richards (1978) have identified these traits as drive, aggression, determination, responsibility, leadership, self-confidence, emotional control, mental toughness, coachability, conscience development, and trust. These authors offer suggestions as to how a coach can help an athlete become stronger in any of these areas. Further they have developed an Athletic Motivation Inventory through which they say assessment of these attitudes within the individual athlete(s) can be made. Science Research Associates are now marketing these concepts as the Athletic Motivation Program.

It would prove helpful to discuss a few of these traits more specifically. The first attitude, desire or drive, of course, is that which we have been referring to as "adnauseam"/achievement. World class athletes possess extra-ordinarily high needs for achievement (Cratty, 1975; Murray, 1979).

Leadership, occasionally referred to as need to exert authority, is common among coaches more so than athletes. Interestingly, those individuals who demonstrate the authoritarian personality often have a need to have authority exerted upon them. Athletes who are authoritarian are usually not difficult to coach for this reason (Cratty, 1975).

Emotional control is essential, for in a

stressful situation, competition, the great athletes maintain emotional self-control. World class competitors are individuals whose emotional problems are controlled or who have stable personalities, for were this not true, they would have dropped out of this highly pressurized arena of sport. The coach must demonstrate extra emotional effort to deal with emotionally unstable athletes.

As an individual who had an opportunity to coach world caliber competitors in gymnastics, the quality which most glaringly stood them apart from all other athletes was their self-confidence. Bandura (1977) refers to this as self-efficacy, or the belief in one's personal competence. A self-fulfilling prophecy is accomplished by those athletes who verbally demonstrate confidence. Unfortunately, spectators consider this a "cocky" undesirable trait in professional athletes and demonstrate their distaste by watching the Yankees and hope that someone like Reggie Jackson will strike out. Muhammed Ali is a prime example of the demonstration of this quality. But he accomplished what Flip Wilson's Geraldine referred to as "Don't write a check with your mouth, your body can't cash." The coach should accurately evaluate whether an athlete's poor performance is due to lack of confidence or skill, and Rotella (1978) has suggestions for assessing this. If failure is due to lack of confidence, the coach should:

1. encourage mental rehearsal
2. encourage resolutions or statements of self-effaciousness
3. provide positive feedback
4. occasionally use false feedback to aid the athlete; past performance plateaus (Rotella, 1978).

One of the strikingly important needs in dealing with the exceptional athlete is to determine how they can increase or improve their focus or direct and control their attention. We need empirical studies in this area and you should be referred to the articles by Dr. Rotella, Dr. Harris, and Dr. Bunker for more information regarding focus and attraction.

What do successful athletes want in and from a coach? Massimo (1975) in a study, determined what gymnasts wanted most from or in their coach. According to Massimo, gymnasts desire that a coach:

1. Use minimal verbiage — too many of us over-coach; maybe this is due to an insecurity in trying too hard. "When you're number two, you try harder," and many female coaches have this attitude about themselves; yet we should select only one or two corrections for an athlete to work on in each skill or effort.
2. Have a sense of humor — one must be careful to not overuse this, especially if the humor takes the form of sarcasm. Humor involves laughing at one's self and not at another.
3. Use individual psychology — this implies dealing with each team member as an individual. Some athletes need lots of coaching and attention and others can just about coach themselves. Fairness as a concept is something that female gymnasts, from my experience, seem to get "hung up" on. There is no way a coach can be completely fair. There will always be some athletes who will get more of the coach's attention on a given day than others. But maybe if the team understands why the coach is giving more time to a certain athlete, there will be more of an understanding — this then is communication. All of us have different needs and the coach should attempt to determine these and within his/her own philosophy provide for them.
4. Have technical competency — any one who cares enough to take the time and is willing to learn and can analyze human movement can coach most of our sports. Knowledge of the sport can be acquired.
5. Appreciate the sociology of the team — the coach must not only deal with the individuals on the team, but also must be concerned with how these individuals interact. The coach should know what the team personality is.

In conclusion, coaching and motivating successful athletes isn't very different from coaching any athlete. To be successful, the coach should be aware of individual differences of team members, both physically and psychologically — respect them, accept them, care about them personally; and appeal to their self-respect, common sense, and need to master self as well as their sport environment.

REFERENCES

Bandura, A. Self-efficacy: Toward a unifying theory of behavioral change. *Psychological Review,* 1977, *84,* 191-215.

Cratty, B. J. *Psychology in Contemporary Sport.* Englewood Cliffs, N.J.: Prentice-Hall, 1975.

Massimo, J. 1973 Presentation of New England Gymnastic Clinic, Newtown, Massachusetts, November 1975.

Murray, M. "Achievement motivation in sport." Charlottesville, Virginia: Psychology of Sport Conference, 1979.

Murray, M. *Women's gymnastics: Coach, Participant, Spectator.* Boston, Mass.: Allyn and Bacon, Inc., 1979.

Rotella, R. J. "Dealing with superior athletes." Charlottesville, Va.: Psychology of Sport Conference, 1978.

Rotella, R. J. "Improved attention in sport through relaxation and mental imagery." Stratton Mountain, Vermont: Coaching staff presentation, 1977.

Tutko, T. A. and Richards, J. W. *Psychology of Coaching.* Boston, Mass.: Allyn and Bacon, Inc., 1974.

Tutko, T. A. and Richards, J. W. Athletic motivation program. SRA, Inc., 259 East Erie Street, Chicago, Illinois, 1978.

10

Maximizing Growth In The Gifted Athlete

Robert J. Rotella
University of Virginia

The athletes who are the most likely to provide the coach with instant success as well as long term frustration are those gifted individuals known as the superior athletes. Super athletes may provide the coach with an assortment of motivational and performance improvement problems which vary markedly from the typical athlete. In order to effectively coach these individuals, coaches must understand that they are different and know how to help them reach their potential.

Many psychologists supportive of the research of behavior modifiers have encouraged the importance of the positive effects associated with the judicious use of praise for motivating athletes of all ages and both sexes. It is often witnessed, however, that an overuse of praise may not best fit the needs of the already self-confident and highly motivated superior athlete. Two researchers, Roland Tharp and Ronald Gallimore (1976) have given us an excellent insight into this dilemma. Their systematic study of John Wooden, Ex-UCLA Basketball Coach revealed some interesting and unanticipated findings. It was noted that praise, although present was a negligible part of Wooden's coaching style. Coach Wooden actually scolds (verbal statements of displeasure) twice as often as he praises. But the scolds are almost always loaded with instruction. In addition, the scold-reinstruction is administered in a general sense so that no one is sure who the offending member is; the net impact being that the whole team pays attention to the scold as well as the instruction that most surely will follow. Coach Wooden's instructions were found to be extremely clear. Modeling of the correct way to execute a skill almost always followed a scold. He then imitates the incorrect way the player has just performed, and

finishes with a demonstration of correct execution. Wooden's technique appears to be a most effective way of providing feedback and discriminative training of superior athletes.

It must be emphasized that Wooden's athletes were for the most part highly talented athletes, and that the coaches use of positive and negative comments was highly individualized. For example, as some UCLA basketball players lost confidence, praise was again given in much larger doses with scolds greatly reduced. The coaches rapport before and after practice is warm and concerned. Practice always ends with a joke or a pat on the back. Physical punishment is never used because of his desire to keep practice a desirable activity. (Wooden's examples of dealing with the highly motivated and talented athlete do not necessarily represent techniques which are best for the average or below average self-deprecating individual).

FEAR OF SUCCESS

Superior athletes also tend to have problems when they are the star on a losing team, *especially* when they are *dedicated* to the team. It is quite impossible for such individuals to deny responsibility for the team's failure. Typically this problem will not be pertinent to superior athletes who are more concerned with individual rather than group achievement. Often when involved as a member of a losing team the superior athlete blames himself, with a resulting loss of confidence and the corresponding depression. If these states of mind and body are allowed to remain the athlete will no longer be a superior athlete. The coach must be sure that this athlete is looking at his/her responsibilities accurately. These individuals should be counseled to understand that they can best help by setting an enthusiastic and positive example. They must also understand that they can only do so much, for this reason it is important that their role on the team is accurately understood.

PLATEAUS IN PERFORMANCE

A second motivational problem of pertinence to the superior athlete is related to plateaus in skilled performance. In the early stages of skill acquisition, improvements occur frequently and are quite visible. At this stage it is easy for athletes to be excited and enthusiastic about practicing diligently. But as skills improve there is less room for large gains. Advancements occur less often and are more difficult to attain. Skills tend to stagnate and remain at the same level for increasing periods of time. The period of little or no gain known as plateaus can have a very debilitating effect upon the motivation of the superior athlete. It is most important that these athletes understand that at higher skill levels, increments will occur less frequently. It is precisely at this point in time as a matter of fact that improvements are a matter of becoming more consistent and thus the mental-emotional side of sport begins to play the crucial role. Let us now turn our attention to those cognitive factors and discuss their possible relevance to the superior athlete.

SELF-EFFICACY

One of the most intriguing concepts determining the performance success of the superior athlete is rooted in the theory of self-efficacy (Bandura, 1977). You may be familiar with the positive thinking approach of Norman Vincent Peale which is quite similar. Recent research studies corroborate the assertions of these two men. It appears that if an individual is capable of performing the desired skill and is motivated to do so (incentive) then performance will be determined by one's own belief in personal competence.

Bandura (1977) emphasized this point when he stated that:

Expectations of personal mastery affect both the initiation and persistence of coping behavior. The strength of people's convictions in their own effectiveness is likely to affect whether they will even try to cope with given situations . . . Not only can perceived self-efficacy have directive influence on choice of activities and settings, but, through expectations of eventual success, it can affect coping efforts once they are initiated. Efficacy expectation determines how much effort people will expend and how long they will persist in the face of obstacles and aversive experiences. The stronger the perceived self-efficacy, the more active the efforts (pp. 193-194).

We are all quite aware of the fact that champion athletes who are outspoken braggingly make predictions about their performance that come true. (Namath, Connors, Ali, Jackson). But what can the coach do to help athletes attain this desired mental set? Prior to attempting to aid the athlete it must be ascertained as to whether or not the athlete's problem is one of a lack of confidence or a lack of ability to perform the physical task required. Unfortunately at this point in time there is no standardized assessment instrument designed for this purpose. But there are self-report strategies which can be quite effective (Mahoney, 1977; Rotella, 1977). Some of these are the following:

1. Direct Inquiry — asking the athlete to report expectation for success just prior to the crucial performance.
2. Model Inquiry — asking the athlete to report expectations for success prior to a practice modeled to imitate the up coming contest.
3. Imaginal Rehearsal — asking the athlete to mentally rehearse the future performance and then giving feedback about self-efficacy expectations prior to the start of the contest.
4. Retrospective Reports — having the athlete recall expectations just prior to recent attempts at the task.
5. Dream Report — asking athletes to record and report all dreams relevant to the target performance.

It is strongly advised that all team members and the coach be involved in group dynamics training so as to increase sensitivity to one another and to decrease false reports and inaccurate estimations of self-confidence. The same suggestions are also most appropriate for dealing with the superior athlete who tends to be overconfident. The same suggestions are also most appropriate for dealing with the superior athlete who tends to be overconfident.

Once assessments are completed and it is determined that a lack of confidence is present several intervention possibilities are available:

1. Mental Rehearsal — mentally practicing for future desired performance.
2. Resolutions — continual repetition of self-efficacious statements in preparation for performance.
3. Positive Feedback — the coach provides positive reinforcement aimed at convincing the athlete that the ability to be successful is present.
4. False Feedback — telling the athlete they have surpassed a goal not actually surpassed (set high jump bar at 6′ 10″ and tell the athlete it is 7′), slight exaggeration of coaches estimation of athlete's ability (telling the athlete they are much better than another athlete who has surpassed his/her expectations or actual records). The last technique should be used sparingly and is most effective in helping athletes past some temporary barrier or plateau in performance.

Only the future will unlock the answer to the potential of self-efficacy theory for improving sport performance. As of the present, its possibilities look great.

ATTENTIONAL FOCUS

The last topic to which I would like to direct your interest is attentional focus in athletes. There is probably no variable of more crucial importance to sport performance than the ability to direct and control one's attention. One of the most feasible attempts to understand attention in sport has been offered by Nideffer (1976) who suggests that attention can be conceptualized on at least two dimensions: direction and breadth of focus. Athletes may attend to either internal or external cues, and in terms of its focus attention may be either broad or narrow.

Athletes must be able to concentrate effectively while performing. When necessary they must be able to focus attention on a single external object, at other times they must be able to focus on several external objects as well as be capable of switching back and forth between these two possibilities (shooting a basketball vs. leading a fast break). Based on this line of reasoning more and more sport psychologists are considering the possibilities of training superior athletes to direct and control attention. An as of yet unanswered question is whether the techniques are feasible for only advanced athletes or should be started at an earlier age.

For the moment there are many techniques being attempted to help athletes learn to regulate attention. Which of the techniques are most effective will only be determined with more research and application. Some of the techniques presently being used to help superior athletes are as follows:

1. Practice concentrating by thinking of the immediate present rather than in the past or future.
2. Practice concentrating on a single object while in a relaxed environment.
3. Practice concentrating on a single object for extended time periods while in a stressful (distractable) environment for increasing time periods.
4. Practice the ability to change the direction and breadth of attention — internal to external, narrow to broad and back again.
5. Practice relaxation training and visual imagery.

A variety of insights into the various problems and techniques of pertinence to superior athletes have been presented. It must however be remembered that these superior athletes will benefit as much from techniques designed specifically for their needs, as will athletes at the opposite end of the scale. Again, it appears obvious that coaches must at all times be caring, knowledgeable, and flexible if they wish to be truly effective.

REFERENCES

Bandura, A. "Self-efficacy: Toward a unifying theory of behavioral change." *Psychological Review,* 1977, *84,* 191-215.

Mahoney, M. J. Cognitive skills and athletic performance. In P. C. Kendall and S. D. Hollon (Ed.) *Cognitive-Behavioral Interventions, Theory, Research, and Procedures.* New York: Academic Press, 1977.

Nideffer, R. M. *The Inner athlete: Mind plus muscle for winning,* New York: Thomas Y. Crowell Company, 1976.

Rotella, R. J. Improved attention in sport through relaxation and mental imagery. Presentation to coaching staff at the Stratton Mountain School, Stratton Mountain, Vermont, November, 1977.

Tharp, R. C. and Gallimore, R. What a coach can teach a teacher. *Psychology Today,* 1976, January, 75-78.

Julie Heyward, Charlottesville, Va.

11

The Application Of Locus Of Control To Sport And Physical Activity

Evelyn G. Hall
Louisiana State University

INTRODUCTION

Many principles and theories from social psychological research on locus of control may readily be applied to relationships found in sport and physical activity. A potentially rich area for future research in sport psychology includes consideration of locus of control as a mediator of various performance phenomenon. For example, how is locus of control related to social facilitation theory, the Inverted-U arousal-performance relationship, information processing strategies, or attribution of success-failure outcomes? Moreover, how is locus of control related to leadership styles and group interaction within sport? Unfortunately, the answers to these and other questions can be determined only through much further study.

Locus of control, sometimes referred to as internal-external control, denotes the way in which individuals perceive their control over rewards and reinforcements received throughout life. As a personality variable, internal control refers to a strong expectancy toward "the perception of positive and/or negative events as being a consequence of one's own actions and thereby under personal control" (Lefcourt, 1966a: 207). Whereas, external control refers to a strong expectancy toward "the perception of positive and/or negative events as being unrelated to one's own behavior in certain situations and therefore beyond personal control" (Lefcourt, 1966a: 207). Because of the various types of rewards and reinforcements available in sports, locus of control becomes a salient individual dimension which mediates expectations in various sport-specific situations.

Rotter's (1954) social learning theory provides a theoretical framework for investigating how internal-external locus of control (I-E) interacts with other variables to determine how choices are made from the variety of behaviors available. To determine which behavior has the strongest potential for occurrence, one must consider expectancy for success or failure, reinforcement value, and the psychological parameters of the situation.

As early as 1961, Moss pointed out that situational variables influence only the behavior of individuals who exhibit particular personality characteristics. Consistent with the ideas of Moss (1961), social learning theory regards behavior as determined by *both* situation-specific factors and general dispositional elements to provide a framework for conceptualizing the way in which their relative contributions vary.

"Internals" perceive their own behavior as the determinant of rewards and/or punishments, whereas "externals" perceive themselves as victims of fate or chance or powerful others with outcomes in life not related to effort or skill (Rotter, 1966). In sport, then, internal athletes would attribute winning, personal achievement, or even losing to their own efforts or abilities. In contrast, external athletes would more likely attribute outcomes of certain events, not to their own behavior, but to such external factors as the weather, officials, coaches, teammates, etc.

The instrument which has been used most extensively in past research to assess locus of control has been Rotter's (1966) Internal-External Locus of Control Scale. This scale consists of twenty-nine forced choice items, six of which are filler items. An example of the types of questions found on the scale would be as follows:

6. (a) Without the right breaks one cannot be an effective leader.
   (b) Capable people who fail to become leaders have not taken advantage of their opportunities.

A number of factor analytic studies have shown that Rotter's (1966) I-E scale assesses diverse life needs such as personal fate control, belief in powerful others, luck or fate, and success, to name a few (Phares, 1976). It is obvious, however, that assessment of locus of control within specific sport situations would be sharpened by development of sport-specific scales.

REWARDS, REINFORCEMENT, AND INFORMATION PROCESSING STRATEGIES

It is evident that a clearer understanding of human performance may be gained through systematic investigation, not only of cognitive and physical properties of reward situations within sport, but also an in-depth examination of locus of control as a mediator or how individuals perceive specific rewards. As Pines and Julian (1972) have pointed out, at least two classes of situational variables influence any obtained performance differences: (1) the informational demands of the task, and (2) the social demands of the situation. Either of these two environmental influences may have reinforcement value to an individual, depending upon his/her personality.

A substantial amount of evidence has shown that since internals possess a stronger generalized expectancy that reinforcement is contingent upon their own behavior, they are more active, alert, and directive in attempting to control and manipulate their environments, than are externals. Internals more often describe themselves as active, striving, achieving, powerful, independent and effective (Hersch and Scheibe, 1967; Julian and Katz, 1968).

Several other researchers have also dem-

onstrated that internals are superior not only in acquisition and recall, but also in utilization of information (Davis and Phares, 1967; Lefcourt, Lewis and Silverman, 1968; Lefcourt and Wine, 1969; Phares, 1968; Seeman, 1963, 1967; Seeman and Evans, 1962; Williams and Stack, 1972). Furthermore, work by Getter (1966), Rothchild and Horowitz (1970), and Ude and Vogler (1969) has suggested greater perceptual sensitivity on the part of internals.

In an experiment which varied locus of control, task difficulty, and social evaluation, Pines (1973) and Pines and Julian (1972) found that internals directed more attention to the nature of the task, task difficulty and the consequent pressure for information processing, whereas externals showed more conformity to social demand characteristics of the situation.

Other researchers have shown that externals are more persuasible and conforming to others' expectations, as well as more accepting than internals of information from external sources (Julian, Lichtman and Ryckman, 1968; Lefcourt, 1966; Phares, 1976; Rotter, 1966). These studies imply that externals require greater social reinforcement and extrinsic feedback from performance situations than internals. A distinction must be made, however, relative to skill versus chance situations. Research by Davis and Phares (1967) and Williams and Stack (1972) on the effects of locus of control on information seeking behavior in a skill versus chance situation showed that internals were superior in performance to externals only in skill situations, not in chance situations. Other researchers have found that internals prefer skill-related motor tasks and externals prefer chance-related tasks (James and Rotter, 1968; Lefcourt, 1967; Lefcourt, Lewis and Silverman, 1968; Phares, 1957; Rotter, Liverant and Crowne, 1961).

More recent work by DuCette and Wolk (1972, 1973) employing a simple problem-solving task and a verbal task has demonstrated several ways in which internals performed better than externals: (1) internals were better at using their experience on a task to improve their perception of performance; (2) internals were more accurate in remembering successes when feedback was provided; and (3) internals could more quickly deduce an invariant rule from an ambiguous situation and use this rule to solve a problem.

From the previously cited literature, it appears that internals can readily assemble environmental cues and internalize them to greater advantage for strategically performing a task or solving a problem. Contrary to the self-regulating internal, the external individual would be expected to perform better with external guidance and direction. Obviously, the more cognitively-loaded a motor task or sport happens to be, the more important the role of internal-external locus of control becomes in determining individual responses to situational cues within the environment.

It has been found that externals are more dependent than internals on additional extrinsic reinforcement in the form of praise, in addition to the intrinsic reinforcement inherent in the task. Internals perform just as well without the extrinsic reinforcement (Baron and Ganz, 1972; Kumchy and Rankin, 1975). In three different age groups Baron and Ganz (1972) found superior performance by internals under conditions of self-discovery of success (intrinsic feedback) as compared to superior performance by externals when unverifiable verbal praise was used (extrinsic feedback).

LOCUS OF CONTROL AS MEDIATOR OF SOCIAL FACILITATION EFFECTS

There is strong evidence that, depending upon individualized perception of locus of control, performers may be more task-oriented or more socially-oriented. Externals pay more attention than internals to social stimuli during various task performances. Thus, social facilitation by audiences or co-actors, performing a similar task at the same time, would more likely occur with external performers.

According to general social facilitation theory, the mere presence of others impairs performance during the initial stages of learning. Once a skill has been well learned, however, performance is facilitated by the presence of others. Since internals are more task-oriented than externals, they can more easily block out distractions by audiences or co-actors. No significant differences in performance were found by Hall (1977) be-

tween internals and externals on a novel motor task with no audience or co-actors present. However, when performing in the mere presence of three other co-actors internals displayed significantly better performance than externals on the novel motor task. The greater learning displayed by internals throughout the task performance was explained by their task orientation and lack of concern for extraneous variables such as other performers within the situation.

A substantial amount of research has shown that internals possess a stronger generalized expectancy that reinforcement will be contingent upon their own behavior. Consequently, internals are more active, alert, and directive than externals in attempting to control and manipulate their environment. Internals exhibit a higher level of coping and activity directed toward seeking relevant cues and utilization of information to manipulate situations to achieve more successful outcomes (Davis and Phares, 1967; Lefcourt, Lewis and Silverman, 1968; Lefcourt and Wine, 1969; Phares, 1968; Pines, 1973; Pines and Julian, 1972; Seeman, 1963, 1967; Seeman and Evans, 1962; Williams and Stack, 1972).

Other studies have shown that externals are more conforming and more susceptible to influence by social demand characteristics of the situation. Several studies have shown that externals are more persuasible and more conforming to other's expectations, as well as more accepting than internals of information from other sources. Majorities, peer influence, prestige of communicators, and the social reinforcements of a situation affect externals more than internals (Julian, Lichtman, and Ryckman, 1968; Lefcourt, 1966; Phares, 1976; Pines, 1972; Pines and Julian, 1972; Rotter, 1966). As a result, externals may waste valuable time worrying about external factors during performance instead of concentrating on task relevant information. Because of greater attentiveness to the task rather than the social environment, internals seem to be less influenced than externals by social facilitation effects and thus perform at a higher level than externals while learning a task.

Since externals have a greater desire to please others, this may cause greater anxiety, less confidence, and greater uncertainty during initial phases of task perform-ance. However, once a task has been well-learned, this need to please others could serve as a positive motivator to enhance performance.

Within performers, there are a multitude of personality dimensions which may cause them to interact with audiences in different ways. For example, anxiety, locus of con-trol, introversion-extroversion, field inde-pendence, field dependence, depression, and self-esteem are only a few of the mul-titude of factors which influence the per-former's perception of a particular situa-tion. By the same token, audiences also react to what is happening during a contest in accordance with their own inherent per-sonality predispositions.

LOCUS OF CONTROL AS A MEDIATOR OF THE INVERTED-U AROUSAL-PERFORMANCE RELATIONSHIP

The hope of sport psychologists to pro-vide coaches and athletes with a clearer understanding of the competitive process and individual differences in reactions to success or failure may be facilitated by in-vestigating locus of control and its effects on situational anxiety prior to, during, or after competition.

Rotter's (1954) social learning theory pro-vides a theoretical framework for investi-gating the interaction of locus of control with other variables to mediate individual reactions to specific situations. Within the context of social learning theory, general anxiety and externality are viewed as indi-cative of a high expectancy for punishment or a low expectancy for success in a valued need area (Phares, 1976). Most previous re-search suggests a linear relationship be-tween externality and trait anxiety (Butter-field, 1964; Feather, 1967; Strassberg, 1973; Watson, 1967).

Consistently, the attribution literature has shown attribution of successful out-comes generally to internal factors and fail-ure outcomes to less threatening external sources (Feather and Simon, 1971; Fitch, 1970; Streufert and Streufert, 1969; Wort-man, Costanzo and Witt, 1973). Scanlan's (1977) investigation of high versus low

A-trait subjects relative to success-failure showed that anxiety was an important fac-tor affecting the perception of threat, as measured by A-state levels.

Phares (1976) has predicted a U-shape re-lationship between anxiety and extreme ex-ternal or extreme internal performers. Ac-cording to Phares (1976), extreme internals are overcome with a sense of personal re-sponsibility for failure and therefore experi-ence anxiety prior to performance because they perceive little chance of controlling environmental effects.

Reactions of internals and externals prior to task performance may be quite different from their post-performance reactions. Past locus of control research has indicated that internals cope with success or failure more realistically than externals and have a greater belief in the efficacy of their own ef-forts, thus providing them with a stronger basis for personal adjustment and reduced anxiety, prior to task performance (Phares, 1976).

The concept of internal control is closely akin to Bandura's (1977) theory of self-effi-cacy in which he proposes that people's perceptions of self-efficacy have a strong influence on their success in mastering new behaviors, coping with aversive experi-ences, and remaining persistent in the face of obstacles. Techniques for effective con-trol of bodily reactions and overt behaviors enable people to strengthen their percep-tions of self-efficacy. In the field of physical activity and sport, it may be imminently valuable to help people increase their feel-ings of self-efficacy or internal control.

The notion that some externals have de-veloped an external locus of control belief for defensive reasons has been suggested by several studies (Davis, 1970; Davis and Davis, 1972; Hersch and Scheibe, 1967; Rotter, 1966). Davis (1972) has reported results indicating that internals more often blame personal causes for failure than ex-ternals. Gregory (1978) has reported attri-bution data collected following bogus suc-cess-failure which supports the argument that Rotter's (1966) scale differentiates per-sons who differ in reactions to negative out-comes (failure), but not positive outcomes (success). Hall (1977) studied post-perform-ance state anxiety relative to success-fail-ure outcomes and locus of control. It was found that internals increased more in state anxiety than externals when confronted with failure outcomes. However, externals showed no significant differences in post-performance state anxiety whether succeeding or failing. The notion that failure is more detrimental and anxiety-provoking for some performers merits further investigation in future studies.

IMPLICATIONS OF LOCUS OF CONTROL FOR LEADERSHIP STYLES AND GROUP INTERACTION IN SPORT

Since research indicates that internals view their own actions as the main source of control over reinforcements in life, internal performers would be expected to attribute reinforcements such as winning, personal achievement, or even losing to their own efforts and abilities. In contrast, externals have been shown to focus on external factors and attribute reinforcements received in life to luck, fate, chance or powerful others. Thus, external performers would attribute outcomes, especially negative ones, to such external factors as weather, officials, coaches or teammates, and not to their own behavior.

One area of sport-specific research has dealt with whether or not individual and team sport athletes differ on the locus of control dimension. One study, using young, junior high school athletes has shown that individual-sport athletes are more internal than team-sport athletes (Lynn, Phelan and Kiker, 1969). However, two later studies failed to support such a relationship (Hutchinson, 1972; DiGiuseppe, 1973). For team-sport athletes, of course, teammates are convenient scapegoats on whom to place blame. The very structure of team sports, as compared to individual sports, enables individuals to assume a more external point of view. For example, the disgruntled center forward in field hockey might readily comment, "If the rest of the forward line had done their job, I would have scored my usual three goals today."

On the basis of inferences from locus of control literature, individuals who have a defensive personality make-up (externals) would more likely gravitate toward team sports than individual sports. In individual

sports such as tennis or golf, people cannot blame someone else for their own poor performance. The level of skill displayed in individual sports is obvious for all to see.

Some research evidence strongly suggests that there are two kinds of externals: (1) those who use the external orientation as a defense for their egos, and (2) those who do not (Hochreich, 1974). Individuals who pursue unclear or unrealistic goals in sport or in any other endeavor may become frustrated and find it convenient to blame outside elements for their own lack of perception about realistic goals and reinforcements they wish to pursue in life. Also external individuals may experience a great deal of anxiety in certain achievement-oriented situations because they feel a lack of control over outcomes.

There have been no sport-related studies on coaching styles and how democratic versus authoritarian leadership interacts with locus of control in athletes. It is not clear from the literature exactly which style of leadership works best in sport. No doubt, the pesonality of a coach, which may be very sport-specific, plays an important role in the motivation of athletes. For example, the "hard-nosed" authoritarian coach may be more suited to rough contact sports such as football, ice hockey, or lacrosse rather than to individual sports such as tennis or golf. The "easy going" democratic coach is less likely to be found among contact sports.

It has been suggested by several researchers that an external locus of control predisposes an individual to be more sensitive to the demands of others, especially those in status roles. For example, Phares (1976) has concluded that majorities, peer influence, prestige of communicators, and/or social reinforcements within a given situation have a much greater impact on externals than on internals.

The dimension of locus of control within a coach's personality appears to be highly related to authoritarian versus democratic tendencies. In 1971 Felton found that the "Rosenthal effect," the influence of an experimenter's expectations upon a subject, was maximal when subjects were external and the experimenter internal. Felton's findings imply that internal coaches are best suited for external athletes and vice versa. External athletes would show greater compliance to authoritarian leadership because they are much more concerned with others' expectations. Apparently such individuals would be more willing to take orders, particularly from higher status individuals and to conform to the structure demanded.

Probably there are not as many so-called "problem athletes" as there are problems with communication. In rare cases, a coach must deal with a problem individual to avoid sacrificing the well-being of the rest of the team. But the essential point is that if coaches can understand more fully some of the factors such as locus of control which contribute to certain aspects of athlete behaviors, then athletes can be dealt with more fairly, flexibly, and effectively. For example, extremely internal athletes are very self-regulating and need flexibility to exercise control over their own actions. If the opportunity for self-regulation is eliminated, this may indeed be frustrating for such individuals. It is helpful for coaches to understand that athletes operate differently and possess different levels of anxiety, need for achievement, different reasons for competing, and different goals. Of course there is much less conflict when athletes' personal goals are compatible with group goals.

The basic leadership style of coaches determines how intrinsic and extrinsic rewards and reinforcements are regulated within a sport. It appears that externals depend more than internals upon external reinforcements. For example, Julian, Lichtman and Ryckman (1968) found that externals became more embarrassed and anxious than internals when their performance on a dart-throwing task was criticized by the experimenter.

Kumchy and Rankin (1975) also found a difference in performance between internals and externals in terms of mode of reinforcement. The performance of externals was more dependent than internals on additional extrinsic reinforcement in the form of praise, in addition to the intrinsic reinforcement inherent to the task. Internals performed just as well without the extrinsic reinforcement. The implications for coaching are that externals need more social reinforcement than internals who are more task-oriented.

In studying three age groups, Baron and Ganz (1972) found that internals performed superior to externals under conditions of self-discovery of success (intrinsic feedback), but that externals demonstrated superior performance to internals when unverifiable verbal praise was used (extrinsic feedback).

Moreover, it has been well documented in the literature that, given the opportunity to choose, internals prefer to perform skill-related tasks; whereas externals choose chance-related tasks whenever possible. The fact that externals prefer this chance orientation may be further evidence of their utilization of it as a mechanism against threat to their self-esteem.

Judgments and evaluations of others are significant determinants of reinforcements for externals who believe that fulfilling demands and expectancies of others is the most effective means of controlling reinforcements and rewards. Thus, externals would tend to show a greater need for social reinforcement and extrinsic rewards from coaches or teachers. In contrast, internals focus more on strategic task cues which are most relevant for efficient performance or problem solving. Such individuals are capable of utilizing intrinsic feedback to understand correct or incorrect aspects of their own performance.

CONCLUSIONS

Many new questions can be generated by sport psychologists interested in locus of control as a personality dimension which influences the perceptions and reactions of individuals during receipt of information feedback and other forms of rewards and reinforcements when performing various sport-related skills. Locus of control may be utilized effectively in future sport psychology research by integrating it with other theoretical constructs such as social learning theory to predict individual performance differences.

However, the mindless use of locus of control to explain every situation is a waste of time and implies a simplistic view that behavior can be predicted by one or two variables. To utilize locus of control without some larger theoretical base to provide a complex analysis of the overall situation is to invite a low level of prediction. It is important to recognize that human performance is so complex that it cannot be explained fully by single personality constructs. The strength of an individual's motives, self-confidence, aspirations, and anxieties are interwoven to direct performance.

However, an understanding of how locus of control relates to behavior in general, can aid teachers and coaches in understanding individual behavior. Sports and physical activities by their very nature often place individuals in extremely external situations where participants are likely to feel a loss of control. It is obvious that in order for teachers or coaches to understand the total behavior of individuals, they must examine the demands of the task, the environmental structure, and the personality dispositions of individuals involved in the process.

There are many relevant questions related to locus of control. For example, what types of leadership styles would be most compatible for extreme internals or extreme externals? How would the strict authoritarian coach be expected to relate to the extremely internal or extremely external athlete? How should the teacher or the coach structure rewards and reinforcements within the learning environment? How would having an audience in the vicinity of practice sessions differentially influence internals and externals? Can an individual's percept of locus of control be shaped through modification of teaching and coaching practices? Do internals learn and perform more efficiently than externals? These are some of the questions that become readily apparent when the construct, locus of control, is superimposed onto the world of sport. Unfortunately, the answers can be determined only through further study.

REFERENCES

Bandura, A. Self-efficacy: toward a unifying theory of behavioral change. *Psychological Review*, 1977, *84*, 191-215.

Baron, R. M., and Ganz, R. L. Effects of locus of control and type of feedback on the task performance of lower class black children. *Journal of Personality and Social Psychology*, 1972, *21*, 124-130.

Butterfield, E. C. Locus of control, test anxiety, reaction to frustration, and achievement attitudes. *Journal of Personality*, 1964, *32*, 298-311.

Davis, D. E. Internal-external control

and defensiveness. Unpublished doctoral dissertation, Kansas State University, 1970.

Davis, W. L., and Davis, D. E. Internal-external control and attribution of responsibility for success and failure. *Journal of Personality*, 1972, *35*, 547-561.

Davis, W. L., and Phares, E. J. Internal-external control as a determinant of information-seeking in a social influence situation. *Journal of Personality*, 1967, *35*, 547-561.

DiGiussepe, R. A. Internal-external control of reinforcement and participation in team, individual, and intramural sports. *Perceptual and Motor Skills*, 1973, *36*, 33-34.

DuCettte, J., and Wolk, S. Locus of control and extreme behavior. *Journal of Consulting and Clinical Psychology*, 1972, *39*, 253-258.

DuCette, J., and Wolk, S. Cognitive and motivational correlates of generalized expectancies for control. *Journal of Personality and Social Psychology*, 1973, *26*, 420-426.

Feather, N. T. Some personality correlates of external control. *Australian Journal of Psychology*, 1967, *19*, 253-260(b).

Feather, N. T., and Simon, J. G. Causal attributions for success and failure in relation to expectations of success based upon selective or manipulative control. *Journal of Personality*, 1971, *39*, 527-541.

Felton, G. S. The experimenter expectancy effect examined as a function of task ambiguity and internal-external control. *Journal of Experimental Research in Personality*, 1971, *5*, 286-294.

Fitch, G. Effects of self-esteem, perceived performance, and choice of causal attributions. *Journal of Personality and Social Psychology*, 1970, *16*, 311-315.

Getter, H. A personality determinant of verbal conditioning. *Journal of Personality*, 1966, *34*, 397-405.

Gregory, W. L. Locus of control for positive and negative outcomes. *Journal of Personality and Social Psychology*, 1978, *36*, 840-849.

Hall, E. G. Interaction of locus of control, sex, competition, and coaction during performance of a novel motor task. Published doctoral dissertation, University of Virginia, 1977.

Hersch, P. D., and Scheibe, K. E. Reliability and validity of internal-external con-

72

trol as a personality dimension. *Journal of Consulting Psychology*, 1967, *31*, 609-613.

Hochreich, D. J. Defensive externality and attribution of responsibility. *Journal of Personality*, 1974, *42*, 543-557.

Hutchinson, Bruce. Locus of control and participation in intercollegiate athletics. Unpublished doctoral dissertation, Springfield College, 1972.

James, W. H., and Rotter, J. B. Partial and 100% reinforcement under chance and skill conditions. *Journal of Experimental Psychology*, 1968, *55*, 397-403.

Julian, J. W., and Katz, S. B. Internal versus external control and the value of reinforcement. *Journal of Personality and Social Psychology*, 1968, *8*, 89-94.

Julian, J. W., Lichtman, C. M. and Ryckman, R. M. Internal-external control and need to control. *Journal of Social Psychology*, 1968, *76*, 43-48.

Kumchy, C. G., and Rankin, R. E. Locus of control and mode of reinforcement. *Perceptual and Motor Skills*, 1975, *40*, 375-378.

Lefcourt, H. M. Internal versus external control of reinforcement: a review. *Psychological Bulletin*, 1966, *65*, 206-220(a).

Lefcourt, H. M. Effects of cue explication upon persons maintaining external control tendencies. *Journal of Personality and Social Psychology*, 1967, *5*, 372-378.

Lefcourt, H. M., Lewis, L., and Silverman, I. W. Internal versus external control of reinforcement and attention in a decision-making task. *Journal of Personality*, 1968, *36*, 663-682.

Lefcourt, H. M. and Wine, J. Internal versus external control of reinforcement and the deployment of attention in experimental situations. *Canadian Journal of Personality*, 1969, *1*, 167-181.

Lynn, R. W., Phelan, J. G. and Kiker, V. L. Beliefs in internal-external control of reinforcement and participation in group and individual sports. *Perceptual and Motor Skills*, 1969, *29*, 551-553.

Moss, H. A. The influence of personality and situational cautiousness on conceptual behavior. *Journal of Abnormal and Social Psychology*, 1961, *63*, 629-635.

Phares, E. J. Expectancy changes in skill and chance situations. *Journal of Abnormal and Social Psychology*, 1957, *54*, 339-342.

Phares, E. J. Differential utilization of information as a function of internal-external control. *Journal of Personality*, 1968, *36*, 649-662.

Phares, E. J. Locus of control in personality. Morristown, New Jersey: Silver Burdett, 1976.

Pines, H. A. An attributional analysis of locus of control orientation and source of information dependence. *Journal of Personality and Social Psychology*, 1973, *26*, 262-272.

Pines, H. A., and Julian, J. W. Effects of task and social demands on locus of control differences in information processing. *Journal of Personality*, 1972, *40*, 407-416.

Rothchild, B. A., and Horowitz, I. A. Effect of instructions and internal-external control of reinforcement on a conditioned finger-withdrawal response. *Psychological Reports*, 1970, *26*, 395-400.

Rotter, J. B. *Social learning and clinical psychology*. Englewood Cliffs, New Jersey: Prentice-Hall, 1954.

Rotter, J. B. Generalized expectancies for internal versus external control of reinforcement. *Psychological Monographs*, 1966, *80*, (1, Whole No. 609).

Rotter, J. B., Liverant, S., and Crowne, D. P. The growth and extinction of expectancies in chance controlled and skilled tasks. *Journal of Psychology*, 1961, *52*, 161-177.

Scanlan, T. K. The effects of success-failure on the perception of threat in a competitive situation. *Research Quarterly*, 1977, *48*, 144-153.

Seeman, M. Alienation and social learning in a reformatory. *American Journal of Sociology*, 1963, *69*, 270-284.

Seeman, M. Powerlessness and Knowledge: A comparative study of alienation and learning. *Sociometry*, 1967, *30*, 105-123.

Seeman, M., and Evans, J. W. Alienation and learning in a hospital setting. *American Psychological Review*, 1962, *27*, 772-783.

Strossberg, D. S. Relationships among locus of control, anxiety, and valued-goal expectations. *Journal of Consulting and Clinical Psychology*, 1973, *41*, 319.

Streufert, S., and Streufert, S. C. Effects of conceptual structure, failure, and success on attribution of causality and interpersonal attitudes. *Journal of Personality and Social Psychology*, 1969, *11*, 138-147.

Ude, L. K., and Vogler, R. E. Internal versus external control of reinforcement and awareness in a conditioning task. *Journal of Psychology,* 1969, *73,* 63-67.

Watson, D. Relationship between locus of control and anxiety. *Journal of Personality and Social Psychology,* 1967, *6,* 91-92.

Williams, J. G., and Stack, J. J. Internal-external control as a situational variable in determining information seeking by Negro students. *Journal of Consulting and Clinical Psychology,* 1972, *39,* 187-193.

Wortman, C. B., Costanzo, P. R., and Witt, T. R. Effect of anticipated performance on the attributions of causality of self and others. *Journal of Personality and Social Psychology,* 1973, *27,* 372-381.

12

Persistence vs. Learned Helplessness In Sport

N. Jean Dalton
James Madison University

Researchers and teachers have often noted the ability of some children to learn new activities, but that other children may totally avoid the learning experience. When children have trouble with a new skill, they may utter one of two well known phrases. The first phrase often heard in a learning environment — especially in the area of motor skills — is a relatively personalized approach to the well known defeatist's attitude — "I can't!" Some children use this phrase just to get attention and encouragement. Unfortunately, there are some children who really believe it themselves. They whine "I can't" after, during, or even before an attempt at a new activity. The typical "comeback" for this child's plea may be one of partial understanding. Adults may unknowingly misguide children by telling them that they are *sure* they can do the skill: "I know you can do it. Anyone can do it!" Unfortunately, if the child again fails after he learns that *anyone* can do the activity, he loses all confidence in himself, and feels totally inept in future attempts.

A second phrase which is commonly uttered by unsuccessful children is a fairly general statement which covers most achievement situations, and is heard on a regular basis among children. "That's not fair." This phrase is most often heard when someone else has a special skill or privilege which you lack. Common examples include when an older brother or sister gets to stay up later than you — "that's not fair"; when your next door neighbor has a pool and you don't — "that's not fair"; or when a friend can eat anything she or he wants and not gain weight — "that's really not fair!". The standard comeback for a "that's not fair" experience is often something like —

"That's life! Nothing in life is fair, so you may as well get use to it. There's nothing you can do about it." Once again, it is unfortunate that children may accept this comeback as a universal truth and adapt their performance accordingly. For some children, frustration at failure or poor performance is somewhat eased by assuming that they have no control over what cards life deals out to them. This is particularly true in the area of motor skills. Repeated failure by an uncoordinated child quickly turns into either the "avoid" or "escape" syndromes. The child either refuses to participate at all, or will make a brief attempt and quickly give up, because, after all, that's life! They refuse to stay with an activity — to persist at an activity — because they feel as if they have no real control over their performance outcome. Some educators refer to this growing population of children as "learned helpless" or as suffering from "learned helplessness."

The concept of learned helplessness was first introduced by Seligman (1975) in research with experimental animals. In this research, laboratory dogs were repeatedly exposed to inescapable shock until they failed to avoid the stimulus. At this point, the response contingency was changed so that inappropriate responses by the animal could terminate the electrical impulse. Instead, the dogs refused to respond — they had learned to be helpless in this situation. Theoretically, they had developed a lack of perceived dependency between personal response and the subsequent negative reinforcement. Seligman's work with induced helplessness in animals created an interest by some as to whether or not this state could be induced in humans. Carol Dweck and her colleagues have done extensive research on this condition in children, and have identified a "learned helpless" child as one who lacks persistence in achievement situations (Dweck and Reppucci, 1973). These children usually give up easily on new tasks, or in some cases, may not even make an attempt.

Dweck (1973) investigated induced helplessness in children and the effect that reinforcement responsibility played in creating this condition. After repeated helpless training, children were tested for performance and task persistence. In addition, the "Intellectual Achievement Responsibility" scale was administered to each child in order to measure his perceived reinforcement reponsibility. This scale is a locus of control measure for elementary children. With this test, Dweck attempted to measure a child's perceived cause for his success or failure. Her scoring procedure was revised to allow for specific description of the "internal" control variables of effort and ability. A quick review of Weiner's model of attribution (1972) shows the conceptual framework for these two factors, (Table 1). This model of attribution theory has two basic components: 1) locus of control — either internal or external: and 2) factor stability — either fixed or variable. The commonly used attributions of ability, effort, task difficulty, and luck can each be classified as shown in the diagram. As I mentioned earlier, Dweck's use of the IAR focused on the specific factors of ability (a relatively fixed variable in a specific situa-

Table 1

Perceived Determinants of Success And Failure

STABILITY FACTOR	LOCUS OF CONTROL	
	INTERNAL	*EXTERNAL*
FIXED OR STABLE FACTOR	ABILITY	TASK DIFFICULTY
VARIABLE FACTOR	EFFORT	LUCK

(Weiner, 1972)

tion), and on effort (a variable conducive to temporal fluctuation). Dweck's results showed a decreased tendency for *internal* attribution among the less persistent or helpless children. This would imply that the more persistent children took more personal responsibility for their success or failure. In addition, very little difference was found between the helpless and persistent children in their tendency to attribute their performance to their own *ability;* however, there was a difference in the way the two groups made attributions to *effort.* The more persistent children were more likely to attribute their performance outcome to effort than the helpless children. These results had some interesting implications. Children who have decreased persistence in the face of failure were more likely to attribute their performance to the factor of ability, not effort. Consequently, because ability is perceived to be a more stable or consistent factor than effort, these children may easily perceive themselves to be consistent failures, and thus lack persistence at selected activities.

This ability/effort distinction between persistent and helpless children led Dweck (1973) to develop an attribution retraining program. She identified the children who lacked persistence or were known "quitters" as having learned this helplessness, and developed a training program to direct their attributional patterns toward the unstable variable of effort thereby increasing the possibility of task persistence. Helpless children were placed in one of two training regimes. The first group, operating under the deprivation theory, experienced only successful situations. This group was given constant reinforcement for success in hopes of overcoming a negative reaction to failure by developing self-confidence. The second group received effort attribution training while experiencing both success and failure. After each performance, subjects were encouraged to attribute their success or failure to their personal effort. In this way, Dweck tried to repattern the children's perception of their performance outcome to a personal factor which could be controlled — effort. Her results showed that children who received the effort attribution training were more persistent, were more apt to use the motivational component of effort to define their performance, experienced less anxiety to an achievement situation, and even rated themselves as better performers than did the less persistent children. From these results, Dweck hypothesized that if a child can learn to be helpless, he can also be taught to overcome this helplessness by changing his attributional patterns by effort attribution reinforcement and thus improve his task persistence. This type of research in effort attribution reinforcement has dealt with an academic, or cognitive task.

Dalton (1979) employed similar techniques using a motor skill as a training tool for task persistence. Using Bloom's taxonomy of learning, Dalton theorized that a motor skill could more effectively incorporate the learning of effort attribution because it offers the child a chance to apply this attribution in not only the cognitive, but also in the affective and motor domains. By using a motor skill as a training tool, children could experience a "trial-and-error" approach to attributional patterning. They could attempt to apply effort attribution to a more extensive number of learning domains using a wider variety of feedback information not available in a task which is strictly cognitive. In this manner, subjects would theoretically persist longer at any type of task once the effort attributional patterning had been established using a motor skill.

Dalton (1979) used 96 fifth and sixth grade students from a local elementary school. These subjects were exposed to practice either a mental (cognitive domain) or motor (extended domains) maze task while receiving either general reinforcement or specific effort attribution reinforcement. The "general reinforcement" group (GR) was used as a control group, and received reinforcement for their success or failure which was *not* attributionally specific. The "effort attribution reinforcement" group (EAR) was encouraged to use personal effort as a determining factor in their performance outcomes. After the training period, children were then measured for task persistence at either the same or opposite type of task. This was done in order to control for task novelty, as well as to determine if effort attribution reinforcement could be transferred from one type of task to another, i.e., would children who were reinforced on a *motor* task be more persistent at either activity?

The results of Dalton's (1979) study were quite encouraging and showed that effort attribution reinforcement increased task persistence, with the EAR group persisting approximately 40% longer than those receiving general reinforcement. The EAR children were encouraged to use the unstable factor of effort, and in this manner felt as if they had personal control over the outcomes and thus persisted longer. It could also be hypothesized that the EAR offered *specific* attributional information. Perhaps general reinforcement does not offer enough information on which to base an attributional decision.

This same study also produced some interesting implications for physical educators and coaches. Although not significant at the .05 level, the data did indicate a tendency to support the "extended domain" hypothesis, that is, that the use of a motor skill for training in EAR could increase persistence time at any type of activity (Dalton, 1979). Children who were exposed to the motor skill while undergoing reinforcement tended to persist approximately 20% longer than those exposed to the cognitive skill, regardless of the type of activity on which they were tested. Perhaps the use of a motor skill was more effective in establishing effort attribution patterns and increased task persistence because of the type of information made available to the child. Motor activity generally offers the opportunity for visual as well as kinesthetic and physiological feedback on task performance. This type of information may not be available in a task which is strictly cognitive. Physical feedback information can serve as tangible evidence of personal effort, and thus serve as an additional reinforcement channel for effort attribution. Perhaps a child can learn to persist at new skills by focusing on the *kinesthetic* information made available to him, while it would be more appropriate for the experienced athlete to use the *physiological* information in order to learn to persist at tasks of higher ability. It would be interesting to see if effort attribution reinforcement could be useful to the athlete who has "learned to be helpless" at certain higher levels of competition.

In the meantime, there are several things that a teacher can do to help the "helpless" child overcome his perceptions of the inevitability of his failure in motor learning situations. (Table 2). First, the teacher must try to identify the child's past history in motor learning situations. He should try to determine if a consistent pattern of failure has been established, and, if so, at what level of ability it occurred. Does the child feel capable on a beginning level, but feel helpless at a more advanced level?

Secondly, the teacher should help the child determine what his attributional patterns are — what does the child determine to be the cause of success? or failure? Does the child make appropriate attributions? Inaccurate information may deter appropriately perceived attributional cause. An informal method of determining these patterns may be sufficient. If not, the teacher may want to take a more scientific approach by administering a locus of control measure.

The third suggestion for improving task persistence is to emphasize to the student that personal effort may be a very significant factor in deciding performance outcome. It may determine whether the student experiences success or failure in motor activities. The teacher should be as specific as possible in emphasizing the importance of effort *quality* (trying your best), and *quantity* (continued effort). Both are important in overcoming potential failures. Of course, the teacher or coach must also be realistic in his estimation of the child's ability level. Just because a child is persistent does not make him a superstar! However, a child who won't persist at a task may never reach his fullest potential. You can never learn what you won't try!

So, the next time you hear an "I can't" in the gymnasium or the playing field see if you can turn it into a "I can't if I don't try" attitude. Try to change that "I can't" into an "I'll try!" by encouraging the child to use effort attribution. Think to yourself of the old, well-known idiom:

"If at first you don't succeed, you must attributionally reinforce yourself to try, try again!"

Table 2
Guidelines for Improving Persistence

1. **DETERMINE PAST HISTORY IN ACTIVITY**
   - CONSISTENCY OF FAILURE
   - LEVEL OF CONSISTENT FAILURE
2. **DETERMINE ATTRIBUTIONAL PATTERN**
   - SUCCESS
   - FAILURE
   - APPROPRIATE CONTINGENCY
3. **EMPHASIZE EFFORT ATTRIBUTION**
   - SUCCESS
   - FAILURE
   - INTENSITY   (QUALITY)
   - DURATION   (QUANTITY)

REFERENCES

Dalton, N. J. "Effect of effort attribution reinforcement on persistence of a cognitive and motor task, (an unpublished doctoral dissertation), University of Virginia, 1979.

Dweck, C. S. and N. D. Reppucci, "Learned helplessness and reinforcement responsibility in children," *Journal of Personality and Social Psychology*, 1973, *25*, 109-116.

Dweck, C. S., "The roles of expectations and attributions in the alleviation of learned "helplessness," *Journal of Personality and Soc. Psych*, 1975, *31*, 674-685.

Seligman, M. E. P. *Helplessness: On Depression, Development, and Death*, San Francisco, Ca.: Freeman, 1975.

Weiner, B. *Theories of Motivation*, Chicago, Ill.: Markman Press, 1972.

Julie Heyward, Charlottesville, Va.

13

Goal Setting: The Key To Individual Success

Linda K. Bunker
University of Virginia

The accomplishment of individual goals is the key to each person's success and to the development of their self-concept. To know who you are, and what you wish to accomplish is critical to each person's happiness. Your goals may be to make someone else happy, to finish that report by Thursday, to practice two hours per day or just to take the garbage out! In each case, these goals help to direct your behavior.

Goals are the stepping stones to success. They should help target the desired end product, and create a path to its completion. Based on an awareness of where you are today (present ability), the creation of stepping stones will lead to the goal. The stepping stones may be of different sizes (small/large steps), and can take differing amounts of time to accomplish.

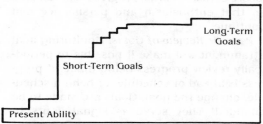

Goals are the stepping stones to success.

Goal setting helps you to answer several questions which are critical to every performer. What is expected or needed in order to perform better? The answer to that question should help individuals evaluate their own skills in relation to those which are needed to be successful. Once these two elements are determined the individual must decide "how important it is to accomplish these goals and to improve." If it is im-

portant, and you know why it is important, it will be easy to keep yourself motivated, especially when you have planned a series of sub-goals or stepping stones to lead you to the desired end.

Personalized goal setting is especially useful because it takes the emphasis off the end product. "It's not whether you win or lose, but how you play the game." You can control how you play, but you can't really control the external product of "winning."

Each person must set their own goals — "personalized." No one can set your goals for you and expect you to perform well. You must believe in them, and perceive them as being attainable. They are also essential because they force each person to set priorities and then to assume responsibility for their accomplishments or for the efforts exerted toward accomplishing the goals.

Notice that the benefits of goal setting are in the energy directed toward accomplishing the goals. The goals may shift or change, but they are part of an ongoing process: evaluate present status, plan to meet goals, measure or evaluate progress toward the goal and then decide on the next step.

Each step or sub-goal should lead toward a larger goal. The goals can be subjective, outcome or product goals, or performance/process goals. They can include goals of such things as social interaction, playing time, improvement of techniques, etc.

Goal setting is a powerful technique because it (1) directs attention and action, (2) helps the individual to mobilize energy, (3) focuses attention, (4) encourages persistence and practice, (5) forces the individual to take responsibility for his/her actions or attributions, and (6) perhaps most importantly, influences expectancies because of the individual's acceptance of responsibility for their accomplishment.

There are many types of goals and many forms of goal statements. But all effective goals share some common elements. They are "growth facilitating," and direct attention toward desired behavior rather than merely saying, "I won't. . . ." They are stated as a desired action, without any alternatives or easy outs, and they represent commitments to work toward their accomplishment.

Effective goals should fulfill the criteria suggested in the ABC's of goal setting: achievable, believable, compatible, controllable, and desirable. Each goal should be achievable, possible, and eventually "probable," given your strengths and weaknesses. An effective goal should also be *believable* and important within your own value system. It must also have a reasonable chance to be accomplished.

ABC's of Goal Setting
Achievable
Believable
Compatible
Controllable
Desirable
Measurable

Each effective goal must also be *compatible* with the rest of your life. Goals should complement each other, and not be mutually exclusive. They must also be within your own control. A *controllable* goal can be accomplished with sufficient concentration and energy, without respect to how others may perform.

One of the most important criteria for an effective goal is that it must be *desirable.* You must be willing to put in the "sweat equity" to accomplish your investment. If you want it badly enough, it will be possible. Are you really willing to work hard in order to accomplish it?

"If you can imagine it
You can achieve it.
If you can dream it
You can become it."
—William Arthur Ward

It is important to be able to monitor your progress toward accomplishing your goals. If goals are "measurable" and carefully spe-

cified, they can be monitored in order to reinforce good progress or identify trouble spots. The goals can be specified in terms of either quantity (how many, how much, how accurate, how far, how often) or quality (form, efficiency, etc.).

Steps in Establishing Effective Goals. In order to be effective in sport, you must be able to identify all of the necessary skills for the activity. What skills are needed in order to be effective? Can you specify them in measurable terms?

You must be able to analyze your own capabilities, strengths, and weaknesses. Rank your behavior in terms of those things at which you are good, and those which need work or improvement. How much change is necessary? How soon? Is it realistic?

Once you know where you want to go, or what goals need to be accomplished you can begin to plan for success. Break down the skill into realistic and sequential steps. Write them down and make a commitment to meet them. "Ink them, don't just think them"! Determine the specific goal, how it will be evaluated, and when it should be accomplished.

Follow up. Once goals have been set and a commitment has been made to accomplish them, it is critical that progress be monitored and reinforced. Both process and product goals should be evaluated. Motivational strategies should be employed (score cards, rewards, progress reports, etc.) so that enthusiasm and persistence can continue.

Periodic Review of Goals. Monitoring goal attainment will make it possible to periodically review progress being made. If progress is ahead of schedule, or behind schedule, change the goal. Goals are made to be changed! They serve as signal lights to focus attention and effort — they are not ends in themselves.

Determine what has been accomplished and what helped lead to that accomplishment. If some things were not accomplished, or insufficient progress was made, then the goal(s) may need to be reassessed. Don't be afraid to change your goals, if you have worked diligently toward them. Goals are made to be changed!

SECTION IV.

Team Motivation

14

Team Cohesiveness, Composition And Success

Evelyn G. Hall
Louisiana State University

Team cohesiveness is viewed as consisting of interpersonal attractiveness of the group as a whole, the sense of belonging to the group, and the desire of members to remain in the group. All of these factors are important since no single index of cohesiveness is adequate to represent the total construct.

How does cohesiveness relate to sport groups, especially team sports? According to Singer's (1975) model for individual performance, performance is equivalent to the additive factors of individual learning plus individual motivation: (Individual performance = Individual Learning + Individual Motivation).

This author has extended Singer's model to include behaviors related to team interaction and the influence of cohesiveness on team performance. This model would be represented as follows:

TEAM PERFORMANCE = TEAM LEARNING + TEAM MOTIVATION + TEAM COHESIVENESS

There are many factors such as age, intelligence, maturation, etc. which relate to the learning aspect of the model. Motivation is influenced by environmental structure, relevance of the task, etc. However, no matter how optimal conditions may be for learning and motivation of individuals within a group, one other factor is essential — cohesiveness. That is, cohesiveness is essential for optimally channeling all of the abilities and efforts of a group to produce the maximum group performance.

Often teams will have tremendous individual talent and may far exceed other teams in ability person for person. However, possessing a wealth of individual talent does not guarantee success for a particular team. Rather, success depends upon how well a team can interweave individual talents. Very often a very cohesive team with less ability and skill may be able to channel the total group effort in the most productive manner. Consequently, such a team may be more highly successful than a team with considerably more talent. An example of this would be the Philadelphia 76'ers who are one of the best professional basketball teams today, player for player.

In comparison, another pro team like the Seattle Sonics may not possess as much talent and experience, but during the past season seemed to have coordinated the team effort more effectively; that is, they seemed to have better team cohesion. There are many examples of teams with less individual talent which have been able to "put it all together" better than other teams who have more unique individuals with higher talent levels.

Clearly, group cohesion is related to both the quality and the quantity of communication within the group. One essential determinant of team cohesiveness is the leadership style of the coach and the coach's personality. Both will play an important role in his/her ability to communicate. If a coach creates an environment which encourages all members of a team to communicate openly, there should be greater cohesiveness and opportunity for enhancing the potential of each individual within the group.

In attempting to promote group cohesion, it is very important to consider the goals of individual group members as well as the goals of the group as a whole. A coach should help individuals set goals and objectives that are compatible with the goals and objectives of the total group or team. In some situations, the coach's goals may not match the goals of individuals. Any potential problems related to this situation may be alleviated by open communication. If it is possible at the beginning for a group to establish mutual goals based upon what everyone would like to achieve, there should be no problem pursuing these common goals in a cooperative manner.

Goals should be clearly defined for all members of a team from the beginning. The extent to which members of a team are able to reach uniformity or cohesiveness will depend upon the extent to which initial differences and goals can be integrated into team goals. The more highly skilled athletes become, the more homogeneous the group is likely to become. Therefore, objectives and goals are likely to become more similar.

The satisfaction that each team member feels will depend upon having determined relevant goals which are compatible with team goals. If, for example, the goal of the team is to win, those individuals who joined the team for social reasons, may find that the group fails to meet their needs. Often the needs of members of a team cannot be accommodated if their goals are inconsistent with those of the team.

Therefore, the needs and motives of individuals on a team must be considered. Individuals have different motives for participating on a team. Some are there for social reasons, some to demonstrate skill and competence in one particular area, others to try a different sport, etc. Whatever the reason, individuals are members of a team, it helps promote cohesiveness when individuals are able to communicate their similarities and differences.

Cratty (1973; p. 4) has written: "The most successful groups it seems are those whose members know each other well enough to be tolerant of their strengths and weaknesses, can communicate effectively, and have a leadership pattern appropriate to the task performance, but whose primary orientation is toward the specifics of the task rather than toward social interaction as an end in itself."

Research from industry, business and other areas indicates that groups which tend to be more task-oriented tend to succeed and, as expected, perform at a higher level. The implications for sports are that coaches must be task oriented in some situations, particularly when time is a limiting factor.

In relationship to the cohesiveness of a group, it is necessary to consider individual characteristics such as differences in personality, need for achievement, locus of control, anxiety, etc. Personality differences may pose a problem in making everyone's goals compatible. It is important for a coach to recognize differences in personality traits and try to channel individual strengths and weaknesses so that different individuals complement each other.

One way to optimize performance, relative to strength and weaknesses of individuals, is to have individuals learn more about the roles of one another. For example, switching the offensive and defensive players during drills or scrimmages to give them insight into the expected roles of other positions on the team, may help the players more fully appreciate other individual's roles. This is one aspect which can help minimize the differences in people's expectations, for as people understand each other, conflict will be reduced.

Clarification of roles of each member of a team is very important to build team cohesion. Every member of a team needs to know exactly what his or her role is during practice, during a contest, and after a contest. If an athlete is uncertain about what his role is in a group, this may make him feel like a misfit and cause others to view him that way also. Coaches must let each individual know the job that each must fulfill.

In relation to roles, or social structure, individuals within a group may emerge with many different statuses. Ultimately the goal of a coach should be to raise the status of every member of the group because players tend to look upon the value of other members in terms of what they can contribute. Usually, this contribution comes in the form of what teammates can do to help reduce the threat of losing a contest since losing is viewed as an external threat to team security. Therefore, it is important to try to raise the skill level of every member of a team. The more every member's skill level is increased or the more clearly individual contributions are recognized the less likely an athlete is to become isolated from the rest of the team.

Coaches need to include everyone, clearly define each person's roles, and let benchwarmers know what their contribution is to the team. For example, at the onset of a season, people who are likely never to start in a contest should be informed and helped to establish other goals. Such individuals may be quite happy to be included as part of the team because they enjoy the friendship and social aspect. Or it may be satisfactory to them to keep on striving and trying to improve their skill in the hopes of becoming a viable performer in the future. Open communication may help alleviate potential problems arising from individuals who do not get to play very much in actual contests.

In many different team sports, there are captains or co-captains who represent the team. Such stratification of certain individuals may not promote group cohesiveness. Rather, it may be better to alternate all members of a team into this role. Election of captains may be a negative thing because individuals are often placed in the leadership role of being a captain when they may not be strong leaders at all. Often the reasons certain individuals are elected captains are because they are "seniors", or they are socially popular. Individuals who are in leadership roles without leadership ability are placed in a very stressful situation because they are expected to assume a great deal of responsibility, but may not be prepared for it.

With regard to status, one factor which unites groups is success. This is an important consideration in terms of scheduling. It is worthwhile to schedule a few easy contests at the beginning of a season to increase the morale, feeling of competence, and success of a group. Everyone likes to succeed and positively reinforce each other. However, there is a danger that egos can become over inflated and expectations unrealistic. For example, we have all seen teams who win, win, win and get too "high on themselves." Then, inevitably, it takes a loss to bring such a team in touch with themselves and make a realistic evaluation of their goals. Occasionally losing can facilitate as much cohesiveness as winning.

There are some examples of negative external forces which unite groups. Losing is one example. Another is a coach who is disliked by the group. Sometimes several cliques may develop within a group because certain members feel that the coach has not dealt fairly with them, or the entire team may even unite against a coach.

Another extremely influential factor in promoting cohesiveness of a team is the manner in which a coach or leader rewards and reinforces individuals in the group. Different sports demand different amounts of interaction by the participants for success. Members of teams such as basketball, lacrosse, field hockey, and soccer, must interact to a very high degree. Such individuals must mix their talents and efforts in the most coordinated manner to insure group benefit. There are other sports which involve parallel competition: bowling teams, golf teams, swimming teams, etc. where performance per se is coactive in nature. That is, in coactive sports, performance does not involve direct interaction with others.

The early research on the topic of team interaction and group productivity was seemingly equivocal. For example, it was found that rowing teams who hated each other personally, still managed to perform extremely well. Later researchers dichotomized the research by looking specifically at the demands of each sport for team interaction. Therefore, it became clear in looking at previous research, that the more interaction a sport requires, the more important group cohesion becomes.

In looking at rewards and reinforcements, if a coach structures a situation so that too much emphasis is placed on extrinsic (external) types of rewards, such as trophies for most valuable player, most rebounds, leading scorer, etc., that situation encourages a lack of cohesiveness and may foster competition within the group rather than cooperation.

Coaches should place more emphasis on rewarding group effort especially in team sports where group effort is most essential. All coaches need to avoid structuring rewards so that teammates are encouraged to compete with each other instead of coordinating their efforts for the benefit of the whole group. However, some degree of rivalry is healthy for a team. There seems to be a trade off — if there is not some intrateam rivalry where players are kept alert with the expectation that someone may replace them, then there may not be as much overall improvement in performance.

If players become too complacent with their goals and performance, this may be detrimental to overall development of skill in that group. Encouraging rivalry in competition can be very positive when it is contained at a level to increase overall quality of performance. However, intragroup competition is negative when it becomes so extreme as to detract from the coordinated efforts of a group.

A distinction should be made by players in when to compete with teammates and when to cooperate. For example, healthy rivalry in practice may be positive, but in a real contest all personalities, tensions, etc. must be put aside for cooperative effort to benefit the total group.

Another important factor which influences group cohesiveness is group size. By necessity, the larger a group becomes, the more authoritarian the leadership must become.

The greater the size of a team, the more a coach must make decisions or delegate those decisions to assistant coaches. In essence, the group decision processes are more controlled by those in power positions. Part of the effectiveness of authoritarian coaches is determined by how well they are able to delegate responsibility to their assistants. When coaching a very mature or highly skilled team, it is often possible for a coach to delegate some responsibility to team members to run certain drills, etc. It is positive to include as many players as possible in leadership roles. The larger the group, the more difficult it is to make contact with everyone and communicate individually with members.

With regard to cohesiveness, a team is only as cohesive as the coaching staff. If the objectives and goals of coaches are not compatible, the team can easily be influenced by this. The coaching staff must be well coordinated in its efforts if they expect the team to coordinate its efforts.

Cohesiveness of a team can also be facilitated by achieving pride in the group. Pride can be established by the use of uniforms and clearly identifiable dress by the team and coaching staff. Identical travel luggage, balls painted in the team colors, school banners and team cheers or chants may be perceived as being a positive influence on group cohesiveness.

The acceptablility of the leadership to the group and the effectiveness of the leader are also important factors. The leader must be extremely perceptive about players' dis-

satisfactions and bring potential problems into the open. When small problems develop, open communication is essential. Sometimes, if a coach lacks perception, even small problems can be blown out of proportion and can be very detrimental.

A coach also must be perceptive about the abilities and special skills of group members in an attempt to optimize these differential skills. It is obviously not very positive to waste the potential of an individual in the wrong position. For example, it is detrimental to place a player at goal keeper if he/she can make a greater contribution elsewhere. This situation often causes individual dissatisfaction as well as team ineffectiveness which can mushroom.

The wise use of positive and negative reinforcements by a coach may contribute greatly to team cohesiveness. For example, coaches need to handle situations individually. If a coach's ultimate goal is to have others value the contribution of each team member, then one thing a coach can do to destroy the individual's value is to belittle a player in the eyes of his teammates. There are situations, of course, when a coach must be negative and punish players who need it — but punishment should be an individual matter. There are also situations where a coach may be misinterpreted. For example, does the coach always give positive reinforcement to one or two members of the group? If so, other teammates may start viewing certain individuals as "coach's pets." It may appear that the coach is always praising certain people because they can do no wrong.

Everyone wants credit and praise for what they do. When players feel that they can make a positive contribution, they usually do — a self-fulfilling prophecy. With constant negative reinforcement or punishment, individuals may feel degraded in the eyes of their teammates. Individual communication by coaches with athletes, is far more personal and acceptable than destroying an athlete's self-esteem in the presence of teammates.

How is cohesiveness measured? The construct of cohesiveness has many dimensions (consider the many determinants). One must expect more than a simplistic method of assessment. However, given the many determinants of cohesion, it is possible that the present instruments used to assess this quality are over simplified. Some of the ways cohesiveness is now measured are as follows:

1. Cohesion may be measured by scales for interpersonal attraction — "friendship indexes." There are several different scales which ask individuals which group members they like the best and with whom they would like to associate.
2. Cohesion may be measured by evaluation of a group as a whole. Each member is asked to rate his liking of the group as a whole.
3. Cohesion may be measured by scales to assess closeness or identification with a group; that is, the strengths of sense of belongingness is measured.
4. Cohesion may also be measured by the individual's expressed desire to remain in a group.

SUMMARY

In summary, some factors which contribute to team cohesiveness are as follows:

1. Cohesiveness is influenced by the extent to which goals are accepted by a group.
2. Previous success and failure also influences cohesiveness. Success is more positive than failure. Failure often causes divisions within a group because certain individuals may blame others.
3. A coach must be perceptive enough to use differential skill within a group to the best advantage. Individual talents and abilities must be meshed together to produce the best results.

Many times individuals may be unhappy with the position that has been selected for them. Just because someone said, "You look like a linebacker;" or to someone else, "You ought to be a wing in field hockey." When individuals get pigeon-holed into roles, they either make the best of it, or they decide to give up the sport.

Allowing players to play different offensive and defensive positions, helps them to find out about the demands on others. It is important for a coach to help individuals to find roles which are compatible to their own objectives and motives to produce maximum cohesiveness.

REFERENCES

Cratty, B. J. *Psychology in Contemporary Sport: Guidelines for Coaches & Athletes.* New Jersey: Prentice-Hall, 1973.

Singer, R. N. *Motor Learning & Human Performance.* New York: MacMillan Publishing, 1975.

15

Cooperation And Cohesiveness: Setting A Winning Personal Environment

Mimi Murray
Springfield College

Success in sport is frequently related to the cooperation and cohesion within a team. The extent to which members of a group are attracted to each other or the group itself is cohesiveness. Middlebrock (1974) found that cohesiveness is positively influenced by the following factors:

1. If membership in a group is limited and occurs after passing difficult entrance requirements.
2. If membership is based upon similar values, interests and beliefs of individual members.
3. Small group size
4. Achievement of group goals
5. External threats to the achievement of group goals

Being a member of the team can fulfill the first criterion for positive cohesiveness within a group. The trying out and making of a team is often a traumatic experience in that the physical and psychological demands of the trials are high. Further, team membership is associated with increased status and lack of it reflects decreased status; thus there are concomitant social ramifications associated with team membership (Coleman, 1965).

To maintain this initial cohesiveness, the coach should evaluate with each team member his/her strengths or weaknesses and initial position or status on the team (bench warmer, starter, almost starter, etc.). There is no more difficult a responsibility associated with coaching than "cutting" a team member. The task is ominous for as we are well aware, a coach is not omnipotent. We are human, and thus subject to commiting human errors. Critical errors in talent assessment of an individual's potential for team contribution may result in

cutting such athletes from a team. It is recommended that a coach use more than one opinion in his/her subjective talent evaluation such as assistant coaches, captains, and/or team members; objective measures such as a skill test; and the athlete's past performance and potential for further growth in selecting a team. In this age of accountability, a written record should be kept regarding each individual trying out for the team. Further, it is each coach's responsibility to discuss with each individual why he/she has been cut from or separated from the team rather than post a list in the dark of night and escape through a side door for a long weekend.

Shared hardships are stimulants for group cohesiveness as was graphically demonstrated to this writer. As a coach of a United States team and member of the USA delegation to international competition in Moscow, I'm well aware that this experience was most significant to those of us who shared it — Russia, Moscow, totalitarianism, bureaucracy, personal discomfort and deprivation, by comparison to our standard of living, created a special camaraderie that we had never experienced before nor have since. Despite our different socioeconomic backgrounds, interests, sports, geographical locations, goals and values, we were one group with esprit de corps — the USA group.

The second criterion for group cohesiveness, membership based upon similar values, interests and beliefs, is associated with some teams. In one of her studies, Sherif (1976) found results which have implications for coaching and this presentation. The subjects consisted of two groups (teams) of boys at summer camps who were continually placed in competitive situations against each other. Team or group solidarity and cohesiveness developed and each group felt extreme prejudice and hostility for the "other" group and its members. In conclusion, the competitive relationships were warm and friendly when those involved shared a common goal. Hostility was saved for opponents or those of other persuasions or having differing goals. The implications for increasing team cohesion are for the coach to ascertain individual goals (team members and coach), as well as team goals. This can be accomplished at an early team meeting or through a questionnaire. During group discussion, common team goals should be established, known, and accepted by all. The team members and the coach should attempt to continually and constantly communicate individual as well as group needs. Cohesion could be destroyed if the coach had aspirations for the team differing from those of the team such as the coach being primarily concerned with developing desirable attitudes and the team concerned with winning at all costs.

Eitzen (1973) studied 288 high school basketball teams and concluded that team success was positively correlated with homogeneity of team members' backgrounds (socio-economics, home neighborhood and religion). From these results, he hypothesized that poor team performance was related to very heterogeneous backgrounds of team members which resulted in cliques within the team, thus reducing cohesiveness.

As previously mentioned (Sherif, 1976), hostility is often present between opponents in a competitive situation. Competition also serves to bring individual members of a team closer together or to become more cohesive; yet in professional basketball play, Phil Jackson (1975) has stated that from his experience, few members of NBA teams are friends for they are constantly competing against each other for fan popularity, increased salaries, coach approval, and more game time. Is this because the end results, winning and money, are far more important than the process? It is proposed (Forsyth and Kolenda, 1966) that team members can be friendly while competitive if they accurately recognize ability differences and control their displays of antagonism for each other. Certainly, the coach should be a key agent in helping athletes to realistically evaluate their own performance, as well as not condoning or permitting demonstrations of personal animosity.

The third criterion for group cohesion deals with group size. The smaller the group, the easier cohesion is to facilitate. Certain individual sport teams (gymnastics, tennis and golf) by their nature are small groups and thus cohesion can more readily be accomplished than with large individual sport teams such as track and field or swimming. Most team sports pose more of a cohesion problem for the coach (football, soccer and lacrosse) due to their inherent large size. A suggestion for coaches of larger teams is to affect smaller groups within the larger groups by delegating responsibility for a smaller group to assistant coaches, team captains, or more talented and experienced team members.

Another suggestion which will be blasphemous to some, includes the coach becoming more democratic within a humane atmosephre rather than the typical autocratic one. George Davis (Amdur, 1971), a successful high school football coach, the basketball coaches at the University of Northern Colorado (Eitzen and Sage, 1978), and the coach of the women's basketball team at Springfield College, are examples of coaches who have given responsibility for selecting the starting lineup to their teams to vote upon.

The achievement of group goals is the fourth factor which can influence team cohesivenes. It is obvious from all of our experiences in sport, if winning is paramount and the team is winning, cohesiveness is fait accompli. In most sport contests, not only is there a winner, but also a loser. What about cohesion in losing? Cohesion tends to disintegrate if the group goal is winning and the team continues to lose. Implications for the coach are thus to help the team set realistic and attainable goals for the group, as well as individual team members. The team should compete against lesser, equal, and better opponents, so that the possibility of wins and challenges is found in the schedule. Most importantly, though, is that the coach and team should become primarily concerned with the process and not the outcome, less goal-oriented (winning). The now hackneyed words of De Coubertain are applicable:

"The important thing in the Olympics is not winning, but taking part. The essential thing in life is not conquering, but fighting well."

Unfortunately, too many of us only give lip service to them. The coach should praise cooperation as a behavior of team members, whether winning or losing. Frequently, when success or winning ceases, so does praise or reinforcement for the demonstration of cooperation.

External threats to achievement of group goals, the fifth factor, is inherent in the competitive process. The opponent serves the function of the external threat, thus aiding cohesion within a team if winning is the group goal. Occasionally, if the coach has different goals from the group, he or she can be perceived as the external threat; thus the team develops cohesion which can be counter-productive. For example, "Let's win in spite of the coach," or "All the coach cares about is winning."

The amount of group cohesion is critical to a successful group. Teams which lack cohesion are inefficient and can be non-productive, or at the other extreme of the continuum, teams which are too cohesive tend to value the group and its maintenance more than goal accomplishment; therefore, as with the ancient Greeks, "nothing in excess." Moderate levels of cohesion should be most efficient and effective for group accomplishment (Middlebrock, 1974).

To reiterate, cooperation and cohesion within a team are means of setting a winning environment. A coach can affect cooperation and cohesion within a team through:

1. constant, continuous, and open communication
2. a well-established criteria and procedure for team selection
3. emphasizing the team members' shared experiences on the team
4. the establishment and acceptance of team goals
5. the acceptance of individual personality differences and the utilization of each person's strengths while understanding and appreciating their weaknesses. Members don't have to like, but need to respect each other.
6. structuring smaller responsible groups in larger groups through the leadership of other coaches and/or responsible team members.
7. providing opportunities for success through:
   a. positive and negative reinforcement
   b. praising the demonstration of cooperation while losing as well as winning
   c. rewarding team effort, not just individual effort.
8. establishing realistic team and individual goals
9. delineating each team member's responsibilities to the team
10. not expecting any more from the team than the coach is willing to give or demonstrate
11. awareness of group interaction (such as using a sociogram on passing in team sports)
12. listening, hearing and being receptive to individual and team needs and suggestions
13. emphasizing the process of goal attainment or achievement, not just the final outcome.

REFERENCES

Amdur, N. *The Fifth Down.* New York: Coward, McCann, and Geoghegan, 1971.

Cartwright, D. and Zander, A. *Group Dynamics: Research and Theory* (2nd Edition). Evanston, Illinois: Row, Peterson, 1960.

Coleman, J. S. *Adolescents and the Schools.* New York: Basic Books, Inc., 1965.

Eitzen, D. S. and Sage, G. H. *Sociology of American Sport.* Dubuque, Iowa: Wm. C. Brown Company, 1978.

Eitzen, D. S. The Effect of Group Structure on the Success of Athletic Teams. *International Review of Sport Sociology,* 1973, *8,* 7-17.

Forsyth, S. and Kolenda, P. M. Competition, Cooperation, and Cohesion in the Gallet Company. *Psychiatry,* 1966, *29*(2), 123-145.

Jackson, P. and Rusen, C. *Maverick: More than a Game.* Chicago: Playboy Press, 1975.

Middlebrock, P. *Social Psychology and Modern Life.* New York: Alfred E. Knupf, Inc., 1974.

Sherif, C. W. The Social Context of Competition. In D. M. Landers (Ed.) *Social Problems in Athletics.* Urbana, Illinois: University of Illinois Press, 1976.

16

Systematic Program For The Development Of Staff Cohesion

Jim Blackburn
Randolph Macon College

Staff cohesion is a necessity if a head coach wishes to develop team cohesion and ultimately insure success for the particular team. This paper will discuss the salient features of cohesion as they apply to a small college football staff, and present a system for creating, enhancing, and maintaining cohesion. Following the presentation of the general plan for the development of staff cohesion a specific program, illustrative of the practical application of the general tenets of staff cohesion, will be introduced.

THE SYSTEM APPROACH

Many important factors regarding cohesion have been explored by sport psychologists, but there seem to be so many different building blocks of cohesion that one fails to see the "big picture." The fundamental questions to be answered however, are these:

1. Can the information we have concerning cohesion be applied to a coaching staff cohesion?

and if so:

2. How can a head coach systematically foster a suitable climate in which a staff can grow together and function effectively?

In developing a general plan for this quality called "cohesion," the author has grouped the many important factors into three general categories that can then be analyzed and systematically implemented into one's coaching and staffing techniques. These three areas to be addressed are labeled as the communication system, the value system, and the professional system. Each of these systems is rather broad based, but the specific characteristics native to each are bound together by the essence of the particular system.

The Communication System

This system involves the communication abilities of the head coach and his assistants, plus the group dynamics inherent in a small group such as a coaching staff. Communication is vital for success in sport. In fact, cohesion in a sport situation is a function of the quality and quantity of communication between members of the staff. The group dynamics are an outgrowth of this communication (or lack of it) and serve as a means to understanding any communication shortcomings and then act as a facilitator to improve group interaction.

Communication is not just the head coach talking to his staff, giving orders, advice, or criticism. It is rather the entire staff talking and listening, and it must be constant, continuous, and open in order to be effective. This quality of communicating is very much a part of the head coach's personality and leadership style. He must possess good perception and intuition and must also listen and be receptive to the needs and suggestions of his staff. By establishing open communication among his staff, the head coach will be able to harness the power of group dynamics to help pave the way to success.

The head coach must be aware of group interaction and must encourage positive interaction as much as possible. This can be accomplished through small group size or structuring smaller groups within the main group. Normally a staff is not particularly large, but the coach must keep the size in mind when setting his staff. Bigger is not always better when one is trying to develop cohesion. If, however, a situation demands a larger staff it is important that the head coach be willing to delegate authority. Smaller groups are naturally more democratic (although not necessarily so) and the head coach should realize that some authoritarian leadership is necessary or the staff could possibly view social interaction as the primary goal of the staff rather than focusing on a task orientation. Coaches by nature are a very proud and competitive group, and the head coach should appeal to this pride and competitive instinct by rewarding group action and effort, encouraging healthy rivalry, and illustrating when cooperation or competition is appropriate. All of these factors coalesce into a driving force when the staff has a shared hardship or external threat such as the upcoming opponent.

A variety of activities can be employed by the head coach in order to improve this communication system. Probably the most important function of the head coach in developing the necessary communication is the formulation of a detailed job description which outlines the requirements, responsibilities, and remuneration for the assistant coaching position. By detailing the myriad of duties of an assistant coach on that particular staff and then using this job description to guide the interview of the prospective coach, the head coach will be communicating all the facets of the job. If a head coach really wants to destroy cohesion he will constantly surprise his assistants with new duties or responsibilities (i.e., "Oh, I forgot to tell you that you are in charge of coordinating all of our recruiting"). The highly detailed job description, with a copy to the prospective assistant, will help avoid problems later on in the season. A follow-up letter to welcome the individual to the staff is suggested also, briefly reviewing the interview process and referring to the job description.

Some additional points relative to improving this communication system are as follows:

1. *Open Door Policy for Coaches* — Quite often head coaches open their doors to players but fail to keep them open to their assistants. It is important for the staff members to know that they too can see the head man if the need arises.

2. *Summer Mail-outs* — Coaches often communicate with their players in the summer or the off-season through a series of mail-outs or more formal newsletters. Inclusion of the coaches on these mailing lists is a good idea also, particularly in the situation where part-time coaches are employed during the season and little contact is made in the off-season.

3. *Evaluation of Coaching Skills* — A post-season critique of the individual's coaching techniques is a very valuable tool in improving the individual's skills plus providing a vehicle for open communication between the head coach and the staff. As staff cohesion grows, and individuals feel less threatened by other members of the staff, the staff as a whole can become involved in the evaluation of each coach (including the head coach).

4. *Cooperative Goal Setting* — Although goal setting is primarily part of what we are referring to as the value system, it can (and will) be a powerful tool in opening the lines of communication and providing for positive group dynamics. By common goal setting the staff will naturally communicate wants and needs and will develop common values and beliefs.

5. *Delegation of Authority* — By delegating responsibility to assistant coaches the head coach is telling them that they are responsible, competent coaches. If coaches feel they are wanted, needed, and valued then they will, of course, feel more positively toward the group. The head coach should guard against having too big a staff because the assistants may feel that their individual responsibilities are too "watered down" and thus prove to negatively affect cohesion.

6. *Brainstorming Sessions* — Staffs need a time when individually and collectively, they can think creatively. The head coach can improve this creativity by establishing an atmos-

phere in which even the most hair-brained, off-the-wall idea is explored constructively. A normal staff meeting is not the situation for such an atmosphere. It must be a meeting separate from the day-to-day preparation for the upcoming opponent.

7. *The Argument-Agreement Example of the Head Coach* — In order for staff meetings to be effective the vigorous exchange of ideas must take place. The head coach must encourage this argument phase and then lead the staff to some form of agreement on the proper manner to deal with the problem at hand. When the staff leaves the meeting they should agree that, of all the options, the one agreed on is the best one to employ. The head coach must serve as an example by being open to the suggestions of others and by actively discounting his own biases, agreeing with the consensus, and then showing his support for that option after the meeting.

The Value System

This particular system has three basic components or factors. These are:

1. The selectivity and uniqueness of the coaching position.
2. The values and goals of the staff members individually and as a group.
3. The social and familial values of the individuals.

These components form the system which is the nucleus of the concept of staff cohesion. While there is a great deal of latitude in the accepted ambience of staff members, there must also be the common thread of this value system woven through the idiosyncracies and nuances of these unique individuals known as the "staff." Disparate value systems have destroyed, and will continue to destroy, seemingly highly qualified and competent staffs. On the other hand, a staff bound together by the cohesive force of a similar value system can easily overcome the technical deficiencies of any of its members.

The first component, "The selectivity and uniqueness of the coaching position," may appear, at first glance, to be out of place when referring to this "value system" and how it affects staff cohesion. Upon closer examination however, this component is the first step toward establishing the values and ideals of a coaching staff, and will serve as a springboard toward a well-defined value system and how it affects staff cohesion. By having a well-established method for interview and selection, the head coach can create a situation, which, while not oppressive, can at least present some trauma for the individual "trying-out" for the staff position. While enduring this somewhat traumatic situation of applying and interviewing for the job, the individual coach must think and rethink his goals, aspirations, needs, and motives for the job and then must communicate these to the head coach. His past performance as a coach, leader, student, player, and as a person, should be taken into account. By passing this "test" of his personal and professional values the coach will then feel wanted and accepted by the group and be reinforced by the knowledge that his value system is consistent with the group's. The incumbent staff members will take heart in the fact that his newest member has "stood the test" and will welcome him openly and genuinely.

The values and goals of the staff members are intrinsic to this system. They do not, however, materialize out of thin air. They must be nurtured and developed (and possibly changed) by the staff and the head coach. The head coach must insure that all goals are: (1) compatible with the group, (2) realistic, and (3) clearly defined, relevant and known to the group. By developing goals for itself and the team, the staff will be reinforcing its individual and group values. In order to enhance the staff cohesion, this value system will include process as well as product into the coaching arena. The idea of "process rather than product" is inimicable to the sport situation in which score is kept. Product will always be important. The inclusion of process though, will help bolster this value system, thus creating staff cohesion, and ultimately, product success.

The third factor in the value system involves the social and familial values that the head coach and each of his assistants bring to the job. The role of the wife and children, girlfriend, or other family members, is fundamental to this value system. If the needs of these social/familial units are not met, then there quite possibly will be a conflict of values and reduced cohesion on the staff. The wise head coach will realize that assistant coaches have (or should have) a deep sense of loyalty to these social/familial units, and he will try to encourage this loyalty. At the same time the coach will attempt to encourage loyalty by these social/familial units toward the sports program of which he is in charge. By encouraging his staff to remain loyal to the responsibilities inherent in a family situation while not negatively affecting job performance the head coach will engender in the social/familial unit a loyalty to him as head coach and to his staff and program. The assistant coach will then feel that he can be both a coach and a "regular person" without jeopardizing either, and will feel much more positively toward the group. While realizing that coaching is very time-demanding, it is imperative that coaches take time off, away from their sport and staff, in order to develop healthy relationships with family and friends outside of the staff itself. The coach must also take time to attend to his individual health, both physical and mental, during the season.

The activities which the coach can employ to positively affect this value system are outlined below:

1. *Goal-Setting as a Group* — The head coach should guide his staff through goal-setting sessions and should provide opportunities to refine and eliminate them as the situation warrants. By actively setting goals for the individuals, the staff will define which values and goals are worthy of their attention and which will help bring the staff together in order to achieve these goals.

2. *Personal Inventory* — The head coach could develop some sort of instrument which the assistant coaches should complete, outlining the physical, mental, and spiritual goals they may have; listing individual assets and liabilities, enumerating priorities and commitments which the coach has; and any other information that would help the head coach and other staff members better know the individual coach.

3. *Illinois Competition Scale* (Martens, 1977) — This instrument would allow the coach an opportunity to gauge his individual staff members' anxiety level, so that he could properly deal with the stressors on an individual basis rather than treating each staff member the same and possibly increasing the stress level for a particular coach.

4. *Qualities of a Coach Questionnaire* — This instrument, developed by the author, lists nine prominent qualities which coaches have mentioned as essential for successful coaching. Each quality is then weighed against the others by the individual taking the test in order to see which qualities that staff assistant feels are most important and which are least important. The head coach can see readily which qualities his staff feels are important, and if there is a big discrepancy between individual's values, he can then open the lines of communication so that individuals will know each other better.

5. *Crisis Simulation* — In staff meetings the head coach can present a crisis to the staff (or have the staff create situations themselves) and then see how the staff would react to the crisis. The reactions of the staff members will be an indication of their values and goals and will also serve as a training ground in order to better handle crises when they actually do occur. If the staff has solved simulated crises together then they will know the procedures to follow when reality strikes.

6. *Cooperative Planning of First Team Meeting* — The first team meeting is the most important one of the season. If the staff has input into the agenda for the meeting and into the details to be discussed they will be much more a part of the team and strong cohesion should ensue. By cooperatively planning this first meeting the staff will also come to realize what other staff members feel are the most important aspects of their program.

7. *Worst/Best Moment Exercise* — In

this exericse the staff members will openly tell the others about the worst and best moments that they have experienced in coaching and how they reacted to them. By opening up in this situation the individual coach entrusts the others with the knowledge of a significant part of his experience, thus bringing the individuals closer together.

8. *Team Captain Qualifications* — Discussing the procedure for the selection of team captains will help the staff identify the leadership qualities which not only captains, but they themselves as coaches, must possess in order to be effective leaders. Here again, the knowledge of the values and goals of other staff members helps to draw the staff together in a cohesive unit.

9. *Staff/Family Functions* — The head coach should develop a definite yearly plan for the involvement of the coaches' families into the program. This should not be a once-a-year picnic, but rather an ongoing function. Free time for coaches, on a regular basis, also should be provided for the staff in order that they can be with friends and families outside of the coaching atmosphere.

10. *Physical and Mental Conditioning Program* — The head coach should see to it that his staff gets proper exercise, nutrition, and rest throughout the season and off-season. This may be accomplished by the introduction of relaxation training, stretching, and actual physical conditioning conducted by the head coach.

The Professional System

The final component in this system approach to developing staff cohesion has to do with the professional aspects of the coaching position. Again, there is some overlap of the points in this particular system and the previously discussed communication system and value system. The professional system is broken down into three main areas: job responsibility, job status and recognition, and professional development. All three deal with the individual coach's perception of his job, its rewards, and the opportunity for advancement in the coaching profession.

Staff cohesion is more easily effected when a clearly defined description of duties and a clear knowledge of other's duties are evident. We have already discussed the importance of a detailed job description, but it is important that the individual coaches know what others on the staff are expected to do also. The coaches should have the freedom to perform those duties in what each feels is the best possible manner. Of course the head coach will have some input into the coaching techniques employed, but the individual coach must feel that he has a great deal of coaching freedom. Most coaches want some important duties to go along with their job and the head coach should affirm, through his actions, that he believes in delegating authority for the implementation of various aspects of his program. If the assistant coaches know that each of them has significant duties to perform and that each job is a valuable one, then cohesion will be more likely to occur. It is imperative, however, that each coach realize that along with these freedoms and responsibilities comes the accountability for the performance of the tasks.

The head coach can aid the staff members in the accomplishment of their various duties by insuring that the entire staff has input into the decision making process. In this way the staff will achieve a meshing of the variety of skills and talents of the staff. What is one coach's strength may be another's weakness, and if the coach knows that he has certain strengths, and that the staff recognizes those strengths and capitalizes on them, he will be proud of his position and will, in turn, work harder toward the accomplishment of the group's goals. The fact that only a limited number of people have his particular assets, and consequently that he is a member of a special group of people, also aids in the development of staff cohesion.

While it is, of course, paramount that coaching tasks be performed adequately, it is also important that the coach be recognized for his accomplishments. There should be some status or recognition inherent in his position. A defensive coordinator, for instance, should be the acknowledged authority on that dimension of the game. The use of position or titles can be helpful if used in a positive manner. The status of staff members can be enhanced outside the group if the head coach makes a concerted effort in this regard. Family, friends, the media, other staff, etc. can all be powerful outside motivators, and the wise head coach will always look for ways to enhance the status of his assistants with those groups. As he is providing the opportunity for success and failure within the staff (failure can sometimes be a powerful teacher for the coach) the head coach must constantly seek means and ways to both positively and negatively reinforce both group and individual effort. The knowledge that effort and production will be recognized is important to developing the unity on the staff necessary for winning.

Often a coach knows that even though he has done a good job there must also be some opportunity for advancement in order for him to become truly satisfied with a job well done. The individual coach can help himself by constantly striving to improve his knowledge of the game and his coaching techniques. The head coach may set a positive atmosphere for this attitude because the improvement in skill level by an individual positively affects the group. He should encourage growth in his assistants and should demonstrate by his actions that the opportunity for increased status within the group exists for those willing to work for it.

The head coach can positively affect this professional system in a number of ways. Among these are:

1. *Developing Well Defined Job Descriptions* — These should be printed and distributed to all the coaches as outlined earlier.
2. *Attending to Staff Structure* — The coach should structure his staff in a manner that is conducive to the delegation of authority and responsibility.
3. *Avoiding In-breeding* — Many staffs have been ruined by having all the coaches alike; same alma mater, same temperament, same coaching style, etc. The head coach should make a conscious effort to bring a variety of experiences, personalities, and styles to his staff, while at the same time attracting coaches of similar values, beliefs, and goals.
4. *Giving Credit to Assistant Coaches* —

Whenever the team wins the head coach should make sure that the assistant coaches get the credit in the media or elsewhere for the coaching success. Whenever the team loses the head coach should take the blame himself. It sounds almost pious, but it is crucial that assistants be sheltered from the "slings and arrows" of defeat, and that they bask in the glory of victory.

5. *Increasing Remuneration* — A pay boost or increase in fringe benefits will do wonders for staff morale.
6. *Supporting Professional Growth Through Clinics* — The head coach should try to finance and encourage attendance at professional meetings and clinics.
7. *Supporting Professional Growth Through Job Advancement* — A head coach who goes out of his way to promote from within, and also who will support and strongly recommend his assistants for other jobs outside his program, will be blessed with a loyal cohesive staff.
8. *Congratulating Family* — A letter of congratulations for an outstanding job, sent to the assistant's home, will not only enhance his status, but will make him want to do more of the same in the future. If an entire staff feels that way then they will be a solid, cohesive unit.

THE SPECIFIC PROGRAM

Recently the present author was appointed head football coach at a small college after a number of years as an assistant at that same school. The upcoming squad had a large number of returnees from the previous year and the team attitude and cohesion was considered excellent. With the hiring of an almost completely new staff the problem of developing cohesion arose in the staff and not necessarily the team (although the two could never be completely segregated). Through the University of Virginia's Sports Psychology Conference the new head coach was introduced to a variety of activities that might be employed successfully in developing a cohesive staff. In a conversation with one of the directors of the Conference two points were made pertinent to this idea of staff cohesion:

1. Nearly all assistant coaches want to be head coaches. And they also know what qualities they would want in their assistants. It is important that their current head coach remind them of this and have them exhibit those same qualities in their present position; and

2. A head coach should communicate to his staff that if they make him successful, then they too will be successful, they will advance professionally, and the head coach will see to it that they advance and progress as a coach.

With these points in mind the author was searching for a vehicle to bring the staff together, to improve communication, to set common goals, and to aid professional advancement; in other words to become a cohesive coaching unit. It was felt that an environment separate from the normal school and athletic office setting was necessary, and that a number of days in a relaxed atmosphere was needed. The idea of a coaches' retreat was considered to be just the vehicle needed to bring this new group of coaches together into a unified, functional, and successful group. A mountain cabin was secured for a period of three days a number of weeks before the actual beginning of summer football practice. This location would allow the staff to be away together in an informal setting before the pressure of the season was upon them.

The idea of a coaches' retreat can be applied to a number of different coaching situations, but it should not be looked on as a vacation, nor as just an opportunity for the head coach to squeeze more hours of work from his staff. It should be highly organized, but in so doing, should allow for some recreational time and relaxation time. It should be patterned after religious and professional retreats in which the individual is refreshed and invigorated mentally, physically, and spiritually.

There are four main areas of concern that will be addressed during the retreat. The first is the developing of friendships among the coaches and providing an atmosphere for fellowship and also teamwork. Just the mere fact that the staff is relatively isolated and must plan and cook meals together can be a tremendous impetus to fellowship and cooperation among the staff. An occasional card game, or perhaps even the cooperative planning of a skit to be presented to the team at the end of summer camp would help in this regard.

The second area deals with physical activity during the retreat. Here the head coach must coordinate a variety of activities to impress the staff with the importance of a regular exercise program. An early morning "dawn patrol" for joggers can be instituted but if the staff has some non-runners it may be better to lead them through the complete stretching and warm-up program that the team will be required to do before practice. Relaxation techniques and stress management programs can be taught also. In addition to these early morning activities it would be fairly easy to schedule time for golf, tennis, swimming, etc. during the day.

The third area is concerned with planning for the upcoming season. This area should not include X's and O's but rather should deal with organizational and administrative matters which can help improve the program. It is here that the staff can cooperatively set goals for the staff and team. These goals will form the cornerstone for the season and the head coach should educate the staff about the proper way to set and manage goals. The staff can also plan that all-important first team meeting, and can continue by planning the preseason, in-season, and off-season aspects of the program. The head coach can also introduce the concept of "brainstorming sessions" and conduct one or two short ones at the same time. The staff and family functions to be held throughout the year should also be planned and the whole idea of the involvement of the family discussed in order to better serve the needs of the coaches' families. Evaluation forms for each coach and for the whole program can be developed jointly at this time also.

Perhaps the most important phase of the retreat is the "Getting to Know You" activities. These exercises will help each staff member know a little bit more about himself and his fellow staff members. These activities have been discussed earlier and they form the backbone of the retreat. There certainly are quite a few activities that would be appropriate but the following have been chosen to better address the needs of a relatively small football coaching staff.

1. *The Personal Inventory* of goals, skills, assets, liabilities, priorities, and commitments of the individual coaches.
2. *Qualities of a Coach Questionnaire* — in order to determine which qualities the staff feels are most important.
3. *Worst/Best Moment Exercise* helps humanize the coach and can serve as an excellent "ice-breaker."
4. *Crisis Simulation* helps each coach see how the others would react under adverse conditions.
5. *Team Captain Qualifications* would help identify and reinforce leadership qualities.
6. *Illinois Competition Scale* (Martens, 1977) — would enable the staff to identify the high anxiety coaches and effectively deal with them.

All of these four areas need to be planned, organized, and integrated into an efficient, effective, and enjoyable retreat, which the staff will view as a positive experience. It should not be so regimented that they cannot relax, but at the same time should be viewed as a time to do something positive to improve the program.

SUMMARY

From this discussion one should realize that staff cohesion does not just happen, but actually can be positively affected by a planned systematic program to promote staff unity. It is important also to realize that staff cohesion can be a negative influence if the staff is socially oriented rather than task oriented. An inverted U hypothesis could possibly be made in the relationship between cohesion and performance. There probably is a middle ground in which cohesion is task oriented and therefore more productive than either the very low and very high cohesion areas.

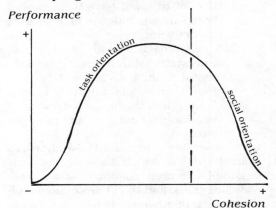

Staff cohesion can also be negatively influenced by the heterogeneity of the staff, the immaturity of the individual coaches, competition among the staff, and forced cohesion.

Finally, it is important to note that the head coach does have some tools to aid in building staff cohesion. He must have a plan and then implement it. If a staff is highly cohesive and task oriented then success will follow. "Cohesion leads to adhesion," and the staff that sticks together will effectively reach its goals.

REFERENCE

Martens, R. (1977). Sport Competition Anxiety Test. Champaign, IL: Human Kinetics Publishers.

University of Virginia photo services

17

Increasing Team Motivation[1]

Robert J. Rotella
University of Virginia

Until now our attention has been centered around individual motivations and goal setting behaviors which affect performance. Let us now turn our attention to social psychological factors which are related to team goal setting behavior and team success.

Anyone who has ever coached has experienced highs and lows in recruiting new team members. Teams that have been consistently successful are usually flooded with potential material while teams with a losing tradition find candidates to be quite scarce. Contrary to the popular American ideal of supporting the underdog, it would seem that most individuals prefer to be associated with a winner.

It appears that several factors may be identified which must be present in order for team membership to be attractive to individuals: there should be some peer status connected with membership, individuals must perceive team membership as being valuable in some way, and individuals must perceive other members in a favorable light. The two factors to which I will focus my presentation affect both team attractiveness and productivity and are thus of crucial importance. Teams must have clearly specified goals and the goals should be attainable; that is the team should have a reasonable chance for success.

One of the major functions of a coach is to overcome conflicts between person-oriented and group-oriented motives for achievement. An athlete who is satisfied by personal success has a person-oriented motive for personal achievement, whereas an individual who is gratified by the group's success has a group-oriented motive for

group achievement (Atkinson and Feather, 1966). In an activity such as sport which is capable of eliciting both motives there are bound to be problems if precautions are not taken. Individuals are most likely to allow a group oriented-motive to dominate when they are allowed to be involved in the goal setting process and when they are given more responsible roles on the team. Members who agree upon a goal for their group become aware that the benefits for all depend upon the efforts of each, and thus a norm to help one another is aroused.

The coach can facilitate this process by involving the team in group discussions designed to make individual members aware of the goals of other group members, assist group members in establishing realistic and mutually satisfying goals, and to bring about member agreement regarding the group goal, referred to as the group level of aspiration. The effective coach will make sure that the goal setting process continues throughout the season. There is a tendency for a team to raise its level of aspiration, following success; there is a tendency to lower it following failure. Coaches should be aware of this inclination and guide the team to adopt goals which are achieveable and satisfying. A goal which is set too low typically fails to generate any feelings or pride even following success and thus has no positive effect upon achievement. Goals which are set too high will most likely result in failure which may adversely effect both perception of member's abilities and the degree of social cohesion. It is evident then that the motivation, morale, and self-evaluation of team members will depend greatly upon the relation between the group's level

[1]This speech was taken in part from an article published in *Motor Skills: From Theory into Practice*, 1978.

of aspiration and its subsequent performance.

It is a well documented fact that group goals are capable of steering the behavior of group members to perform certain activities rather than others. Once a particular group goal has been established, "dedicated" group members are expected to work toward its attainment even when their preferred goal has not been selected. However, when a team adopts a goal and embarks upon a program of actions intended to bring about goal attainment, it may encounter success or failure. If the team's efforts are successful, members who have accepted the group goal have reason to experience gratification. Team members may be expected to increase their evaluation of the team, to become more attracted to it, and set higher aspirations for its future performance. A group that is unsuccessful in attaining its goals encounters quite a different situation. Members are likely to experience frustration, to decrease their evaluation of the group, to become less attracted to it, and to set lower goals for its future performance. Group failure also stimulates members to engage in a variety of coping behaviors designed to minimize the negative consequences of failure. Such behaviors include efforts to shift responsibility for the group outcome from oneself to others, depreciation of the value of the unattained goal, and derogation of the criteria employed in evaluating the performance of the group and its members.

These factors clearly point to the importance of the setting of specific and realistic goals by sport teams. They further add support to the notion that coaches should make sure that teammates are aware of each others goals and should continuously remain involved in the process of setting goals for the team if it is desirable to have all team members adopt group aspirations.

REWARDING THE ATTAINMENT OF GROUP GOALS

Now that the team goals are established the next most important job for the coach in terms of motivation is to make sure that rewards are dispensed contingent upon group performance rather than individual performance. Far too often it is witnessed that coaches preach team goals but then reward individual performance. This contradiction is further amplified by the fact that rewards are usually given to the outstanding performers who have already received their "payoffs" in the forms of prestige, recognition, and affection. In essence then, a situation is created in which most rewards are given to those individuals least in need of them and are administered in a manner encouraging individuality rather than team work. Coaches would be wise to keep in mind the fact that the rules controlling the awarding of payoffs will have significant motivational consequences for the members and for the functioning of the team as a whole. If a team operates under a policy whereby the magnitude of each member's payoff depends directly upon the quality of the group's performance, members will contribute to attainment of this end (such as practicing deligently, helping teammates improve, building confidence in teammates, making suggestions about ways to improve the group's efficiency, or even playing "second string"). A much different motivational situation would be present if each member's payoffs were contingent upon the quality of his own individual performance. In this situation, it is to each person's advantage to be concerned with his own performance alone; no incentive is provided for helping others, seeking ways to improve the group's efficiency, or doing anything that might lower his level of performance.

This situation suggested above in which rewards are contingent upon group output but dependent of individual scores, labeled cooperative interdependence, provides an environment in which whenever one member performs an act beneficial to himself he simultaneously benefits all other members. Thus, athletes will be willing to accept specialized roles on the team as well as a readiness to help teammates develop to their potential. The development of the perception among teammates that working hard with other group members will lead to fulfillment of both individual and group achievement needs will in turn cause all members to increase their effort and maximize the chances of the team reaching its potential.

ACHIEVEMENT MOTIVATION AND ATTRIBUTION THEORY: IMPLICATIONS FOR IMPROVING SPORT PERFORMANCE

Researchers in sport psychology have long been concerned with the relationship between achievement motivation and sport performance (Klein and Christiansen, 1969; Ogilvie, 1976; Willis and Bethe, 1970). An abundance of empirical studies have been generated from the resultant achievement motivation model (Atkinson, 1964) and have resulted in the subsequent development of both projective measures (McClelland, Atkinson, Clark, and Lowell, 1953; Mandler and Sarason, 1952) and objective measures (Mehrabian, 1968, 1969) of achievement motivation.

This achievement model describes high achievers as individuals with a stronger motive to achieve success than a motive to avoid or fear failure. Low achievers are conceived as having a stronger motive to avoid failure than to achieve success.

Researchers interested in personality variables have successfully identified characteristics related to individuals with high and low achievement motivation. High achievers have been characterized as having a realistic aspiration level, preferring intermediate risk situations, being better able to delay gratification, and attempting to finish tasks they undertake. High achievers also appear more likely to persevere at a task, and have proportionately better recall of their mistakes or weaknesses following a test situation.

In contrast, low achievers have more extreme aspiration levels, either low or high, prefer extreme risk situations (e.g. very easy or very difficult tasks), tend to prefer immediately gratifying activities which do not necessarily lead to any future goals or rewards, and are not concerned with closure in the tasks they undertake. Low achievers, additionally, are less likely to persevere at a task, have poorer memory of incomplete tasks, and recall proportionately more successes or strengths following a test situation (Mehrabian, 1968).

The most frequently mentioned researchers in achievement motivation theory, McClelland (1961, 1971, 1973) and Atkinson (1964) have made frequent reference to

sport. Both authors linked the achievement motive with interest in competitive athletics, both as spectators and participants. Currently, it is commonplace to see the term high achiever used to describe all athletes. Research suggests that this practice is at best highly questionable (Weinberg, 1976; Rotella, 1976). Highly successful athletes at both the high school and college levels have been found to display a variety of achievement motivation scores, ranging from high to low.

At first glance it might appear that the individual with low achievement motivation (one who is dominated by fear of failure) would not even be motivated to enter into the domain of sports where success and failure are so publicly evaluated. However, the low achiever's entrance into sport can be easily explained on the basis of extrinsic rewards (trophies, scholarships, parental and peer praise) which are constantly handed out for athletic participation. Indeed, it can be easily understood in light of the fact that sport is one of the few avenues in which a young person can achieve and be recognized for that achievement prior to adulthood (Weiss, 1969).

The low achievement motivated athlete typically displays a self-concept reflecting a perception of lack of ability combined with a tendency to actively circumvent failure and/or worry about failure. The belief system and action preferences of these individuals remains unchanging over time and across situations in the face of contradictory facts. It seems that achievement motivation is independent of, and unaffected by, external reinforcement (Sarason and Spielberger, 1975). Fortunately, this holds true also for the high achievement motivated individual facing consistent failure.

Heckhausen (1975) has stated that "What appears to be a deficient reality orientation and a lack of openness to relearning, is not a simple result of reinforcement history. That is to say, the fear of failure motive is not the outcome of poor ability causing failures, and of failures causing negative external reinforcement by the social and physical environment. There is no notable difference in intelligence test scores, for instance, between high and low achievement motivated individuals." (Heckhausen, 1975, p. 121).

Achievement motivation development is

an extremely subtle and complicated process. Success or failure experiences are the result of evaluated cognitions, which early in life are established in a person's motive system. Therefore, it becomes clear that definitions of success or failure are highly individualistic and subjective. Each athlete in a competitive situation will set goals or levels of aspiration against which the actual outcome will be compared. If the outcome exceeds the standard, it is perceived as a success. If it remains below the standard, it is peceived as a failure (Kanfer, 1971).

In order to completely understand the development of fear of failure and the problems of the athlete motivated by avoidance motivation, we must go one step further. The role of causal attribution for success or failure as they are determined by the comparison process must be understood.

ATTRIBUTION THEORY

In recent years an abundance of literature has been gathered, which is relevant to an attributional analysis of achievement motivation. Many studies have been stimulated by the writings of Weiner (1972), who combined Rotter's (1954) distinction between internal and external locus of control and Heider's (1958) differentiation between stable and unstable forces into a four-fold table of causal factors. The causal factors identified were ability, a stable and internal factor; effort, a variable and internal factor; task difficulty, a stable and external factor; and luck (good or bad), a variable and external factor (Weiner, Frieze, Kukla, Reed, Rest, Rosenbaum, 1971).

Weiner's (1972) analysis has detailed the relationship among goal setting behavior, causal ascriptions, and achievement motivation. The low achievement motivated athlete will prefer extremely high or low goals. When this athlete is attracted to a low goal situation, success is highly likely. However, the success will be clearly attributed to the ease of the task. Obviously, this is a factor external to the individuals, so that the individual will not be able to take credit for the success. If high goals are sought after, success is unlikely, yet, if it is attained the success will be attributed to luck, an external factor, rather than internal factors such as ability and effort. The high achievement motivated individual, on the other hand, sets realistic goals in which there is a 50-50 chance of success and failure. This preference results in the high achievement motivated individual attributing success to internal factors, ability and effort, and failure to either bad luck or effort. When the high achievement motivated athlete attributes failure to lack of effort, the result is an increase in effort in the future because there still remains full confidence in one's ability.

It becomes increasingly more apparent that by their goal setting performance low achievement motivated athletes create situations that minimize their personal responsibility for success and yet, blame their failures on lack of ability rather than effort or external factors such as task difficulty or bad luck. The opposite is true for the high achievement motivated athlete. Lack of ability is seldom the explanation for failure. If an internal factor is warranted a lack of effort will be utilized. In the future this athlete will simply work harder in order to be a success.

In summary, the causal interpretation of success or failure of high and low achievement motivated athletes are biased. Low achievement motivated athletes tend to blame failure on a lack of ability explanation. High acheivement motivated individuals perceive failure as due to a lack of effort attribution. Clearly, the effort one expends is capable of being modified. Ability is quite permanent. If one looks separately at internal causes, lack of ability has a more detrimental effect in self-reinforcement than lack of momentary effort (Meyer, 1973). Obviously, the low achievement motivated athlete digs a hole that gets deeper and deeper. Even under comparable conditions, athletes with high achievement motivation credit themselves more for their successes than for their failures and low achievement motivated athletes credit or blame themselves more for their failures than for their successes.

IMPLICATIONS

Due to the nature of todays sports, a low achievement motivated athlete can be a success in sport if blessed with enough ability. Coaches are frequently disturbed at the motivational deficit apparent in many of their superior athletes (low achievement motivation). It is clear that these athletes will never attain their maximal potential. Many coaches find it difficult to comprehend how such a talented athlete could have a motivational system dominated by fear of failure. Often this is the crux of the problem. It is not that the athlete is simply lazy.

The solution to the problem is not merely providing the low achievement motivated athlete with consistent experiences which the athlete may already be experiencing. Rather, a planned program must be implemented for changing goal setting and causal attributions.

The first phase involved in the motive change program is to test all athletes on achievement motivation and allow the athletes to self-score themselves and determine their motivational level. The use of the Mehrabian 1969 Achieving Tendency Scale for Males and Females (Mehrabian, 1969) is suggested.

The second phase of the program involves providing information relevant to achievement motivation and goal setting behavior as well as causal attribution and its relationship to ascriptions for success and failure in competitive situations (as detailed above). This information should be presented in a manner which will allow for complete understanding. It is usually quite beneficial to encourage group discussion and questions. An additional tool effective in helping athletes accept this new knowledge and change their motive system is to provide guest speakers, such as notable coaches or athletes who would be viewed as attractive models. These models should speak on the importance of realistic goal setting, confidence in one's ability, and a belief in the feasibility of improving oneself by expending more effort.

The third phase consists of helping the athlete in the process of setting realistic goals. Both terminal goals and a list of sequential goals to help the athlete achieve the terminal goals need to be carefully identified. Athletes, coaches, and teammates work together in helping each other in this process. It is important that attainment of these goals require an abundance of effort. Yet, they must not be so difficult

that even with maximal effort the individual will be frustrated. It should be emphasized that the honesty and accuracy of goal setting is of crucial importance. All individuals involved must be willing to spend time in setting the goals.

Low achievement motivated athletes must be taught the value in setting small sequential improvements in order to realize long range ambitions which must be perceived as more valuable than immediate gratification. Far too often the low achievement motivated athlete never plans out how to attain a goal which is 1-5 years in the future. Consequently, the skill of even the most gifted athlete becomes stagnated and never gets significantly better.

In phase four the coaches and athletes draw up a master list of all the skills required for reaching the desired level of success (physical skills, conditioning, strategies, etc.). The list should be very specific. Each athlete, with the help of coaches and teammates must deal in sequential order of their weakest skills (many times coach and athlete disagree on weaknesses and if teammates interact and discuss openly will have to admit to inaccurate self-perception). When this list has been completed a specific amount of time will be allocated daily for practicing on individual weaknesses only.

The fear of failure motivated athlete tends to spend most time practicing strengths, especially when surrounded by teammates or coaches. As the athletes weakest skill is improved and alleviated this time is spent on the next weakest skill. This time period should be followed by a 10-15 minute time period during which each athlete works on their favorite or best skill which are often one in the same.

Finally, it must be stressed that the coach must be aware of the importance of player-coach interactions on motivation and causal attribution. Emphasis on developing confidence in one's ability should be stressed following both victory and defeat. Encouragement and reinforcement should be given to athletes for increases in effort. These self-perceptions are extremely important in helping athletes to maximize their potential.

ACHIEVEMENT MOTIVATION AND FEMALE ATHLETES

Achievement motivation appears to be of

particular significance to women. For years it has been recognized that women do not achieve as much as men in the fields of science, the humanities, and the arts (Astin, 1973, Commission of the Status of Women, 1970; Maccoby and Jacklin, 1974; Rossi and Calderwood, 1973). The same is true for women in sport.

The research of Bardwick (1971) indicates that the model of achievement motivation developed by Atkinson and Raynor (1974) and McClelland (1971) is not appropriate for women. Alper (1974) suggests that female achievement motivation possesses an illusive quality. Bardwick (1971) suggests that the problem is centered on the women's need for both achievement and affiliation and their fear that success in one rules out success in the other.

Horner (1968) studied the avoidance of achievement in women which she calls "fear of success." Horner discovered that most women had less fear of success when competing against themselves, than when they were competing with other students. The opposite was true for most males.

Lipman-Blumen (1972) argues that many women choose to achieve vicariously through the successes of important male persons in their lives rather than directly achieve on their own merits. (The female who wishes to be manager, statistician, cheerleader of the team or girl friend of the star athlete). Through this approach the woman may avoid responsibility for success or failure (external control) and yet still benefit from the success of the team or friend.

It is quite clear that any discussion of achievement motivation and females in general and female athletes in particular will be somewhat confounded by variables difficult to completely control. Most likely the sex related differences found in the achievement motivation literature are to a great extent a result of sex-role stereotyping (Mischel, 1966; Reese and Lipsitt, 1970). It is obvious that the distinctions between male and female achievement motivations are a result of factors other than biological. The dissimilarities are, therefore, susceptible to change.

Although present research findings on the athletic and achievement motivation patterns of women are not complete enough to provide highly specific directions to coaching practice, they are sufficient to pro-

pose some general ideas for coaches interested in increasing achievement motivation in women athletes. Young female athletes should be presented with successful, non-traditional role models. Successful women athletes and/or coaches should be invited to speak or visit with students. Role models may also be presented through group discussion, films, or printed material. Black women who reportedly have very low fear of success and home career conflict (Gump and Rivers, 1975), should also be useful for females experiencing motivational conflicts.

Coaches should also take an active role in teaching parents how to recognize and reduce sex-role stereotypic behavior. Coaches and parents can encourage females to actively attempt to achieve in athletics. Coaches must be sure that females receive as much recognition for their athletic success as males usually receive.

Female athletes will start developing their potential to a maximum when they start realizing that it is perfectly acceptable to be assertive and successful in any endeavor they choose. When males as well as females completely accept their attitude, women's potential will no longer be engulfed in half-true myths. Most likely a single model of achievement motivation will successfully apply to male and female athletes and female athletes will no longer be dominated by a "fear of success."

SUMMARY

All persons involved in sport are not high achievement motivated and do not attribute success and failure to causes capable to modification. For these reasons many athletes never manage to attain their maximum performance level. Through the utilization of a motivational change program coaches can help athletes experience joy of realizing one's full potential.

REFERENCES

Alper, T. Achievement motivation on women: now-you-see-it-now-you-don't. *American Psychologist*, 1974, 29, 194-203.

Astin, H. S. *Preparing women for careers in science and technology.* Paper presented

108

at the Massachusetts Institute of Technology Workshop on Women in Science and Technology, Boston, May, 1973.

Atkinson, J. W. *Motives in fantasy, action and society.* Princeton: Van Nostrand, 1964.

Atkinson, J. W., and Feather, N. T. *A theory of achievement motivation.* New York: John Wiley & Sons, 1966.

Atkinson, J. W., and Raynor, J. O. *Motivation and achievement.* Washington, D.C.: V. W. Winston & Sons, 1974.

Atkinson, J. W., and Reitman, W. R. Performance as a function of motive strength and expectancy of goal attainment. *Journal of Abnormal and Social Psychology*, 1965, 53, 361-366.

Bardwick, J. *Psychology of Women.* New York: Harper & Row, 1971.

Bird, Anne M. "Applications from Attribution Theory: Facilitating Sport Group Performance." Paper presented at the Joint NACPEW/NCPEAM Conference, Orlando, Florida, January, 1977.

Commission of the Status of Women. *Participation of women in the economic and social development of their countries.* New York: United Nations, 1970.

Deutch, Morton. Some factors affecting membership motivation and achievement motivation in a group. *Human Relations*, 1959, 12, 81-95.

Gump, J., and Rivers, L. The consideration of race in efforts to end sex bias. In E. Diamond (Ed.), *Issues of sex bias and sex fairness in career interest measurement.* Washington, D.C.: U.S. Government Printing Office, 1975.

Heckhausen, H. *The anatomy of achievement motivation.* New York Academic Press, 1967.

Heckhausen, H. Achievement motive research: Current problems and some contributions toward a general theory of motivation. In W. J. Arnold (Ed.), *Nebraska symposium on motivation 1968.* Lincoln, Nebraska: University of Nebraska Press, 1968.

Heckhausen, H. Fear of failure as a self-reinforcing motive system. In Sarason, S. B. and Spielberger, C. (Eds.), *Stress and anxiety*, Hemisphere Publishing Corporation, Washington, D. C.: A Halsted Press Book, John Wiley and Sons, New York, 1975.

Heider, F. *The psychology of interpersonal relations*, New York: Wiley, 1958.

Horner, M. *Sex differences in achieve-ment motivation and performance in competitive and non-competitive situations.* Unpublished doctoral dissertation, University of Michigan, 1968, No. 69-112, 135.

Kanfer, F. H. The maintenance of behavior by self-generated stimuli and reinforcement. In A. Jacobs and L. B. Sachs (Eds.), *The psychology of private events*, New York: Academic Press, 1971.

Klein, M. and Christiansen, G. Group composition, group structure, and group effectiveness of basketball teams. (Trans. D. E. Kenyon). In J. W. Loy and G. S. Kenyon (Eds.), *Sport, culture, and society*, London: MacMillan, 1969.

Lipman-Blumen, J. How ideology shapes women's lives, *Scientific American*, 1972, 226, 34-42.

Lott, Albert and Bernice Lott. Group cohesiveness as interpersonal attraction. *Psychological Bulletin*, 1965, 54, 259-309.

Maccoby, E. and Jacklin, C. *The psychology of sex differences*, Stanford, California: Stanford University Press, 1974.

Mandler, G. and Sarason, S. B. A study of anxiety and learning. *Journal of Abnormal and Social Psychology*, 1952, 47, 166-173.

McClelland, D. C. *The achieving society*, Princeton, N.J.: Van Nostrand, 1961.

McClelland, D. C. *Assessing human motivation*, New York: General Press, 1971.

McClelland, D. C. What is the effect of achievement motivation training in the schools? In D. C. McClelland and R. S. Steele (Eds.), *Human motivation*, Morristown, N.J.: General Press, 1973.

McClelland, D. C., Atkinson, J. W., Clark, R. A., and Lowell, E. L. *The achievement motive*, New York: Appleton-Century-Crofts, 1953.

Mehrabian, A. Male and female scales of the tendency to achieve, *Educational and Psychological Measurement*, 1968, 28, 493-502.

Mehrabian, A. Measures of achieving tendency, *Educational and Psychological Measurement*, 1969, 29, 445-451.

Meyer, W. U. Leistungmotiv and Ursachenerklarung von Erfolg und Misserfolg, In Sarason, S. B. and Spielberger, C. (Eds.), *Stress and anxiety*, Hemisphere Publishing Corporation, Washington, D.C., A Halsted Press Book, John Wiley and Sons, New York, 1975.

Mischel, W. A social learning view of sex differences in behavior, In E. E. Maccoby

(Ed.), *The development of sex differences,* Stanford University Press, 1966.

Ogilvie, B. C. Psychological consistencies within the personality of high-level competitors, In A. C. Fisher (Ed.), *Psychology of sport: Issues and insights.* Palo Alto: Mayfield, 1976.

Ogilvie, B. C. and Tutko, T. A. *Problem athletes and how to handle them,* Palham Books: London, 1968.

Reese, H. W. and Lipsitt, L. P. *Experimental child psychology,* New York: Academic Press, 1970.

Rossi, A. and Calderwood, A. (Eds.), *Academic women on the move,* New York: Russell Sage Foundation, 1973.

Rotella, R. J. *An analysis of the relationship between primary sport participation and reduction of psychological conflict over the child-training practice of achievement,* Unpublished doctoral dissertation: University of Connecticut, 1974.

Rotter, J. B. *Social learning and clinical psychology.* Englewood Cliffs, New Jersey: Prentice-Hall, 1954.

Weiner, B. *Theories of motivation,* Chicago: Markham, 1972.

Weiner, B., Frieze, I., Kukla, A., Reed, L., Rest, S., and Rosenbaum, R. M. *Perceiving the causes of success and failure,* New York: General Learning Press, 1971.

Weinberg, W. T. *A comparison of resultant achievement motivation levels of college athletes and non-athletes.* A paper presentation at the 1976 Convention of the American Alliance of HPER, Milwaukee, April 4, 1976.

Weiss, P. *Sport: A philosophical inquiry,* Carbondale: Southern Illinois University Press, 1969.

Willis, Joe D. *Achievement motivation, success, and competitiveness in college wrestling,* unpublished Ph.D. dissertation. The Ohio State University, 1968.

Willis, Joe D., and Bethe, D. Achievement motivation implications for physical activity, *Quest,* 1970, *13.*

Zander, A. Group Aspirations. In D. Cartwright and A. Zander (Eds.), *Group Dynamics,* New York: Harper and Row, 1968.

University of Virginia photo services

18

The Successful Coach: A Leader Who Communicates

Robert J. Rotella
University of Virginia

What is the best leadership style for coaches to utilize who wish to maximize the potential of their team? In recent years this question has come under close scrutiny.

Coaches exist as mediators in many ways: between athletic potential and actual performance, between parent and child, and between theory and practice. Their power is formidable because they govern an area of considerable emotional investment — that of sport — for both parent and child. Therefore, the means they choose to reach the end they perceive as important is crucial. Their methods can, and will, have ramifications since in sports, coaches deal with young athletes for whom some models are critically important. Hence, the coaches' choice is critical simply because their actions will have a larger consequence.

Several authors have stereotyped coaches as authoritarian leaders (Scott, 1971; Tutko and Richards, 1971). These scholars see coaches as more interested in power and manipulation than in humanism. Supposedly coaches are efficiency experts who demand unquestioned commitment to their philosophy. Ogilvie and Tutko (1970) have conducted research which has found that coaches tend to score high on measures of need for achievement, aggression, abasement and endurance — traits generally associated with getting ahead and succeeding but not necessarily most advantageous for character development. These qualities also typify the authoritarian leader. Anderson (1959) describes the authoritarian leader as one who uses authority to control others, issues orders to others in the group, tries to have things done according to the accepted rules, acts in an impersonal manner, punishes members who disobey or deviate, decides upon division of labor, determines how work should be done, and judges the soundness of ideas.

George Sage (1973) believes that the authoritarian coach is very similar to leaders who follow the Scientific Management model of leadership designed by Frederick Taylor in the early 1900's. Such leaders tend to treat team members as objects in a machine-like environment. They desire to manipulate player behavior not only in practice and games, but also outside of practice time (curfews, hair length, dating).

Possibly there is good reason for coaches to lead in an authoritarian manner. Several tentative explanations have been given: (1) coaches perceive their role as authoritarian, thus they form into the mold; (2) coaches are persons who have high needs for control of others and have gravitated to sports to fulfill their needs; (3) stressful leadership situations that arise in most sports call for control of the participant by the coach; (4) certain athletes seek authoritarian behavior from the coach so the coach acts to meet the athlete's needs (Cratty, 1973). Some coaches attempt to fulfill the father role as well as the coach role and thus feel the need to instill discipline (Beisser, 1967; Massengale, 1974), and some coaches are authoritarian because they are unsure of themselves and do not wish to be questioned.

It is quite possible with many athletes that any leadership style other than an authoritarian style would be highly unsuccessful due to the high expectations for this type of behavior. This thought may be particularly pertinent to children from low socioeconomic level families where an authoritarian approach to child-rearing is more typical. It is also quite likely that even these expectations could be modified if one desired to do so. Most likely this would only happen if coaches placed as much emphasis on personality development and morale as they did on winning.

More assuredly it is understandable if one suggests that the authoritarian style presented by many major university coaches is a direct result of the "win at any cost" philosophy of the university administration. A study by Mudra (1965) astutely demonstrated that major university level coaches view learning as a process of habit formation rather than a process of differentiating, generalizing, and reconstructing the psychological field. Such coaches with a stimulus-response as opposed to a cognitive orientation, out of necessity, display an authoritarian style of leadership. These coaches clearly fail to place much confidence in athletes' ability to make decisions.

Although the tendency has been to criticize the authoritarian style of leadership there possibly are some advantages to its use. Some of these advantages are: (1) the insecure athlete may feel more secure and protected in a stressful situation; and (2) time may be used more effectively, especially in the earlier organizational stages and during actual practice time when an authoritarian style is used. This may be especially important in light of the limited time available for pre-season practice.

Other research has found many coaches to be democratic in their leadership style. "Democratic leaders generally act in a friendly, personal manner; allow the group as a whole to plan the agenda; allow group members to talk with one another without permission . . .; accept suggestions about how the work shall be done; and talk only a little more than the average group member" (Anderson, 1959, p. 202). In general, research suggests groups with a democratic leadership style, whose members participate in determining their goals, will have higher morale and more commitment to the group than those directed by authoritarian leaders (Cartwright and Zander, 1968). Certainly coaches have been successful using a democratic approach to coaching. George Davis, a high school football coach, uses a democratic leadership style and his teams have won over 45 straight games. Coach Davis contends that as a result his athletes have developed increased confidence, cohesion, responsibility, leadership and mo-

tivation (Eitzen and Sage, 1978). Of course we could find many successful coaches who have used an authoritarian leadership style who also feel they have developed "character" in their athletes.

At the present time it is really impossible to determine conclusively whether one style is more effective in terms of team success than another. However, it appears that coaches would be wise if they attempted to utilize the strengths of both leadership styles. As George Sage (1973), the leading researcher in this field, has suggested:

It is nonsense to suppose that every step in coaching can be democratic. It is obvious that in task-oriented groups such as one finds in sports where decisions frequently have to be made, quickly and on the basis of experience, a pure democratic leadership cannot effectively prevail. That a leader may have to unilaterally make decisions for the group does not necessarily diminish his sensitivity and humanism for the member (p. 39).

Coaches would do well to be authoritarian during the actual practice sessions and during game sessions when efficiency and decisions under stress need to be made. Yet, use a democratic leadership style in dealing with athletes before and after practice and in the off-season. This is an ideal time to gain the trust and respect of the athletes which is needed for efficient leadership and communication. Doc Counsilman, head swim coach at the University of Indiana, has stated that "the mature, intelligent, emotionally stable athlete cannot identify with the autocrat. The coach should be fair, but firm about rules and practice schedules and yet treat athletes as individuals and adults."

It will probably be many years before it will be possible to identify more exactly the leadership style which will guarantee success. Possibly it will be an endless search. Obviously, the ability of team members will always be a very influential factor. But if there is one quality that appears to be consistently important it is the ability of the coach to communicate with the team members. So let us now turn our attention to communication and some ways in which coaches can develop a greater rapport with their players and in general become more encouraging people.

COMMUNICATION AND FLEXIBILITY: THE KEY TO SUCCESS

Clearly, if one set coaching style is not appropriate for coaching all situations, coaches are going to have to be able to adjust to the situational demands and meet the needs of the different athletes within a team.

Coaches can only meet these needs if they know what they are, so it is crucial for the coach to communicate effectively with their players and encourage them to communicate with the coach and the other players. Following a thorough review of pertinent research Marcini and Agnew (1978) found that communication was crucial in coaching — even more crucial than in teaching. These authors further state that interpersonal interactions are very important in sports, and that "communication is the key to success in leadership" (1978, p. 283), particularly coaching.

Too often, coaches think that a tough, forbidding exterior is most effective, because it will keep the players in line. Although there is some truth to this, such a style also discourages players from communicating freely. Players get the impression that they are better off keeping to themselves, so their ideas and complaints may never be voiced. Keeping problems bottled up inside never solves them. The coach, while maintaining control, must still establish an atmosphere in which players feel free to communicate. Better morale and greater success (any way you define it) are likely to result.

When there is an open line of communication between the leader and group members, self-awareness of learning and motivational problems on both sides are likely to be enhanced. Some coaches fail miserably at communicating with those they are to teach, while others are incredibly successful. But it seems that most of those who are successful are so by merit of some talent they naturally possess without any real understanding of the process. The following will attempt to provide some techniques that have been found to be helpful in improving the quantity and the quality of communication between athletes and coaches and teachers and students.

In 1955 two experts in group dynamics, Luft and Inghom, illustrated relationships in terms of awareness with what has been called the Johari Window (see Fig. 1). The model can be viewed as having four separate quadrants. Quadrant 1, the area of free activity, or open area, refers to behavior and

	Known to Self	Not Known to Self
Known to Others	1 Open	2 Blind
Not Known to Others	Hidden 3	Unknown 4

motivation known to others. In a new group or team, Q1 is very small; there is not much free and spontaneous interaction. As the group remains intact for extended periods of time, Q1 grows larger, and in general people are more likely to be freer to be more like themselves and perceive others as they really are. Quadrant 2, the blind area, is where others can see things in ourselves of which we are unaware. Q2 very slowly shrinks in size because often there are "good" reasons of a psychological nature to blind ourselves to certain things we feel or do. Quadrant 3, the avoided or hidden area, represents things we know but fail to reveal to others (often weaknesses or skills we feel sensitive about). Q3 is reduced in size as Q1 expands. As an atmosphere of mutual trust is developed there is less need to hide pertinent thoughts or feelings. Quadrant 4, the area of unknown activity, points to the area where neither the individual nor others are aware of certain behaviors or motives. We can however assume these exist because with time some of these things become known. It is at this point in time that we realize that unknown motives and behaviors were influencing our relationship all along.

A basic intent of group dynamics is to increase the area of free activity in Q1 and reduce the size of quadrants 2, 3, and 4. The largest reduction will occur in Q3 with the smallest decrease in Q4. The likelihood of much greater use of the knowledge and skills of members of the group being utilized will be increased with greater openness. Group morale will also be greatly facilitated. Opinions and ideas will be communicated more

114

often and less time will be spent on self-defensive behaviors.

CHANGING GROUP PROCESSES

The stated results of improved communication no doubt appear to be quite positive. How then do we go about the process of change; where do we start?

In the early stages of group formation, group members will think and feel in an independent manner. In other words, each member tends to rely on one's own feelings, impressions, and judgments as a guide to behavior. There will always be times when independent action will be required, but an important quality of the mature group is interdependence of members upon one another.

Leaders who wish to improve the communication in their groups must be willing to open themselves up to other members of their group. Communication will not change if this doesn't happen. Communication is a two-way street. The coach must be willing to be flexible and group members must become flexible and open.

The early pre-season is usually the best time of year to meet with your team and start group discussion. Groups should ideally not be larger than 8 or 10 and should be arranged in a circular fashion. Usually it is best if the coach or teacher starts the discussion process by asking questions and then as openly as possible responding to them and then asking all other team members to respond to them.

The following is a listing of questions that have been used to improve communication and awareness with a wide variety of sport groups. You can be assured that if you try them out you will know your athletes much better and they will know you and each other much better. The result will be a happier and more effective learning and performance atmosphere.

Questions for Sport Groups

1. What has been the most satisfying sport experience that you have ever experienced?
2. What was the most disappointing sport experience that you have ever experienced?
3. What is your greatest strength as an athlete?
4. What is your major weakness as an athlete?
5. When are you the most confident during competition?
6. When are you the most anxious during competition?
7. How do you feel you best get ready for a contest?
8. What are the typical problems of players sitting on the bench?
9. What are the typical problems of being a starter?
10. What are things that coaches do that tend to decrease your motivation — in practice — games?
11. What are things that coaches do that help you?
12. What are things that players do that turn off or motivate the coach?
13. What do you concentrate on while performing your sport?
14. What are things that distract you?

ENCOURAGING THE INDIVIDUAL ATHLETE

By far the most difficult communication problem facing each and every coach is that of individual communication. To the coach who wishes to develop all athletes, each individual athlete is perceived to be as important as the team. Don Dinkmeyer and Rudolph Dreikurs (1963) have listed four assumptions which are of crucial importance to the encouragement process:

(a) the individual exists as a social being
(b) the individual functions as a whole, complete person, not as a series of parts
(c) the individual has goals, purposes, and values that motivate his or her behavior
(d) the individual acts according to the way he or she views the world.

In order to effectively respond to these basic assumptions, coaches must be willing to put forth the time and energy to help each and every individual on their team develop. Many coaches question whether there is enough time or energy for encouraging each team member. It is helpful to recognize that encouraging each player in need will in the long run save rather than waste energy.

Attention and feedback are often given in plentiful supply to the successful and confident athletes. It is quite natural for this to occur. Such athletes by their very presence make communication happen. Unfortunately, these are the athletes least in need of encouragement. The discouraged or depressed athlete needs your help and energy the most.

The next time that you have a team practice, pick out an athlete who you have not given much attention to in the past, who perhaps you don't happen to like a great deal, or who is discouraged. Give this athlete special attention. Let the athlete know you care and wish to help. Watch what happens to your relationship as well as to the athlete's peformance.

If you will do this every day with your athletes you will find your athletes starting to encourage themselves and turning themselves on. Soon you, the coach, will find that encouragement and sensitivity to the needs of your athletes will become second nature to you. It will no longer be something you have to plan and it will require less and less time and energy. Soon you will find that athletes trust and respect you and will be more open to your coaching suggestions. You will begin feeling more positively about your players and will be more willing to listen to them as a result. Often the coach will realize that an athlete once thought to be lacking in motivation was actually discouraged. Often such athletes have come to perceive the situation much differently than the coach and actually think that attitude and effort aren't important.

BUILDING CONFIDENCE AND ENTHUSIASM

Great leaders believe in their athletes. They expend energy, convincing their athletes that with enough effort and motivation they have the ability to be a success. These coaches are successful partially because they build confidence in all of their athletes by both their actions and words which build self-promoting rather than self-

defeating thoughts and actions (Bandura, 1977; Losoncy, 1977; Dinkmeyer and Dreikurs, 1963).

Because of the way they foster development in their athletes, encouraging coaches set an environment which encourages athletes to speak openly about their problems and discouragements. Such coaches show their sincere interest and care for their athletes by responding to their ideas, effort and successes and failures with enthusiasm. If coaches really care about their athletes it is impossible to respond without enthusiasm.

"Encouraging people are not afraid of their positive emotions and can express them to other people. You as an encourager should be aware of how vital are your reactions to the discouraged person's ideas after he 'took a risk' and told you. This is healthy and a real compliment to you. An enthusiastic, non-evaluative response to his feelings will give this person the courage to take a risk again. Your reaction to what he says may determine whether or not he pursues goals (growth) or gives them up (stagnation). A comment uttered in a monotone or a neutral or disinterested facial expression can really turn off someone who is already in doubt about his or her abilities and worth." (Losoncy, 1977, p. 94)

DEVELOPING THE SKILL OF ENCOURAGEMENT

Exercise 1: Begin to develop perceptual alternatives. Try to recall the last time that you had a disagreement with one of your athletes or coaches. Remember their position on the issue. Put yourself in that person's position, including their experiences and knowledge which are quite different from yours. Try to understand the athlete's perspective. You are developing perceptual alternatives if you are beginning to understand the athlete's point of view. You need not agree with but if you can understand their different perspective you perhaps will be patient enough to be a more encouraging coach.

Exercise 2: Imagine that you are one of

116

the best players on the team that you coach. Now from that athlete's perspective, write a paragraph about what you see, think and feel about the coach.

Exercise 3: Imagine that you are one of the bottom line players on your team. Now from that athlete's perspective write a paragraph about what you see, think, and feel about the coach.

Exercise 4: Think for a moment of two different athletes on your team. One that you really enjoy coaching and one that you really can't stand and have little patience with. Write down some of the characteristics that you feel they have — first the athlete you enjoy and then the athlete you don't enjoy.

Look carefully at the lists you have developed. Did you tend to see positive qualities in one athlete and negative qualities in the other? It is quite possible that you have been focusing mainly on positive qualities in the athlete you enjoy and thus encouraging him and focusing mainly on negative qualities in the athlete you don't enjoy. Chances are that if you are seeing only negative qualities in the athlete, you have not been very encouraging to the athlete. It is probably reflected in how often you smile, respond enthusiastically, and provide confidence-provoking statements to this athlete. Most likely you are discouraging this athlete. Try to focus on some positive qualities in this person and express it to the athlete in your interactions with him. Continue to do so and watch what happens to the communication between the two of you and the athlete's performance.

Exercise 5: Constantly look for other ways in which you have possibly helped to discourage athletes. See if you can do something different that can encourage them.

CONCLUSION

There are no magic answers to the complex problem of developing success in the world of coaching. But certainly being open and receptive to new ideas, attempting to have a degree of flexibility in your leadership style, developing open lines of communication within your team, and constantly striving to encourage each and every athlete will help you develop your team to its fullest potential.

REFERENCES

Anderson, R. C. Learning in discussion: A resume of the authoritarian-democratic studies. *Harvard Educational Review, 29,* 1959.

Bandura, A. Self-efficacy: Toward a unifying theory of behavioral change. *Psychological Review, 34,* 1979, 191-215.

Beisser, A. *The Madness in Sports.* New York: Appleton-Century/Crofts, 1967.

Cartwright, D. and Zander, A. *Group Dynamics: Research and Theory.* Harper and Row Pub., New York, 1968.

Cratty, B. J. *Psychology in Contemporary Sport: Guidelines for Coaches and Athletes.* Englewood Cliffs, New Jersey, Prentice-Hall, 1973.

Dinkmeyer, D. and Dreikurs, R. *Encouraging Children to Learn: The Encouragement Process.* Englewood Cliffs, New Jersey: Prentice-Hall, 1963.

Eitzen, S. and Sage, G. *Sociology of American Sport.* Dubuque, Iowa: Wm. C. Brown Company, 1978.

Losoncy, L. *Turning People On: How to be an Encouraging Person.* Prentice-Hall, Inc., Englewood Cliffs, New Jersey, 1977.

Luft, J. and Ingham, H. The Johari Window, a graphic model of interpersonal awareness. University of California, Los Angeles, Extension Office Proceedings of the Western Training Laboratory in Group Development, August, 1955.

Marcini, V. and Agnew, M. An analysis of teaching and coaching behaviors. In W. F. Straub (Ed.) *Sport Psychology: An Analysis of Athlete Behavior.* Ithaca, New York: Mouvement Publications, 1978.

Massengale, J. Coaching as an occupational subculture. *Phi Delta Kappan,* 1974, *56,* (2), 140-142.

Mudra, D. E. A critical analysis of football coaching practices in light of a selected group of learning principles. Unpublished doctoral dissertation, University of Northern Colorado, 1965.

Ogilvie, B. C. and Tutko, T. A. Self-image and measured personality of coaches. In *Contemporary Psychology of Sport.* Edited by G. S. Kenyon. Chicago: Athletic Institute, 1970.

Sage, G. The coach as management; Organizational leadership in American sport. *Quest,* 1973, *19,* 35-40.

Schein, E. and Bennis, W. *Personal and Organizational change through group methods: the laboratory approach.* New York: Wiley, 1965.

Scott, J. *The Athletic Revolution.* The Free Press, 1971.

Tutko, T. A. and Neal, P. *Coaching Girls and Women: Psychological Perspectives.* Boston: Little, Brown and Co., 1970.

Tutko, T. A. and Richards, J. *The Psychology of Coaching.* Boston: Allyn and Bacon, 1971.

19

A Model Of Attributional Conflict In Sport *

Walter J. Rejeski, Jr.
Wake Forest University

In the last decade, literature in sport psychology has clearly documented a growing interest in the relationship between coach and athlete. The diversity in both empirical and theoretical study has been broad. For example, while initial investigations focused on identifying young athletes' perceptions of coaching behaviors (Percival, 1971; Danielson, Zelhart and Drake, 1975), more recent thinking has examined the congruence between coaches' overt behaviors and children's perceptions of these behaviors (Smith, Smoll and Hunt, 1977; Smoll, Smith Curtis and Hunt, 1978), role compatability of coach and athlete (Carron, 1978), and the mediational role of expectancies on athletes' performance (Rejeski and Hutslar, note 1).

A common theme, either implicit or explicit, in the foregoing research has been that the coach-athlete relationship is complex and often troublesome. Many problems besetting this dyadic interplay can be directly attributed to attributional divergence. That is to say, coaches and athletes often hold different views as to what caused a particular behavior. For example, a common situation is one in which the coach blames an athletes' failure on carelessness, while the athlete ascribes the outcome to deficits in training. The conflict which arises from differences in causal interpretation has important implications for both the individual and the team. Yet to date, no formal sport specific theoretical approach has been developed to assist in delineating the dynamics of this process.

The intent of this paper, then, is to propose and analyze a model of attributional conflict in sport. To facilitate explanation, discussion centers on one type of interaction in which the athlete is the actor and the coach is the observer.

ATTRIBUTION, INTERPERSONAL PERCEPTION, AND CONFLICT IN SPORT

A promising paradigm in social psychology — known formally as attribution — offers an auspicious point of departure for examining interpersonal perception and in particular the coach-athlete relationship. Attribution theory, as originally posited by Heider (1958) presents a framework for understanding the layperson's causal interpretation of his/her world. A basic assumption of the theory is that people are motivated to seek order and to have some sense of control over the future. This objective is achieved by attributing events to stable dispositions of the person (e.g., ability) and/or the environment (e.g., task difficulty); in short, by attributing *meaning* to behaviors.

For example, in an effort to locate the source of a team's problems, coaches discuss and critically examine each facet of team structure. The eventual outcome is that circumstantial and/or personal causes are identified. In the ensuing weeks, training and/or personal changes are made. At various points throughout this chain of events, the potential for conflict exists. In other words, interpersonal perception or the attributions which coaches and athletes

Reprinted with permission from *J. Sport Behavior*, 1979, 2, 156-166.

make for behaviors may serve as catalysts for volatile interpersonal interactions.

The relevance of attribution theory is enhanced by both the high level of involvement (Jones and Davis, 1965) and the problematic nature which characterizes sport (Kelley, 1967). That is, the outcomes of sport are valued by both coach and athlete, and the very nature of competition demands decisions which are subject to immediate evaluation.

PERCEPTUAL DIVERGENCE: THE BASIS OF INTERPERSONAL CONFLICTS

The major theoretical premise supporting a model of attribution conflict is the divergence extant in actors' and observers' perceptions of behavior. Jones and Nesbitt (1972) have proposed that there is a general tendency for actors to perceive the causes of behavior in the situation, but for observers to attribute the behaviors of actors to internal dispositions. The suspected origin of this difference is perceptual in nature. That is, for the actor the situation is perceptually salient, while for the observer the actor is perceptually salient.

Laboratory research on this issue is equivocal to say the least. While several investigators have supported Jones's and Nesbitt's proposal (Duval and Wicklund, 1973; Storms, 1973; and Miller, 1975), an equal number of contradictory results exist (Bell, 1964; Miller and Norman, 1975; and Taylor and Koivumaki, 1976).

According to Monson and Snyder (1977), the experimental methodology employed to investigate social perception has in many cases created conditions which elicit situational attributions. It was this analysis which led them to predict that: "Actors should make more situational attributions than should observers about behavioral acts that are under situational control; by contrast, actors' perceptions of behaviors that are under dispositional control ought to be more dispositional than the perceptions of observers" (Monson and Snyder, p. 96). The implication for sport is that athletes' attributions are more veridical than those of coaches. Indeed, athletes are often aware of facilitative forces and perceptual cues to which the coach is blind. However, a caveat is issued here.

Monson's and Snyder's position is firmly rooted in an informational interpretation of attribution. In the presence of motivational bias their proposition may not hold. For example, although athletes may realize that failure resulted from some miscalculation on their part, ego involvement may preclude attribution to this personal shortcoming. Rather, they may displace the cause of failure on the state of the environment or other situational factors.

One of the most definitive statements on actor-observer differences in person perception has been provided by Daryl Bem (1972). Several specific points which Bem raised are important in understanding why athletes and coaches might diverge in their causal interpretation of behavior. First, consistent with Jones and Nesbitt (1972), Bem discussed what he termed an *insider-outsider difference*. The notion expressed here was that self-perceivers have special access to their own perceptual cues. Borg's research on perceived exertion during physical work (1970), and subsequent investigation by Rejeski and Lowe (in press) in the domain of attribution and sport achievement are relevant to this issue. In particular, when tasks result in increases in metabolic function, self-perceivers have direct perceptual feedback regarding effort expenditure. Hence, whereas coaches must assume intentionality for behavior solely on the basis of inference, athletes have quantitative cues to guide their attributions (see Kelley, 1971).

The second point Bem entitled the *intimate-stranger difference*, denoting that actors have unique access to personal history. Theoretically speaking, athletes have distinctiveness information (Kelley, 1967). They know how they have performed across various entities and are in a position to discount non-plausible causes (Kelley, 1971). For example, an athlete's inconsistencies in motivation may lead him/her to the attribution that an atypical performance was triggered by variation in effort. The coach, however, may perceive that the athlete's performances appear to covary with the level of competition. This latter datum becomes salient to the coach and will most likely result in situational attributions (Feather, 1969; Feather and Simon, 1971;

and Simon and Feather, 1973). Of course, the extent of this effect will vary with both the nature of the behavior and the degree to which the coach understands the athlete. Nevertheless, the *intimate-stranger difference* presents a potential source of conflict particularly when the coach and athlete have had limited experience together and/or possess divergent attitudes.

Finally, Bem (1972) defined a motivational bias labeled the *self-other difference*. This divergence in actor-observer perception is based on the belief that people have a basic need to maintain their self-esteem; a point which has theoretical precedent in Heider (1958) and recent support from the sport literature (Scanlan and Passer, 1978). The implication is that actors possess a tendency to make environmental rather than personal attributions for failure.

The Topic of actor-observer difference serves as the core for understanding and explaining attributional conflict in sport. There remains, however, a number of specific antecedents and consequences of conflict which enhance comprehending the dynamic nature of this process.

A MODEL OF ATTRIBUTIONAL CONFLICT

Since the subject of attributional conflict is complex, a prerequisite for both theoretical and practical clarity is a schemata integrating relevant variables. The following model provides such a tool. The supporting literature describes the antecedents and consequences of attributional conflict and identifies a number of important mediating variables in this process. Let it be clear at the onset that attribution involves the search for *meaning* in behavior by ascribing causality to attributes of the person (e.g., needs, ability, and motivation) and/or the environment (e.g., field conditions, refereeing, and the weather).

Behavioral Cues in the Attribution Process. Kelley (1967) has provided a succinct theory on the specific cues which overt behavior contribute to the perception of causality. Briefly, Kelley suggested that perceivers function as naive psychologists, logically combining distinctiveness, consensus, and consistency in formation. Hence, when an athlete behaves in a manner which is typical of most athletes, *high consensus,* and the behavior is exhibited only in the presence of particular entities, *high distinctiveness,* then the tendency is to perceive situational control. Conversely, if an athlete engages in a behavior which is atypical, *low consensus,* and he/she does so across most entities, *low distinctiveness,* then the behavior will be perceived as personally caused.

Consistency, the third behavioral criteria, influences the specific type of environmental or personal disposition employed to explain behavior. When consistency is *high,* attributions will generally relate to *stable* causes such as an athlete's ability or the level of competition. Conversely, when consistency is *low,* the perceived causes of behavior will be *unstable* in nature. Likely personal or environmental causes might be effort or luck, respectively.

Consensus and distinctiveness information may differ in their potential threat as catalysts to conflict. Due to league records and the wide publicity which sport receives, consensus information is a readily available source of data for *both* the actor and the observer. Not so for distinctiveness. Recall, that the athlete is in a superior position to determine the status of historical information and other personal dimensions. Thus, the different cues employed by athletes and coaches to arrive at distinctiveness creates a potential site for interpersonal conflict.

Behavioral and Situational Antecedents of Conflict. It is obvious that conflict does not occur in every situation. What then are some possible antecedents? First, negative behaviors of athletes can lead to biased attributions on the part of coaches. Athletes whose nonverbal behaviors present threats to authoritative coaching styles represent classic examples of this phenomenon, since there is a tendency for coaches to perceive these athletes as personally responsible for failure or team unrest (see Orvis, Kelley, and Butler, 1976).

Second, the failure of athletes to reach prescribed goals or disagreement on the means utilized to reach goals may generate conflict (Deutsch, 1969). The competitive element in sport places an inordinate importance upon the outcome. Hence, failure will trigger motivational biases and coaches and athletes will search for scapegoats. Unfortunately, as is often the case, coaches and athletes blame one another. As a se-

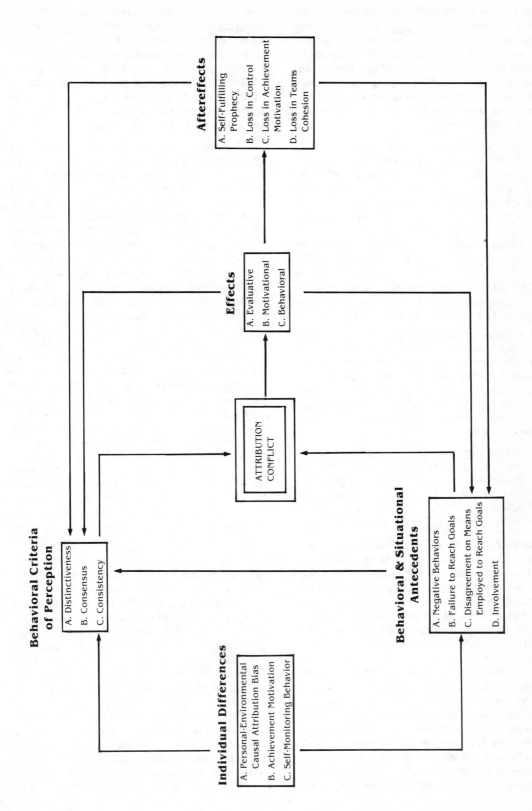

Figure 1. A Model of Attributional Conflict

quel to failure, coaches and athletes often begin to sharply disagree on the means utilized to reach goals. In short, the coach has lost credibility and alternate strategies, which diverge from those of the coach, appear warranted. Attributional conflict thus increases in intensity and, as we shall see, can be detrimental to both individual and team achievement.

Finally, conflict should increase as a function of involvement. Jones and Davis (1965) suggested that individuals are biased in their perceptions of behavior when affected by the consequences — a construct known as *hedonic relevance*. Thus, for example, there should be a general tendency for coaches to judge athletes' negative behaviors harshly, since these behaviors may hinder team success, an outcome which is salient to the coach. Furthermore, the severity of the conflict should increase when a crucial game or highly valued issue is at stake.

An even greater danger of perceptual bias is triggered when an observer senses that the consequences of an act were intended for him/her. This condition, known as *personalism*, may in reality not be true. The role of coach optimizes the possibility for personalism, or what in certain circumstances might be termed paranoia.

In some sense, every institutional structure creates a hiatus between the leader and those led. In sport, group cohesion and performance are ultimately coaching responsibilities. It is this institutionalized hierarchy which perpetuates personalism.

Individual Difference Measures as Mediators of Conflict. At this juncture, it is important to recognize that the *perception* of behavior and the *onset* of situational and behavioral factors which trigger conflict may both be influenced by individual difference variables. In particular, from the viewpoint of the observer Low, Medway, and Beers (1978) have provided an instrument known as the Personal Environmental Causal Attribution Scale (PECA). Their theoretical contention is that, irrespective of objective data, observers differ in the strength of their tendencies to perceive *both* personal and environmental causality. As with other generalized measures (see Rotter, 1975), prediction with the scale is best in novel or ambiguous situations. Since the causes of failure in sport are often unclear, it is logical to propose that a coach may bring inherent bias to the situation. Presently, little is known about the profile of individuals who score high and low on the personal and environmental dimensions. A future task of sport research is to define these characteristics and investigate their relationships to the dynamics of the sport group.

Idiosyncratic behaviors and perceptions of the actor (athlete) may also contribute to the attribution conflict. For example, low achievers are prone to behavior styles which increase the possibility for failure. It may well be that low achievers overtly appear to lack in motivation. Such self-presentation could easily be interpreted by coaches as negative behavior. Further, Weiner and his colleagues (Weiner, Frieze, Kukla, Reed, Rest and Rosenbaum, 1972) have provided evidence that level of achievement motivation mediates causal attribution for achievement outcomes. Specifically, while high achievers appear predisposed to take personal credit for success, low achievers assume more responsibility for failure. Although at present, this proposition is not generalizable to sport — in fact, there is some question as to its validity in intellectual achievement (Medway and Lowe, 1976) — current directions of investigation attest to the perceived importance of the achievement literature to sport behavior (Scanlan and Passer, 1978). If it is found that low and high achievers differ in their perceptions of sport outcomes, then it follows that these perceptions may act as precursors to conflict in the coach-athlete relationship.

Finally, Snyder (1974) has proposed a Self-Monitoring Scale which predicts that whereas some individuals are situationally guided in locating causes for their behavior (high self-monitors), others ignore environmental cues and look internally (low self-monitors). The implication is clear. Athletes who attend to situational cues and interpersonal advice should be more "coachable." Whereas the cognitive and behavioral styles of high self-monitors should reduce conflict, the opposite is true of athletes who are low self-monitors. This does not imply that high self-monitors are better athletes than low self-monitors, rather it points to the flexibility and understanding required of the coach.

THE EFFECTS OF ATTRIBUTIONAL CONFLICT

Although there is an obvious tie between attribution and Asch's (1946) research on impression formation, the *evaluative effects* of interpersonal conflict deserve special consideration. The proposed relationship is that attributional conflict can lead to the formation of negative impressions which bias future attributions. For example, attributional conflict in the presence of an athlete's apparent lackadaisical posture may lead a coach to the conclusion that an individual has an "attitude problem." This negative evaluation distorts future perceptions of the athlete and may even result in the coach unconsciously singling out this person to vent his/her frustrations in other seemingly unrelated situations. These factors combine to sustain the athlete's undesired behaviors and promote more deeply seeded problems.

Conflict may also lead to a number of reactions intended to release frustration and/or protect athletes and coaches — *motivational effects*. While responses may include traditional defense mechanisms such as displacement and projection, Horai (1977) has expounded on a number of verbal coping strategies particularly relevant to attributional conflict. For example, athletes may call attention to circumstances surrounding their behavior, as if to indicate that they had no alternative. Another defense, disassociation, represents a clear denial of responsibility. "You have the wrong person." Additional verbalizations may include attributions to unstable causes, "I had an unlucky day."; to rationales, "I had to do it, can't you see, the entire team expected it to be that way."; or justifications, "Tell me what would you have done?" Similarly, coaches will often physically punish their teams after defeat. In effect, the coach may be saying, "If you are at fault, then how can I be?"

Perhaps the most obvious outcome of conflict is overt *behavioral reaction*. Due to role relations in sport, the initiation of conflict resolution is primarily a coaching responsibility. In fact, behavioral reactions by players may be reacted to quite negatively. It is not uncommon to hear coaches say, "Listen, your job is to score points. Let me worry about what works and what doesn't." Within the context of sport the coach is the master strategist. It is rare for athletes to contribute significantly to training methods or technical issues. Yet, it is apparent this may not be the most constructive reaction by coaches. The literature on learned helplessness (see Seligman, 1975) is replete with examples demonstrating the negative effects which lack of control can have on performance. It is this very issue together with the evaluative and motivational effects which further complicates the dynamics of conflict.

Aftereffects. In discussing the effects of attributional conflict, it becomes evident that several disruptive aftereffects are plausible. For example, it is argued that coaches' negative evaluations can lead to impressions which bias future interactions with athletes. The underlying principle here is rather simple. As a result of social interaction, expectancies regarding individual personalities are formulated. These expectancies play an important role in determining how we approach people in the future. Actually, in a covert sense, our interactional patterns function to elicit specific behaviors from others. Through a similar process then, coaches' negative impressions may in fact account for developing and sustaining the very behaviors in an athlete which are unwanted — *self-fulfilling prophecies*. More than likely, the result will have adverse effects on the athlete, both creating emotional problems and stifling performance.

In addition, psychological defenses which promote external attributions and coaches' authoritative reactions to conflict can lessen athletes' personal control. The inherent danger is that loss of control inhibits behavior change. There are two main reasons for this effect. First, the athlete may simply believe that there is little to gain from alternate behavior; a condition of apathy. Or second, the athlete may well sense that the mechanisms of change are either obscure or manipulative. If the conflict exists because of differences of opinion over training methods or game strategies, then the athletes' loss of control may cause decreases in situationally specific achievement motivation. In short, aspiration levels, task orientation, concentration, and effort expenditure may all decrease.

The most catastrophic result, of course,

124

is that the above effects undermine group cohesion. Whether or not loss of cohesion destroys team achievement remains a moot point. However, at many levels of sport where the purported focus is the process as well as the product of sport involvement, a loss in group cohesion carries particular significance.

Feedback from Effects and Aftereffects. As a final component of the model, the feedback system, from the consequences to the antecedents, clearly indicates that attributional conflict is best characterized as a dynamic process. In short, behaviors do not occur in isolated units. The motivational, evaluative, and behavioral effects, together with their aftereffects — loss of team cohesion, self-fulfilling prophecies, loss of personal control, and decreasing achievement motivation — each affect the *data* of future perception and contribute to the *onset* of those behavioral and situational factors which optimize the potential for conflict.

Employing the feedback concept to attributional conflict complicates the issue from an empirical perspective, yet demonstrates the potential crippling effect of poor interpersonal relations. At the same time, it explains the evolution of major problems for coaches and athletes. Isolated behaviors may at times seem insignificant. It is however, the covert role which these behaviors play in more general mechanisms that reveals their *significant* character.

SUMMARY

The proposed model integrates several areas of research relevant to interpersonal conflict in sport. Even after a cursory glance, it is apparent that there are a number of empirical issues deserving attention. The integration of these variables within the model offers a potential paradigm for conceptualizing the antecedents and consequences of attributional conflict. There is little doubt that the relationship between coach and athlete has emotional as well as performance based ramifications. It is for this very reason that the model presented has practical merit.

REFERENCES

Asch, S. E. Forming impressions of personality. *Journal of Abnormal Social Psychology,* 1946, *41,* 258-290.

Bell, L. G. Influence of need to control on differences in attribution of causality by actors and observers. (Doctoral dissertation, Duke University, 1973) *Dissertation Abstracts International,* 1974, *34,* 4401.

Bem, D. J. Self-perception theory. In L. Berkowitz (Ed.) *Advances in Experimental Social Psychology.* New York: Academic Press, 1972.

Borg, G. Perceived exertion as an indicator of somatic stress. *Journal of Rehabilitative Medicine,* 1970, *2,* 92-98.

Carron, A. V. Role behavior and the coach-athlete interaction. *International Review of Sport Sociology,* 1978, *2,* 51-64.

Danielson, R. R., Zelhart, P. F., and Drake, C. J. Multidimensional scaling and factor analysis of coaching behaviors as perceived by high school hockey players. *Research Quarterly,* 1975, *46(3),* 323-343.

Duval, S. and Wicklund, R. A. Effects of objective self-awareness on attribution of causality. *Journal of Experimental Social Psychology,* 1973, *9,* 17-31.

Deutsch, M. Conflicts: productive and destructive. *Journal of Social Issues,* 1969, *25(1),* 7-41.

Feather, N. T. Attribution of responsibility and valence of success and failure in relation to initial confidence and task performance. *Journal of Personality and Social Psychology,* 1969, *13,* 129-144.

Feather, N. T., and Simon, J. G. Attribution of responsibility and valance of outcome in relation to initial confidence and success and failure. *Jrnl. of Personality and Social Psychology,* 1971, *18,* 173-188.

Heider, F. *The Psychology of Interpersonal Relations.* New York: Wiley, 1958.

Horai, J. Attributional conflict. *Journal of Social Issues,* 1977, *33(1),* 88-100.

Jones, E. E., and Davis, K. E. From acts to dispositions: The attribution process in person perception. In L. Berkowitz (Ed.) *Advances in Experimental Social Psychology.* New York: Academic Press, 1965, Vol. 2.

Jones, E. E., and Nesbitt, R. E. The actor and the observer: Divergent perception of the causes of behavior. In E. E. Jones, D. Kanouse, H. H. Kelley, R. E. Nesbitt, S. Valins, and B. Weinder (Eds.) *Attribution:*

Perceiving the Causes of Behavior. New York: General Learning Press, 1972.

Kelley, H. H. *Attribution in Social Interaction.* Morristown, N.J.: General Learning Press, 1972.

Kelley, H. H. Attribution in social psychology. *Nebraska Symposium on Motivation,* 1967, *15,* 192-238.

Lowe, C. A., Medway, F. J., and Beers, S. E. *Individual Differences in Causal Attribution: The Personal-Environmental Causal Attribution Scale.* Paper presented at the Annual Meeting of the American Psychological Assn., 1978.

Medway, F. J., and Lowe, C. A. The effects of stimulus person valence on divergent self-other attributions for success and failure. *Journal of Research in Personality,* 1976, *10,* 266-278.

Miller, A. G. Actor and observer perceptions of learning a task. *Journal of Experimental Social Psychology,* 1975, *11,* 95-111.

Miller, D. T., and Norman, S. A. Actor-observer differences in perceptions of effective control. *Journal of Personality and Social Psychology,* 1975, *31,* 503-515.

Monson, T. C., and Snyder, M. Actors, observers, and the attribution process. *Journal of Experimental Social Psychology,* 1977, *13,* 89-111.

Orvis, B. R., Kelley, H. H., and Butler, D. Attributional conflict in young couples. In J. H. Harvey, W. J. Ickes, and R. F. Kidd (Eds.) *New Directions in Attribution Research* (Vol. 1). Hilldale, N.J.: Erlbaum, 1976.

Pecival, L. The coach from the athlete's viewpoints. In J. W. Taylor (Eds.) *Proceedings, Symposium on the Art and Science of Coaching.* Toronto: Fitness Institute, 1971.

Rejeski, W. J., and Lowe, C. A. The role of ability and effort in sport achievement. *Journal of Personalioty* (in press).

Rotter, J. B. Some problems and misconceptions related to the construct of internal versus external control of reinforcement. *Journal of Consulting and Clinical Psychology,* 1975, *43,* 56-67.

Scanlan, T. K., and Passer, M. W. Factors related to competitive stress among male youth sport participants. *Science and Medicine in Sports,* 1978, *10*(2), 103-108.

Scanlan, T. K., and Ragen, J. T. Achievement motivation and competition: Perceptions and responses. *Science and Medicine in Sports,* 1978, *10*(4), 276-281.

Seligman, M. E. *Helplessness: On Depression, Development, and Death.* San Francisco, California: W. H. Freeman and Co., 1975.

Simon, J. G., and Feather, N. T. Causal attributions for success and failure at university examinations. *Journal of Educational Psychology,* 1973, *64,* 46-56.

Smith, R. E., Smoll, F. L., and Hunt, E. A system for the behavioral assessment of athletic coaches. *Research Quarterly,* 1977, *48,* 401-408.

Smoll, F. L., Smith, R. E., Curtis, B., and Hunt, E. Toward a mediational model of coach-player relationships. *Research Quarterly,* 1978, *49,* 528-541.

Snyder, M. The self-monitoring of expressive behavior. *Journal of Personality and Social Psychology,* 1974, *30,* 526-537.

Storms, M. D. Videotape and the attribution process: Reversing actors and observers point of view. *Journal of Personality and Social Psychology,* 1973, *27,* 165-175.

Taylor, S. E., and Koivumaki, J. H. The perception of self and others: Acquaintanceship, affect, and actor-observer difference. *Journal of Personality and Social Psychology,* 1976, *33,* 403-408.

Weiner, B., Frieze, I., Kukla, A., Reed, L., Rest, S., and Rosenbaum, R. M. Attribution: Perceiving the causes of success and failure. In E. E. Jones, D. E. Kanouse, H. H. Kelley, R. E. Nesbitt, S. S. Valins, and B. Weiner (Eds.) *Attribution: Perceiving the Causes of Behavior.* Morristown, N.J.: General Learning Press, 1972.

REFERENCE NOTE

1. Rejeski, W. J., and Hutslar, S. The mediational role of expectancies in the acquisition and performance of sport skills. Manuscript submitted for publication, January 1979.

SECTION V

Stress In Sport

20

The Coach And Stress

Robert J. Rotella
University of Virginia

Stress — it's what makes some people tick and others have heart attacks.

Long days and pressure are a part of every coach's job. The pressures of visibility and responsibility to the family, team, school and community are plentiful. Undoubtedly, stress is a problem that increasingly limits the productivity and effectiveness of both head and assistant coaches. Because people's jobs and their health are closely related it is crucial to give our attention to the issue of coaching stress.

Role conflicts, incompatibilities between two roles simultaneously occupied by the same person, or between two or more behaviors required in a single role, can have a major impact on health status (Kahn, 1969). These role conflicts in coaching must be carefully evaluated (Kahn, 1964a, 1964b).

The environment of any coach consists largely of formal organizations or groups. Such groups — athletic department, coaching staff, team, family, church, etc. affect a coach's physical and emotional state and are major determinants of his behavior.

To understand the relationship between the coach and these organizations it is necessary to look at the coach's association with others within the organization in which he/she works. These other individuals constitute the coach's *role set* (Kahn, 1964).

A role set typically includes the coach's supervisor, immediate supervisor, subordinates, and some colleagues of equal rank. But the coach's role set may also include close friends, family, alumni, respected models and any others who are concerned with the coach's job performance.

All members of a coach's role set depend in certain ways upon his performance. Either they require it in order to perform their own tasks or they are rewarded by it. Thus, each of these individuals form attitudes and ex-pectations about what the coach should or should not do in his role. The members of the coach's role set also communicate their role expectations, either directly (athletic director instructs coach) or indirectly (athlete or assistant coach expresses admiration or disappointment).

One of the most prevalent anxiety producers in coaching occurs when different members of one's role set have quite different expectations for the coach. These differing expectations demand conflicting behaviors which lead to tension.

Often a coach believes that one leadership style is appropriate but his supervisor feels that another style would be best. Of course this same type of conflict could occur between coach and assistant coach or coach and athletes. In either case, such a conflict is labeled *inter-sender* conflict. A second type of conflict, *intro-sender* conflict, occurs when a single member of the role set places incompatible pressures on the coach. An example might be the athletic director demanding that the coach win but not giving the coach the available money, facilities, or time to build a winning program.

Sometimes, pressures connected with membership in one group conflict with pressures that stem from membership in another group. Working late at night during the season, as well as on weekends and during the summer may conflict with family affairs. The coach's role as worker then conflicts with the family role as husband or wife, or in the case of the single coach with loneliness and time for dating. In any case such conflicts are labeled inter-role conflicts (Kahn, 1964a).

Of course, it appears that there is a great deal more conflict and pressure if the team has been losing, the salary is low, and there is little community support and praise for the coach and spouse to bask in. This prediction leads to the likelihood of more conflicts for so called "minor sport" coaches who are not winning.

Still other types of conflicts come from disparity between environmental pressures and internal forces. These are called *person-role* conflicts. Person-role conflicts occur when a person's role requirements violate his ethical values. For example, the pressure to win may lead a coach to play an injured player or to intentionally try to inflict injury on a member of the other team which is in opposition to the coach's personal code of ethics. Another example might be a coach lying or selling his soul to a recruit who will help insure a winning season.

No matter what the type of role conflict, it is typical for pressure to be exerted by members of a role set to change the coach's behavior. The greater the demand for change, the greater the internal conflict.

The emotional and psychological costs of role conflict are severe. They include anxiety, low job satisfaction, low confidence in the organization and high tension. A common response to role conflict is to avoid those seen as creating conflict. The coach may reduce communication with his athletic director, assistant coaches, or players, or family. The coach may also assert, often unrealistically, that these individuals lack power over him. Such withdrawal which is a defense mechanism, often reduces the possibility of arriving at later cooperative solutions to the conflict.

Because a major health hazard resulting from conflict is stress, let us turn our attention now to this issue. Stress is the environmental stimulus or signal which leads to anxiety, a psychological response and increased arousal, the physiological response. The environmental stimulus need not really be dangerous to provoke the "fight or flight" response. It only needs to be perceived as a danger.

In order to completely understand the issue at hand, recognize that stress is not necessarily bad for coaches. Most certainly stress is one of the most important motivating or driving forces available. For most individuals involved in athletic coaching it is actually the perception of the contest as being stressful that makes it so pleasurable. Most coaches and athletes actually thrive

on stress. Without stress the sport world would be quite boring and mundane. It is helpful to consider this positive use of stress as "EUSTRESS" (Selye, 1974).

It is only when stress gets out of control and our particularly individualistic pressures and problems mount that stress becomes a negative force, "DISTRESS." Under distress our defense systems begin to break down which cause all kinds of illnesses real and imagined: insomnia, hypertension, depression, alcohol and drug abuse, marital collapse, and heart attack.

For many years a wide variety of scholars have studied stress responses (Sarason and Spielberger, 1975; Selye, 1952, 1974; Shultz and Luthe, 1959; Jacobson, 1934). One of the earliest to do so was Soren Kierkagaard, the progenitor of the modern era of the study of anxiety. In his work, "Begrebet Angest" in 1844 (translated in 1944 under the name "The Concept of Dread") he suggested that as Christianity declined, man's sense of individuality increased. This strong individuation and self-awareness led to an increase in man's freedom and therefore an increase in his responsibility for his choices. Kierkgaard argued that it was this awareness of one's need to make choices, with the possibilities of failure and guilt, that led to anxiety (Sarason and Spielberger, 1975). Based on this concept it is easy to understand how coaches who are constantly placed in situations where they must take responsibility for their actions might become distressed (Erikson, 1964).

An opposite view of the origins of anxiety and distress has been proposed by Seligman (1975). He has argued that it is the perception of a lack of control over events which leads to a feeling of helplessness and anxiety. Seligman (1975) argues that when an individual believes that there is a high probability that the outcome of an event will be the same irrespective of their particular response the individual feels helpless. Recognize though that it is the *perception* of control that is important. It does not matter whether or not there is indeed control. The implication is that when one is placed in an uncontrollable situation one is more likely to respond with fear and anxiety.

Seligman (1975) has also argued that controllability is related to predictability; people are more confident and relaxed in predictable situations. If the sport experience is looked at closely it is clear that the coach often percieves that he/she is in contests which are out of personal control and/or are quite unpredictable. Therefore, if coaches are frequently placed in such situations it is likely that problems with the management of stress are likely to surface.

ADAPTATION TO STRESS

Fortunately, the body and mind have a tremendous ability to adapt to stress. One of the leading researchers on stress, Hans Selye (1952), has developed an all-encompassing term for the stress adaptation syndrome called the GENERAL ADAPTATION SYNDROME (G.A.S.: *general* because it is produced only by agents that have a general effect upon large portions of the body; *adaptive*, because it stimulates defense and thereby helps insure the body to hardships; *syndrome*, because its signs are coordinated and partly dependent upon each other). This entire syndrome evolves through three stages: (1) the alarm reaction, (2) the stage of resistance, and (3) the state of exhaustion. Any time that we are exposed to a stressful stimuli or we *perceive* that we are exposed to a stressful event, an alarm reaction is set off with physiological and psychological responses which typically cause a loss of appetite, strength and ambition. Continuous exposure to any noxious agent capable of setting off this alarm reaction is followed by a stage of adaptation or resistance. It appears that disease is not just suffering, but a fight to maintain the homeostatic balance of our tissues when they are damaged. So that the resistance stage initiates many of the exact opposite reactions that occurred during the alarm reaction.

For example, during the alarm reaction, the adrenal cortex discharges into the blood stream secretory granules that contain hormones. Consequently, the gland depletes its stores. In the resistance stage, the cortex accumulates an abundant reserve of secretory granules. Again, in the alarm reaction, the blood volume diminishes and body weight drops; but during the stage of resistance the blood is less concentrated and body weight returns to normal (Selye, 1952).

Interestingly, it appears that after prolonged exposure to any noxious agent the body loses its learned capacity to resist, and enters the stage of exhaustion. Exactly how long the body can maintain itself in the third stage is unknown. But Selye (1974) proposes that an organism has a finite level of energy which it can use to resist stressors. How long an organism can last in the third stage depends upon the amount of adaptation energy the organism has, and also on the severity of the stressor. Eventually, if the individual faces continuous exposure to the stressor, exhaustion will follow.

PSYCHOLOGICAL EFFECTS OF STRESS

Sarason and Spielberger (1975), two of the most noted researchers in the field, believe that anxiety is closely linked to self-preoccupation. These authors suggest that this preoccupation with one's self is characterized by self-awareness, self-doubt, and self-depreciation. In other words when an individual is anxious in a test or competitive situation there is a tendency to emit self-centered interfering thoughts and behaviors. Included are worry and second-guessing oneself. In addition, anxiety will narrow attentional focus on environmental cues (Sarason and Spielberger, 1975). Anxiety can also diminish the coach's ability to control the direction and/or width of attention. The effects can therefore distort encoding processes and strategy planning, thereby inhibiting responses that are selected to cope with these anxiety producing situations (Nideffer, 1976).

Another noteworthy theory posited by Sarason and Spielberger (1975) argues that "a central interpreting or appraisal process codes situations in life as potentially harmful according to possible undesired consequences. Anxiety, according to this view is seen as internally generated cycles of connotative signals elicited by external stimuli" (p. 50).

Information is presented to the central cognitive processing system by each cycle of signals. As an individual becomes more anxious, the amount of information presented to the system is increased, and therefore a greater number of cognitive operations are required which leads to an increased information load on the system.

For many coaches, if they gain in confidence in their ability to successfully manage potentially unpleasant situations, such stimuli will become habituated or extinguished (Bandura, 1976; Rachman, 1978). But if the coach loses confidence and the potentially harmful (shame, embarrassment) stimuli do not become habituated or extinguished, then a wide range of stimuli may continue to elicit over-differentiated and over-elaborated systems of unpleasant, aversive, and threatening signals.

As a result, the coach with the more differentiated and elaborated aversive memory structures will generate more task *irrelevant* information. In effect an overactive retrieval system will present excessive information to a code-analyzing and response-organizing system. As a result of the excessive amounts of information pressing for central processing, performance will suffer.

PERSONALITY AND YOUR HEALTH

The effects of too much stress can be quite detrimental to your coaching and social performance, as well as your physical and psychological health. Two cardiologists, Friedman and Rosenman (1974) have determined that a majority of their coronary heart disease patients exhibit a particular behavior pattern which they have termed "Type A Behavior." This pattern characterized by aggressiveness, ambition, drive, competitiveness, and a profound sense of time urgency is closely related to many of the characteristics consistently ascribed to coaches (Ogilvie and Tutko, 1970; Sage, 1973). Drs. Friedman and Rosenman labeled the absence of the Type A emotional interplay Type B, but they realized that it was difficult to clearly differentiate the two. Therefore, it seems logical that we take a close look at the potentially negative effects of coaching stress.

According to their findings, you fit into the Type A behvaioral pattern:

1. If you have (a) a habit of explosively accentuating various key words in your ordinary speech even when there is no real need for such accentuation, and (b) a tendency to utter the last few words of your sentences far more rapidly than the opening words. The vocal explosiveness betrays the excess aggression or hostility you may be harboring. The hurrying of the ends of sentences reflects your underlying impatience with spending even the time required for your own speech;
2. If you *always* move, walk and eat rapidly;
3. If you feel an impatience with the rate at which most events take place, particularly if you express it to others. You are suffering from this sort of impatience if you find it difficult to restrain yourself from hurrying the speech of others and resort to the device of saying very quickly over and over again, "uh, huh, uh huh" or "Yes, yes, yes, yes" to someone who is talking, unconsciously urging him to speed up. You are also suffering from impatience if you attempt to finish the sentences of people speaking to you before they can.

Other signs of this sort of impatience: if you become *unduly* irritated or even enraged when you feel that a car ahead of you is going too slow; if you find it anguishing to wait in a line or to wait your turn to be seated at a restaurant; if you find it intolerable to watch others perform tasks you know you can do faster; if you become impatient with yourself if you are obliged to perform repetitious duties (making out bank-deposit slips, writing checks, washing dishes, and so on) that are necessary but take you away from doing things you would rather be doing; if you find yourself hurrying your own reading or always attempting to obtain condensations or summaries of truly interesting and worthwhile literature;
4. If you indulge in polyphasic thought or performance, frequently striving to think of or do two or more things simultaneously. For example, if while trying to listen to another person's speech, you persist in continuing to think about an irrelevant subject, you are indulging in polyphasic thought. Similarly, you're exhibiting polyphasic performance if

while golfing or fishing you continue to think about your business or professional problems; or if while using an electric razor you attempt also to eat your breakfast or drive your car; or if while driving your car you attempt to dictate letters to your secretary. Polyphasic activity is one of the most common traits in the Type A man. Nor is he always satisfied with doing just two things at one time. We have known persons who not only shaved and ate simultaneously but also managed to read a business or professional journal at the same time;

5. If you *always* find it difficult not to talk about subjects that especially interest and intrigue you, and when you can't steer the conversation your way you pretend to listen but really remain preoccupied with your own thoughts;

6. If you almost always feel vaguely guilty when you relax and do absolutely nothing for several hours or several days;

7. If you no longer observe the more important or interesting or lovely objects that you encounter in your world. For example, if you enter a strange office, store, or home, and after leaving cannot remember what was in them, you no longer are observing well — or, for that matter, enjoying life very much;

8. If you do not have any time to spare to become the things worth *being* because you are so preoccupied with getting the things worth *having;*

9. If you attempt to schedule more and more in less and less time, and in doing so make fewer and fewer allowances for unforeseen events. Along with this tighter scheduling comes a chronic sense of time urgency, one of the core components of Type A behavior pattern;

10. If, on meeting another severely afflicted Type A person, you find yourself compelled to "challenge" him instead of feeling compassion. This is a telltale trait because no one arouses the aggressive and/or hostile feeling of one Type A person

more quickly than another Type A person;

11. If you resort to certain characteristic gestures or nervous tics. For example, if in conversation you frequently clench your fist, bang your hand on a table, or pound one fist into the palm of your other hand to emphasize a point, you are exhibiting Type A gestures. Similarly, if the corners of your mouth spasmodically jerk backward slightly, exposing your teeth, or if you habitually clench your jaw or grind your teeth, you are subject to nervous tics. These muscular phenomena suggest the presence of a continuous struggle, which is the kernel of the Type A behavior pattern;

12. If you believe that whatever success you have enjoyed has been due largely to your ability to get things done faster than your fellow men and if you are afraid to stop doing everything faster and faster;

13. If you find yourself increasingly and ineluctably committed to translating and evaluating not only your own but also the activities of others in terms of "numbers;"

On the other hand, you possess the Type B behavior pattern:

1. If you are completely free of all the habits and exhibit none of the traits we have listed that harass the severely afflicted Type A person;

2. If you never suffer from a sense of time urgency with its accompanying impatience;

3. If you harbor no free-floating hostility and feel no need to display or discuss either your achievements or your accomplishments unless such exposure is demanded by the situation;

4. If when you play you do so to find fun and relaxation, not to exhibit your superiority at any cost;

5. If you can relax without guilt, just as you can work without agitation.

It is well documented that if you have a Type B personality you have a very small risk of ever developing coronary heart diseases. If, on the other hand, you find that you have many characteristics of the Type A personality pattern you should begin to

134

learn how to modify your behavior (Friedman and Rosenman, 1974, Rosenman & Friedman 1966; Quinlan, Barrow, et al, 1969; and Russek and Russek, 1972). Even though this behavior pattern is quite stable over time it is possible to modify your cognitive and behavioral response to stress.

MANAGING STRESS

Stress certainly is not necessarily bad. In fact, as stated earlier it can be very helpful and beneficial to you. The key appears to be in learning to manage stress. The development of methods of coping with stress can be growth experiences based on sound physiological and psychological principles which can be mastered on your own. Certainly they would be utilized most effectively if they were used as a preventive measure.

There are many methods for coping with stress (Jacobson, 1963; Benson, 1976; Schultz and Luthe, 1959; Ellis, 1962; Michenbaum, 1978). Some of these techniques are more effective but probably none are simpler than regular exercise or physical labor for rejuvenating an overly stressed individual (Ulrich, 1956; deVries, 1975). However, the more sophisticated techniques for dealing with stress such as progressive relaxation, autogenic training, relaxation response, biofeedback, controlled imagery, and the various cognitive therapies are especially efficient and beneficial and should be regularly utilized to prevent or remediate a stress-related problem.

The regular use of these techniques will not prevent you from having as intense a reaction to stress as people who do not practice, but they will teach you to cope and recover more readily and prevent *distress* from occurring. It would be wise to combine these techniques with regular exercise.

One of the first benefits of the stress management techniques is that they foster a feeling of controllability and predictability which as stated earlier are so crucial to your perception of a potentially stressful event (Seligman, 1975; Rachman, 1978). People who thrive on stress and successfully manage it have the objective feeling that they can manage the stressor. They believe that they are in control. Such individuals anticipate their stressors and plan

ahead of time how they will effectively cope with them. In other words, they are always prepared (Michenbaum, 1978; Rachman, 1978). In addition, they attempt to look at their stressors in an intellectual-rational manner rather than in an emotional way (Ellis, 1962).

In essence, the trick for coaches is to realize that due to their personality and the chosen career there is a great deal of potential for stress. This stress, if out of control, can cause both physical and psychological dangers which can and should be prevented. Coaches, through the use of coping strategies can perform their jobs more effectively, remain healthier, deter job stress from carrying over into the family and social life and prevent stress from becoming distress.

REFERENCES

Bandura, A. (Ed.) *Social Learning Theory.* New York: Prentice-Hall, 1976.

Bandura, A. Self-efficacy: Toward a unifying theory of behavioral change. *Psychological Review, 84:* 191-215, 1977.

Benson, H. and Klipper, M. *The Relaxation Response.* New York: Morrow, 1976.

deVries, H. A. A review of the tranquilizer effect of exercise. *Journal of Physical Education and Recreation, 46:* 53-54, 1975.

Ellis, A. *Reason and Emotion in Psychotherapy.* New York: Lyle Stuart Press, 1962.

Erikson, E. *Insight and Responsibility.* Norton, 1964.

Friedman, M. and Rosenman, R. H. *Type A Behavior and Your Heart.* Greenwich, Conn.: Fawcett Publications, 1974.

Jacobson, E. *You Must Relax.* New York: McGraw-Hill, 1934.

Jacobson, E. *Tension Control for Businessmen.* New York: McGraw-Hill, 1963.

Kahn, R. L. et al. *Organizational Stress: Studies in Role Conflict and Ambiguity.* John Wiley and Sons, Inc., 1964a.

Kahn, R. L. and Bouldings, E. (Eds.) *Power and Conflict in Organizations.* Basic, 1964b.

Kahn, R. L. Stress — from 9 to 5. *Psychology Today,* Vol. 3, No. 4, pp. 34-38, Sept. 1969.

Michenbaum, D. *Cognitive-Behavior Modification: An Integrative Approach.* Plenum Press, New York and London, 1978.

Nideffer, R. M. Test of attentional and

interpersonal style. *Journal of Personality and Social Psychology,* 1976, *34:* 394.

Nideffer, R. M. *The Inner Athlete: Mind Plus Muscle.* New York: Thomas Crowell, 1976.

Ogilvie, B. C. and Tutko, T. A. Self-image and measured personality of coaches. In *Contemporary Psychology of Sport.* Edited by G. S. Kenyon, Chicago: Athletic Institute, 1970.

Quinlan, C. B., Barrow, J. G., et al. The association of risk factors and coronary heart disease in trappist and benedictine monks. *Proc. of Conf. on Epidemiology.* The American Heart Association, New Orleans, March 3, 1969.

Rachman, S. J. *Fear and Courage.* W. H. Freeman and Company, San Francisco, 1978.

Rosenman, R. H. and Friedman, M. et al. Coronary heart disease in the western collaborative group study: a follow-up experience of two years. *Journal of the American Medical Association, 195:* 86-92, 1966.

Sage, G. The coach as management, organizational leadership in American sport. *Quest,* 1973, *19,* 35-40.

Sarason, S. B. and Spielberger, C. D. *Stress and Anxiety.* Hemisphere Publishing Co.: Washington, D.C., 1975.

Schultz, J. H. and Luthe, W. *Autogenic training.* New York: Grune and Stratton, 1959.

Seligman, M. E. P. *Helplessness: On Depression, Development, and Death.* San Francisco, Calif.: Freeman and Company, 1975.

Selye, H. *The Story of the Adaptation Syndrome.* Montreal: Acta, Inc., Med. Publ., 1952.

Selye, Hans. *Stress Without Distress.* J. B. Lippincott Co., New York, 1974.

Ulrich, A. C. Measurement of Stress evidenced by college women in situations involving competition. Unpublished doctoral dissertation, University of Southern California, 1956.

21

Role Conflict
And Athletic Coaching

Tom Perrin
University of Virginia

Use of the terms "role" and "role conflict" are popular among social scientists who seek to provide a better understanding of human behavior in social settings. These concepts are perhaps most frequently applied by educational sociologists and psychologists in examining aspects of school society (Parsons, 1951; Becker, 1953; Getzels and Guba, 1954; Gross et al., 1958; Getzels, 1963). Most notably, educational researchers have commonly used the role and role conflict constructs in analyzing the teaching profession (Merton, 1957; Wilson, 1962; Westwood, 1967; Grace, 1972).

But while teaching has provided a valuable model for expositions of these concepts, little research has attempted to employ them in analyzing the behavior of another important group of individuals in the educational setting, namely, athletic coaches. Although the term role does appear frequently in coaching and physical education textbooks, its use in these contexts tends to be exhortative and normative in nature, rather than analytical and empirical. What theoretical attempts have been made to study coaching behaviors and interactions through the use of role and role conflict theory has focused almost exclusively on the role of "teacher/coaches" (Locke and Massengate, 1978; Templin et al., 1980).

The purpose of the present paper is to examine role conflict theory and briefly make application of this theory to athletic coaching. The professional literature pertaining to role theory is vast and somewhat confusing. In particular, the concepts of "role" and "role conflict" have been formulated in varied and sometimes contradictory ways, although important attempts have been made to produce conceptual order (Biddle and Thomas, 1966; Biddle, 1979). In any event, an attempt to discuss all of the as-

pects of role analysis within the scope of this paper would result in a very cursory presentation.

It is surprising that very little research has focused on role conflict in coaching not only because of the popularity of role conflict theory in educational research, but also because coaching as a profession seems to be eminently suited to analysis as a social role and exceptionally vulnerable to the role-related conflicts that affect other members of the educational community as well. Besides, conflict should be a vital concern to coaches as well as to everyone affected by coaching behavior. Conflict can negatively affect the attitudes and behaviors of coaches which, in turn, can detrimentally impact the quality of the experience that coaches provide to their athletes. Coaches who are more cognizant of role conflict and better prepared to deal with it will ultimately be better able to positively affect the lives of their athletes.

ROLE CONFLICT

Every individual occupies a number of "social positions" in the society in which he lives. A social position is simply an identity that designates a commonly recognized set of persons such as a coach, teacher, athlete, parent, etc. For each position there is a set or pattern of expectations that dictates appropriate and normative behavior for that position by prescribing some acts and forbidding others. This set of expectations comprises the rights, privileges, and obligations of an individual occupying the given position.

In sociological terms, this set of expectations is called a social "role." Merton (1957) has defined a role as "a pattern of expectations which apply to a particular social position and which normally persist independently of the personalities occupying the position." It is perhaps more accurate, however, to define a role as a pattern of expected *behaviors* common to everyone who holds a specific position (Locke and Massengale, 1978). For, in essence, expectations determine behaviors.

In any event, it is common for individuals to experience problems and conflict in attempting to maintain or occupy social roles. Not only is it difficult to fully conform to different expectations for a single role, but roles often interfere with one another as well.

In role theory, role conflict is a term used, in a general sense, to denote problems that an individual experiences in occupying a social role. Despite its variations — role "strain" (Goode, 1960) and role "stress" (Westwood, 1967) — the central component of role conflict is *incompatibility* (Grace, 1972). Conflict occurs when an individual perceives and/or experiences his role expectations as incompatible to some degree. Specifically, as Biddle (1979) states, "an individual experiences role conflict when they are subject to two or more contradictory expectations whose stipulations they cannot meet in behavior."

Generally, role conflict can be categorized into two types, *inter-role* and *intra-role* conflict (Grace, 1972; Biddle, 1979). Inter-role conflict arises when an individual occupies two or more roles that demand contradictory skills or incompatible behavior. Because roles commonly overlap, such as teaching and coaching, an individual who occupies "multiple" roles may experience conflict if the roles demand dissimilar skills and behavior. In a case such as this, the "perceived legitimacy" of the roles becomes a major factor in determining the degree and intensity of the role conflict. The more legitimate or important that each role is to the individual, the more that the individual will want to meet the obligations and expectations that each role demands (Grace, 1972). But this is impossible, of course, if these obligations are incompatible in nature. And yet, to the degree that individuals choose to define themselves in terms of one role over another, unequal role commitment will occur and, hence, role conflict can again result.

A somewhat typical example of inter-role conflict in coaching occurs when a coach, as part of his coaching responsibilities, is expected to scout games on the weekend; yet, as part of his responsibilities as parent and spouse, is also expected to spend time with his family.

Templin et al. (1980) have examined the nature of inter-role conflict in teacher-coaches and found what they consider to be a "predictable sequence" leading to dysfunction between the roles. This sequence provides a good example of how inter-role conflict may develop between other roles as well.

1. If one role demands that the individuals possess the skills and inclinations needed to deal with relatively large numbers of clients who are unmotivated, often hostile, relatively heterogeneous for ability and present under compulsion (as in teaching); and
2. if one's other role, occupied simultaneously, demands that the individual possess the skills and inclinations required to deal with relatively small numbers of clients who are highly motivated, relatively homogeneous for ability, and present as volunteers (as in coaching); then
3. it follows that the two roles may not be equally attractive or compatible when linked together and it is not unexpected that one would become the preferred role, leading perhaps to dysfunction in the non-preferred role.

In contrast to inter-role conflict, intra-role conflict arises when an individual occupies a "single" role for which different groups or individuals expect incompatible behaviors. To better understand this form of conflict, it is necessary to discuss the concept of "role set" within role theory.

The term role set was first introduced by Merton (1957) to designate the total complement of role relationships in which a person becomes involved by virtue of their occupying a particular social position. "Role behavior always occurs within the context of an actual, imagined, or anticipated relationship with another person (Coakley, 1982)." Each role that an individual occupies is articulated and defined in a network of other roles representing different social positions with which the individual interacts. These so-called other roles are referred to as "counter-roles" and the individuals who occupy them are called "role partners." For every role, there is at least one, and probably more, counter-roles.

Every role set holds a potential for conflict to the extent that members of the role set (i.e., role partners) occupy different social positions. More specifically, the potential for role conflict within any role set increases depending on the extent of the "diversity" of the role set and the extent of the "responsibility" associated with the role in question (Snoek, 1966).

Role partners are simply people with whom an individual, in any given role interacts on a regular basis. They occupy positions that are affected, directly or indirectly, by the behavior of the individual in question. Either they are rewarded by this behavior in some way, or they require it in order to perform their own tasks (Rotella, 1981). In any event, because of their interest in and dependency on this particular role, role partners form attitudes and expectations about how the individual in the given position should and should not behave. Hence, the greater the number of counter-roles with which an individual must interact, the more likely it is that the given individual will experience conflicting goals, values, and expectations held by these role partners with regard to their role behavior. Very simply, when expectations for behavior are presented from a variety of different sources, there is a greater potential for strain and conflict in trying to please everyone.

Not only does the "number" of counter-roles and role partners with which an individual must interact affect behavior, but so too does the extent of the "responsibility" associated with the role in question. For the greater the responsibility associated with a particular role, the more strongly the individual feels obligated to "appropriately maintain" relationships with the role partners. But to do so, of course, involves meeting their expectations. And attempting to satisfy a wide variety of conflicting values and goals is difficult. Hence, it is likely that the individual will experience conflict to some extent (Snoek, 1966).

While inter-role conflict relates to problems experienced as a result of multiple role obligations, intra-role conflict occurs within a single role and grows out of dysfunction or disturbance in the role set. As just discussed, an individual will experience conflict such as this when faced with several contradictory or conflicting expectations caused by a diversified role set. The degree and intensity of intra-role conflict is greatly determined by the perceived legitimacy of the "expectations" held by role partners, and the perceived level of responsibility associated with the given role. The more expectations that are "accepted" by an individual as legitimate, and the greater responsibility "perceived" to be associated with his position, the greater the potential for conflict.

Before discussing the application of role conflict theory to athletic coaching, it should be noted that experiencing some degree of role conflict is normal and perhaps unavoidable (Merton, 1957; Goode, 1960; Grace, 1972; Biddle, 1979; Coakley, 1982). In this discussion of role strain, Goode (1960) states that, in general, an individual's total role obligations are "over-demanding." Hence, it is simply impossible to fulfill all the responsibilities of multiple roles or all of the expectations of a diversified role set.

ROLE CONFLICT IN COACHING

Coaches are extremely susceptible to both inter-role and intra-role conflict because of the nature of their roles and their tendency to assume occupational roles in addition to coaching.

Inter-Role Conflict:

It is common for coaches at all levels of interscholastic and intercollegiate athletics to occupy roles within the educational setting in addition to coaching. In most cases, coaches are required to do so as part of their job description. At the public school level, coaches frequently assume additional roles as teacher or school administrator. At the collegiate level, it is also common for coaches to teach, although many will also occupy positions as athletic director, assistant athletic director, or athletic trainer.

In occupying multiple roles, coaches become vulnerable to role conflict because of the possibility that one role will interfere with another. In examining inter-role conflict with teacher/coaches, Locke and Massengale (1978) presented a model for identifying the types of conflicts that are most frequently experienced with multiple role obligations. This model, outlined below, provides a conceptual framework for identifying the potential areas of conflict for coaches as they attempt to fulfill multiple role obligations within or outside the educational setting.

Potential Conflict Areas

1. *Values:* It is possible that coaches will experience incompatibility between the values that they are expected to uphold in their coaching and those that are expected to be upheld in another role, such as teaching or administration.
2. *Status:* It is possible that coaches will experience conflict because of a perceived or experienced difference between their status as a coach and their status in another role (i.e., community peer or faculty acceptance).
3. *Self-Other:* It is possible that coaches will experience conflict with regard to their potential for career advancement in coaching or another role and their ethical commitment to fulfill all roles to the best of their ability and in the best interests of others. It may be more difficult for individuals to "get ahead" in coaching if they have to fulfill other role obligations.
4. *Workload:* This is perhaps the most common area for potential conflict. It is possible that coaches will experience conflict over their ability to adequately fulfill the obligations of multiple roles within given time and energy demands.
5. *Skill:* It is possible that coaches will experience conflict due to differences in the type of skills and training required to perform each role (i.e., coaches are often experts at teaching sport skills, yet teaching in a classroom may demand different skills and training in order to be effective).

Intra-Role Conflict:

Just as coaches are very susceptible to inter-role conflict, it is also likely that they will experience intra-role conflict due to their typically extensive diversified "role set" and due to the degree of responsibility associated with their task. Coakley (1982) has identified what might be considered a typical role set of many high school and college coaches. Listed below are those individuals who might occupy "counter-roles" within this role set.

- players
- players' parents
- school administrators
- news media personnel
- faculty and students
- other coaches
- athletic director
- national and state athletic coaches associations
- support staff — trainers, managers, doctors, etc.
- fans — alumni and booster clubs

Certainly, there may be some variation in this role set from one school to another, but, nevertheless, most coaches are required within their roles to relate with a wide variety of role partners. It should be kept in mind, however, that expectations coming from counter-roles will not automatically be dissimilar. In fact, many of the values and goals held by the above-mentioned individuals in the coach's role set may be quite similar with regard to the coach's role. Yet, considering that there are so many counter-roles and that these role partners range in social position from players to fans, to school administrators and news media, there is a great deal of "potential" for conflicting goals and values.

Further role conflict is precipitated by the extent of responsibility placed on the shoulders of coaches. The following is a hypothetical example of a typical conflict situation faced by coaches (Coakley, 1982). It indicates the tremendous amount of responsibility that coaches must try to uphold and the kinds of contradictory expectations they are expected to fulfill.

"Fellow faculty members expect the coach to be an educator and to give priority to the academic needs of stu-

140

dent athletes; players' parents expect priority to be given to the social and personal development of their sons or daughters; alumni expect the coach to field a winning team regardless of anything else; administrators expect the coach to handle a team and players in a way that will provide good public relations for the school; players expect special treatment or the opportunity to express themselves as individuals both on and off the field; those in other counter-roles have additional expectations."

In addition to the fact that coaches frequently face many incompatible and overdemanding expectations, such as those noted above, it is typical for members of the coach's role set to also hold the coach "totally accountable" for fulfilling each of their specific desires. This is a tremendous source of conflict. For, as Edwards (1973) has discussed, athletics is an activity characterized, above all else, by "uncertainty." In attempting to meet a wide variety of expectations, "a coach is asked to control events that are ultimately uncontrollable; to display self-confidence and certainty when forced to operate on the basis of hunches, guesses, and probabilities; and to ensure success when outcomes are influenced by human error, luck, the calls of officials, and performances of athletes who are subject to injuries, fatigue and personal problems (Coakley, 1982)."

It is obvious that the extent of a coach's responsibility, involving "limited control but complete liability," is an important source of strain and conflict.

REACTIONS TO ROLE CONFLICT

Consciously or unconsciously, individuals who experience role conflict will respond in some way. The specific action that they take will depend on the nature and intensity of the conflict, the specific context in which it occurs, and the characteristics of the individual. Generally, however, reactions to role conflict take the form of "adaptation" or "retreatism."

Adaptation to Incompatibility

Responses to mild or moderate forms of role conflict will frequently take the form of adaptation. Whether it be in regard to inter-role or intra-role conflict, the process will include the selection of one role (inter-role conflict) or one set of expectations (intra-role conflict) as being more important. This selection is made at the expense of other roles or expectations (Getzels and Guba, 1954; Grace, 1972). The particular role or set of expectations is frequently chosen by one of the following procedures.

Expedient orientation: In this approach to decision making, the individual considers/weighs "costs" and "rewards" and selects the given role or set of expectations that conforms to the persons or duties considered to be most important.

Moral orientation: In this case, the individual bases his decision on the role or set of expectations that are considered most "legitimate," regardless of self-interest.

Moral-expedient orientation: In this case, the individual seeks to balance considerations of legitimacy and self-interest and choose the specific course of action best suited for all involved.

In general, adaptation to role conflict involves compromises and sacrifices. The individual either selects one role (or set of expectations) as more important and attempts to *totally* conform to that position at the expense of others, or the individual selects one role (or set of expectations) as more important, yet attempts to conform only *in part* in the hope that the "sanctions" applied by the other position will not be too severe (Getzels and Guba, 1954; Grace, 1972).

In his examination of teacher/coaches, Edwards (1973) has pointed out that these individuals are "socialized" to prioritize their coaching role over their teaching position. Because of an unequal reward system in which teacher — coaches are primarily hired and fired for coaching performance, these individuals realize that if they are to survive professionally, they must place greater emphasis on their coaching responsibilities.

Yet, making a choice such as this often makes role conflict worse. For in selecting their coaching role as more important, teacher/coaches often neglect their teaching role to some extent and, in turn, are criticized for it (Edwards, 1973).

Role Retreatism:

Reactions to more severe role conflict will result in avoidance and withdrawal. Initially, the individual is likely to reduce his commitment, intentionally or unintentionally. In many cases, it appears that the individual simply loses interest when, in fact, he has purposely attempted to reduce the intensity of his conflict through delegating responsibility, avoiding conflict situations, or choosing alternative reference groups, etc.

When a reduction in commitment fails to adequately resolve role conflict, an individual may then seek to abandon the role or roles altogether. This type of reaction may be "functional" in that the individual "strategically" withdraws, or this response may simply result unintentionally from an individual's desire to quit.

It should be kept in mind that role conflict is not necessarily bad. It can be a source of positive change or what Grace (1972) calls "productive transformations." Any of the aforementioned reactions to role conflict can be functional in nature if the individual is stimulated to analyze his problems and seek to change the situation in which troubling incompatibilities exist.

DYSFUNCTIONAL CONSEQUENCES OF ROLE CONFLICT

Similar to the potential reactions or responses to role strain, consequences of unresolved conflict will vary depending on the nature and intensity of the conflict, the context in which it is found, and the characteristics of the individual exposed to it (Grace, 1972). In general, exposure to long-term or on-going conflict can have severe emotional, psychological, and physical costs for the individual. The major health problem resulting from this type of conflict is "stress." The potentially negative effects of stress on the individual are well docu-

mented (Sarason and Spielberger, 1975; Seligman, 1975; Selye, 1974; Shultz and Lutke, 1959; Jacobson, 1934). It is not the purpose of this paper to discuss these effects, although negative psychological, emotional, and physical manifestations might inlcude the following:
— sense of helplessness
— perception of loss of control
— insomnia
— hypertension
— depression
— alcohol and drug abuse
— anxiety
— low job satisfaction
— burnout
— heart attack
— marital collapse
(etc.)

Resolving Role Conflict in Coaching

Ideally, a coach would like to be competent in all of the roles that he occupies and be able to meet all the expectations placed on him. But expecting to meet all obligations is simply unrealistic and most coaches are aware of this. In his discussion of problems and conflict in coaching, Coakley (1982) provides some general guidelines that can be used by coaches to assist them in taking more specific action to reduce role conflict.

Generate Support:

It is imperative that a coach first attempt to properly "sell" his program to those who potentially may place incompatible expectations on him. To do so effectively, a coach must not only describe his program clearly and simply, but he must also convince others that he has confidence in his own ability. When a coach can recruit the support and backing of individuals occupying counter-roles, it is less likely that these individuals will place conflicting demands upon him.

Maximize Control:

In addition to generating support, a coach must attempt to maximize control if he is to effectively control role conflict. To do so, a coach should take a number of steps. First, he should attempt to elicit some guarantees of autonomy from individuals who supervise his position, such as the athletic director or school principal. Second, a coach should attempt to create the "impression" that he is unapproachable when it comes to taking suggestions on how to do his job. Third, a coach must be willing to demand obedience and, when necessary, simply tell others to keep their expectations to themselves. And, finally, a coach must be willing to "avoid" conflict situations whenever possible. Coakley (1982) does not advocate total avoidance of personal contact with others who may hold incompatible expectations for his behavior but, rather, avoidance of situations where the coach may have to "simultaneously" respond to contradictory obligations, values or goals.

Exercise Expedience:

Role conflicts are inevitable to some extent even when a coach attempts to maximize control. As a result, a coach must be willing to compromise. He should not expect to fulfill all role obligations nor live up to all expectations demanded of him. Instead, a coach should closely examine the costs and benefits involved with alternative behaviors and choose the one he feels is most appropriate.

Discussion of role conflict theory has been popular among educational researchers in examining aspects of school society. At the same time, however, there has been little systematic study of the role conflict construct related to the athletic coaching profession.

Clearly, additional research concerning role conflict in coaching is needed. Coaches certainly do play a very important role in determining the quality of the experience that athletes gain in sport. And yet, by virtue of their position, coaches are extremely vulnerable to the types of role-related conflicts which can have a detrimental impact on their ability to provide for athletes. Further research in this area, however, might provide coaches with a better understanding of the problems that they encounter in their role, as well as ways to deal with these conflicts. In this way, they might also be better able to provide effectively for athletes.

REFERENCES

Biddle, B. J. *Role Theory: Expectations, Identities and Behavior.* New York: Academic Press, 1979.

Biddle, B. J. and Thomas, E. *Role Theory: Concepts and Research.* New York: Wiley, 1966.

Coakley, J. J. *Sport in Society: Issues and Controversies.* St. Louis: C. V. Mosby, 1982.

Edwards, H. *Sociology of Sport.* Homewood, Illinois: Dorsey Press, 1973.

Getzels, J. W. "Conflict and Role Behavior in the Educational Setting." In W. Charters and N. Gage (Eds.), *Readings in the Social Psychology of Education.* Boston: Allyn and Bacon, 1963.

Getzels, J. W. and Guba, E. G. "Role, Role Conflict and Effectiveness: An Empirical Study." *American Sociological Review,* 1954, *19,* 164-175.

Goode, W. J. "A Theory of Role Strain." *American Sociological Review,* 1974, *39,* 567-578.

Grace, G. R. *Role Conflict and the Teacher.* London and Boston, MA: Routledge, Kegan and Paul, 1972.

Gross, N. et al. *Explorations in Role Analysis.* New York: Wiley, 1958.

Jacobson, E. *You Must Relax.* New York: McGraw-Hill, 1934.

Kahn, R. L. et al. *Organizational Stress: Studies in Role Conflict and Ambiguity.* New York: Wiley, 1964.

Locke, L. F. and Massengale, J. D. "Role Conflict in Teacher/Coaches." *Research Quarterly,* 1978, *49*(2), 162-174.

Marks, S. R. "Multiple Roles and Role Strain." *American Sociological Review,* 1977, *42,* 921-936.

Massengale, J. D. "Researching Role Conflict." *JOPERD,* 1981, *52*(9), 23.

Merton, R. K. "The Role Set: Problems in Sociological Theory." *British Journal of Sociology,* 1957, *8,* 106-120.

Rotella, R. J. "The Coach and Stress." In L. Bunker and R. Rotella (Eds.), *Sport Psychology: Psychological Considerations in Maximizing Sport Performance.* 1981.

Sarason, S. B. and Spielberger, C. D.

Stress and Anxiety. Washington, D. C.: Hemisphere Publ. Co., 1975.

Seligman, M. E. P. *Helplessness: On Depression, Development, and Death.* San Francisco, CA: Freeman and Company, 1975.

Selye, M. *Stress Without Distress.* New York: J. B. Lippincott Co., 1974.

Shultz, J. H. and Lutke, W. *Antogenic Training.* Greene and Stratton: New York, 1959.

Sieber, S. D. "Toward a Theory of Role Accumulation." *American Sociological Review,* 1974, *39,* 567-578.

Snoek, J. "Role Strain in Diversified Role Sets." *The American Journal of Sociology,* 1966, IXXI(4), 363-372.

Templin, T. J. et al. "Teacher/Coach Role Conflict: An Analysis of Occupational Role Dysfunction." Paper presented at the annual meeting of The Indiana Association for Health, Physical Education, Recreation and Dance, Vincennes, Indiana, October, 1980.

Toby, J. "Some Variables in Role Conflict Analysis." *Social Forces,* 1952, *30,* 323-327.

Westwood, L. J. "The Role of the Teacher — I." *Education Research,* 1967, 9(2), 122-134.

Wilson, B. R. "The Teacher's Role: A Sociological Analysis." *British Journal of Sociology,* 1962, *13,* 15-32.

22

Stress-Related Problems In Developing High Level Athletes

David Ojala
Stratton School, Vermont

In 1980 at the Winter Olympics at Lake Placid many world class athletic performances will be seen. We've seen many in the past. In 1976 Franz Klammer supplied us with, what some people consider, the most exciting televised sports experience ever. In 1978 we saw back-to-back World Cup wins at Stratton in both Slalom and Giant Slalom by the twins from Whitepass, Washington, Phil and Steve Mahre. Last winter we saw Abby Fisher win a World Cup Slalom in Italy and seventeen-year-old Heidi Preuss finish second in the World Cup finals at Furand, Japan.

In the winter of 1977 I worked as a coach with the U.S. Ski Team. I considered this to be quite an opportunity, and in fact it was; however, for me the format was not particularly satisfying. I felt more responsible for the logistics of travel arrangements than I did for the development of ski racers. Following that season I went back to development. The process of developing young athletes, attempting to maximize their talent, hopefully sending a few on to World Cup competition, is a process I find most intriguing.

Currently, I am working at the Stratton Mountain School, and I would like to briefly describe it for you because I feel that it is a fairly unique situation in athletic development in America today. (Incidentally, Abby Fisher and Heidi Preuss, the two successful World Cup skiers whom I mentioned earlier, have come out of our school and we expect that they will be racing at Lake Placid in the 1980 Olympics.)

Stratton Mountain School has ten coaches, fifteen teachers, and sixty racers (twelve cross-country racers and the rest alpine racers: slalom, giant slalom, and downhill).

It is a fully accredited co-ed private boarding school. The campus is at the foot of Stratton Mountain in Southern Vermont, with classrooms and dorms in the former Hotel Tyrol, within walking distance to the lifts and the training hills. The school has its own private Poma lift which services the World Cup Slalom trail, a ski deck, which is an inclined revolving carpet to stimulate skiing, and a fully equipped gymnasium.

The goal at Stratton School is to maximize ski racing potential while experiencing a quality education. In Europe there are a number of sports academies, but academics are not really stressed in the same way that the athletics are. The athletic and academic success in Stratton's seven year history has been quite good. While a good handful of skiers have gone on to become World Cup competitors, I might add, many more have gone on to some of the best schools in the country, many of whom have ski teams.

The school schedule begins on August 20 and goes through June 1. In the fall and spring the schedule starts at 6:30 in the morning for "Morning Sport." That's a light run, stretching, a swim, at the right time of year, or maybe a little bit of indoor soccer. At 7:00 a.m. we have breakfast, at 8:00 a.m. classes start, lunch at 1:00 p.m. In the spring, lunch is at 2:00 p.m. because the kids work for the Mountain Corporation for their season lift passes. At 4:00 p.m. we have dryland training. This might be anything from a run, a hike, soccer, weight training, gymnastics, volleyball, etc. At 6:00 p.m. the kids have supper, study from 7:00 until 9:00 p.m., an hour of free time and then it's bed. It's a fairly demanding day. In the winter, ski training occurs in the morning. This is because our northern exposure gives better light at that time of day. Consequently, classes are after lunch. Classes start at 1:00 p.m. and go until 6:00 p.m., and the evening schedule is the same as the fall.

A "typical day" may not be an appropriate term — the kids are in and out of school all the time. In the fall we have two European training camps. The top fifteen international competitors in the school go for six weeks to Hintertux, Austria. Hintertux is a glacier where many of the top national teams are doing their fall training. The kids get to ride up the lift with Franz Klammer and there is a whole lot of positive visual imagery. They learn a lot by osmosis. We have a three week camp for fourteen and fifteen year olds. This year it looks like we will be going to Tignes, France. We'll have two coaches and one teacher going with fifteen kids to Hintertux, and one teacher and one coach going to Tignes. These are not only training experiences, they are rather good cultural experiences.

In the winter the competitive season begins. The kids are gone much of this time of year also. Some are skiing with the U.S. Ski Team, some go out to the Junior Olympics, which are held every year at Squaw Valley, some go to the Senior National Championships and some race on the Nor-Am circuit. It's not unusual for a kid to leave the first week in January and come back in the middle of February. The winter calls for a less strenuous academic schedule. This is why we start in August in an effort to complete as much of the academic work before Christmas as possible. At the end of the ski season we have a two week break in April, we come back to an academic sprint with training and a June 1 graduation.

This life style presents and intensifies many problems common to athletic development. It does provide more time to try to deal with the athlete in given situations. Adolescents aspiring world class athletes are seen in many situations beyond training and competition. This can be a draining or a stimulating experience, both in terms of sport performance and overall development.

Keep in mind that I am addressing problems and not necessarily solutions. The following problems or areas of consideration would be listed: communication, motivation, concentration and training facilities. Also I would like to discuss the conflict be-

tween athletics and academics, health guidelines, sex roles, and keeping sports enjoyable for our athletes. Finally, I would like to assess the development program at Stratton School.

Considering communication, we see that skiing is a very individualized sport, therefore, it requires much individual attention. Each of the 60 kids must be able to communicate with at least one of the eight coaches on our staff. Each individual athlete must likewise be hearing a compatible message from each coach. This is the importance of a uniform, systematic, and comprehensive presentation of information.

At times, communicating may be more effective if it is non-verbal. Words get worn, especially in the middle of February. Six months into the program it can be difficult for the coach to verbally stimulate the desired response. An an illustration — if an athlete is to shoot into the corners of the goals and all but the lower corners of the goal are barricaded, you really don't have to tell him where to shoot the ball to score. The same thing can be accomplished with gate placement for slalom, giant slalom, and downhill.

Let's take a look at motivation. In the fall there is really no problem. Some of the kids are excited about going to Europe and all of the kids are excited in the anticipation of the upcoming ski season. This time of year it is not difficult to convince the individual of the benefit of group momentum. During the competitive season, motivating the individual, in many cases may depend on the degree of the individual's success. In May, the post competition season, the road gets a little rougher. The kids have been in a fairly intense situation from August 20 through the middle of April and they feel they've earned the right to do as they please. At this point orientation is relied upon heavily. Skiers are encouraged to focus on their goals for the following season so that the Spring off-season training becomes a little more meaningful. Motivation is affected by influences other than the season of the year. Motivating the athlete who has had success early in his career, say at thirteen or fourteen, is hard because most often he will attribute his success to ability. This is a reasonable assumption since he or she has probably enjoyed an early physical maturity. It is our job to try to convince the athlete of the importance effort will play when he gets into higher levels of competition.

Concentration is definitely a learned skill. Some skiers come to school and they have already learned it, others haven't. Athletes must learn how and when to focus their attention. Coaches must know if the athletes are maximizing their performance in training and competition. But as a school director, I also have to be concerned with the coach's presentation of information and the structure of individual training blocks. For example, are these presentations worthy of the athletes' concentration and attention?

A coach needs to supply the best training opportunity available to the means of his program. Is the training time spent efficiently? Is the training program getting the athlete ready for the physical and the psychological demands of competition? How can European racing conditions be simulated? Ski racing is the kind of sport that happens on your home field very seldom. It's not one game away, one game home. It's more like nine games away, one game home. That's why it's interesting that the 1980 Olympics are in the U.S. at Lake Placid. This "home field advantage" phenomonen is similar to the problem that Dr. Harris mentioned concerning the U.S. Field Hockey women verses British women. Our European ski training camps definitely help, because they stimulate the terrain, the language and the culture, but it's not a racing situation.

The academic versus athletic conflict is a special consideration at a place like Stratton Mountain School. How does the student/athlete fill the requirements of a training program geared toward World Class competition while at the same time trying to fulfill the requirements of an academic program geared toward the toughest universities, while at the same time trying to minimize stress? Teachers and coaches need a well thought out systematic, mastery approach in their own areas to maximize the result of the time spent by the student/athlete in each of their areas.

HEALTH GUIDELINES

The fall is really no problem. Students are typically motivated and very busy. The winter becomes a problem for some of the less successful athletes. It seems every time you pick up the paper some prominent athlete is reported to be connected with the negative side of drugs, marijuana, alcohol, tobacco, getting adequate rest or maintaining a nutritionally sound diet.

How does an athlete in today's society accept guidelines concurrent with peak performance in his or her sport when they are constantly reading about and meeting with role models whose actions are not in agreement with these guidelines? Our athletes have trouble understanding that only a few extremely gifted athletes might succeed without sound training habits.

Finding a comfortable sex role is a problem for some of the adolescents in our program. This seems to be potentially a problem especially with female adolescent athletes. Remember, our school is co-ed, even in training and travel situations. A female participant competing at a high level in a traditionally male dominated field, often overestimates her social female role expectations. Unfortunately, this can cause problems with self concept and oftentimes is not the healthiest basis of social interaction or relationships.

Keeping sports enjoyable can be difficult in a community aiming at excellence. Reasonable goal orientation is very important in this area. It's obvious to me, that of the hundred or so skiers that pass through our school every four years, we'll be lucky if a handful progress to the National 'A' Team or Olympic Team. This realization that not all of the kids will "make it," comes slow to some of the kids. It comes even *slower* to some of the parents. It *never* comes to some of the parents. Next year we plan to have a preventative workshop in this area for the parents. Hopefully, they will realize that the process of working toward a goal is a very important lesson to learn.

The assessment of a development program is the last problem to be discussed. Measuring the actual skiing achievement is easy enough. There is the FIS point list. The FIS is the governing body of World Amateur skiing and the point list is a complicated, but accurate way of ranking anyone finishing in the FIS sanctioned race against everyone else in the world, including the best in the world. *Positive* use of this is best done in an indirect, competitive nature. But it is also important to measure the effectiveness of our training program in order to constantly improve or maintain its effectiveness. This year we tried to measure the effectiveness of our training program by establishing a psycho-biological profile for each of our racers. This program was designed and implemented by Drs. Rotella, Billing and Wakat and was worked in conjunction with the coaching staff at the Stratton Mountain School.

We were trying to assess the physiological and psychological state of the individual and by compiling that data could get a feel for the state of the group and thus assess the state of our program. We had some limitations — geographic, lab facilities, set up and break down time, but these were far outweighed by the rapport between the coaching staff, the kids, and the testing team. The implementation of this psycho-biological profile system was set up in a way that we tested three times a year: September, which is when we first come in contact with the kids on a full-time basis; December, which is the beginning of the competition season; and April, which is the end of the competition season.

Let's look at a chart which catalogues the physiological information (see Chart A). The maximum oxygen uptake is listed under "VO_2." Moving from left to right across the top of the chart we see strength and endomorphy — body fat. Line "y" is the mean of the male population at the Stratton Mountain School. Line "x" is three standard deviations above the mean of the population of the men at Stratton Mountain School, and line "z," three standard deviations below the mean for the men at Stratton Mountain School. What we did find from the data collected was a trend where the better skiers, based on their FIS point ranking, scored well in four categories; that was in the VO_2, the leg strength, the reaction time and the flexibility. If those four values added up to 100% of predictive value, 60% was given to VO_2. That tells us what we ought to be emphasizing in our training program. The physiological data is what we use most at this point. As coaches, we feel more comfortable counseling in the physiological area right now, than we do in the psychological areas. In the psychological area we work primarily on an individual basis.

Looking across the psychological profile (Chart B) it is set up again, the population being the males at Stratton Mountain School, line "y" is the mean, and it goes three standard deviations above ("x") and below ("y") the mean again. The areas that we measure, if you look from left to right, is trait anxiety, state anxiety, achievement motivation, sport specific achievement motivation, two sub scales of the personal orientation inventory and a self concept scale. A low reading in any of these categories gives us information pertinent to dealing with individual athletes.

Using this data it was possible to measure each individual against every other individual, thus providing the capability of using this information in an indirect or direct competitive fashion. We choose to counsel on an indirect fashion. It gives us an asessment of the overall training period from one period to the next, and because this is hopefully a long range program, it will give us an assessment from one year to the next. It helps us to design or modify our training program. It helps us counsel the individual athlete, which is very important for motivation.

I remember about a month ago we had two of our girls going out to train with the National 'A' Team at Bend, Oregon. This is a fairly select group and the first such experience for either of these two girls. They were two of the first girls to whom I showed the physiological information. That was a Thursday evening and there were academic tests on Friday. One of the teachers had organized a cookout at her house which was about seven miles away from our dorm. It was raining pretty miserably that evening and the cookout was taking the place of Thursday's athletic training. Well, the two girls ran the seven miles in the rain to go to the cookout. So the positive motivational value of that kind of information is really something that you should consider for your program.

It's very helpful in establishing a reasonable goal orientation for programs and for individuals. And lastly, it helps to design an individual training effort with emphasis in the appropriate areas for individual athletes.

In conclusion, it seems like we've answered some questions, but we still have a lot of questions to answer. I'll leave you with the

thought that I do believe that a program
like this can help young athletes evolve into
who they are trying to become.

CHART A
PHYSIOLOGICAL PROFILE
MALES

Name_____   Date_____

		VO_2	VO_2K	FX	LST	RTAV	AS	ENDO
Line X	3 SD	5.07	68.6	26.9	1576	33.0	2.2	
		4.74	65.3	25.9	1464	35.8	2.12	
	2 SP	4.41	62.0	24.8	1344	38.6	2.04	.16
		4.08	58.7	23.8	1128	41.4	1.96	.81
	1 SP	3.75	55.4	22.7	1112	44.2	1.88	1.46
		3.59	53.8	22.2	1054	45.6	1.84	1.79
		3.42	52.1	21.7	996	47.0	1.8	2.11
		3.26	50.5	21.1	938	48.4	1.76	2.44
Line Y	MEAN	3.09	48.8	20.6	880	49.8	1.72	2.76
		2.93	47.2	20.1	822	51.2	1.68	3.09
		2.76	45.5	19.6	764	52.6	1.64	3.41
		2.59	43.9	19.0	706	54.0	1.6	3.74
	-1 SD	2.43	42.2	18.5	648	55.4	1.56	4.06
		2.1	38.9	17.5	532	58.2	1.48	4.71
	-2 SD	1.77	35.6	16.4	416	61.0	1.4	5.36
		1.44	32.3	15.4	300	63.8	1.32	6.01
Line Z	-3 SD	1.11	29.0	14.3	184	66.6	1.24	6.66

CHART B
PSYCHOLOGICAL PROFILE
MALES

Name_____   Date_____

		T. Anx.	S. Anx.	A. Not.	SSA	Ptc.	P.I.	S. Con.
Line X	3 SD	31.3	29.0	99.5	16.9	25.3	111.4	295
		29.5	27.2	87.0	14.8	23.5	106.0	290
	2 SD	27.6	25.3	74.5	12.7	21.7	100.6	285
		25.8	23.5	62.0	10.6	19.9	95.2	280
	1 SD	23.9	21.6	49.5	8.57	18.2	89.7	276
		23.0	20.7	43.3	7.54	17.3	87.0	273
		22.1	19.8	37.0	6.50	16.4	84.3	271
		21.2	18.8	30.8	5.47	15.5	81.6	268
Line Y	MEAN	20.2	17.9	24.5	4.43	14.6	78.9	266
		19.3	17.0	18.3	3.40	13.7	76.2	264
		18.4	16.1	12.0	2.36	12.8	73.5	261
		17.4	15.1	5.8	1.33	11.9	70.8	259
	-1 SD	16.5	14.2	-0.5	0.29	11.0	68.1	256
		14.7	12.4	-13.0	-1.78	9.26	62.6	252
	-2 SD	12.8	10.5	-25.5	-3.85	7.48	57.2	247
		11.0	8.7	-38.0	-5.92	5.70	51.8	242
Line Z	-3 SD	9.1	6.8	-50.5	-7.99	3.90	46.4	237

NAT LIST - Nov. 15, 1979
FIS LIST - Nov. 1, 1979

STRATTON SCHOOL POINT LIST

| | | SLALOM | | GS | | DOWNHILL | | |
AGE	SUBJECT	NAT	FIS	NAT	FIS	NAT	FIS	EASTERN #
14	1	279.78		222.91		259.31		1787555
18	2	143.11		121.54		170.65		2832962
16	3	128.36		128.97		145.65		2100774
12	4	279.78		222.91		247.68		2359131
15	5	119.04	128.33	97.42		151.54		2039436
15	6	209.63		184.13		191.72		2837417
17	7							
18	8	128.58		130.64		151.33		2559441
16	9	98.44	108.82	105.43	119.49	146.89		2656338
18	10	69.56	72.11	53.91	65.03		52.69	2007284
15	11	142.76		145.50		251.54		
16	12	243.96		206.31				2832939
18	13		24.65		24.09		41.64	1116524
16	14	125.69		142.44		171.59		2611127
17	15	377.21		230.17				2832947
17	16		80.19	65.22	76.33	218.34		0860965
16	17	138.34		153.51		237.41		1415009
15	18		124.87		115.32	319.49		1510361
16	19		65.53		74.33	179.89		1344506
19	20	155.76			104.38	36.71	43.53	1033174
19	21	82.03	86.11		42.56	44.68	54.63	2368512
17	22	67.12	89.75		65.70	125.29		2760569
16	23	160.48		146.19		144.72		2705846
15	24	187.42		115.96		129.05		2333441
16	25	106.21	142.91	112.71		79.62	107.99	1755982
18	26	160.41		129.15		176.74		2556579
16	27	131.02		111.41		121.02		2738417
15	28	154.80		152.13		184.61		2310183
19	29	45.31	48.27		37.20		74.33	0646703
17	30	133.23		153.30		180.04		2202067
15	31	155.50		133.26		143.16		2253649
19	32	60.84	85.42	80.38	86.16	302.78		1445382
20	33	50.02	54.42		32.63	115.95		1364363
18	34	42.41	49.33	52.99	56.53	64.73	71.88	2570315
16	35	193.38		157.87		197.62		
16	36	169.41		155.18		120.32		2402014
15	37	190.48		200.67		164.08		2555910
14	38	265.05		210.53		222.91		3032331
16	39	95.12	105.03		56.06	106.43		1376052
19	40	93.86	135.75	89.75	123.47	94.97		1376045
18	41	85.68		73.18	82.28	190.65		1629336
19	42	113.82	118.17	49.24	46.44	113.21		2565869
16	43	161.25		184.96		123.65		2737237
15	44							
16	45	159.68		144.10		125.31		2315737
16	46	89.50	107.51		68.33	102.37		1751692
15	47	168.26		161.70		147.89		2858298
15	48	253.59		355.92		206.08		2793750
17	49	88.42	111.75	95.73	119.04	101.15		1226703
18	50	134.41		134.71				

23

The Effect Of Anxiety And Arousal on Performance "Psyching Them Up, Not Out"

Linda K. Bunker
University of Virginia

Many teachers and coaches believe that the best way to be prepared for a new learning situation, or especially for an athletic contest, is to increase arousal and motivation levels to their maximum. Too often the view is held that if athletes are not "sky high" or "psyched up," they are not mentally prepared to learn or perform. Seldom is it realized that the prepared and self-confident learner or athlete is the relaxed or only moderately aroused individual.

It is now a well established fact that individuals, whether students or athletes, do not necessarily perform all skills most effectively when arousal levels are extremely high. Coaches and teachers must be able to identify the optimal levels of arousal required to produce maximum performance results. Once these levels have been identified it may be possible to determine how best to control and/or manipulate the arousal levels. In general, it has been found that for each and every sport or skill, an individual needs to be aroused to a level above his or her normal, resting state, but not too high. The implication of this concept is obvious, in that persons who are apathetic or under-aroused may require experiences that cause an increase in arousal levels, while performers (especially athletes before game time) whose arousal levels are already quite high may profit most from reducing anxiety.

Measurement of the intensity of arousal can be accomplished through several different systems. The physiological responses to arousal can be assessed through such measures as skeletal muscle functioning and tension, or measures of autonomic activity (including pulse rate, respiration, electro cortical activity and skin conductance). The nature of each separate response varies with the specific stimuli or environmental situation, as well as organic factors within each individual. It is however clear that it is the total organism, the entire person, who responds to arousal or activation.

The early concepts of arousal centered on the notion of "energy mobilization" during stress or emotional situations, originally thought necessary for either defending oneself or fleeing — the fight or flight mechanism. This idea has since been expanded to include the intensity dimension of behavior, or the overall degree of excitation (Duffy, 1951). The degree of internal arousal can be viewed as lying along a continuum from low levels (i.e. during sleep) to high levels (i.e. during great emotional excitement), and can be evaluated by the previously mentioned physiological indices. Unfortunately, the outward manifestations of arousal in terms of its effect on performance, are not as easily observed or placed along a continuum. Oftentimes the high levels and low levels of arousal have similar effects on behavior.

The relationship of arousal and athletic performance is an excellent example of the hypothesized Inverted-U relationship. This concept implies that for optimal performance, each individual must attain an intermediate or moderate level of arousal. At the two extremes, either very low or high arousal levels, the performance or behavior may appear quite similar. For example, a basketball player performing optimally may be able to make 90% of the free throws attempted. But under different conditions may perform at a 60% level of efficiency. Given the Inverted-U hypothesis, this could

152

be the result of either under arousal (X_1) or over arousal (X_2).

BASKETBALL FREETHROW EXAMPLE

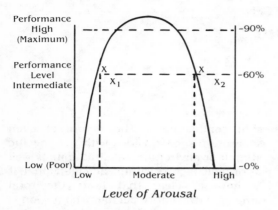

Inverted-U Hypothesis Relating to the Interaction of Arousal and Performance

be used to predict shooting accuracy, and found that if the difference was 9 points or more, shooting percentage was 55%, whereas if 5-8 points differed, shooting percentage was 72%; and if 1-4 points, the percentage fell to 53%.

The impact of specific degrees of activation on performance also appears to be affected by a number of factors, including the nature of the task to be performed, and certain characteristics of the individual. This interaction of individual and situation is a key principle which may account for the unique effect of each individual's performance at what appears to be similar conditions or situations, individuals differ in both the degree of induced arousal, as well as the sensitivity of response (i.e. speed of response and later return to the former level of functioning).

Similarly, the player referred to as a "good practice player," but one who apparently "clutches" or "chokes" at game time, may simply be the player who becomes over aroused. A good coach or teacher would recognize this pattern and help the student learn to control the level of activation in order to maximize performance.

Physiological measurements made in a wide variety of situations have shown correspondence between the degree of arousal and the apparent significance of the situation. This significance is obviously differentially ascribed to a situation by each individual, and related to such things as the incentive value, the perceived danger, the social importance, or the evaluative potential of a situation. For example, we can all identify with the changes in arousal levels and performance when some important figure comes to observe, or when the "arch rival" is the opponent in a contest. On the other hand, low arousal levels can be observed to have a negative effect on such things as the last game of the season when the team is already in last place, or when the basketball score is quite far apart. For example, Ahart (1973) found that for one high school team the score differential could

INDIVIDUAL CONSISTENCY OF RESPONSE

Individuals respond to varying levels of activation in very individualistic ways. Both the degree of arousal and speed of response have been shown to vary from individual to individual (inter-individual variability). However, there is also a great deal of evidence to suggest a level of consistency of response within each individual (intra-individual consistency). That is, individuals who tend to respond with greater intensity in one situation will, in general, respond with greater intensity in other situations when compared with other individuals. Different individuals appear to vary in terms of their central tendency to be responsible with those who are easily aroused, or more responsive, consistently showing their responsiveness in many different forms. These individual levels of responsiveness seem to be quite highly related to the notion of anxiety, and can be discussed in relation to the general "trait anxiety," or over-riding characteristic, of individuals.

A truly stressful situation is not required for these reactions to surface. It is the athlete's perception of the situation that is most important. Whether the explanations for becoming emotionally aroused are realistic or imaginary does not matter. In either situation the reaction will be the same. As athletes grow anxious they will begin to worry. Worry will always relate to a negative state of affairs: What if I lose? Will I be embarrassed? What if I don't play well? Often worry will cause the contest to take on significance far in excess of its true meaning. Often this is simply a result of responding at an emotional rather than at a controlled cognitive level (Meichenbaum, 1975). The result is that the body is stimulated by the brain to go into a state of preparedness for danger which is typically called the "fight or flight" syndrome. This automatic response to perceived danger which was originally handed down to us as a survival mechanism may still be helpful to us in emergency life or death situations. But it is often a detriment to athletes who are attempting to relax and affectively focus their attention during a sport performance.

THE PHYSIOLOGY OF ACTIVATION

As stated above, the concept of arousal or activation can be thought of in terms of both psychological and physiological factors. In relation to the physiological components, activation can be defined as the degree of neural activation with the individual, and this activation is directly related to the arousal function of the reticular activating system (Sage, 1971; Fisher, 1976).

The ascending reticular activating system (ARAS) is a column of nervous tissue which extends upward from the medulla and branches to the thalamus and hypothalamus, and finally into the entire cerebral cortex. This network of nerve fibers is generally stimulated by input from the collateral sensory receptor fibers, and consists of two distinct parts: (1) the brain stem reticular formation responsible for long lasting periods of activation, and (2) the thalamic nuclei responsible for transitory periods of activation.

The descending reticular activating system (DRAS) also plays an important role in controlling motor activity, as it extends downward from the brain stem into the spinal cord. This system stimulates the proprioceptors associated with specific muscles, to cause the muscles to contract.

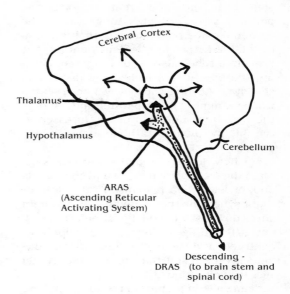

The Interaction of Various Neural Structures in the Activation Process

These two systems, ARAS and DRAS, are both involved in several feedback loops which allow the cortex to control some components of the arousal conditions by either stimulating or suppressing the RAS. It is particularly important to recognize that cognitive processes can therefore be used to exercise control over the RAS and concomitantly to help control the level of individual arousal.

The implications of the effect of the RAS are quite important in relation to motor performance. For example, when athletes perceive a real or imaginary threat, a signal is sent along the ARAS to the posterior hypothalamus which functions as a central switchboard for body and brain action. The hypothalamus releases a hormone that triggers the nearby pituitary gland. The pituitary in response releases the potent hormone ACTH, which transmits a message through the rest of the body and stimulates your adrenal glands which stimulates several endocrinal responses, including an increased release of epinephrine (adrenalin), cortisone, norephinephrine and the consequent increased arousal level.

The accumulated result of the stimulation of the various hormones is to prepare the body for a stressful situation: to stay there and fight, or to flee from the stress. There is a general increase in muscle tension, heartbeat, and breathing rate. The panting allows athletes to eliminate the carbon dioxide building up in their system. In addition, the muscles surrounding the bronchial tubes also tend to tighten, causing the breath rate to become faster and shallower. Anyone who has ever been scared while swimming in deep water understands the resulting shortness of air. In essence, the highly anxious athlete does indeed choke.

But how do these reactions to stress explain the feelings of nausea and cold hands and/or feet? As a response to the fight or flight syndrome the entire digestive system shuts down, since food digestion is not salient at this time. Therefore, the esophogus contracts and the gastric juices stop flowing with the result that many athletes feel sick to their stomach.

Meanwhile in preparing for danger, blood is diverted to the larger muscles which will be required in the "fight or flight." The smaller blood vessels at the extremities and near the surface shut down as a partial defense against bleeding to death. It is this response which causes circulation to slow down and the sensation of cold to be experienced.

Of course the reaction just described would be an extreme response. An athlete would have to be very fearful for it to occur. The "fight or flight" may even be helpful to athletic performance at specific moments in competition but most often the response is a detriment. The tensing of inappropriate muscles and the loss of concentration and rational judgment can definitely disrupt athletic performance.

SPECIFIC EFFECTS OF AROUSAL ON PERFORMANCE

Increased levels of arousal produce a general increase in neurological activation throughout the organism. This effect on neural activity implies that moderate arousal levels may have a facilitating or organizing effect on behavior since neural transmission will be enhanced. On the low end of the arousal continuum, the lack of neural excitation has been hypothesized to inhibit the transmission of impulses, while at the higher levels, arousal over-activates and therefore disrupts the system's ability to integrate sensory input with skillful, purposeful motor output.

The Inverted-U hypothesis has previously been utilized to explain the potential effects of varying levels of activation on arousal and performance. This theory suggests that optimal performance will be possible when arousal levels are moderate, but that with high or low levels, performance will be poor.

Two theories have been suggested to explain the specific influence of arousal on various types of performance: (a) drive theory and (b) the Inverted-U theory. Historically, the drive theory suggested that as drive (and therefore arousal) increased, the dominant response would be emitted (Duffy, 1957; Malmo, 1959). Thus, during early practice or learning, since there is a higher probability that the performance will be incorrect, this dominant, incorrect, response will be emitted, while during performance of well learned skills, the dominant response will generally be the correct response. This principle implies that increased arousal or drive facilitates performance of well-learned skills, but hampers learning or acquisition of new skills, strategies, or applications, and is sometimes referred to as the *dominant response theory.*

The drive reduction theory has some implicit validity based on real experiences. However, it seems to lack hard scientific evidence, since it is difficult to operationally determine both levels of drive and also determine when a task can be classified as well-learned (Martens, 1971, 1977).

This inverted-U hypothesis (originally postulated by Yerkes and Dodson, 1908), has also been used to explain the relative effect of various levels of arousal on easy vs. difficult tasks. As early as 1908, the Yerkes and Dodson Law postulated that "an easily acquired habit, that is, one which does not demand difficult sense discriminations or complex associations, may readily be formed under strong stimulation, whereas a difficult habit may be acquired readily under relatively weak stimulation." This law (although originally written in terms of motivation and not arousal) would indicate that with very difficult motor tasks, arousal should be held reasonably low for maximum performance, while for easier tasks, the arousal level can be raised slightly (Malmo, 1959; Spence and Spence, 1966).

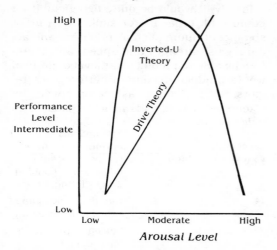

The Relative Effect of Arousal on Performance Based on the Drive Theory Versus the Inverted-U Hypothesis.

Experience as a Modifier. The general effects of increased arousal levels on motor performance have been previously discussed. The negative effects of stress seem to be particularly apparent with beginners, or with performers who are not proficient in performance (Carron, 1965). This may have been predicted since beginners are more likely to make mistakes (there is a high probability of an incorrect response occurring), and therefore the "dominant response" would be elicited when aroused, and in this case it would be detrimental to performance. On the other hand, the dominant response of proficient, well-experienced performers will perhaps be the correct response, and may therefore be facilitated by increased arousal levels (up to a point).

The fact that high arousal levels are not conducive to beginners, or to anyone learning a new skill, has several implications for teaching. During the introduction of new material, or practice of new skills, arousal levels should be held at a low level. Practice and learning sessions should be interesting, well organized and enjoyable. Competitive situations (i.e. games and relays) should be used for motivational purposes with great caution, since the increased individual activation may retard learning and/or performance of the newer skills.

This experience concept can also be used to explain several interesting behaviors of novice vs. experienced athletes. For example, "pre-game jitters" and the approach/avoidance conflict have been reported to be quite different for beginners as compared to advanced wrestlers (Sullivan, 1964). Beginners tend to be quite excited about upcoming contests and generally have high feelings of "approach" the night before, but as the time of the meet draws near, the "approach" response is lowest. On the other hand, experienced performers tend to "save" the maximum approach feelings until the actual time of the competition.

In addition to the actual skill level of the performer, each individual's *self-perception* of competence may also affect the interaction of arousal and performance level. If a performer's self-assessment of his or her skill or preparation for a specific contest is low, the effect of any increase in arousal may be magnified. That is, if the learner is already highly aroused, any increase in arousal may have a detrimental effect on performance or learning potential. This effect may be the direct result of the stress produced by the incongruence of the perceived demand of a situation compared to the perceived capabilities of the individual (McGrath, 1970).

Stress can therefore cause changes in arousal levels, and may be used as a way to evaluate and predict the consequences of certain situations. McGrath (1970) and Martens (1977) have suggested four events which are critical to studying stress:

1. the individual's perception of the demands of a situation and his/her response choices
2. the physical or social environment
3. the organism's actual response
4. the response consequences

Another concept related to the second factor listed above deals with the individual's *social perception* while performing. A great deal of information is now available which relates to "social facilitation" effects on performance. For example, it has been shown that beginners tend to perform at lower levels when other people are present, especially if they are serving in an evaluative capacity. On the other hand, more proficient athletes may respond positively to socially facilitating situations. A similar finding exists when proficient athletes attempt to perform newly acquired skills while

156

under competitive stress and find their performances inhibited. These results may be directly affected by the increased arousal levels caused by the changed social situations.

Task demands and situational characteristics modify arousal and performance interactions. According to the Yerkes-Dodson Law, simple tasks can be performed well when drive is high, compared to complex tasks which are performed better at lower levels of drive. Unfortunately, the specific effects of arousal are not clearly addressed by this law, but have been subsequently studied.

The relative level of task complexity is a critical variable in evaluating the interaction of arousal and performance. The dominant response theory has already been discussed, and indicated that under stressful or highly aroused conditions, the most probable or dominant response will be elicited. As tasks become more complex, it becomes less likely that the dominant response will be of high quality (especially during early learning).

The specific nature of the task also has an effect on the interaction of arousal and performance. It has been shown that high levels of arousal affect balance and precision tasks more negatively than skills requiring strength or power.

The stories of almost un-human feats of strength after tragic accidents (i.e. examples of mothers lifting cars off trapped children) seem to reflect the generally facilitative effect of arousal on strength. In terms of athletic feats, this concept would suggest that skills requiring pure strength (i.e. maximum weight lifting, performing an iron cross in gymnastics, etc.) or pure speed (100 meter swim or run) may be performed maximally under higher arousal levels.

The somewhat oversimplified generalization that high levels of arousal may facilitate tasks requiring strength and speed, must be carefully and cautiously applied to most motor skills, since there are few skills in sporting situations which require massive strength alone. Most performance tasks require some degree of accuracy and/or decision making, from the preceding discussion it is obvious that these skills may be interfered with if arousal levels are too high. For example, a defensive lineman in football must be mentally alert and pre-

pared to make split second decisions, as well as produce strength and power.

Ideally, it would be quite beneficial if we could rank order motor skills in terms of some continuum such as precision and accuracy vs. strength and speed, and therefore be able to predict what level of arousal would produce maximum performance results. Such a listing has been proposed by Oxendine (1970) and an example is provided below:

Level of Arousal	Sports Skills most optimally performed
#5 (extremely high)	football blocking, consecutive pushing, weight lifting, etc.
#4	running long jump, races, judo, wrestling
#3	boxing, gymnastics, basketball
#2	baseball pitchers and batters, fencers, driver
#1 (slightly aroused)	archery, bowling, golf strokes, precision ice-skating

Unfortunately, such a classification system, based on strength and accuracy, does not adequately take into account such things as task complexity, perceptual requirements of the skill, cognitive decision-making components, etc. In addition, many "sports" contain many different skills and/or requirements, which may respond differently to arousal. For example, the basketball defensive skills may be very different than offensive skills such as shooting, dribbling, and rebounding.

It has been suggested that the nature of the task, in terms of all requirements, in-

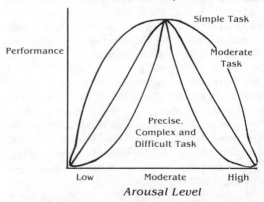

The hypothesized effect of task difficulty and arousal levels on performance (modified from Fiske and Maddi (1961) and Martens (1977).

cluding difficulty, might change the shape of the inverted-U curve. Fiske and Maddi (1961) have suggested that the more difficult the task the narrower the inverted-U, and consequently the smaller the range of arousal levels which will produce optimal results. This concept suggests the complex interaction of such things as strength or energy requirements combined with task difficulty to even further reduce the range of optimal arousal. The implications here are obvious, with certain sports skills, i.e. gymnastics apparatus activities, which are high in both dimensions, being particularly difficult to attain.

In addition to the specific characteristics of the task, the *environment* in which the task is to be performed may also affect its level of execution. If performance is to take place in a new or strange environment, this may add to the general arousal level of the performer. The implication for educators is obvious. Participants should be given accurate and complete information about the environment, or preferably, be given an opportunity to practice in the new situation (i.e. college teams try to arrive at least one day early in order to practice at the opposition court or field). This becomes particularly critical when arousal may be in part due to the unknown quality of equipment to be used (i.e. different characteristics of diving boards, tennis court surfaces, artificial lighting, synthetic turfs, etc.).

Individual personality factors also effect the interaction of arousal and performance. For example, high anxiety vs. low anxiety, extroversion vs. introversion, high need achievement vs. low need achievement, etc., are all potential interactive personality variables. The interference effects of highly emotional, arousing situations has a greater effect on tense or highly anxious persons than on persons with lower anxiety levels.

The explanations for the divergent reactions of persons of varying personality structures are very complex. One of the key factors may be the fact that different situations are perceived differently by each individual. That is, the goals and motivations may be entirely different! The elements in any situation can affect individuals in many different ways depending on the predisposition and past experiences of each performer. The implications for this fact are obvious. No single situation will be received with equal arousal potential within each individual. Group "psych-up" techniques and pep talks designed to increase all arousal levels must therefore be critically evaluated. Not only is it likely that they do not generate the same increased activation in each performer, but even if they did, it would probably mean that some individuals would be aroused beyond their optimal level, while others may remain underaroused.

The concept of individual differences must be of paramount importance. Conditions which facilitate performance for some learners, may be detrimental to others. Many sport psychologists now believe that many of the team oriented motivational techniques may be more harmful than good.

An individual's unique personality can have a marked impact on athletic performance. This influence has generally been thought to be the result of either transient shifts in personality patterns, (i.e. *state* model), or as a result of latent, stable dispositions (*trait* model). In general then, personality variables are often conceived to reflect either stable traits, or transient states.

Traits have been thought to reflect internal determinants of behavior, which are general and enduring predispositions to respond, and do not vary in relation to specific situations, or specific stimuli (Allport, 1937; Cattell, 1957, 1965). These basic units of personality are thought to provide for the consistency and relative predictability in human behavior. Trait theorists would therefore believe that the principle determinants of behavior lie within each individual and remain relatively stable over various situations.

Unfortunately, however, we now recognize that personality factors seem to vary in relation to specific situations, and that conversely, situational factors must be considered in interpreting personality. Situations therefore influence behavior both by providing a set of stimuli which provoke responses, and also as specific environmental conditions which prescribe certain actions in order to meet the demands of the situation (Icheiser, 1943). This theory of personality conceives of *state,* or *immediate,* environmental conditions as a major determinant of personality. In its extreme form, this belief in environmental influences may be called *situationism,* and emphasizes that situational factors are the prime determinants of behavior.

Modern social theory tends to recognize a compromise position which suggests there is a reciprocal *interaction* between each individual situation and each unique person (Endler, 1977). It is obvious then that the issue is not a question of individual personal factors versus external situational determinants, but rather a question of "How do experiences or situations interact with individual characteristics in shaping behavior?"

Anxiety. As a personality variable, anxiety has been felt to have a tremendous impact on behavior and performance. Anxiety itself has been described and defined in various ways, including "an emotional state, with the subjectively experienced quality of fear or a closely related emotion (terror, horror, alarm, fright, panic, trepidation, dread, scare)" (Lewis, 1970, p. 77). This emotion of anxiety may be accompanied by performance decrements, manifest bodily disturbances, and physiological states of activation. Anxiety, arousal and activation have sometimes been used interchangeably. They do however refer to slightly different concepts. Martens (1971) has differentiated between the concepts by stating that arousal refers to the intensity dimension of behavior, which may vary on a continuum from deep sleep to intense excitement. This arousal is very similar to the terms activation and energy mobilization. State anxiety on the other hand can be used to refer to both the intensity and direction of an event, and is always felt to have a negative effect.

Each individual is thought to have a certain level of internal anxiety which is specific to their own personality constellation and reflects a chronic predisposition or trait (A-trait), as contrasted to a component of transitory emotional functioning (A-state) (Cattell and Scheier, 1961; Speilberger, 1966, 1972). The temporary state of anxiety is generally categorized by consciously perceived levels of tension and apprehension which may be linked to various autonomic nervous system reactions (i.e. increased heart rate, elevated blood pressure and rapid respiration rate). This two-process concept of anxiety is sometimes referred to as Spielberger's state-trait theory (Spielberger, Gorusch and Lushene, 1970) which emphasizes the interaction of personal charac-

teristics with certain situational characteristics. For example, persons who are high in A-trait anxiety perceive ego involving situations as threatening and therefore respond with higher A-state arousal than would persons with low A-trait anxiety levels. It has also been shown that highly anxious individuals tend to be characterized as self-centered, and focused on self-worry and self-evaluation in a very cognitive fashion.

In tennis for example, we would predict an interaction between the A-trait facets of social evaluation and the "congruent" ego threatening or social evaluation facets of a competitive tennis match, and therefore produce increases in A-state. Simultaneously we would predict that the A-state increases would be greater for higher A-trait athletes than low A-trait participants, (Martens, 1977).

One new concept which may prove to be quite significant in relation to sport is the notion of Competitive Anxiety (Martens, 1977). This concept refers to a "tendency to perceive competitive situations as threatening and to respond to these situations with feelings of apprehension or tension" (Martens, 1977, p. 23). The Sport Competition Anxiety Test (SCAT; Martens, 1977) has been designed to assess this *trait*. There is some evidence that this trait may be a critical component in determining the relationship between sport and anxiety, and/or arousal, since in a competitive situation high competitive A-trait persons will manifest higher levels of A-state than low competitive A-trait persons.

Individuals who are exceptionally responsive to the environment will continue to vary in their own response levels based on the personally ascribed importance of the situations. The general tendency toward a high degree of arousal does not in itself determine which aspects of the environment will be positively responded to or approached, versus those situational events which will be avoided, or which will cause large increases in arousal levels. Each individual's tendency toward responsiveness may also be related to the development of aggression or withdrawal, enthusiasm or anxiety. For example, it has been shown that stress has a greater negative effect on balancing ability (Carron, 1965) and steadiness (Eysenck and Gillen, 1965) for high versus low anxious males, especially during early learning. Overall, in tasks with low difficulty, high anxious subjects were found to be superior to low anxious performers, whereas low anxious performers tend to do better on new or difficult tasks (Carron, 1965).

Since it has already been established that situational and motivational factors such as anxiety have a marked influence on performers, it is important to deal with the interaction of each individual performer in various situations. That is, we must determine how the athlete peceives a particular situation in order to determine its potential impact on performance. If a person who is high on social evaluation A-trait perceives a particular situation to be one in which social evaluation is likely to occur, we know that his A-state is likely to increase. If this increase proved to be detrimental to performance, it might be wise to aid the performer in re-evaluating or altering his perception of the situation or shifting his focus to task orientation (i.e. through modeling, positive reinforcement, cognitive reappraisal) (Meichenbaum, 1975). It thus becomes important for education to carefully evaluate all three factors in each activity: the individual, the task situation, and the interaction of the team.

Anxiety among specific sport groups. A great deal of research has been conducted to determine if athletes differ from non-athletes in terms of anxiety. When all athletes are considered, it is generally felt that as a group they represent a normal range of A-trait levels (see Hardman, 1973 for an excellent review). Similarly, individual versus team-sport participants do not seem to differ, neither do contact versus non-contact athletes (Hardman, 1973). Another interesting finding has been that beginners have higher anxiety levels than superior athletes. In addition, Ogilvie (1968) has also suggested that superior athletes are emotionally more stable, and have greater resistance to emotional stress. Unfortunately, several other researchers have evaluated the literature to conclude essentially no differences in A-trait between varying skill-leveled participants on non-participants (Martens, 1977).

In general it is now believed that highly anxious performers may require calming down rather than "psyching up." But unfortunately, the overly anxious athlete often is accused of lack of motivation or not being "ready" because of their poorer performance. Coaches and teachers often mis-diagnose the cause of this decrease in level of attainment and attempt to increase the motivational drive or stressors, and thereby cause even worse performance. It is a vicious cycle — poor performance causes greater stress which causes even poorer performance (Sage, 1971; Fisher, 1976).

ESTABLISHING DESIRED AROUSAL LEVELS

The inverted-U hypothesis has been proposed as an explanation for the non-linear affect of arousal on performance. In the earlier example, it was shown that basketball players may shoot 60% of their free throws under either of two arousal levels, slightly underaroused or slightly overaroused. The teacher or coach must therefore attempt to ascertain the particular athlete's arousal level. One approach might be to systematically increase or decrease the arousal level and observe changes in performance. If performance improves with increased arousal, the initial level would be determined to be less than optimal. On the other hand, if performance deteriorates, it might be suspected that the earlier level was already too high for maximum performance or learning.

Several factors have been discussed and must be understood in order to identify the effects of various levels of arousal on performance:

1. Individual personality traits of each performer (i.e. trait anxiety);
2. Initial level of learning (i.e. beginner vs. advanced performer);
3. Task requirements, including: complexity, physical fitness demands, accuracy or precision demands;
4. New or unusual environmental factors;
5. Self-perception or self-assessment of the individual's competence;
6. Social-facilitation effects on arousal and therefore performance;

The implications here should be obvious to both the teacher and coach. In order to expect both optimal learning or acquisition of new skills, or performance of formerly learned skills, the evaluation and adjustment of arousal levels must be a conscious consideration. The following sections are therefore devoted to a discussion of techniques which may be used to control or alter individual activation levels with the emphasis on techniques designed to help athletes lower arousal levels.

DEALING WITH ANXIETY AND AROUSAL IN SPORT

As the popularity and the importance of sport has grown over the last decade more and more athletes are in need of techniques designed to help them regulate their emotions. For far too long coaches and athletes have been led to believe that increasing their arousal level would improve their level of performance. The result has been a very high percentage of athletes who never reach their athletic potential because of an inability to deal with anxiety.

Concentration is a necessity for success in athletics at an advanced level. It is quite impossible to truly concentrate when one is anxious or tense. To concentrate one must be relaxed and able to focus attention on the present. Thoughts which focus attention on the past or future are distracting and detrimental to attention (Bunker and Rotella, 1977).

Inexperienced competitors are often intimidated by an opponent's calculated display of confidence. Often, such individuals find it difficult to relax and be as self-assured as desired. Consequently, these athletes do not perform as well as they might. Excess tension results in many athletes being unable to move in a free and relaxed fashion which characterizes the performance in a more relaxed situation. It is therefore imperative that you have confidence in your players.

Similarly, sport experiences must emphasize the positive. The practice environment should lead the young athlete to leave practice with feelings of pride rather than shame. By utilizing this approach to coaching, we will motivate athletes to continue to be attracted to sports participation. Furthermore, the athletes coached in this manner are likely to be desirous of learning what their weaknesses or mistakes are and be willing to work to improve on them. Don't threaten — encourage!

Young athletes have had a limited range of experiences. They do not yet know if they possess great, average, or poor athletic ability. The youngsters who are constantly told by the coach that they are talented, and are made to feel that way often will start believing that they are, indeed, very talented. The athletes who believe they are talented will often perform as if they are — a self-fulfilling prophecy. What the athletes believe about themselves is often more important than the ability each individual actually has.

Initially the young athlete should receive frequent and consistent reinforcements in the form of verbal praise, pats on the back, and smiles of approval for their efforts. An abundance of criticism will cause the child to lose confidence in his ability and therefore lower his level of aspiration. It takes a special kind of coach to be able to find something good to say to each child. Anyone can find a way to crush a child's ego with — "Lyn, you blockhead, can't you catch anything but a cold" or "Oh brother, we've got butterfingers Bobbie on our team." Such comments can have a devastating effect on the young athlete's self-concept and desire to participate.

It is critical that we find ways to make all children feel good about themselves, even if it is only in relation to how well they look in their uniform, or how well they run the bases or block. With time however, positive reinforcement and rewards should be handed out with greater selectivity, and less frequently. Praise should be given only when the young athlete has improved, and truly deserves it. This approach will increase the athlete's motivation to achieve, and will make the coach's rewards more significant. The result should be an increase in the effort and enthusiasm displayed in practice and games.

Many colleges and professional coaches tend to use criticism, sarcasm, threats, and punishment to motivate their teams. The youth coach must recognize that there are important differences between the way high level athletes can be motivated and the techniques most effective for young athletes. The frequent use of threats and punishment can have a very detrimental effect on the young athlete. Few athletes at this time in life have the overabundance of confidence necessary for these techniques to be effective motivators.

If situations arise in which threats or punishments must be used, be certain that they are appropriate and follow through with them. Threats of punishments may be somewhat useful if the athletes are winning consistently and are becoming overconfident and less coachable. This approach should most certainly be the exception rather than the rule.

Awards and motivation. Youth sport teams typically provide a wide variety of awards in the form of trophies, plaques, jackets, ribbons, certificates, etc., to motivate team members to practice harder. We must carefully consider the possible positive and negative effects of these rewards on both the immediate and future performances of young athletes. Athletes who participate in sport because they really enjoy it, wish to master and have control of the skills, or display and feel competent are likely to practice diligently over extended periods and perform at a higher level. These athletes are considered to be internally controlled and self-motivated, in contrast to athletes who participate mainly for some reward. Participants who play because of external rewards are extrinsically controlled, and not as likely to be as highly self-directed as the internally controlled athletes.

Most children enter into youth sports with a high level of intrinsic motivation. It appears that a child's intrinsic motivation might be detrimentally affected by the frequent distribution of awards that is so commonplace in today's youth sport programs. Most likely we are unintentionally causing many youth who were originally intrinsically motivated and attracted to sport to become extrinsically motivated.

The extrinsically motivated child would be apt to display an increase in immediate performance when awards are presented. Extrinsic rewards for children under seven years appear to be quite effective. At this young age reward is viewed as a bonus. But after the age of seven, children begin to view rewards given merely for participating as a bribe which causes a motivational decrement. In addition, the long range effects of extrinsic motivation are not nearly as appealing as are the effects of intrinsic motivation. It would be expected that the extrinsically motivated child would withdraw from participating if the rewards were eliminated. Hopefully, the youth sport coach recognizes that lifelong performance and enjoyment are more important than temporary goals.

Unfortunately, many young athletes never benefit from these rewards. Many do not perceive themselves as having the ability to ever attain the awards. If we desire to help each athlete reach his maximal potential it would appear quite important to make it possible for each child to receive an award, or better yet, to set individual goals. At the beginning of the season the coach should sit down with each athlete and together with the young athlete set down specific individualized goals which must be attained in order to earn the desired award. Care should be taken to insure that each child must practice diligently in order to achieve the award, and that the goals, are not so difficult that the child who expands an abundance of effort cannot attain them.

In general, children over the age of seven should not be presented with awards for merely participating. Awards given on the basis of individually established, and short term goals based on the quality of performance, tend to increase intrinsic motivation as long as the child believes he is physically able to attain the award.

Reducing anxiety in children. Sports by their very nature contain many elements which are likely to produce anxiety. Whenever a young athlete is faced with a competitive situation, anxiety in the form of doubts as to the outcome of the contest are apt to surface. This uncertainty about the outcome causes many of us to spend the days and nights prior to a contest worrying about whether or not our skills are sufficient to allow us to win. A second element found to produce anxiety in all sports is strategy. All teams plan and practice strategies supposedly designed to ensure success. Much anxiety is produced due to concern over the effectiveness of these strategies.

A third element inherent in any sport which is likely to cause anxiety is luck. The outcome of any sport contest may be influenced to varying degrees by good or bad "breaks." Luck may take the form of a good or bad bounce, an unfortunate injury, a mistaken call by the umpire or referee, a gust of wind, or the sun getting in the athlete's eyes. Whatever shape luck may take, it is always unpredictable. If we think about it rationally, we would realize that the good and bad breaks will, by the law of averages, eventually even out. Unfortunately, most of us dwell on the bad breaks we receive rather than the good breaks. Bad luck accounts for many losses, but wins are usually because we worked harder! By blaming luck for our defeats we may allow our emotions to control us — a situation which can be detrimental to one's athletic performance as well as one's ability to make coaching decisions effectively.

The overly anxious athlete will not be able to concentrate or focus attention on the appropriate object. The player may begin to worry about what others are thinking or become too cognitively involved, as attention drifts. During competition the athlete's attention becomes misdirected. The overtly anxious athlete may direct attention to the actual mechanics of the task, or on the anticipated consequences of poor performance. "What will others think of me if I lose?" "Does my coach think I'm terrible?" "Are my friends laughing at me?" "Am I letting my teammates down?" "Will my parents be upset with me?" The athlete who has been performing poorly may also further impair his or her performance by worrying about the effectiveness of their skill techniques. The more often the basketball shooter misses, the more she worries about her elbow position, wrist position, follow-through, or the more often he worries about the spin of the ball, or who he's supposed to block out for the rebound. The more the athletes worry about these problems the more their concentration will be misdirected which will result in a continued decrease in performance. Clearly, it becomes a circular problem.

The coach should be sure that practice sessions are designed so as to allow each team member to acquire new skills and build confidence. Care should be taken to encourage enthusiasm and avoid frustration for each athlete. We must remember that young athletes develop to their potential at different ages. We must be sure to avoid emotionally upsetting the young athlete who might not be very highly skilled.

Whenever new skills are being learned, practice drills should be conducted in a relaxed atmosphere. Fans and/or parents should be discouraged from attending practices until skills have been well mastered. An audience can have a very detrimental impact on the learning of new skills. Likewise, competitive drills should not be incorporated into practice plans until an advanced skill level has been attained.

Additionally, it appears most appropriate that in the initial stages of skill acquisition, the young athletes be encouraged to experiment with the skills, and be given opportunities to try to figure out on their own how to perform or apply the skills in new situations (i.e. problem solving). As the athletes explore and attempt to perform the skills the coach should give verbal feedback and encouragement to each athlete. The athlete should be told which aspects of the skill he is performing correctly, followed by corrections and refinements of the skills. As the skills improve, refinements and demonstrations of correct skill execution, as well as opportunities for practicing the skills correctly, should be provided. By requiring the active problem-solving involvement of each athlete, and by ensuring an environment which will maximize success for all, anxiety and frustration which can interfere with skill development and performance will be eliminated.

In summary — We must psych ourselves and others up, not over and out!

REFERENCES

Ahart, F. C. *The effect of score differential on basketball free throw shooting efficiency.* Unpublished Master's project, Ithaca College, New York, 1973.

Allport, G. W. *Personality: A psychological interpretation.* New York: Holt, 1937.

Bunker, L. K. and Rotella, R. J. Getting them up, not uptight. In Thomas J. R. (Ed.) *Youth sports guide for coaches and parents.* Washington, D.C.: AAHPER Publications, 1977.

Carron, A. V. *Complex motor skill performance under conditions of externally induced stress.* Unpublished Master's thesis, University of Alberta, 1965.

Cattell, R. B. *Personality and motivation structure and measurement.* Yonkers-on-Hudson, New York: World Book, 1957.

Cattell, R. B. *The scientific analysis of personality.* Chicago, Illinois: Aldine, 1965.

Cattell, R. B. and Scheier, I. H. *The meaning and measurement of neuroticism* and anxiety. New York: Ronald, 1961.

Duffy, E. The concept of energy mobilization. *Psychological Review,* 1951, *58,* 30-40.

Duffy, E. The Psychological significance of the concept of "Arousal" or "Activation." *Psychological Review,* 1957, *64,* 265-275.

Endler, N. S. A person situation interaction model for anxiety. In D. C. Spielberger and I. G. Sarason (Eds.) *Stress and anxiety* (Vol. 1). Washington, D.C.: Hemisphere Publishing Corp. (Wiley), 1975.

Endler, N. S. The role of person by situation interaction in personality theory. In I. C. Uzgiris and F. Weizmann (Eds.), *The structuring of experience.* New York: Plenum Press, 1977.

Endler, N. S. and Okada, M. A multidimensional measure of trait anxiety: The S-R Inventory of General Trait Anxiousness. *Journal of Consulting and Clinical Psychology,* 1975, *43,* 319-329.

Eysenck, H. J. and Gillen, P. W. *Facts and fiction in psychology.* Baltimore, Md.: Penguin, 1965.

Fisher, A. C. *Psychology of sport.* Palo Alto, Cal.: Mayfield Publishing Co., 1976.

Fiske, D. W. and Maddi, S. R. (Eds.) *Functions of varied experience.* Homewood, Illinois: Dorsey, 1961.

Hardman, K. A dual approach to the study of personality and performance in sport. In H. T. A. Whiting, K. Hardman, L. B. Hendry and M. G. Jones. *Personality and performance in physical education and sport.* London: H. Kimpton Publishers, 1973.

Icheiser, G. Misinterpretations of personality in everyday life and the psychologist's frame of reference. *Character and Personality,* 1943, *12,* 145-160.

Lewis, A. The ambiguous word "Anxiety." *International Journal of Psychiatry,* 1970, *9,* 62-79.

Malmo, R. B. Activation: A neuro-psychological dimension. *Psychological Review,* 1959, *66,* 367-386.

Martens, R. Anxiety and motor performance: A review. *J. Motor Behavior,* 1971, *3,* 161-179.

Martens, Rainer. *Sport competition anxiety test.* Champaign, Ill.: Human Kinetics Publishers, 1977.

Meichenbaum, D. H. A self-instructional approach to stress management. A proposal for stress innoculation training. In C. D. Speilberger and I. G. Sarason (Eds.),

Stress and anxiety (Vol. 1). Washington, D.C.: Hemisphere Publishing Corporation (Wiley), 1975.

McGrath, J. E. A conceptual formulation for research on stress. In J. E. McGrath (Ed.), *Social and psychological factors in stress.* New York: Holt, Rinehart and Winston, 1970.

Ogilvie, B. Psychological consistencies within the personality of high level competitors. *J. American Medical Association,* 1968, *205,* 780-786.

Oxendine, J. B. Emotional arousal and motor performance. *Quest,* 1970, XIII, (Winter), 18-22.

Sage, G. H. *Introduction to motor behavior: A neuropsychological approach.* Reading, Mass.: Addison-Wesley, 1971.

Spence, J. T. and Spence, K. W. The motivational components of manifest anxiety: Drive and drive stimuli. In Spielberger, C. D. (Ed.), *Anxiety and behavior.* New York: Academic Press, 1966.

Spiegel, H. Spectrum of hypnotic and non-hypnotic phenomena. *American Journal of Clinical Hypnosis,* 1963, July.

Spielberger, C. D. The effects of anxiety on complex learning and academic achievement. In C. D. Spielberger (Ed.), *Anxiety and behavior.* New York: Academic Press, 1966.

Spielberger, C. D. Anxiety as an emotional state. In C. D. Spielberger (Ed.), *Anxiety: Current trends in theory and research* (Vol. 1). New York: Academic Press, 1972.

Spielberger, C. D., Gorsuch, R. L., and Lushene, R. E. *Manual for the state-trait anxiety inventory.* Palo Alto, Calif.: Consulting Psychologist Press, 1970.

Sullivan, E. Emotional reactions and grip strength in college wrestlers as a function of time competition. Unpublished Master's thesis, University of Massachusetts, 1964.

Suinn, R. H. Behavior rehearsal for ski racers. *Behavior Therapy,* 1972, *3,* (No. 519).

Suinn, R. H. Muscle relaxation exercise for athletes. *Nordic Sports Medicine Journal,* 1972, *3.*

Suinn, R. H. Anxiety management training for general anxiety. *The innovative therapies: Critical and creative contributions,* in R. M. Swinn and R. G. Weigal (Eds.), New York: Harper and Row, 1975.

Suinn, R. H. Visual motor behavior rehearsal for adaptive behavior. In J. Krumboltz and K. Thoresen (Eds.) *Counseling Methods.* New York: Hold, Rinehart and Win-

164

ston, 1976.

Suinn, R. H. Body thinking: Psychology for Olympic champs. *Psychology Today,* 1976, July, 38-43.

Yerkes, R. and Dodson, J. The relation of strength of stimulus to rapidity of habit formation. *J. Comparative Neurology and Psychology,* 1908, *18,* 459-482.

Julie Heyward. Charlottesville. Va.

24

Problems Of Aggression In Sport

Dorothy V. Harris
Pennsylvania State University

What do we mean when we say, "He's an aggressive athlete?" Is this a desirable trait? We speak of aggressive salesmen, of aggressive women, of aggressive professionals. Are we complimenting them or are we criticizing them? Violent, aggressive behavior in sport has become a real problem in today's society. Professional sport has provided the model for collegiate, high school, and even pee wee league sport. Is sport just reflecting society's general attitudes toward violence as a way of resolving conflict? Can we expect sport to be different from society in general with regard to aggression and violence?

One cannot read the sports page or view sports on television without acknowledging that violent, aggressive behavior in sport is escalating. The problem appears more severe in team sports. Popular sports magazines have published articles on brutality in football. Basketball and even baseball have both had their share of physical aggression and injury. Ice hockey is another sport that hardly has a game played that does not include some aggressive, violent action. When one hockey player was charged with a felony for his behavior on the ice the sports world exploded. The reaction was that the courts have no right to interfere.

The severity of the problem can be seen in the attitudes of participants. One coach said "We have to police our own." "We do not have to go to court." "I do not think the law can dispense justice in sports," while another said "If they cut down violence too much, people won't come out to watch." "It is a reflection of our society." "People want to see violence."

Physical brutality has now invaded women's sports. The injury rate has increased tremendously with increasing in-terest and support of women's sports. Last spring at the U.S. Women's Lacrosse tournament many players were walking around with broken noses, facial lacerations, broken or lost teeth, etc. How did sport get to this point? Can we change it? If so, how?

Eysenck (1975), commenting on the so-called "killer instinct" that some say is essential for athletic success, said, "The drive stimuli of the killer instinct are those feelings that you would experience if you hated your opponent and wanted to kill him." "But, killing your opponent is one thing, beating him in tennis another, and the habits appropriate to the former are in-appropriate for the latter. In fact, they interfere with it and performance suffers." John Paul Scott put it another way when he said that one of the first principles of competitive sport is that a person who loses his temper is likely to lose the game either because he loses his judgment or through violation of the rules.

Aggression in sport has not been studied systematically; most of the discussion and writing about it has been based on general work in psychology on aggressive behavior. As a result, the theories of aggression in sport are the same theories that psychologists use for general aggression. The major theories are: (1) aggression is innate or instinctive; (2) the frustration-aggression theory; and (3) aggression is a learned form of behavior. Research has generated more support for the social learning theory of aggression than other theories. This theory also has implication for sport.

Once aggressive responses have been acquired, a number of different conditions and factors operate to ensure their persistence. As long as these acts provide important tangible rewards, the behavior will continue. Continued social reward and approval will also insure the continuation of aggressive behavior. One of the primary means of maintaining the behavior is to "pat oneself on the back." Another is reinforcement. As an example, think what reinforcement 80,000 people give to a defensive lineman who has just wiped out the quarterback!

fans

Perhaps the most important implication for the social learning theory is the optimistic framework for creating situations where aggressive behavior is not tolerated, therefore never learned. Further, since aggression is viewed as a learned form of behavior, it can be modified or unlearned through many procedures. Social learning theorists do not view human beings as constantly driven toward violent behavior; they believe that aggression occurs only under specific conditions that tend to facilitate such a response. Thus, it is argued that if the conditions are altered, aggression may be prevented or reduced.

Aggressive behavior is frequently elicited by conditions of the social environment. Frustration has been considered the social antecedent of aggression most often. Sport provides many situations where the blocking of ongoing, goal-directed behavior serves as a catalyst to aggression. The action of Woody Hayes during the bowl game of Ohio State in 1978 is a good example of that.

Direct provocation from others, especially physical provocation, tends to make individuals who are already aroused, reciprocate in a similar fashion. Sport provides many such situations. Also, exposure to aggressive models serves as a catalyst for overt aggression.

Environmental factors such as loud and irritating noises, uncomfortably warm temperatures, crowded conditions, and behavior of others around, also generate aggressive behavior. Individual and personal conditions set the stage for aggressive behavior as well. An athlete under the influence of drugs, medication, alcohol, marijuana, or even an injury can have his or her arousal state altered beyond control. Behavior under these conditions may be entirely different from the normal behavior of an athlete.

While the current situation involving aggression and violence associated with sport is far from encouraging, the fact remains that socialization through games and sport can provide effective methods for the control of these behaviors if social learning theory is put into practice. According to John Paul Scott, games and sports provide ways of organizing life along non-violent directions. Games and sports learned in childhood and adolescence create opportunities for practice and training in living according to group rules. However, adult intervention and control effectively prevent this socialization from occurring when they make all the rules and do all the decision-making for the children.

In addition to providing situations where children can learn social interaction and decision-making in non-threatening ways, games and sports can psychologically influence behavior in another manner. Disallowing overt physical aggression is a strong inhibitor to fighting. The best way to control aggressive behavior is never to allow it to occur, to be learned, in the first place!

Modifying the rules so the penalty for aggressive behavior is not worth the risk, also inhibits aggressive behavior. This would take the cooperation of all to enforce; there are examples of this approach being utilized in the changes of some of the rules in football.

Continued pressure on the media to eliminate the over-play and replay of violent action in sport must become the responsibility of all of us. This would contribute to the decrease in the modeling effect that television has in influencing children's behavior. If they see professional athletes demonstrate aggressive behavior and get rewarded for it through attention, replays, etc., children begin to think that is the way to behave as a professional.

In conclusion, perhaps sport and/or play can help in teaching individuals not to be aggressive, to assist in teaching them to control aggression. Aggression in sport is not simply determined, it involves many conditions and previous experiences. It may be the result of frustration, pain, previously learned behavior, or modeling. To learn more about predicting who might be overtly aggressive we need to know something about the aggressor, the situation, and the target of the aggression.

It is clear that competitive sport has many inherent qualities that make participation frustrating and many conditions

168

that are conducive to aggressive behavior. The encouraging aspect of the problem is that behavioral research demonstrates that individuals learn to be aggressive, therefore they can also learn to give non-aggressive responses in aggressive situations. When individuals observe non-violent behavior and are reinforced for such behavior, they are likely to continue to behave non-violently. Therein lies perhaps our only hope for saving sport. Our goals must be to model non-violent behavior, to reward non-violence, and to no longer tolerate violence of any form in sport.

REFERENCES

Eysenck, M. W. (1975). Arousal and speed of recall. *British Journal of Social and Clinical Psychology, 45,* 269-277.

Scott, J. P. Source unknown.

25

Aggression In Sport

B. Thomas Duquette
University of Virginia

Participation in sport at some level or to some degree is a nearly universal phenomenon in America today. For many this participation is directed toward the primary goal of besting an opponent. At issue in this paper is not whether this emphasis on winning is good or bad; rather it is accepted that at certain levels of competition winning is the goal, and certain behaviors are necessary to attain it. Primary among these is aggression. The immediate impact of the word and its behavioral connotations is negative. It is difficult to deny, however, that in certain sports, at least as their rules stand today, aggressive behavior is essential for success. If such behavior is requisite for success, what can be done to increase the frequency with which it is manifested properly? To answer this question it must first be understood what aggression is, where it comes from, and how it becomes exhibited. These questions will be answered from a social learning perspective, and hopefully their answers will shed some light on the teaching of situationally specific aggression.

Baron (1977) defines aggression as "any form of behavior directed toward the goal of harming or injuring another living being who is motivated to avoid such treatment" (p. 7). It should be noted that this definition does not preclude psychological harm or injury. Viewed initially within the context of this definition it seems difficult to argue that aggression is an acceptable behavior anywhere, even in the athletic arena. Zillman (1977) has dichotomized aggression in a way which makes it more relevant to sport. He speaks of "annoyance-motivated" and "incentive-motivated" aggression. The former deals with aggressive behavior undertaken in response to an aversive stimulus; the latter with aggressive actions performed in the pursuit of a goal. Here the

goal is of primary importance and the injury caused in its achievement is incidental. In sport, where the goal is winning, the second half of this dichotomy seems particularly pertinent. Aggression is a most effective means to a very specific end.

Prior to analyzing aggression as a social learning phenomenon a brief look at two other theories of aggression is warranted. Historically aggression was first viewed as an instinctive behavior. Freud (1920) explained aggression as the necessary redirection of man's desire for self-destruction. Ethologist Konrad Lorenz (1966) in his best-selling book *On Aggression* hypothesizes that aggressive behavior is the result of an accumulated and innate drive to aggress in conjunction with an appropriate aggression releasing stimulus. An interesting adjunct to this is his explanation for the level of man's destructiveness. He reasons that man, since he is not equipped with the physical tools to do harm (claws, teeth, etc.), did not develop any form of submissive behavior which would allow an encounter to end short of the death of one of the participants. In instinct theory the only way to control aggression is to vent it. Lorenz (1966) in fact saw sport as an ideal vehicle for this. Recent research runs counter to this notion of catharsis as a controller of aggression, hence it has few proponents today.

A second and still widely held view of aggression sees it as the result of an elicited drive. This theory, whether it is the Frustration-Aggression Hypothesis of Dollard, Miller, Sears, et al. (1939) or the aggressive cues of Berkowitz (1964), attributes aggressive acts to external forces which elicit a drive to harm or injure. Both the instinct approach and the elicited drive approach are very pessimistic as to the possibilities for control of aggression. Man either has it within him or is driven to it by something without, and neither offers him much of a chance. It is for this reason that a social learning approach seems to make such good sense. Albert Bandura (1973) expressed the possibilities afforded by a social learning approach as follows:

"Man is endowed with the neurophysiological mechanisms to enable him to behave aggressively, but activation depends on appropriate stimulation and is subject to cortical control, therefore the specific forms that aggressive behavior takes, the frequency with which it is expressed, the targets selected for attack are largely determined by social experience. . . . Since aggression does not originate internally and its social determinants are alterable, social learning theory holds a more optimistic view of man's capacity to reduce the level of human destructiveness" (p. 43 & 59).

Bandura's final statement about "reducing the level of man's destructiveness" can be inverted. If man can learn to reduce this level, then he can also learn how to exhibit "destructiveness" at the proper time and in the proper place. How is aggression learned? Bandura (1973) breaks this process into three parts — acquisition of the behavior, instigation of the behavior, and maintenance of the behavior. For aggressive behavior to be demonstrated properly all three must be addressed completely. Omission of one could lead to aggressive behavior which is inappropriate to the situation or improperly expressed.

Where does aggression come from? The social learning view holds that it is acquired in two ways, direct experience and observational learning (Bandura, 1973). In its most basic form learning by direct experience is instrumental conditioning (Baron, 1978). Behaviors which are reinforced will continue to be engaged in and those which are not will be eliminated. The reinforcement consequences become paired with the behaviors which obtained them. If direct experience were necessary for learning we would all be very limited in the behaviors we would exhibit. A great percentage of our learning, however, is done observationally (Bandura, 1977). Behaviors which are seen to be rewarding for others will be incorporated into our own behavior hierarchies. The

cognitive awareness of response consequences, either direct or observed, serves two important functions. It serves to inform us of what behaviors must be engaged in to be rewarded, and additionally serves to motivate us to engage in these behaviors. The addition of new responses to our behavior hierarchies does not, however, guarantee that these responses will be performed (Bandura, 1977).

What factors serve to instigate aggressive behavior? Four social antecedents of aggression will be discussed here — modeling influences, incentive inducements, instructional control, and the presence of an audience (Bandura, 1973; Baron, 1977). The modeling influence exerted here is primarily one of contagion. What one is doing and having success by doing is likely to be copied (Bandura, 1973). Research on the kind of model (aggressive or passive) most likely to be imitated seems to indicate that the degree of success that the model is experiencing is more important than the characteristics which the model may possess (Epstein and Rakosky, 1975). These characteristics may be important in having the model attended to initially (Zimbardo, 1978), but success is what will ultimately bring the result of imitation. Bandura (1965) speaks directly to the issue of using a model in instigating aggression, stating that "response inhibition and disinhibition can be vicariously transmitted through observing the reinforcement consequences for the model" (p. 593). Incentive inducements are also powerful instigators to aggress. Buss (1969) states that "rewarding aggression or showing that it can lead to a goal is a potent determiner of aggression" (p. 161). In the sport context this incentive motivated aggression is of primary concern. If the goal is perceptible and is important enough the behavior necessary to attain it will be instigated. Incentive inducements and modeling influences are closely allied with the motivational aspects of direct and observational learning. Expectation is the key.

Instructional control is another powerful instigator of aggression. The actions of the SS guards at Nazi concentration camps provide a most vivid example of this. Almost to a man, their reason for perpetrating such horror was that they were told to do so, and their respect for authority was so great that they did. Without too much effort the German attitude toward authority can be related to an athlete's attitude toward his coach, especially a young athlete. As will be discussed later this puts the coach in a position of incredible power. This power must be exercised wisely. A second form of instructional control is that which is exerted by groups. Borden (1973) describes this phenomenon as follows: "People can be dared, cajoled, and excited to the point where they will execute a group's hostile intentions" (p. 360). The final instigator of aggression, at least for the purpose of this discussion is the presence of an audience. Baron (1977) observes that in general audiences can exert either a positive or negative influence on aggressive behavior. Borden (1975) is a bit more specific. He states that it is not merely the fact that someone is watching, but who is watching and how the performer perceives their expectations. A most vivid example of this audience influence on aggression was box lacrosse. It was promoted as violent, the fans expected violence, and they got violence. The sport was inherently rough, but the spectators demanded excessive violence. As can be seen many factors serve to trigger aggressive behavior and an understanding of them is essential if aggression is to be displayed at the proper time.

The final theoretical question to be answered is how is aggressive behavior maintained. The key word once again is reinforcement. According to Bandura (1973) aggression is maintained and regulated through external rewards, vicarious reinforcement, self-reinforcement, and neutralization of self-punishment. With the first two, rewards are accrued directly, or the giving of them to others for the same behavior is witnessed (Bandura, 1973). Self-reinforcement is the most involved regulatory mechanism. It can take the shape of an internal pat on the back, or the expectancy of a tangible reward at a later time (Bandura, 1973). Dangers begin to creep in, however, with the neutralization of self-punishment. Individual actions which are inconsistent with established behaviors are often punished internally (Bandura, 1973). The possibilities for reducing the need for self-punishment are potentially very dangerous. In war when aggression is necessary for survival these techniques may have a place, but all too often they are applied on the athletic field. Bandura (1973) discusses diffusion of responsibility and dehumanization of the victim as two disinhibitors of aggression. Others include moral justification and displacement of responsibility. These are all essentially rationalizations for aggressive acts. The dangers inherent in them are the possibilities that the behavior will generalize to inappropriate situations.

How can this theoretical framework be put to practical use? Before embarking on any behavioral change program several questions must first be answered. What type of aggressive behavior is desired? How, when, and where should it be exhibited? As should be evident by now the key to the whole social learning concept is expectancy. The process of building these expectations is crucial for having the behavior exhibited in the proper way. Since incentive-motivated aggression is of concern here we must first establish a goal or goals for the behavior. In the sport context the goal will usually deal with winning. The visibility of this goal is essential for all phases of the social learning process as it is the basis for all expectancies. A goal has been set and the behavior necessary to attain that goal has been described. It is important that the behavior be both experienced directly and observed. Care should be taken to provide an acceptable, at least at first, as well as successful model. Jeffery (1976) indicates that retention of observed behaviors can be facilitated through the use of symbolic rehearsal. This seems to be as valuable in learning to exhibit aggression in the proper manner as it is in the performance of a motor skill. The direct experience must also be carefully controlled. The behavior should be properly shaped by rewarding those behaviors which get closer and closer to the target behavior. The ultimate goals and the reinforcement of the correct responses are what should be stressed. There should be as little negative feedback as possible in the initial learning situation to give the desired behaviors a chance to surface. Implicit in all this is the role of the coach. His selection of models is critical to the success of the whole program. He must also exercise the moral judgment to decide what is the proper behavior and then be certain that the reinforced behaviors begin to approximate this standard.

Proper models within the sport team will serve as instigators as well. Their behavior, and their success with it, will serve to make others engage in similar behavior. Expectancy is the ultimate instigator, however. If the goal is pertinent, the learned behaviors will be exhibited in attempting to attain it. With great care the coach can exercise some instructional control over aggression. It is essential that this approach be used only by those who know why they are doing it. For others to use it would be folly. Group instructional control can also be utilized, but it too must be used with care. The influence can be great and on one unprepared, potentially disastrous. The presence of an audience could be of tremendous value, but their expectancies may need changing before they can exert a positive influence on the participants.

The regulators of aggression offer the most chance for abuse. Those regulators which should be stressed are those involving reward: those either internally or externally administered which tend to reinforce the proper behavior as it relates to goal attainment. Dehumanization, diffusion or responsibility (and the rest) are fine in time of war but have no place in sport. An emphasis on these factors would seem to lead to anything but situationally specific aggression.

Aggression is a difficult topic to deal with. Its connotations are extremely negative, but in certain situations it is a very desirable trait. If aggression is acceptable in certain situations, sport principle among them, it is imperative that we teach why, where, when, and how to aggress. To leave the teaching of something as potentially destructive as aggression to chance is absurd.

REFERENCES

Bandura, A. *Aggression: A Social Learning Analysis.* Englewood Cliffs, New Jersey: Printice-Hall, Inc., 1973.

Bandura, A. Influence of Model's Reinforcement Contingencies on the Acquisition of Imitative Responses. *Journal of Personality and Social Psychology,* 1965, I, p. 589-595.

Bandura, A. *Social Learning Theory.* Englewood Cliffs, New Jersey: Prentice-Hall, Inc., 1977.

Bandura, A., Ross, S. A. and Ross, D. Vicarious Reinforcement and Imitative Learning. *Journal of Abnormal and Social Psychology,* 1963 C, p. 600-607.

Bandura, A., Underwood, B., and Fromson, M. E. Disinhibition of Aggression through Diffusion of Responsibilities and Dehumanization of Victims. *Journal of Research in Personality,* Vol. 9, 1975, pp. 253-269.

Baron, R. A. *Human Aggression.* New York, New York: Plenum Press, 1977.

Baron, R. A. Threatened Retaliation from the Victim as an Inhibitor of Physical Aggression. *Journal of Research in Personality,* Vol. 7, 1973, pp. 103-115.

Borden, R. J. Witnessed Aggression: Influence on an Observer's Sex and Values on Aggressive Responding. *Journal of Personality and Social Psychology,* Vol. 17, 1971, pp. 342-349.

Borden, R. J. and Taylor, S. P. The Social Instigation and Control of Physical Aggression. *Journal of Applied Social Psychology,* Vol. 4, 1973, pp. 354-361.

Buss, A. H. Instrumentality of Aggression, Feedback, and Frustration as Determinants of Physical Aggression. *Journal of Personality and Social Psychology,* Vol. 3, 1966, pp. 153-162.

Epstein, S. and Rakosky, J. The Effect of Witnessing an Admirable Versus an Unadmirable Aggressor upon Subsequent Aggression. *Journal of Personality,* Vol. 44, 1975, pp. 560-576.

Eron, L. D., Walder, L. O., and Lefkowitz, M. M. *Learning of Aggression in Children.* Boston, Massachusetts: Little, Brown and Company, 1971.

Freedman, J. L., Carlsmith, J. M., and Sears, D. O. *Social Psychology.* Englewood Cliffs, New Jersey: Prentice-Hall, Inc., 1970.

Freud, S. *A General Introduction to Psycho-Analysis.* New York: Liveright, 1920.

Jeffrey, R. W. The Influence of Symbolic and Motor Rehearsal in Observational Learning. *Journal Research in Personality,* Vol. 10, 1976, pp. 116-126.

Lefkowitz, M. M., Eron, L. D., Walder, L. O., and Huesmann, L. R. *Growing Up to be Violent: A Longitudinal Study of the Development of Aggression.* New York, New York: Pergamon Press, 1977.

Zillman, D. *Hostility and Aggression.* Hillsdale, N.J.: Lawrence Earlbaum Associates, 1977.

26

Assertiveness
In Sport

Mimi Murray
Springfield College

The antecedents, consequences, and ramifications of aggression need to be discussed in order to appreciate the need for assertiveness in sport. The difficulties most concerned with aggression in sport are the semantic nature of the term itself and the lack of empirical evidence regarding aggression in the sport milieu. There is no universally accepted definition or theory of aggression and often a definition is dependent upon the results of the act or behavior, whether positive or negative. For the purpose of this presentation, aggression will be defined as the desire to, and or action of, inflicting harm on another person.

Research on aggression in sport has been limited. Thus, sport sociologists and psychologists have borrowed general theories and information from the academic disciplines of psychology and sociology and generalized these to sport. The primary theories are instinct, sociobiology, frustration-aggression, and social learning. A simplistic and succinct discussion of these theories and criticism of them will follow.

INSTINCT THEORY

Instinct theory was originally proposed in the psychoanalytic approach by Freud and has since been supported by the works of ethologists Ardery (1961, 1966), Lorenz (1966), and Morris (1967). Aggression according to Freud, is innate and relates to the "death wish" (the instinct to commit violence against oneself or others). In similar fashion, aggression is instinctive and relates to humankinds' "animal nature" (Ardery, 1961, 1966, Lorenz, 1966; and Morris, 1967). Thus aggression is a necessity of the Darwinian approach, survival of the fittest, and survival for humans predicated upon

aggressive behavior. A constructive outlet for aggressive instincts is critical for the maintenance of societies. The process for this constructive outlet is termed catharsis. Lorenz (1966) was a leading proponent of the catharsis function of sport.

The criticisms of the instinct theory of aggression revolve around the age-old argument, still unanswered, regarding instincts — What are instincts, and do humans have instincts? If humans have instincts and aggression is common, why is it necessary to train or teach individuals how to agress against others, i.e., the military. Further, do women release aggressive tension? Since women have fewer cathartic opportunities than men, one could hypothesize that the suicide rate for women should be greater than for men, yet it is not. The theory overlooks women.

Even more criticism surrounds the research methodology and supportive information of instinct theory since most of it has been gleaned through animal research. How much, and can we in fact generalize the results of animal research to humans?

More recently Lorenz was quoted in an article in *Psychology Today* (Evans, 1974) as questioning the cathartic value of sport for players and fans. Yet, sport leaders and coaches frequently justify sport and sport value as that of positive catharsis for aggression — an outlet. Rather than catharsis, does sport serve as a nurturant environment for aggression?

The results of a study by Sipes (1973) further refutes the catharsis theory and indicates a high positive relationship between combative sport and war (aggression). He found that two out of ten peaceful societies had combative sports and that nine out of ten warlike societies had combative sports. In addition, some of the worst race riots have occurred during war times (Allport, 1958). Consequently, it would appear that warlike societies neither drain away intra-societal aggression by fighting other groups or through participation.

Aggression serves to lead to more aggression and the sight of violence may increase aggressive behavior. Moreover, some aggressive behavior may actually be a consequence of sport involvement (Berkowitz, 1972; Martens, 1975; and Hughes, 1976).

Sociobiology. A new theory of behavior which attempts to explain aggression is sociobiology. Sociobiology can be conceptualized on a continuum between Lorenz (humans as captives of aggressive instincts) and Skinner (humans are maleable and behavior can be environmentally shaped). Sociobiology stresses the effects of the innate on our behavior and makes allowance for the influence of the environment. Conflict within the family is seen by sociobiologists as the essence of life. The key is reaching the right level of aggression for too little might cause an individual to lose out while too much could cause death or loss of time and energy. Aggression pays off when the cost-benefit ratio is positive for the aggressor. Since controlled aggression is the important factor in this theory, and if sport teaches one to control aggression in sport participation, then aggression in sport could be justified. Yet one of the major problems confronting sport today is the lack of control of aggression as evidenced by the increasing number of injuries to athletes in certain sports. Sport provides models through which aggression is learned and sanctioned.

Frustration-Aggression. Dollard et al. (1939) proposed the frustration-aggression theory. The tenets of the theory are rooted in and occur when an individual's progress toward a goal is interrupted, the consequence of this interruption is frustration which causes and results in aggression. The fallacy of this theory is that aggression is not always caused by frustration (there are other causes of aggression, i.e. overcrowding, noise, emotional arousal, and pain), and frustration does not always result in aggression (there are other outlets or alternatives for frustration besides aggression). In this theory sport is seen as a safe outlet for aggression, a resultant of frustration. There is no evidence to support this hypo-

thesis. Sport, in effect, causes fatigue which does not eliminate the source of frustration, nor the possibility of other forms of aggression (non-physical). Participation in sport could increase an individual's frustration if her/his reason for participation is goal-oriented (winning) rather than process-oriented (involvement). Because the loser will be thwarted from her/his goal attainment (winning), frustration results, which could lead to increased aggression. Thus sport does not serve as an outlet for aggression but may serve to increase the level of aggression.

Social Learning. According to social learning theorists aggressive behavior is learned and assumes cultural characteristics. This approach to aggression is more universally accepted by social scientists than the previous three theories. This theory is certainly more palatable for educators. Yes, fortunately sports fans, there is hope. This approach to aggression has implications for sport. Since sport is a social institution, behaviors are learned and demonstrated in the sport environment. Thus, sport could serve as a medium for the learning of controlled aggression. Currently though, sport appears to serve as a training ground for aggression (Zillman, et al., 1974, and Fletcher and Dowell, 1971).

Sport is violent (Runfola, 1975) as evidenced by 1040 NFL players in the 1974-75 season who suffered 1101 injuries severe enough to prevent their return to the game or practice; the use of the "brushback" in baseball; and the intentional provocation of aggression in ice hockey. Because sport is so pervasive in our culture, professional athletes and their behaviors serve as role models for athletes at other levels of participation. The identification and emulation of professional athletes' behavior have serious consequences. Smith (1974) found that athletes who choose violent role models demonstrated more violent behaviors than those who selected less violent models. Thus the prevalent and popular sports in our society and the athletes of these sports, through the social learning process, are teaching and encouraging aggression.

Can we as educators and humanists justify, encourage, accept, condone, and reinforce the demonstration of aggression in sport? What can be done to control and lessen violence in sport? The possibilities include: an emphasis on the process in sport; greater penalties for violence; a change in the semantics, motivational techniques, and behavior of players and coaches; and a consciousness raising in the media.

The Process in Sport. Sport is a mirror of society and winning or achievement at any cost (which might include injuring another) is an important quality in our way of life or culture. We don't like losers. Maybe we over-emphasize winning because we haven't been taught in our social institutions (family, school, church) to enjoy the doing or the process. We tend to value only that which is achieved through hardship and persever-ence. Why can't we value and teach the doing — the fun of participating, the joy of effort, the process of accomplishing?

Many of the sports we participate in de-veloped as an expressive function during the Industrial Revolution, as well as an es-cape from the "humdrum" of daily exist-ence. Our society has changed greatly since then. Sage (1974) concludes that highly competitive sport is not preparation for contemporary life in America, for sport com-petition requires hard physical struggle, su-periority, and dominance over others, as evidenced by our founding fathers' need to dominate this vast country. In contrast, the present demands for success in life are per-sonal initiative and cooperation in relation-ships. George Leonard (1974) suggests "New Games" can be played by all ages of people and all sizes of groups in which cooperation rather than competition can be emphasized. In many youth sports programs across our country, participation, sportsmanship, and cooperation are being emphasized more than winning. In these programs, no perma-nent records or scores of individuals or team performances are kept; however, dur-ing the contest the score is kept, for this is the only way to determine skill improvement or performance level not on the final result, but on how one arrived at it — the means and not the end — the process.

Penalties. Since professional athletes and their behaviors are imitated by aspiring athletes, there should be greater controls placed on athletes such as the institution and enforcement of severe penalties for in-jury-causing tactics, flagrant fouls, and un-sportsmanlike acts; and outlawing the use of stimulants and controlling this through saliva or urine tests (suggested reading:

Mandell, *Nightmare Season,* 1976 — an ex-pose of the use of drugs in the NFL, estima-ting that 60% of the players are using am-phetamines to induce a "pre-psychotic par-anoid rage state").

Semantics. The primary motive in sport is to win or succeed. This focusing is frequently justified by the Darwinian approach of sur-vival of the fittest, or the strongest will win. Unfortunately, this approach is accom-plished by taking advantage of one's op-ponent. Coaches actively promote within their athletes the value of winning through locker room incentives (posters, slogans, etc.), humiliating losers, and glorifying winners. Terms such as "hate," "kill," "smash," "destroy," and "hurt" are com-monplace in sport. There are coaches who realize that contact sports are best played in a state of "controlled anger" so they en-courage and promulgate the usage of such words and the behaviors these terms define. They motivate their athletes by inciting negative feelings and hate toward their op-ponents.

Coaches should be using the terms and the associated behavior of ASSERTIVENESS rather than encouraging aggressiveness; that is, reinforcing athletes to positively af-firm their prowess through the demonstra-tion of their own skill and expertise — not through the harming or injuring of an op-ponent. Coaches and players need to estab-lish a new evaluative criteria whereby per-sonal athletic excellence is based upon in-dividual improvement and performance rather than being compared to another in-dividual's performance or skill.

Coaches should further realize the impact they have as role models and must learn to control their aggressive behaviors includ-ing the use of boisterousness and denigrat-ing language and gestures in regard to op-ponents, officials, and spectators.

The Media. The media must be educated so as to affect a consciousness-raising in terms or responsibility to individuals and society. The media should refrain from the sensationalism of showing violent acts and the resultant of such behaviors (a case in point: Daryl Stingley's injury) over and over again. The media should de-emphasize ag-gression in all televised sports, thus provid-ing a real service to society, sport and sport's participants.

Ideally and in conclusion, if we provide

178

for positive fun, and success-filled experiences for all of our participants in sport, we will have more winners. To provide for more winners, sport should be designed for expressive rather than instrumental results. Competition within internal standards of excellence, rather than external standards of excellence, would provide for competition and cooperation in the same sporting context. Specific suggestions might involve utilization of indirect competition (Billings, 1978); educational sport (Sheehan, 1978); new games (Shasby, 1978); sports for fun, recreation, and fitness.

For those sports which are well established reflections of our culture the emphasis should be on ASSERTIVENESS, not aggression.

REFERENCES

Allport, G. W. *The Nature of Prejudice.* New York: Doubleday and Co., Inc., 1958.

Ardrey, R. *African Genesis.* New York: Dell Publishing Co., Inc., 1961.

Ardrey, R. *The Territorial Imperative.* New York: Atheneum Publishers, 1966.

Berkowitz, L. *Social Psychology.* Glenview, Ill: Scott, Foresman and Co., 1972.

Billings, J. *Proceedings, Psychology of Sports Conference.* University of Virginia, Charlottesville, 1978.

Coakley, J. *Sport in Society.* St. Louis: The C. V. Mosby Co., 1978.

Dollard, J., et al. *Frustration and Aggression.* New Haven, Conn.: University Press, 1939.

Eitzen, D. S. *Sport in Contemporary Society.* New York: St. Marten's, 1979.

Evans, R. A conversation with Konrad Lorenz, *Psychology Today,* 8(6): 82-93, 1974.

Fletcher, R. and L. Dowell. Selected personality characteristics of high school athletes and non-athletes. *Journal of Psychology,* 77(1): 39-41, 1971.

Goldstein, J. and R. L. Arms. Effects of observing athletic contests on hostility. *Sociometry,* 34(1): 83-90, 1971.

Hughes, R. H. The social organization of heavy contact sports and the incidence of aggressive behavior. Unpublished paper, 1976.

Leonard, G. B. *The Ultimate Athlete.* New York: The Viking Press, 1974.

Lorenz, K. *On Aggression.* New York: Harcourt Brace Jovanovich, Inc., 1966.

Martens, R. *Social Psychology and Physical Activity.* New York: Harper and Row, Publishers, Inc., 1975.

Morris, D. *The Naked Ape.* London: Jonathan Cape, Ltd., 1967.

Runfola, R. Violence in Sport: Mirror of American Society? *Vital Issues,* 24(7): 1-4, 1975.

Sage, G. H., Ed. *Sport and American Society.* Reading, Mass.: Addison-Wesley Publishing Co., Inc., 1974.

Shasby, G. New Games. *Proceedings Psychology of Sport Conference.* University of Virginia, Charlottesville, 1978.

Sheehan, T. J. Educational Sport. *Proceedings, Psychology of Sport Conference.* University of Virginia, Charlottesville, 1978.

Sipes, R. G. War, Sport and Aggression: an empirical test of two rival theories. *American Anthropologist,* 75(1): 64-86, 1973.

Smith, M. D. Significant others influence on the assaultive behavior of young hockey players. *International Review of Sport Sociology,* 3-4(8): 45-56, 1974.

Wilson, E. *Sociobiology: The new synthesis,* 1975.

Zillman, D., R. Johnson, and D. Day. Provoked and unprovoked aggressiveness in athletes. *Journal of Research in Personality,* 8(2): 139-152, 1974.

SECTION VI

The Management of Stress in Sports

Julie Heyward, Charlottesville, Va.

27

Psychology For
Superior Performers

Dorothy V. Harris
Pennsylvania State University

The psychology for superior performers is probably not significantly different from the psychology for non-athletes. All may have problems or situations which give them some difficulty in performing to the level they might desire. Psychological services should be directed toward maximizing the potential of each individual so that they can function at an optimal, efficient, and satisfying manner.

The percent of sport performance that may be related to the psychological aspect has not been determined. Regardless of the percent, this aspect of performance may be the critical one. It is relatively easy to assess the mechanical and the physiological efficiency of an athlete and predict what their accomplishments will be. However, one can arrange a race which includes ten runners who are predicted to run a sub-four-minute mile based on their physiological and biomechanical efficiency. One will win. Is this where the psychological difference is apparent? Perhaps.

The European countries, especially the Eastern Bloc countries started utilizing psychological techniques to maximize the athlete's performance long before the U.S. Only since the 1976 Olympics in Montreal have we begun to structure procedures whereby athletes might have some assistance in the psychological area. The U.S. Olympic Committee is just beginning to function by appointing a sub-committee in Sport Psychology within the Sports Medicine Committee. As a member of that committee, I am pleased to say that the focus will be toward helping the athlete develop relaxation skills, attentional and concentration skills, and other skills related to mastery and control of anxitey.

The research efforts in psychology for superior performance will be to help answer questions concerning the most effective means of developing psychological processes underlying athletic success. There is need for better descriptive information with regard to the nature of psychological profiles of superior athletes and specific characteristics of the athletes. There is also need for specific instruments that will tap situationally specific behaviors that contribute to athletic success.

The biggest task ahead is probably that of convincing the coaches that psychological skills should be taught and practiced like any of the sport skills. These skills should be included in regular practice sessions and not as "rainy day" practice or a one time only proposition. A lot of coaches are leery about anyone intervening or interfering with the authority and control they have over their teams. It is difficult to convince a coach that one may have to incorporate skills other than those involving a basketball to produce a better basketball player. Generally, when performance has not met the coach's expectations the reaction is to increase both the duration and the intensity of the practice. It just might be that the skills needed are psychological ones rather than the techniques of the sport.

The individual who is working with the development of psychological skills must know the sport that the athlete is playing. A thorough understanding of what the behavioral demands are on the player is essential. Without that knowledge it is difficult to assist the athlete in learning coping skills.

The sport psychologist must also work closely with the coach and establish a sense of trust because he or she will know the athletes better and will be in a position to refer problems and discuss situations they have observed where a particular athlete may have difficulty. Communication and discussion with the coach is essential to cooperative effort in assisting athletes.

Individualized communication with the athlete is also important. Group efforts can be directed toward learning skills like relaxation, imagery, attention and concentration. However, many other skills need to be individualized, depending on the problem or problems that the athlete may be having. Both the coach and the psychologist should work with the athlete in individualizing goals to work toward change and improvement. Both need to provide the athlete with reinforcement and encouragement. Records need to be kept so the athlete has accurate feedback as well.

Asking the athletes to keep a log of their own experiences, reactions and thoughts will also help the athlete to become sensitized to his/her feelings about playing, practicing, etc. The log can remain private with the athlete; that is, the coach should never request that they be turned in, but those athletes who wish may do so. Keeping a log helps the athlete focus and internalize on some of the aspects of his/her involvement in sport that would not be considered without such an assignment. This process also helps in the personal growth and development of the athlete.

The primary goal is to make the athlete feel that he/she has the necessary skills to regulate and control anxiety in any situation. Most of the techniques have been borrowed from clinical or cognitive psychology. Relaxation techniques are probably basic to all others.

Relaxation techniques should be included in the regular practice sessions. When athletes are learning to relax, the instruction is probably most effective following the physical workout of a practice. Once the athlete has learned the skills, the practice should start with a period of relaxation to prepare the athlete for concentration and focus during the practice. A coach could probably reduce the time in practice if maximal concentration could be maintained throughout the period of practice time. Relaxation can help concentration and focus, thereby reducing the amount of time needed to learn and perfect a technique.

Another way to incorporate some of the relaxation and concentration skills into the regular practice is to do them during the stretching for warm-up and preparation for practice. Relaxation increases the stretch and the flexibility of an athlete.

Knowledge of any difficulty an athlete is having with sleep is also important. Little is known about the sleep patterns of athletes. We know that some athletes get very little sleep prior to an event; others sleep very little after an event. Relaxation techniques will also aid in getting proper rest and sleep.

Every coach talks about concentration and the need to concentrate, yet very few offer any suggestions to the athletes with regard to improving that skill. Obviously, attentional focus varies with each sport and with positions within the sport. As an example, a kicker or a quarterback must have attentional skills that are more focused than those of a lineman. Relaxation techniques and imagery can assist in developing better concentration skills. Anxiety tends to dissipate concentration and performance so anything that will assist in controlling anxiety will assist in better concentration. If any of you have "blanked out" on an exam, then you know what anxiety will do to your concentration.

A coach needs to learn these skills as much as the athlete. There are coaches that are good "practice" coaches who see everything in practice and can provide helpful comments, suggestions, and analyses. Many coaches, however, get quite anxious during a game and cannot see the action. When there is a timeout or a break in the action, they have little to offer the players because their own anxiety has prevented them from concentrating sufficiently to do their job. Books such as the *Inner Athlete* and *Sports Psyching: Playing Your Best Game All of the Time* are good references to increase your understanding and awareness of the relationship of anxiety and performance.

In the late 1970's there has been a great deal of discussion about the relationship of exercise and anxiety and depression. It appears that regular vigorous exercise tends to dissipate anxiety and to reduce depression. Athletes do generally get sufficient exercise, yet depression and anxiety are also observed in athletes. Little is known about depression in athletes; most feel that it is not a real problem. Depression becomes a problem with the injured athlete; there is evidence to suggest that injured athletes are more neurotic and depressed than non-athletes with similar injuries. This is not surprising in light of the fact that others have suggested that individuals can become addicted to regular exercise and without it, they become less well and depressed. Not enough attention is paid to the psychological aspects of injury and rehabilitation of that injury.

Coaching from the sidelines should be discouraged. If the athlete is really concentrating on the game (and that is what one hopes is happening) the coach should not continually try to disrupt the concentration and attract the attention of the athlete for additional coaching. The coaching should be done before the game, not during it. If an athlete is really concentrating as he/she should, those comments yelled from the sidelines should not be heard.

Nutritional concerns should be given some attention. There are many nutritional fads and myths in sport. Slight allergic reactions to food can affect behavior. A psychological problem may be only a nutritional one. As coaches, you should become knowledgeable about nutrition and about the eating patterns of your athletes. You should also provide some guidance to them concerning nutrition and eating habits.

One of the things that the Eastern Bloc countries are doing is attempting to reduce all the unknowns regarding an athletic event so that the only unknown is the outcome of the game. To do this, they do a lot of simulation, trying to rehearse every aspect of the event as it will occur. If the athlete has practiced everything in just the way it will occur, then the only unknown that can arouse any anxiety will be the outcome of the game. Let me give you an example: I have been working with the U.S. Women's Field Hockey Olympic Team and have introduced them to many of the psychological skills that I have discussed. Two years ago they were going on a tour and were scheduled to play England at Wembley Stadium. How do you prepare a team for playing in a stadium that will seat over 70,000 when they have never played before more than a couple hundred spectators? How can you simulate that? Our answer to that problem was to obtain the film of the last U.S.-England match played in Wembley Stadium and have the players view that over and over. They were asked to concentrate on the sound track so that they

would know what it would sound like playing in front of all those English cheering for the opponents. They were also asked to study the surroundings, the stadium, so that they would know what it looked like and they would not be overwhelmed when they first walked into it. This was the closest we could come to staging a practice in the stadium. I think the techniques were pretty effective; certainly the response was good from the players. Many said they felt like they had been there before when they arrived.

With the sophistication of telemetry equipment, opportunities to obtain much more information from athletes during the actual competition will increase. At Penn State we have already done some research on fencers, and bowlers during practice and competition. Monitoring heart rate and comparing that to perceived anxiety and performance provides some interesting information. As an example: We learned that two of the bowlers had extreme high heart rates during competition. One of them continued to bowl her usual high average, however, the other one's performance suffered. After teaching the second bowler some techniques for anxiety management, she no longer "choked" but was able to control her anxiety through relaxation and attentional skills and to maintain her usual bowling average, regardless of the competition. I should add that this team went on to win the Nationals!

We are now using feedback equipment to help in teaching relaxation and to try to determine how much one can literally "think with their muscles." This is all quite preliminary so we do not have any results to discuss as yet.

In summary, any techniques that serve to assist athletes in "getting their act together" will improve performance. Most of these techniques have been used by clinical psychologists working with individuals who have difficulty functioning in a normal world. Even though athletes do not have difficulty in normal function, they may have difficulty in competitive environments. The principles of altering behavior are the same regardless of the degree of difficulty of the problem. Point in fact, athletes should make faster progress in learning to control their anxiety because it is less severe and usually situationally specific.

The differences in performance among

184

athletes of relatively equivalent skills appear to rest on a person's ability to cope with the perceived stress of the competitive situation. The stress reaction produces an anxiety syndrome that has specific physiological as well as psychological components that inhibit performance. A multifacted and integrated approach utilizing self-regulation skills, relaxation and other psychological approaches can be viewed as an appropriate way of overcoming individualized performance stress responses. This view draws together knowledge of skill learning and psychological conditioning from the fields of sport psychology, exercise physiology, and clinical psychology. Motivation, psychological self-awareness, and an internal sense of one's own physiological feedback underlie much of the effectiveness in obtaining self-mastery and regulation of competitive anxiety.

REFERENCES

Nideffer, R. M. (1976). *The inner athlete: Mind plus muscle for winning.* New York: Thomas Y. Crowell, Co.

Tutko, T., & Tosi, U. (1976). *Sports psyching: Playing your best game all of the time.* Los Angeles: J. P. Tarcher, Inc.

28

Strategies For Controlling Anxiety And Arousal

Robert J. Rotella

As the popularity and the importance of sport has grown over the last decade, more and more athletes are in need of techniques designed to help them regulate their emotions. For far too long coaches and athletes have been led to believe that increasing their arousal level would always improve their ability to perform. The result has been a very high percentage of athletes who never reach their athletic potential because of an inability to effectively control their arousal level.

Concentration is a necessity for success in athletics at an advanced level. When arousal is too high or too low, concentration may be hindered. It is quite impossible to truly concentrate when one is anxious. To concentrate one must be in a controlled state both mentally and physically and able to focus attention in the present. Thoughts that focus attention on the past or future are distracting and detrimental to attention.

Inexperienced competitors are often intimidated by opponents' calculated displays of confidence. Often, such individuals find it difficult to control arousal level and be as self-assured as desired. Consequently, these athletes do not perform as well as they might. Excess tension results in many athletes being unable to move in a free and effortless fashion which characterizes their performance in more relaxed situations.

The focused concentration displayed by outstanding performers can be developed in all athletes through the use of the techniques described in this paper. The techniques will not make superstars out of all athletes. The purpose of the various techniques discussed within this paper are intended to help athletes consistently perform up to their potential. A variety of individuals have found these techniques to be ad-

vantageous. Professional, olympic, collegiate, high school, and young athletes in both team and individual sports have improved their performance by incorporating them into their training schedules. In addition, teachers and coaches may find these techniques an important addition to their practice strategies.

HYPNOSIS

Hypnosis has a long and successful record of effectively controlling anxiety. Yet, even today most individuals would be unable to define or explain hypnosis. Historically, hypnosis has often been confused with sleep, when in fact these two experiences are complete opposites. (Hyponosis should only be related to sleep as a possible treatment for insomnia.)

Hypnosis is not black magic and it is not some mysterious power given to a few select individuals (Marcuse, 1964). Hypnosis is simply the utilization of an innate capacity that most individuals possess. Dr. Herbert Spiegel, a professor of psychiatry at Columbia University and considered by many of America's leading hypnotherapist, likes to describe hypnosis or the trance state as a "state of aroused intensive concentration, the very opposite of sleep although there is an illusive similarity" (Spiegel, 1963). Most individuals also experience a sensation of heightened awareness. Often the concentration is so intense that hypnotized individuals may appear oblivious to the world. One's mental focus is so restricted that there is no room for concentration on anything else. Obviously, this at least partially explains why hypnosis has been so frequently confused with sleep.

In reality, everyone has experienced the

hypnotized state. When people concentrate deeply on a book and become totally absorbed in its contents, they are not asleep even though they are not aware of events going on around them. They are in a sense hypnotized. In sleep, rather than alert concentration there is a loss of conscious awareness. Athletes also experience a form of hypnosis when completely absorbed in catching a football, shooting a basketball, or hitting a tennis ball or baseball. This state only occurs in athletes when they are performing well, are fully confident, and relaxed.

It is clear to coaches, teachers and athletes that attaining this relaxed state of confidence in one's ability is crucial to success in sports. Some athletes never do experience this state and grow increasingly lacking in confidence. Coaches too often recognize the problem, but lack a solution. Frequently, their only suggestions are to shout "relax" or to emphasize positive thinking. The result is usually a confused, anxious, and depressed athlete. The picture painted is definitely not reflective of the self-concept of the successful athlete. Hypnosis is one possible starting point for athletes who are highly anxious and lacking in self-confidence.

Becoming hypnotized is essentially a matter of shifting gears mentally to narrow the focus of attention to one specific aspect or element at the expense of everything else. Many experts believe that all hypnosis is actually self-hypnosis (Freese, 1976). These individuals have classified the hypnotic states as formal or customary hypnosis, self-hypnosis, and spontaneous hypnosis.

Formal hypnosis almost always consists of four basic phases. Phase I involves the induction of the hypnotic state. In Phase II, the hypnotic state, subjects give up some of their executive control to the hypnotist so that they will be open to suggestions. The suggestions will be acted out immediately or at some later time. The hypnotist will use the trance state to accomplish some end such as relaxation and/or overcoming fear or pain. Phase III involves waking the individual with a predetermined signal from the hypnotist. The fourth and final phase is the post-hypnotic phase. Frequently, the suggestions given in the hypnotic state are expected to affect the subject in Phase IV. Formal hypnosis is clearly an un-

attainable state without the cooperation of the subject being hypnotized and therefore is a form of self-hypnosis.

In *self-hypnosis* people merely go into and come out of the trance state by their own volition, at their own time and in their own way. *Spontaneous hypnosis* is the type that people drift into unintentionally and which ends in the same manner. Spontaneous hypnosis explains athletes who are so intent on their game that they never feel the pain of a broken bone until the game is over and they let their concentration lapse. The same rationale explains athletes who never know they have been cut until they see the blood or until the game ends.

There are a wide variety of opinions as to the number of people who are susceptible to formal hypnosis. Most experts suggest that somewhere between 75-90% of humans can be hypnotized. However, some experts believe that given the right time, the right circumstances, and the right hypnotist, everyone can be hypnotized. There is much more agreement on the degree of hypnotizability. It is most likely that only about 10-25% of the population have the capability of being hypnotized into a deep enough trance to allow such things as major surgery. The limits of trance capability are greatly affected by individual motivation. Quite clearly, athletes in great pain can accomplish more than their trance capacity would suggest. It is becoming increasingly clear that individuals wishing to be hypnotized most likely will be.

There do not appear to be any sex differences in trance capacity. Age, however, does make a difference. Children are highly susceptible from about the age of 5 and peak at about 9 or 10. Susceptibility decreases steadily until the mid-forties. There appears to be another decline after about 65 years of age. But, once again, motivation to be hypnotized cannot be overlooked. Individuals of all ages with the necessary need and desire have been successfully hypnotized.

For many athletes hypnosis can be a useful technique. In many cases, athletes who cannot maintain a confident state, overcome the weakness by placing faith in the power of the hypnotist. The belief in the "supernatural" power of the hypnotist often allows athletes to overcome problems and markedly improve their ability to control anxiety. This is not to suggest that athletes can use hypnotism or direct suggestions to improve muscular strength and/or endurance. Hypnosis is not particularly effective in producing long-range physical performance effects, although under certain conditions it may facilitate immediate performance.

Probably the greatest strength of hypnotism is athletes' belief in the "supernatural" power by the hypnotist. Unfortunately, this may also be its greatest weakness in terms of benefitting athletes. It is this faith that allows athletes to overcome their problems and improve their performance. Yet, if athletes are to be self-confident, they must be able to function without the hypnotist. Without this important step the value of hypnotism is seriously limited for athletes (Nideffer, 1976). Morgan (1973) also argues that another major weakness in utilizing this technique is the necessity of properly trained personnel. This, however, may not be as crucial as the need for responsible personnel. The actual process of learning hypnotism is not so difficult. Most coaches could learn to use the technique properly and under the proper circumstances in a few days of intensive training.

However, due to the above-mentioned weaknesses of hypnosis, attention will now be directed to a variety of self-hypnotic techniques from which athletes can gain the same benefits without ever having to become dependent on a therapist or other external "powers."

SELF-MANAGEMENT TECHNIQUES

An assortment of self-management techniques, which are variations of self-hypnosis, have been developed to allow athletes to gain self-control of anxiety and arousal level in sport. Several of the techniques are discussed below.

Autogenic Training.

Autogenic training utilizes autosuggestion in the control of psychophysiological processes. It was originally devloped as an alternative to hypnosis, by Dr. Johannes H. Schultz, the German physician, around 1900. But Schultz's book *Autogenic Training* did not appear in America until 1959. The ad-

vantage of autogenic training is that it places responsibility on the individual learner or athlete rather than on a teacher, coach, or clinician. The therapeutic advantages of self-control of anxiety is of utmost value.

Autogenic training utilizes verbal formulas by which feelings of heaviness and warmth are to be experienced. Individuals systematically progress through the use of verbal cues, from concentrating on specific muscle groups, to inducing heaviness and then warmth. Once the standard exercises have been mastered, the performer may proceed to meditative exercises that emphasize visual imagery.

Autogenic training involves practicing a series of exercises each day. It has been argued that the maximum effect is generated by practicing at least three times a day; however, recent evidence suggests that once a day may be of equal effectiveness (Peters, Benson, Porter, 1977). On the first day the performers passively concentrate on heaviness in their dominant arm for 60-90 seconds. They either sit or lie quietly with their eyes closed and silently keep repeating to themselves "My right arm is heavy, I am at peace . . ." Then their arm muscles are stretched on the count of one, take a deep breath on the count of two, and open their eyes on the count of three. Individuals enact three of these 60-90 second passive concentration periods in each training session. Once they are successful in developing the feeling of heaviness in their right arm, they move to the left arm. When they can rapidly relax both arms within a 60-90 second period, they repeat the procedures with their legs. The process then is repeated on other parts of the body. At the end of about four months, they can go through all the standard exercises within 90 seconds. Subjects then sit down, close their eyes, and begin thinking something like this: "My arms and legs are heavy and warm, my heartbeat is calm and regular, my breathing is deep and slow, my solar plexus is warm, my forehead is cool."

Once subjects have mastered the standard exercise, they can begin to induce the same feelings under more anxiety-provoking situations. Athletes who practice diligently can successfully control arousal and anxiety in just a few seconds even under highly stressful conditions.

Many olympic athletes from European teams, especially Austrian ski jumpers and alpine skiers report that autogenic training reduced nervousness, increased relaxation, improved their relations with their friends and teammates, and gave them better technical control. Other athletes report that autogenic training is equally successful for sports such as golf, baseball, cycling, hockey, diving, tennis, track, and judo.

Yoga

Yoga has frequently been described as a three-fold path of development: physical, mental, and spiritual. The goal of yoga is to bring each individual to the highest state of achievement in each of these areas. There are many different paths in yoga, but all begin with hatha yoga, the philosophy of physical well-being.

The name "hatha" is made up of two Sanscrit roots: ha meaning sun, and tha, meaning moon. The traditional interpretation of the name is that the flow of breath through the right nostril is controlled by the sun, while that through the left is controlled by the moon. The word yoga means union or joining and, though it may be taken in the larger sense, referring to man's ultimate union with God or the universe, it here signifies the joining of the two breaths.

Breathing is the basis of hatha yoga. Complete control of the breath is essential to proper development and most of the movements of asanas (bodily positions) practiced are associated with deep breathing. Mental concentration is also essential, for development of the constructive power of the mind is a vital part of thinking. Yogis believe that the air we breathe is informed with a quality known as prana (life-force or absolute energy). This force, this extra something, that might be compared to vitamins in food, has not yet been seen or measured by scientific instruments, but it is taught that if complete control of prana is achieved, eventually life itself might be controlled. Control of prana comes through control of the breath.

Besides teaching breath control, the practice of yoga also develops flexibility (suppleness of the spine and joints), stimulation of the glands, relaxation of the nervous centers, and improvement of the digestive and elimination powers of the body. These are achieved through a group of asanas, of

which there are 84 in number, gestures, exercises, and breathing cycles.

Although hatha yoga is known as physical yoga, it is not only limited to the body. The mind and the body are equally involved. The ultimate aim of yoga is the liberation of the spirit, but in western countries only a few practice it for this purpose. Several of the yoga techniques involve mental processes involving will power, imagination, and self-hypnosis.

However, because hatha yoga is based on breathing, one of the main objectives is the achievement of breath control. Yogis believe that through such mastery people could eventually learn to control life itself. This is done through controlling the prana or life force which yoga teaches is in the air we breathe (deVries and Adams, 1972).

The pranic theory must be accepted by all students who really desire to make progress, for it is a fundamental part of the yoga philosophy. The higher forms of training are all devoted to the control of breath, and advanced students spend more time in breath control techniques than in physical exercise.

According to yoga teaching, prana can be stored in the body and then directed by the mind to different parts, with revitalizing effects. The seat of vital energy in the body is the solar plexus, and this is the storage place for the prana. There are many breathing exercises that direct prana to this center and others that send it to different parts of the body with revitalizing effects. Nothing can be done without the cooperation of the mind and will power. In most cases, the breathing exercises themselves are very easy to perform. The really difficult part is to control the mind and train it to work with and for you.

This is the very same problem that athletes engaged in competitive athletics must learn to control. That is, they must be able to control their mind and train it to work with and for them. Anyone who has ever engaged in sports is well aware of the fact that when they get nervous their breathing tends to become very rapid and very shallow. Unfortunately, if anything, their bodies need more air than normal when they are nervous while engaging in vigorous sport. Basically, tension causes athletes to constrict muscles in the diaphragm, chest, and throat so that athletes do in this sense "choke."

Through the use of yoga breathing techniques while participating in sports, athletes can learn to regain control of their tension levels. Through the deep breathing techniques the athletes will be better able to regulate their arousal level as well as their joint flexibility and, therefore, more consistently perform at their maximal level of proficiency (Kraus and Roab, 1961; Rathbone, 1969).

Zen

The Zen system of thought is based on the idea that when people are tense there is a splitting of the mind. In other words, the mind is distracted and does not concentrate on the appropriate activity.

Relaxation allows the mind to eliminate distractions according to the Zen approach. The Zen system teaches its practitioners to apply thought to action. It is believed that concentration is being completely absorbed in the present. There is no awareness at the moment to events past or future. Zen meditation teaches its followers to deal with tension by the practice of focusing attention on one's present activity. Students devote much time to sitting quietly and relaxed, and breathing deeply. Through concentration on only the immediate present practitioners of Zen will be able to allow the body to "let go" and react spontaneously (Herrigel, 1953; and Watts, 1957).

According to Suzuki (1970) the Japanese samurai warriors were especially attracted to the Zen way of life. "Zen discipline is simple, direct, self-reliant, self-denying; its ascetic tendency goes well with the fighting spirit. The fighter is to be always single-minded with one object in view: to fight, looking neither backward or sidewise." (Suzuki, 1970, 62).

PROGRESSIVE RELAXATION

Progressive relaxation is based on a few important premises. When muscles are freed from tension, anxiety will be eliminated. In other words, tension and relaxation are direct opposites. They cannot be experienced at the same time because the mind and the body work in a harmonious relationship. This seems logical when one considers that a reduction in proprioception in the skeletal muscles would reduce stimulation of the reticular activating system. Progressive relaxation as well as a complementary technique known as differential relaxation were developed by Edmund Jacobson, a physician in the 1930's (Jacobsen, 1938, 1972).

Jacobsen (1938) argues that the human body has a limited supply of energy available to it. When people are tense they waste much of this energy on muscles not requiring it. The energy wasted due to excess tension is often called "effort error."

Jacobson believes that the anxiety process can be revised by eliminating muscle contractions. He taught muscle relaxation through a series of alternate muscle tightenings and relaxations. These differ from other forms of relaxation because you start from a state of deliberately heightened tension. The momentum built up in this manner allows the attainment of a deeper state of relaxation. The muscle tension has an additional advantage. It increases self-awareness of how and where you experience your tensions. This awareness can function as a cue for intentional relaxation when tension is experienced in various life situations.

It allows athletes to control their own tension levels. Through its use athletes can learn to prepare themselves individually, prior to and during competition, so as to best produce peak performance levels.

Through the techniques of progressive relaxation (Jacobson, 1938, 1970) athletes can learn to discriminate between muscular tension and the release of tension in specific muscle groups. Lying down in a supine position at first, athletes learn to systematically contract and relax specific muscle groups starting with the right arm and progressing to the left arm, right leg, left leg, stomach, chest, neck, forehead, eyes, cheeks, jaws, total face, and total body. Through this systematic procedure, general relaxation is eventually attained. Athletes may next proceed to do the exercises while seated.

Once general relaxation is accomplished, *differential relaxation* is taught. Differential relaxation teaches athletes to minimize extraneous tension or energy not necessary for a specific sport movement. Athletes learn to be sensitive to tension patterns necessary for each skill they perform, called *primary tensions*, as well as other tensions

190

not required for skilled performance. These tensions may distract the athlete and waste energy (effort error). Through this process athletes learn to use those tensions that are primary for skilled movements while avoiding excesses in them. At the same time athletes learn to completely relax distracting extraneous tensions.

Clearly, Jacobson's techniques do more than just teach athletes how to rest and sleep (these, however, are important uses for high-strung athletes on the night preceding or immediately prior to an important contest). The combination of progressive and differential relaxation will help athletes improve their performance through economy of energy (Jacobson, 1970).

Jacobson has noted the importance of differential relaxation to the mastery of motor skills: "In aesthetic and ballet dancing relaxation plays a conspicuous role. The individual who holds himself rigid in these acts fails in his effects. A particular exercise is repeated until grace is attained. This means that those muscles alone are used that are needed for the act and that no excess tension appears in them or in others" (Jacobson, 1970: 118).

Several other authors have detailed the value of progressive relaxation techniques for improving athletic performance in a wide variety of team and individual sports from golf to football (Tutko and Tosi, 1976; Nideffer, 1976). Its effectiveness remains unquestioned by those willing to give it a chance.

TRANSCENDENTAL MEDITATION

In recent years transcendental meditation (TM), an Eastern meditation procedure based on the Hindu discipline of yoga, has grown increasingly popular in the United States. Transcendental meditation appears to be quite easy to learn and effective in inducing relaxation (Maharishi, 1966).

Investigations designed to determine the effectiveness of TM have been impressive. The findings of several researchers (Wallace and Benson, 1972; Benson, 1974; Blasdell, 1974) have revealed the following: (1) reductions in oxygen consumption, (2) a marked decrease in the blood lactate level, (3) slowing of the heartbeat, (4) a considerable increase in skin resistance, (5) a sig-

nificant decrease in systolic and arterial blood pressure, (6) an electroencephalogram pattern of intensification of slow alpha waves with occasional theta-wave activity, (7) subjects who practiced TM performed significantly faster in mirror star tracing when compared to nonmeditators.

TM training programs are staffed by individuals certified to meet the requirements of the Maharishi himself. The instructor prescribes for each student a secret word, sound, or phrase called a *mantra* which is individualized to the student's neurological organization and is to be perceived inwardly. Students sit quietly and repeat the mantra over and over. Students "passively concentrate" on the mantra twice a day for 15 to 20 minutes. When the mind is distracted, students are taught to experience the distraction and simply let the mind return to the matter.

Many athletes have adopted the techniques of transcendental meditation. Pro athletes such as Joe Namath, Bill Walton, Arthur Ashe, Steve Hrubosky, and ex-Olympic diving star, Craig Lincoln, have all utilized TM and praise its value. In spite of its strengths, there are important aspects that leave it subject to question. Proponents of TM argue that the individually prescribed "mantra" which is repeated to induce the meditative state can only be identified by their trained staff. Research on the various forms of relaxation have shown us that the "mantra" or word repeated is actually of little importance. In essence, any word could be used. The same benefits will still be derived. It appears that because other techniques of self-induced relaxation are available in a relatively inexpensive book or cassette tape and are just as effective, they should be preferred over TM (Benson, 1975).

THE RELAXATION RESPONSE

The "relaxation response" was assimilated from transcendental meditation and other relaxation techniques. Dr. Herbert Benson of Harvard Medical School and director of the hypertension section at Boston's Beth Israel Hospital, developed the technique originally as a therapeutic treatment for hypertensive patients other than medication.

Although the relaxation response is similar to other relaxation techniques, it is the opposite of progressive relaxation in that it works from the mental to the physical. The muscles are not tensed and then relaxed. Instead the mind's attention is placed on a mantra and kept free from disturbing thoughts with the body automatically relaxing itself. Compared to transcendental meditation (TM) the advantages of Benson's relaxation response method are: (1) it is outside of religious teaching, (2) it can be taught in a matter of minutes, (3) it is physiologically sound, and (4) it is inexpensive — the price of Benson's book.

POSITIVE MENTAL REHEARSAL

Mental rehearsal involves a process of systematically and repetitively thinking about past or future performances in the form of visual images. It is based on the premise that thinking about how you have played in the past will have an impact on how you will play in the future (Tutko and Tosi, 1976; Nideffer, 1976).

It has frequently been noted that successful and confident athletes think about successful performances prior to competition. Ineffective athletes often have negative mental pictures of past experiences and, as a result, have many negative thoughts about future performance. Research, however, has been lacking in the area of mental rehearsal and, for this reason, it is impossible to be completely confident that it will improve athletic performance for all athletes. We can be quite confident that most athletes can improve their ability to mentally rehearse in a fairly short period of time.

An abundance of pro athletes in football, basketball, baseball, skiing, golf, and tennis systematically utilize mental rehearsal prior to and during sport contests. Mental rehearsal is typically used for two basic purposes: (1) to aid in the learning of new skills and (2) to create positive experiences to help athletes develop relaxed confidence and identify the important cues that otherwise could only be learned through many years of playing experience.

The second use is most appropriate for aiding athletes in attaining a relaxed state of improved performance. Typically rehear-sal techniques will have athletes identify a peak performance or a day when they performed flawlessly, or felt relaxed and their concentration never wavered. Distractions were never experienced and concentration was not forced. Athletes are asked to try and visualize their bodies moving fluidly and easily.

Usually athletes utilize one of the relaxation procedures prior to mental rehearsal. It is believed that mental rehearsal is more effective when the body and mind are relaxed. Athletes then systematically rehearse, in a sequential fashion, their strongest skills in their most relaxed situation to their weakest skill in their most anxious situation. In the last step, athletes might mentally rehearse a situation such as shooting a one-and-one free throw shot in the final second of a championship game with their team two points down and playing in the opponent's band box gym filled with hostile fans. It is amazing how familiar athletes can be made to feel in situations they have rehearsed. Mental rehearsal can help to make relaxed "veterans" out of nervous "rookies."

MODEL TRAINING

More and more sport coaches are recognizing the importance of having their athletes experience stress situations in practice which are similar to those that will be experienced in the "real" game situation (Cratty and Vanek, 1970). Model training is based on the theory of adaptation to stress (Selye, 1956). Clearly, mental rehearsal is a form of model training done in the imagination for the very same purpose.

Typically there is much more tension in the game situation than in practice. The belief is that through frequent experiences in which athletes have to perform under stress they will learn to handle stress more effectively in the games. Model training may involve using referees in practice, using scoreboards, wearing game uniforms, keeping statistics, piping in ground sounds, or actually practicing in front of a large vocal audience.

Model training can also take the form of strategy practice. This method might involve the practice of responding to various game situations, (i.e., game with 30 seconds left, 2 points ahead with 2 minutes left in the game, "running out the clock" or protecting the lead.

SYSTEMATIC DESENSITIZATION

Systematic desensitization refers to a specific type of psychotherapy which in practice is a combination of the relaxation techniques discussed earlier and mental rehearsal techniques. Systematic desensitization was popularized by Swiegard (1956), who suggested the imagine action method which utilized autosuggestion through the use of words that reinforce visual imagery suggestive of specific muscle group relaxation. The technique emphasized the role of muscle lengthening imagery as opposed to muscle shortening imagery. Hubbard (1947) describes desensitization procedures developed by Yates during World War II. Autosuggestive techniques were utilized to train Navy pilots to avoid freezing at the stick during the stress combat. Yates' method consisted of using a key word connotating relaxation such as "calm" and then visualizing an image that complimented the key word (floating on a cloud, sitting in a row boat on a still pond). Once a general state of relaxation was mastered utilizing the imagery method, combined with Jacobson's progressive relaxation techniques, the pilots would concentrate on visualizing an anxiety-creating situation (being shot at) and attempt to remain relaxed while thinking of the stressor, thus, desensitizing themselves from the specific stressors.

Wolpe's (1958) systematic desensitization technique compliments the Yates method by combining relaxation exercises and mental cues. It is based on the concept that neuromuscular tension compliments anxiety and that deep conscious relaxation will counteract anxiety elicitation. Wolpe's systematic desensitization method consists of: (1) adaptation of Jacobson's techniques; (2) a formulation of an anxiety hierarchy, progressing from least anxiety provoking to most; (3) coupling the relaxation technique with each anxiety-provoking image, progressing from lowest to highest ends of the anxiety hierarchy. Thus, athletes systematically desensitize themselves from individually specific anxiety provoking stimuli by coupling deep conscious relaxation with an anxiety hierarchy. Systematic de-

sensitization is designed to help athletes to effectively overcome particular fears. It might be a fear of heading a soccer ball in a crowd, a fear of returning to play following knee surgery, a fear of bodily contact while trying to reach high to catch a football, a fear of being hit by a pitched ball in baseball, a fear of coming to the net in tennis, or a fear of missing a dive from a 10 meter board. It is probably obvious by now that most fears that can be identified can be overcome through systematic desensitization.

Once the fear is identified a fear hierarchy that consists of defining and ranking 8-10 situations that elicit sequential increases in the amount of fear they elicit must be developed. The first step is to master one of the relaxation techniques. At this point the actual desensitization procedures can begin. Athletes are asked to visualize the lowest situation on the fear hierarchy until they can maintain a relaxed state while doing so. Slowly, athletes progress one step at a time along the fear hierarchy until they can maintain a relaxed state while doing so. Slowly, athletes progress one step at a time along the fear hierarchy until they can remain in a relaxed state while performing the desired skill.

Systematic desensitization has been found to be effective in eliminating between 70 and 90% of the fears pertinent to athletes (Nideffer, 1976). It has great promise for helping athletes successfully return to competition following injury. Too often injured athletes are thrown back into competition without any mental preparation, often resulting in poor performance and a loss of self-confidence. Far too often these athletes never attain their past level of performance due to improper mental preparation. Desensitization procedures will also be of benefit to many athletes who have never tried certain sports or skills within a sport due to specific fears. Recent years have seen biofeedback techniques combined with systematic desensitization procedures with reports of remarkable effectiveness. There is, however, a definite need for research in this area.

ANXIETY MANAGEMENT TRAINING

Anxiety management training (AMT) for

general anxiety is a conditioning method involving (1) the use of instructions and cues to arouse anxiety responses and (2) the training of the client in developing competing responses, such as relaxation or competency (Suinn, 1972). AMT is based on the premise that anxiety responses may be viewed as discriminative stimuli and that athletes can be conditioned to respond to these stimuli with responses that effectively remove the stimuli through reciprocal inhibition.

Anxiety management training was developed to overcome some of the weaknesses of desensitization techniques. Systematic desensitization demands the identification of anxiety stimuli for the establishment of fear hierarchies. This process often requires a great amount of time and effort. A second weakness of systematic desensitization is that it does not prepare athletes to successfully deal with future anxieties not included in the previously established fear-hierarchy (Suinn, 1972, 1976). Anxiety management training rectifies the weaknesses of desensitization techniques in an effective manner as well as broadening its serviceability.

Anxiety management training consists of three phases: (1) in Phase I the athletes are introduced to AMT and Jacobson's relaxation procedures. The objectives of anxiety control and a treatment schedule are presented here. Phase I takes between 45 minutes to one hour and is available on audiotapes (Suinn, 1976).

Phase II must be conducted "live." The anxious athlete is at this time aided in the process of identifying situations that arouse anxiety, relaxation, or competency. Sometimes athletes are simply asked to recall anxious feelings from the past. This phase usually involves specific treatment in anxiety, breath control, and imagery.

Phase III involves actual conditioning of the athletes. Athletes are relaxed, anxiety is aroused, and anxiety is terminated through deep breathing and relaxation responses.

BIOFEEDBACK

Biofeedback uses biological recording devices to record each individual's bioelectric potentials. Athletes can use this biofeed-back information to control particular body functions (i.e., hearing your own heartbeat and learning to voluntarily slow it down). Athletes are capable of a very high level of motor skill learning as a result of the well developed feedback mechanisms within their bodies. It would indeed be difficult to perform very effectively without auditory, visual, or kinesthetic feedback (Morris, 1976).

For years it has been thought that athletes could only gain "willful" control over activities regulated by the voluntary neuromuscular system. Today, through the use of biofeedback instruments it is growing increasingly possible to consciously control processes previously thought to be outside of voluntary regulation.

Biofeedback systems are in reality fairly simple instruments. They always include the following sequence: (1) a physiological response capable of being assessed, then fed to (2) an external amplifier, filter, etc., (3) to a controlled display panel whereby (4) the person may perceive and interpret the signal that the display sends out and finally (5) a path is needed to return the subject's response back to the recording device (Mulholland, 1975).

Far too often athletes do not become aware of increasing arousal until it is too late and they are already out of control. Clearly then self-awareness of tension and relaxation is of utmost importance. Athletes often deceive themselves into thinking that their muscles are indeed relaxed prior to or during competition. Most performers are deceived as a result of the physiological action of adaptation. Tension is experienced so frequently that the athlete is unable to effectively differentiate between genuine relaxation and the apparent state of relaxation (Brown, 1974).

Biofeedback promises to provide athletes with a very direct way of learning what their bodies are doing and how to control them. Electromyographic techniques have enabled many individuals to record minute levels of electrical activity from specific muscle groups. It is even possible to teach subjects to control single motor units through electromyographic feedback.

Electromyographic feedback is particularly effective because with increased muscle tension there is an increase in electrical activity. Similarly the frontalis, forearm, or

194

masseter musculature have been used by researchers in a electromyographic feedback studies as the "barometer" with the frontalis muscle being the most desirable.

Similarly, the electrical activity in the form of energy is amplified. The energy runs a light or tone generator to which the subject will respond. The subject through listening to changes in the tone or seeing changes in light intensity aware of fluctuations in muscle tension.

In actual training, electrodes (sensitive discs which pick up the electrical activity of the muscles) are attached to the muscles under study. This requires a simple, painless procedure to temporarily attach a small piece of metal to the surface of the skin. The electrical current from the pertinent muscles is picked up by the electrodes. The energy is then transmitted to an amplifier that magnifies the energy until it is of sufficient intensity to operate the feedback device. The subject is typically asked to listen to the tone (if a sound device is used) and attempt to increase the pitch that initiates increased tension or decreases the pitch, which indicates decreased tension or relaxation.

These electroencephalograms (EEGs) have also been used to teach relaxation since the EEG can record brain wave activity. Athletes are usually taught to produce alpha waves associated with the relaxed, nontense state. This technique however still has room for improvement. It is questionable as to whether or not all people can produce alpha waves at will, let alone produce or control them while engaged in sport activities (Nideffer, 1976).

DEALING WITH POST GAME ANXIETY

So far emphasis has been placed on the psychological preparation of athletes prior to a contest. Let us now turn our attention to considerations related to the post-competition psychological state of athletes.

In general it may be stated that the likelihood of problems following an unexpected or embarrassing defeat are far greater than following victory or expected defeat. But once again it becomes obvious that all athletes cannot be treated similarly. While it

might be quite helpful to initially talk to all athletes as a group, it is of crucial importance to treat individual athletes differently. It makes no more sense to treat all psychological problems following a contest as a group than it would to treat all physical problems the same. Clearly, different problems require different treatment.

It can be reliably stated that emotional stability is extremely important to consistent success in high level athletes. Therefore, it is most appropriate that athletes are not allowed to experience extended states of depression or elation following a contest. Most certainly the locker room atmosphere should be such that coaches and athletes can realistically talk about positive and negative aspects of their performance and its effects on future goals and performances.

Athletes should always leave the locker room in a stabilized frame of mind ready to prepare for the next contest.

Stabilization of psychological states following competition may be especially important in sports where there may be 2 or 3 contests per week. Prolonged highs or lows will be hazardous to performance.

In summary, close attention must be paid to individual psychological states following a contest. Allowing athletes to remain elated for extended time periods can be just as potentially dangerous as extended depressions. Athletes must be treated not only as a group, but also as individuals. By the time athletes leave the locker room their emotional level should be stabilized. Depending on the situation, it may require the utilization of relaxation techniques as presented earlier or the use of a pep talk designed to rebuild confidence in expectations of success in future performance.

REFERENCES

Freese, A. (1976). *How Hypnosis Can Help You.* New York: Popular Library.

Jacobson, E. (1962). *You Must Relax.* New York: McGraw-Hill, Inc.

Jacobson, E. (1970). *Modern Treatment of Tense Patients.* Springfield, IL: Charles C. Thomas.

Jacobson, E. (1938). *Progressive Relaxation.* Chicago, IL: University of Chicago Press.

195

Marcuse, F. L. (1964). *Hypnosis Through-out the World.* Springfield, IL: C. C. Thomas.

Nideffer, R. M. (1976). *The Inner Athlete: Mind Plus Muscle for Winning.* New York: Thomas Y. Crowell Company.

Peters, R. H., Benson, H., & Porter, D. (1977). Daily relaxation response breaks in a working population: Effects on self-reported measures of health, performance, and well-being. *American Journal of Public Health, 67,* 946-953.

Spiegel, H. (1963). Spectrum of hypnotic and nonhypnotic phenomena. *American Journal of Clinical Hypnosis.*

Suinn, R. M. (1976). Body thinking: Psychology for olympic champs. *Psychology Today, 10*(2), 38-43.

Suinn, R. M. (1972). Behavioral rehearsal training for ski racers. *Behavioral Therapy, 3,* 519-520.

University of Virginia photo services

29

Facilitating Athletic Peformance Through The Use And Coping

Robert Rotella
University of Virginia

Christopher Malone
Cortland State University

David Ojala
Stratton Moon

...hletes, coaches, and sport psy-
...sts are considering the role of psy-
...ogical factors in athletic performance.
...l are working toward one common goal —
maximizing athletic performance during
practice and competition.

The science of cybernetics has great potential for helping athletes maximize their
performance. Cybernetics is a science
which explains how the mind programs the
body to respond in a manner similar to
computers. More specifically, every time
athletes experience something, they create
new response patterns in the brain or
strengthen response patterns which already
exist. These response patterns are stored in
the brain (like tape in a computer) and can
be replayed whenever a past experience is
recalled. Athletes can learn how to recall
successful past experiences which may
help their performance in similar competitive situations.

Programming the mind with the correct
responses in order to improve athletic performance is an effective method of pre-race
mental preparation. One way to develop
successful response patterns in the mind is
through the use of imagination. Through
the use of the imagination, the mind may
be programmed to help the body respond in
successful ways.

There are several types of imagery training. Two kinds of imagery training that athletes are using successfully today, mastery
rehearsal and coping rehearsal, will be discussed in detail in this article.

Mastery rehearsal can be best understood
as athletes imagining themselves performing perfectly and without stress and anxiety.
On the other hand, coping rehearsal involves athletes imagining themselves in situations, where they are experiencing difficulty or a temporary loss of emotional and
mental control prior to and during performance and then regaining control and concentration.

By combining mastery rehearsal and coping rehearsal during mental practice, athletes can facilitate the development of correct response patterns in the brain. By learning how to recall these response patterns
when performing during competition, athletes will be better able to maximize their
performance potential.

MASTERY AND COPING TAPES

One method of practicing mastery and
coping rehearsal is through the use of tapes
(typically cassette tapes). Mastery and coping tapes are tapes produced by athletes
for the purpose of providing a relaxing and
anxiety-reducing method of mental preparation for competition.

Reprinted with permission: *J. United States Ski Association.*

Mastery tapes consist of scripts produced by athletes which describe their performance under perfect conditions. Their performances are completed in a non-stressful environment. Coping tapes contain scripts in which athletes describe themselves performing under stressful conditions and overcoming these conditions through the utilization of pre-planned strategies.

... perfect performance." This thought process in itself can facilitate performance since it helps athletes develop self-awareness of all aspects involved during their competition. Also, this thought process may help athletes focus their attention on what they should be concentrating on during performance. In this manner, the thought process develops self-coaching and self-management strategies which are important in helping athletes develop a sense of self-control.

After athletes have considered what their "perfect performance" involves, it is a good idea for them to talk with their coaches about their thoughts and ideas regarding their "perfect performance." This is important because athletes must be sure that their "perfect performance" is realistic relative to their abilities and past experiences in competition. While mastery rehearsal is visualized perfect performance, it is the striving for this perfect performance by athletes which must be emphasized. Remember, athletes are attempting to program their minds and bodies to perform effortlessly and flawlessly while at the same time realizing that they may never achieve a "perfect performance."

Once athletes have progressed to the point where they understand what their mastery rehearsal tape should include, they can begin to write a script. A script is a written version of their "perfect performance" from which their tape will be made. After athletes have written their scripts, it is again a good idea to have other athletes or coaches review them.

There are several points to consider when writing a script. Athletes should attempt to dramatically describe how their body feels during all aspects of performance. For example, how does the body feel as a skier waits in the starting gate, or how do the leg muscles feel as the skier races down the slope. Furthermore, athletes should include other sensory information such as how objects look, the vividness or dullness of colors, and what they hear as they perform. The more athletes can include body feelings ... become. ... mental conditions ... a tape is to describe ... the ... ance will take place. By describing athletes ... ment and its unique conditions, ance. ... "e" for their perform-

To help facilita... athletes should use ... apply to their performan... focus their attention on term... is meaningful for them. This focu... tapes, tention will help promote concentrat... the right things as athletes listen to the... tapes over and over during mastery rehearsal.

Another way to make tapes realistic is to have athletes make their performances exactly the same length as the time they have decided is their "perfect performance." For example, if athletes have decided that the time for their perfect race is 60 seconds, then the race on the tape should last for 60 seconds. However, some athletes may mentally visualize their performance in slow motion. If athletes visualize their performance in slow motion they need not be concerned about the length of time their race takes on the tape. The tape should include all pre-race preparation — not just the 60 second race.

Many athletes may want to use introductory or background music on their mastery tapes. This is a good idea as long as athletes feel that the music enhances confidence and concentration. Besides music, the type of voice used on the tape must be considered. Some athletes may choose to use a very soft, mellow voice while other athletes may prefer a loud, boisterous voice. Either extreme is useful, as long as athletes demonstrate an emotional involvement in what they are saying on the tape. This emotional involvement through music and voice will elicit mental images that will lead to enhanced confidence and performance.

The most important aspect of making a "good" tape is to realize that each athlete is an individual and will perceive situations differently. When describing how athletes feel about something or look at something, their descriptions may vary greatly. Therefore, it is important to keep in mind that it is reasonable to expect athletes to have sensory and perceptual differences. On the other hand, there are certain sensory feeling or concentration cues which all athletes should include in their tapes. Coaches should help insure that both individual differences and team commonalities are considered.

AN EXAMPLE OF A MASTERY SCRIPT

As I wake up this morning, feelings of excitement fill my head. It is a good feeling as if I am about to do something special. Today is the first Nor-Am Giant Slalom Race of the year. For me to succeed today I will have to break into the Top 10. This is a big race for me, but I am not nervous because I have prepared both physically and mentally for this race throughout the entire training and racing season. I have worked hard for this race and I know I will succeed. Everything seems to be going right for me this morning, even when I ran I could feel my muscles energize with every stride. I feel that I am ready to succeed. Today when I get to the lounge my equipment is ready, especially my skis. Last night I tuned them so they would be clean and fast on the hard packed snow. I also waxed and scraped my skis so they would move fast over the snow. I get my bib at the race registration. I am running 38th which is pretty far back, but it doesn't bother me because I know I will move up on my first run. I will succeed. I feel confident about breaking into the Top 10. I get to the top of the course for my race inspection. As I look over the course I try to pick up the key points. I feel the course is fast and that is how I like it. Subconsciously I know the other racers will have to ski fast today to beat me, because I am feeling very good. These key points are places in the course where I can pick up time on other racers. I like the flats and long sweeping turns where I can gain momentum through the turns and use my strength to explode out of the turn and gain speed. I am ap-

proaching my run, I must think now of what I have to do to beat these other racers. I've trained all year and I am confident I will succeed. Now it is up to my mind to prepare myself for the up and coming run. I know what I have to do both physically and mentally. I am confident I know how to go about succeeding. I have seen the first skiers go down and they look good. But I know I can be just as good, I want to succeed. My start is coming up now, I think back to the key places on the course where I have to precisely balance over my skis to go through clean. I know I have to keep my eyes on the course and not the people on the side. I must be clean and smooth throughout the course to succeed.

I am now in the starting gate, my energy is building and I am getting psyched. The starter gives me the count, 5, 4, 3 . . . I push out of the starting gate. I ski to the first gate and I am on my way. Think, think, I start to get my rhythm on the first couple gates. Think smooth from turn to turn. On the top part of the course I feel good. I come to the hard turns on the course, I think balance, balance. Drive those hands. I feel fast. I will succeed. The following gates are open. I feel clean. I feel good. I feel fast. I know I am doing well. I come to the flats. I must keep my line straight as possible without sacrificing speed. Let those skis run. I know I'm doing well. I know I'm doing well coming closer to the finish now, going over the last row. Keep on concentrating. I know I am doing well, and I go through the finish. As my time comes out I see that I have done well for my run. Count up nine times better than me. I know I can do better now. I will succeed.

All I have to do is to do the same routine just a little smoother and a little cleaner. I know I can do it. I have prepared for this all year both physically and mentally. I grab my clothes at the bottom and get ready for the second race.

During lunch I just relax and have a good time. I just think to myself that I will succeed. As I go for my second run inspection, I talk with my friends to get extra input on the course so I can correct my mistakes on my first run. The second course seems to be almost the same as the first, maybe a little faster. I feel good about this; and I know I will succeed today. Think fast, fast. Where can I pick up speed? I know I can't on the steeps. I must be rounder than on my first run because I know this is where I lost speed on my first run. Round, round, think round. I will succeed. On my free ski run I run on a trail next to the course, make long and fast sweeping turns as if I were running a race course. I feel good and I feel confident that I will succeed. As I wait up for my run, I sit by myself watching the first five racers go down. I go over the course in my mind. I place myself inside their bodies. I try to see how fast, how smooth I can be. I ought to be as clean as possible. I psych myself up as I did in my first run hopping around, getting ready for the physical aspects of the course. The starter motions me into the starting gate and starts to give me the countdown. Get into the beat . . . 2, 1, I'm off. Rhythm, rhythm, smooth, clean. Look for speed. I can feel the snow under my skis. I feel fast. I feel good. I am confident. I am confident when I come to the steeps. I take the gates round and clean, better than before. I will succeed. Look ahead. My legs are getting tired but it doesn't bother me. I must drive, drive. I will succeed. The transition onto the flats must be taken well to carry my speed. Yes, I feel the speed gradually gaining as I go skimming down the run. Think fast, fast. Let these skis run wisping my body against the gates. I am coming over the last hump to the finish. I am extending my body to its limits, driving my body through the gates, looking for the most speed possible. I know I will succeed. I will succeed. I'm almost to the finish now, I get into my tuck and through the finish. Inside I know I have succeeded. I just wait for my time. My time comes up. I can only count six better times on the board. I have succeeded on what I have come here for. I am proud of myself.

MAKING A COPING TAPE

Coping tapes are different from mastery tapes in that athletes mentally rehearse performing under stressful conditions and responding emotionally to negative and anxious thoughts. They are not rehearsing a "perfect performance." However, coping tapes also provide mental strategies which are repeatedly rehearsed in order to prepare athletes to perform successfully in any competitive situation in which they might find themselves.

More specifically, coping tapes include all types of problems and stressful situations which athletes might encounter prior to and during competition. These stressful situations may be anxiety provoking and thereby distract athletes from completing their performances as successfully as possible. Typically, as skiers become anxious they become preoccupied with negative self-thoughts which might include such statements as, "I won't ski fast today because I used the wrong wax," "I can't ski well in this type of weather," or "How can I expect to race well today, my parents are watching me, and if I make a mistake I'll never live it down." These types of statements may cause athletes to focus their attention on the wrong things and may cause performance to suffer.

If athletes think carefully about all types of situations which might occur prior to and during competition, they can begin to plan strategies for coping with these situations. By anticipating all types of situations which athletes might encounter and how they will cope with them, athletes can begin to make effective coping tapes.

SAMPLES OF STRESSFUL EXPERIENCES CAPABLE OF ELICITING ANXIOUS THOUGHTS AND FEELINGS: (For use on coping tapes)

Extended Pre-Race
1. Poor physical condition — diet, rest
2. Rehabilitation from injury
3. Poor past performance
4. Questioned commitment
5. Equipment limitations
6. Team relationship problem
7. Peripheral pressures (academic, peers, family)
8. Limitations on social life
9. Personal desirability of upcoming race site
10. Interruptions in training (poor weather, scheduling problem, etc.)

Last Week Pre-Race
1. Physical condition problems
2. Minor injuries become major
3. Bout with flu interrupts training

4. Overtired and/or overtrained
5. Poor past performance
6. Recent failure on same or similar mountain
7. Lack of specific training needed for race (downhill, cross-country, etc.)
8. Total lack of specific training.
9. Poor timing on tapes
10. Equipment limitations
11. Broken ski
12. Binding problems (recent pre-release)
13. Boot problems
14. Modify or break in new boots
15. Racing suit (FAST)
16. Waxing problems
17. Team relationship problems
18. Feel you have become non-productive or impasse point with coach
19. In stiff competition with your teammate
20. Quarreling with teammate(s)
21. Too much input from coaches
22. Disagreement on coaching
23. Philosophies on training and tapering
24. Peripheral pressures girlfriend-boyfriend problems
25. Pressures from non-skiing peers who question your commitment
26. Parental pressures for success
27. Academic pressures causing physical and mental drain
28. Personal desirability of upcoming race-site in strange or foreign country
29. Uncomfortable with foreign food or language
30. Must travel too far
31. Jet lag problems
32. Regionally poor snow conditions
33. Reputation of poor race organization
34. Undesirably flat or steep terrain for personal preference
35. Interruptions in training
36. Poor surface or weather conditions
37. Scheduling conflict at home training site
38. Outside commitments
39. Illness or injury

Eve of Race
1. Physical condition problems
2. Disagreeable meal
3. Sleep interruptions
4. Menstrual cramps

5. Nervous sleeplessness
6. Poor time zone adjustment
7. Fear of oversleeping
8. Poor past performance
9. Dwelling on anxious thought and memories
10. Thoughts of failure, embarrassment
11. Unsatisfactory last training
12. Equipment limitations
13. Last minute problems with skis, boots, binding and unsatisfactory replacement of the above
14. Lack of confidence in wax selection
15. Team relationship problems
16. Uncomfortable with assigned roommate
17. Unable to find and talk to coach
18. Ridiculed by teammates or coaches (real or imagined)
19. Peripheral pressures — parents or other important friends show up for race
20. Unsettling phone conversation
21. Failure of academic test
22. Personal desirability of upcoming race-site
23. More or less intense version of previous column
24. Poor runs on training course
25. Not happy with weather forecast
26. Uncomfortable sleeping accommodations

Race-Day Pre-First Run
1. Physical condition problems
2. Tired, tight, upset stomach, unsatisfactory breakfast or sleep
3. Muscle fatigue and soreness
4. Bruised bones (shins, etc.)
5. Poor past performance
6. Intimidated by opposition
7. Not feeling "on" in early warm-up runs
8. Equipment limitations
9. A boot fit problem
10. Ski tuning problem (edge too sharp/too dull)
11. Wrong wax
12. Broken pole or binding at start
13. Wrong goggle lens
14. Team relationship problems
15. Negative statements by teammates just prior to start
16. Overcoaching in starting gate
17. Losing confidence because respected teammates have performed poorly

18. Negative course reports by team-mates or coaches
19. Peripheral pressures coping with unknown competition
20. Coping with known and impressive competition
21. Coping with efforts by opposition to psych you out
22. Real or imagined advantages possessed by the opposition for competition (better equipment, coaches, facilities)
23. Parent or important others unexpectedly show up at a race
24. Unaccustomed to media coverage
25. Altercation with area management or ski patrol (i.e. problem in lift line)
26. Personal desirability of upcoming race-site
27. Cope with steep-flat (icy-snow covered, fast-slow, etc.)
28. Interruptions in training
29. Warm-up course unavailable
30. Free skiing, limited or unavailable
31. Chair breakdown making skiing impossible
32. Too little time for course inspection

Starting Gate Thoughts
1. Too late for adequate warm-up and preparation
2. Missed start-out of sequence
3. Provisional required
4. Equipment failure at last minute
5. Last minute negative radio course report
6. Coping with thoughts of success or failure
7. Coping with course conditions
8. Coping with a hold on course
9. Coping with changing weather or course conditions

In Between Race Runs
1. Coping with a good or bad run
2. Coping with eating, inspecting, and maintaining or adjusting your physical and mental preparedness
3. Coping with new starting position
4. Coping with your own and others evaluation of your first run
5. Coping with necessary equipment changes or modifications (i.e. re-waxing, etc.)
6. Maintaining concentration irrespective of being ahead or behind

7. Developing a realistic and general second run strategy and sticking with it

Athletes can help each other by openly discussing anxious situations which might occur prior to and during competition. Athletes experience different distractions in competition based upon their age, level, and exposure to coaching. Since different experiences occur at different stages in athletes' careers, sharing past experiences can help younger athletes anticipate further competitive situations which they may not have yet considered since they have not yet experienced them. Furthermore, coaches who are willing to talk about their past experiences can also help athletes plan strategies for situations they are likely to encounter later in competition.

Once the athletes have decided which situations prior to and during competition affect their performance, they can plan to cope with these situations. Athletes should employ the following four-step approach when planning their coping strategies:

1. recognize the distraction;
2. think "stop" to themselves;
3. breathe deeply — "let go" of muscle tension;
4. use concentration word to bring them back to concentrating on task, i.e., "think" or "respond."

Recognizing the distraction is facilitated through the process of considering and anticipating all situations prior to and during competition which could affect performance. This thought process helps athletes to quickly become aware of distractions.

As soon as athletes recognize distractions they can initiate their coping strategies by first ridding themselves of the distracting thoughts by saying "stop." Then athletes should immediately breathe deeply and "let go" of any muscle tension that has been created by the distraction. Finally, athletes can once again attend to the task at hand by using a concentration word — a cue word, such as "think positive," "I'm good," "I'm ready," "respond," etc. It is not important which word or phrase the athletes use, but they should consistently use the same word or phrase throughout their tape. This cue word or phrase should then be followed by athletes' coping strategies.

Athlete coping strategies are based on positive self-talk. Positive self-talk functions are counter statements to the negative self-talk which athletes think to themselves. The counter statement might be, "I can race in any kind of weather; I've trained in similar conditions and my opponents haven't." Athletes should create a positive counter statement for all the stressful situations they have anticipated.

Before athletes make their coping tape they should write out the script and discuss it with other athletes and/or coaches who helped with their mastery tape. Once again, athletes should include only those aspects of sport competition which are pertinent and realistic to them. Not all the same situations are stressful for all athletes. Therefore, each athlete's coping tape is individualistic. Athletes should also follow the same suggestion for graphically describing feelings and other sensations which occur to them prior to and during competition as was suggested for the mastery tape.

AN EXAMPLE OF A COPING SCRIPT

It is one week prior to the Senior National Giant Slalom. This is a big race for me, the biggest of the year. Giant Slalom is my best event and I have finally arrived at a level in skiing where a top ten performance is a very reasonable goal. I have a problem. I slightly twisted my ankle yesterday. Why did it have to happen now? Isn't that just my luck. I might as well forget the Nationals for this year. Wait a minutes — STOP —. Let Go — Think. I've had minor twists like this before. I've always recovered quickly. There's hardly any swelling and my ski boot immobilized the ankle completely. OK, I guess that ankle really is no big deal BUT the Nationals are in Colorado! I've got a super pair fo skis for the Vermont Race at Stratton but they'll never work on the soft, deep stuff in Colorado. Why couldn't the Nationals have been held in the East this year. STOP — Let Go — All right, now I've got to think about this logically, one of my better Giant Slaloms this year was on fairly soft snow on these same skis. Yeah, I suppose I really do have a chance in this race after all I've had some of the best training and my best results over this year. If I can get just three

good days of Giant Slalom training this week I could be ready for peak performance. Three good days! That's impossible. I have to travel to Colorado on Wednesday so that will foul up at least one day of training if not more. I might as well forget this whole thing — STOP — Let Go — Think. Almost everyone else will have traveled one day this week also and besides I'm well prepared. If I approach this right — the plane trip can be a refreshing diversion and besides I could stand a day off skis. OK, maybe I just better relax and get to sleep.

Pause. Later at the hotel in Colorado the night before the race.

Well, everything's gone OK so far. I'm glad I had a chance to go up on the race hill today and make a few turns. My skis really felt good on the snow, but I probably shouldn't have taken so many runs. I wonder if I overtrained. Actually, I do feel a little tired now that I think of it and also we are at a much higher elevation. Oh, now I've done it. I know I've spent too much energy. There's no way I can recover in time to have a peak performance tomorrow. — STOP — Will you please relax and Let Go. I know my conditioning program has been good. I know my strength maintenance program has been more honest than ever. I know I'll have plenty of energy to put in a great effort tomorrow; and, if I'm a little fatigued now, that's all the better, I'll be able to sleep tonight. I'll be ready tomorrow. In fact, I'm anxious for tomorrow's opportunity. Good night!!

Pause. It's morning.

This is the BIG day. Let's take a look out the window. OH, NO! New snow. I don't believe it! How the heck am I supposed to race in this stuff. — STOP — Let Go — Think. Well, maybe it's not such a big deal. There are only about four inches and it's so light it will be side slipped off the course. OK, no big deal. Well, I better go down to the dining room and have breakfast. . .

What's the smell? NOT PANCAKES! I can't eat those things. They sink to the bottom of my stomach like a cannon ball. I have to eat. What am I going to do? Nothing's going right. Well, I should have known that this race would be a disaster. STOP — Let Go — Think. Ah, waitress, do you think I could substitute two scrambled eggs for these pancakes? See, I have this big race today and — Oh, sure, no problem. Hey that wasn't so bad. Well maybe that's a good omen. OK, well I better finish this breakfast and get up on the hill.

I don't believe it — they've got me listed out of order by about 20 racers on this start order. Soft snow and they screw up my number. The way this trip is going I might as well head for next week's race site right now. — STOP — Let Go — Think. Sure enough, that was an unofficial misprint. I should have known that my coach would already have the situation under control.

The top part of this course looks great, lots of fast sweeping turns. I wonder what this lower section's going to be like. Hey, that turn looks a little tight and then right into the flats to the finish. You've got to be kidding. I'm going to lose all my speed for the finish right there. I can't stand it — STOP — Let Go — Think. I suppose I could turn this thing around. The same gates are for everyone. Probably everyone has or will react to seeing that combination the same way I did. So maybe if I inspect well, I could actually make time on most of the field in this very combination. OK, well I better go warm up with some free skiing.

Here I am at the starting gate. I've got about 15 racers till I go. I better do a last minute warm-up routine. I don't believe it. Everyone is saying that tight gate before the flats is spoiling a lot of good runs. I knew it, I could see it when I inspected. Well, I guess it just wasn't meant to be my day. STOP — Let Go — Think. Those are self-defeating thoughts. When I inspected the course I recognized then that this would be a place for me to make time on the rest of the field. Well now, I've got my chance. OK, one more racer, then I go. I hope I do well. Oh, I probably won't. STOP — Let Go — You don't have time. You can do it now. Just do it. 10 seconds . . . 5, 4, 3, 2, 1, GO! Explode — look ahead — BALANCE — DELAY — look ahead, delay — step — hustle — look ahead — get ready for that tight gate — look ahead — delay the tight one's coming — look ahead — step up — get ready — get up — drop in — now hustle to the finish line — hup hup — alright — I'm home.

Now to get my time. I've got to CATCH my breath. ALL RIGHT, 87:65 — that's good time. I can only count 6 better times on the board! That's a good run and my starting position for the second run will move up about 24 slots. I better get a quick snack.

. . . Well, I've got about 15 minutes until the start of my second run. The second course is similar to the first. I've got a great starting order — I hope I don't blow it. I mean, really — what are the chances of me having two good runs in a row — especially when they really count. I'll blow it — I know I will. STOP — Let Go. This course is very much like the first course. I had a great run on the first and I can do it again here. I'm going to do it. That's right. I'm going to concentrate on the right things and I'm going to conquer my self-doubts in this run. I did it once, I'll do it again. . . . 10 seconds . . . 5, 4, 3, 2, 1, GO! EXPLODE — look ahead — step — delay — complete — balance — look ahead — hustle — blance — step — get ready to make a good move into the flats — set up — drop in — hustle home — hup hup — hustle — cross the finish line. AHH. It should be a pretty good run. I felt OK. Come on, get my time up there. Come, 86:43. Alright. Let's see. That totals up to the fifth best overall in the race. This is my best ever.

CONCLUSION

Using mastery and coping tapes provides a relaxing and anxiety reducing method of mentally preparing athletes for competition. By picturing images in the mind, athletes can influence performance. The mind programs the body to perform. By programming the mind to give successful responses through the use of these tapes, athletes can facilitate their performance.

It is natural for athletes to think positively when their performances are successful. On the other hand, athletes can begin to think negatively when performances become bad. The mind responds to positive and negative experiences. Therefore, there is a need for developing self-control and self-awareness to help athletes program their minds to respond in effective-positive ways rather than ineffective-negative ways. Through the use of mastery and coping tapes, athletes can develop self-awareness and self-control and employ successful coping skills which may facilitate performance.

The important thing for coaches and athletes to keep in mind is to let performance flow when things are going well. However, when performance is not good, then have the skill and ability to cope and focus attention in a positive way. Athletes and coaches can help develop these skills and abilities by using mastery and coping tapes.

Mastery tapes are appropriate at the beginning of the season or pre-season. By developing and using mastery tapes early, athletes can build and establish a positive mind set and self-confidence. Some athletes may suggest that mastery tapes are not reality, that performance doesn't always happen that way. Therefore, athletes must prepare themselves to anticipate any situation which might affect their performance. For this reason, coping tapes are appropriate.

When athletes develop and plan out strategies prior to competition, it can help create self-confidence on the day of competition. Athletes can believe in themselves in the sense that they are better prepared than their opponents in coping with all types of situations which may occur during competition. However, athletes and coaches should not allow anticipation of situations to become an excuse for failure. They should use this anticipation as a strength.

Mastery rehearsal and coping rehearsal tapes are another way athletes can mentally prepare themselves for competition. By programming the mind with the correct response patterns the body can perform correctly the skills required in competition. Furthermore, by preparing the mind and body to perform correctly under various stressful situations which might occur during competition, perhaps athletes will be able to come closer to their "perfect performance."

30

Sport Psychology And Christianity: A Comparison Of Application

David L. Cook
University of Virginia

Our world is located 92,000,000 miles from the sun. If we were but 100 miles closer or further away, there would be no life on our planet. What are the odds that this happened just by chance? A trillion to one?

The moon is 182,000 miles away from the earth. If it were 100 miles closer or further away there would be no life on this planet (because of the importance of the gravitational force it exerts upon our oceans). What are the odds that it was positioned just so, by chance? A trillion to one?

The earth is spinning at a constant speed around its axis (approximately 1500 mph). If it were spinning but one mph faster or slower there would be no life on this planet as we know it today. What are the odds that this happened just by chance? A trillion to one?

What are the odds that on our earth several elements, carbon, hydrogen, oxygen, nitrogen, calcium, and phosphorus, came together to form man (the same substances that are found in a shovel full of dirt)? And within this form, 60 trillion cells working independently from each other, give us life. Within this form there are also 60 thousand miles of veins, arteries, and tubing which transport our lifegiving blood. And within this form there is a three-pound globe of mass, the brain, which harbors 13 billion nerve cells which enable this form to think, perceive, see, hear, talk, taste, and smell. What are the odds that all these things happened just by chance? So that man indeed exists today? Several trillion to one?

What does all this mean? That from a researcher's viewpoint, you couldn't prove that you exist? You wouldn't come close to being significant at the .05 level. In other words, you could never get published in any research journal.

Why did we bring this up? Because when you bring up topics such as religion and faith and belief, "non-scientific" topics, many people immediately turn off, because you can't scientifically put your finger on the source.

This chapter discusses the subject of religion in sport. Before we go one sentence further we must clarify a few misconceptions. Many people have strong biases against religion for one or several reasons. During this chapter when religion is referred to, it must be understood we are not talking about the following as being religious experiences:

1. "I go to a Christian school, therefore, God is obviously on our side, we'll win;"
2. "I don't have to practice, God will help me perform, He'll let me win because I'm religious;"
3. "I went to mass this morning, of course we'll win;"
4. "Everything is predestined. I have no control. Why practice? I'm helpless."
5. "Prayer before game will get God on our side;"
6. "I must remember to cross myself before I shoot my freethrows, so they will go in."

Each of these things *can* possibly increase confidence and even motivation sometimes, but they all miss the essence of what religion is all about, which hopefully you will see as this progresses.

This chapter is not here to sell religion, but to give you understanding of this phenomenon in our sporting world.

Religion in sport is a fascinating area to focus in on. As prospective coaches, it is a phenomenon that will touch your life many times down the road. As educators and researchers in a scientific world this non-scientific topic has never been discussed openly in a text on sport psychology or coaching. Today as we begin to notice that many logical things can't be statistically proven, we tend to say, "Wait a minute. Research can't be performed on everything we wonder about, and what's more, we can't disregard "non-scientific" entities due to the fact that they can't be researched." It is from this new and logical thinking pattern that this chapter has evolved.

Many religions take form in our world. This causes us a problem right off the bat in defining the word. Basically religion is the belief in a superior being.

This chapter will focus in on only one of the many religions from across the world. It must be remembered that many of the religions may have similarities and similar effects, but each must be studied in depth to know for sure how they affect athletes.

Today, Christianity is the most prevalent of the many religions in our country. It helped form our country and many of its principles helped our leaders fashion the Constitution, the Declaration of Independence, and the ruling bodies of our country. Christianity therefore makes an incredible impact on our society and our sport world.

It must be understood that we aren't talking about any particular denominations. What we are talking about is an individual who has a one-on-one relationship with God and is deeply devoted to their God, not necessarily religion. This is a key point to understanding this chapter.

The Fellowship of Christian Athletes, Athletes in Action, Pro Athletes Outreach, Sports Ambassadors, Sport Chapels, and the Institute for Athletic Perfection are all Christian organizations which have their outreach in athletics. As this chapter discusses the effects of Christianity on sport, think back in your life or to the life of someone close to you. What role did religion play? Was it an asset? Can it all be explained scientifically or psychologically? Were the effects real or imagined?

To begin with, it is amazing to note the compatibility of sport and a belief in Chris-tianity. Many of the principles, values, and goals of each are very similar to the other. Therefore each in someway contributes to the success of the other. Gary Warner, author of *Competition,* writes, "The qualities that can be derived from athletic competition have, I believe, strong carry-over values to what it means to be a full-fledged follower of the Lord."

Sports promotes the building of character. It is assumed that as one learns to be diligent, to sacrifice, and to overcome pain in the pursuit of a goal in certain sports, a strong sense of accomplishment, pride, and responsibility are learned which contribute strongly to the development of character. Douglas MacArthur once said, "Sport is a vital character builder. It molds the youth of our country for the future roles as custodians of the republic."

Christianity also stresses the building of strong moral character. One is to emulate the life and teaching of Christ. As a Christian gets closer and closer to becoming the person God created them to be, a sense of responsibility and commitment help to form this strong character. Warner says, "In the same way His followers are also called upon to bear the cross, and that is precisely what it means to be a Christian. Just as Christ maintained His communion with the Father by His endurance, so His followers are to maintain this communion with Christ by their endurance (by their character)."

Sport requires self-discipline and striving for excellence. It is through self-sacrifice, prioritizing, hard work and dedication that excellence can be reached in athletics. There is no place for laziness or striving for mediocracy.

Christianity can facilitate the development of this attribute through the importance of self-discipline.

A commitment to Christ and to people through devotion and caring demands a self-discipline to overlook selfishness and pride and instead, give to others. It takes a great deal of self-discipline to turn away from the materialistic lure of this society. It is the ultimate in self-discipline training to become self-disciplined in the physical, mental, and spiritual parts of the body at the same time. Gary Warner says, "Self-discipline, commitment, right priorities and growth — these are the marks of responsibility, and these are the signs of a mature competition (in Christ)."

Both sport and Christianity have an interesting phenomenon, "improvement through pain." In sport the harder one trains, the more pain is involved. Pain becomes seen as improvement — "no pain, no gain."

Christianity talks of "dying to self." One must become totally unselfish. It is the pain of swallowing selfish human pride which brings one to a closer relationship to their Creator. L. Pearce Williams, history professor at Cornell, says. "I like pain. Pain raises sport from the level of entertainment to that of human achievement, and I consider it central to a humane education . . . it is the difference between play and sport. I had a healthy fear of pain, but I realized that through a competitive sport this fear could be overcome and that the man who could overcome it had a distinct advantage over those who lived in its thrill. Pain, of one sort or another is everywhere . . . and I am convinced that learning to live with and transcend physical pain can give one the strength to conquer the mental variety . . . To know of what one is capable, both mentally and physically, is to know the scope of one's freedom."

After reviewing these characteristics of sport and Christianity we can immediately see a couple of things. Number one is that sport and Christianity are very compatible, and number two — we can see that they can strengthen each other because their philosophies are so similar.

Certainly such a belief can help athletes in their search for their athletic potential.

As we look into the playing mind of the Christian athlete we can note thought patterns which correspond very closely with sport psychology strategies. In sport psychology athletes are helped to reach their potential through the use of attentional control, positive perception of the situation, mastery and coping rehearsal, relaxation training and other types of thought control strategies. It is intriguing to see how the Christian athletes have already been using variations of these techniques, but from a little different frame of reference, or how they take these and build them into their faith. For example, the first strategy is that of maximizing attentional control and focus. It is the ability to concentrate on the task at hand and alleviate unwanted distrac-

tions. Athletes must be able to concentrate totally on their performance to reach their peak performance. To the Christian athlete attentional control would be taken from Scripture, "Keep your eyes focused on Christ." In doing this during competition one's total concern is to give their best to God. In its purest form, distractions such as social consciousness, intermediation of others, living up to others' expectations, ego, pride, etc., will not distract from concentration. When competition is performed under one goal, to give one's best for God, then many of the "inside of the mind" distractions are eliminated.

Another strategy is that of positive perception. Perception of situation can be one of the strongest indicators of performance. Many outside factors can influence one's perception of the situation, many times causing it to become out of control. It is safe to say that an altered perception is the seed to many anxiety problems in sport and even in life. Many times the Christian athlete will enter an important contest with this perception:

> "I have practiced hours and hours for this event. I'll give it everything I have; I know that God will be there to give me that little extra when I really need it. I must remember that winning this event is not my number one goal in life. My goal is to become more like Christ in all that I do. Therefore, I want to compete fiercely, play with the attitude of Christ, and remember that I am an example for Him at all times. I don't have to worry about anything. I'll give it my all, a total release of my energy and ability, and the outcome is in God's hands. If I win or lose, make a mistake or make a great play, I'll be happy and positive, because I know that everything that happens to me happens because God wants me to learn and grow, and everything has a lesson or reason. It is not by sulking in defeat or boasting over victory that growth occurs, but it is learning from each which helps me to come closer to God's potential for my life."

This perception of the situation is so positive and anxiety-free, and if followed this individual will likely play great and reach his or her potential. Many times athletes tend to get anxious about an upcoming event and these thoughts will follow:

"This is the most important event of my season. I'm so anxious about playing well. Will I make a dumb mistake in front of everyone? My competition is going to be tough. What if they blow me out and make a fool out of me. Will coach like my performance? Will I let my team down? Will my skills break down? If we lose this one, it's all over. I'll hate myself if we lose. How will I be able to face my parents and friends if we lose and I play bad? We've got to have luck on our side for a change. I'm so anxious. I hope I do well."

It is interesting to see how important perception is as we try to set our athletes up for success. It is important for them to know that: No. 1, the "work of worry" is destructive; No. 2, defeat isn't the end of the world; and No. 3, giving 100% is all any coach can ask for. The Christian athlete's philosophy is a great way to get there. It is a totally positive perception of this situation.

A third strategy is that of rehearsal. There are two kinds, mastery and coping. Mastery rehearsal is a confidence-building strategy. It requires one to think through an upcoming performance (a day before, five minutes before, or just prior to next shot or play during a game). Many times athletes have to lie to themselves about competing successfully, and therefore mastery rehearsal will most likely be inefficient. Mastery rehearsal will help alleviate anxiety when one has practiced thoroughly and successfuly for the event. When one has done all they can to prepare, and they know realistically what they expect to do, then mastery rehearsal is a set-up for reaching potential through *confident* performance. The Christian athlete realizes that God helps those who help themselves. Gary Player responding to his 1974 "Master's" victory said, "I knew I was going to win on the first tee. It is the best golf I've ever played in a major championship all the way. I derive a lot of strength from my belief in God. I'm a Bible puncher. When I work for something, I expect it to happen. No one works as hard at golf as I do. No athlete has ever traveled so much as I have. I say all this only to try to make everybody understand what it means to me to win. There is no way to properly describe

the gratification from working so hard, and then being rewarded for it." The Christian athlete feels that it is their responsibility to practice hard and diligently, so that their specific talent can be maximized.

When the big contest comes and the "chips are on the table" they are confident during their rehearsal of the event. Mastery rehearsal can be realistic for them. They know that God will surely be with them during competition, which will give them a little extra boost. They believe that they will be successful, and mastery rehearsal will help them.

Probably the most important of the rehearsal strategies is that of coping rehearsal. It is very common for an athlete to approach a contest very anxious about "what could possibly happen this time to mess me up." It is so helpful to visualize all the things that could possibly go wrong and devise a solution for each. This is incredibly important to one's confidence, not detrimental in that they know that they will not face something that they are not prepared for.

Many think that it is absurd to think of anything but positive thoughts, but coping rehearsal has proven to produce positive results. The Christian athlete is told to be prepared that they will face many trials. They certainly don't believe life is all roses. The Christian is aware of the possible traps and problems by thinking ahead and they prepare a solution, knowing that God will lead them through all situations if they are faithful.

The final strategy of great importance is that of relaxation training. In today's athletic world filled with pressure and stress, relaxation techniques, if used properly, can alleviate tension and anxieties which are detrimental to performance. Many Christian athletes (CAs) say that they don't need it or want it. Some sport psychologists or coaches may take offense to this attitude, but they must try to understand the CA's perspective. No one lives up to God's ideal for life, but many are leaning in the right direction. The ideal existence is one that is lived in a completely relaxed, confident state. The CA really believes that life is but a brief moment in time compared to eternity. They live on the promise of eternity in heaven and strive to get there. They understand that all of the problems and decisions of life boil down to one question when it's all over: "Did I believe through faith that Christ was indeed God's way of reaching down to us, and did I live a life in this faith?" In knowing that you have eternal life, the problems and stresses of this world tend to look smaller and many times insignificant.

On the other hand, most people of the world feel like this life is it — you only go around once. Problems and decisions of this life become immensely important. Trying to live up to the world's definitions of success provokes increasing anxiety. The way we teach these people to relax is through relaxation training, where their minds can escape the rat race for a few moments. But the Christian athlete's mind isn't in the rat race to begin with — their inner mind is in another world, if you will. So instead of using these techniques they will meditate on Scripture and prayer. But you see, they are actually partaking in relaxation training. It just hasn't been referred to as such for the past 2,000 years.

One of the most difficult problems in life, and especially in sports, is that of identity crisis. This may come in the form of the ending of a career from organized sports at the high school, college, or pro level. The most difficult way to have a career ended is through that of a traumatic injury. This is one of the ultimate tests of the sport psychologist and sport psychology principles. Many people are scared to deal with this type of individual because of the total unpredictability of the situation. Some athletes see this as the end of life and would as soon be dead, and often may contemplate suicide.

I read in *Sports Illustrated* a story of a young man who had grown up an athlete who was confined to a wheelchair through an accident. He tried for years to cope with this new life, but it was so different from the one he had lived before. One day he had some friends drive him to a secluded place where he shot himself in the head. Other confined athletes have nervous breakdowns or severe fits of depression. Others disappear. They don't want anyone to see them in this state and they become a recluse. Still others see this as a challenge, an obstacle to overcome, the ultimate challenge of their faith, themselves, or God.

It's through traumatic injury that some people for the first time understand or even contemplate the meaning of life. For the first time they may realize that life isn't a football game. For the first time they may realize that life, too, like a game, will end. Why does life end? What happens to them then? Why did this happen to me? What does life have to offer now that my career has ended? Who cares about me now? Is there a God? Does He care? These questions and more bombard the athlete as he seeks a new identity, a new way of life, a new beginning.

At this point, more than any in life, faith seems to play an incredibly important role. It doesn't matter if the athlete had a "belief" before or not. It is at this time that they are reaching for something solid to lean on, not fragile like the talent that they had depended on so much in the past. It is at this point that faith gives them many answers to their questions. It is at this point many times that faith in God is their last and only hope.

It is at this point in life that psychology can't give all that a person needs. Sport psychology can be an asset in that goals can be redefined, coping strategies can be instigated, pain management techniques can help, attitudes that made them a great athlete can be encouraged to continue to help them overcome this problem, and positive thinking and motivation can help them through the painful process of rehabilitation, if rehabilitation can be instigated. These are very helpful ways in which sport psychology can be an asset.

But sport psychology can't *promise* anything. Sport psychology can't answer many of the questions about life that they have been forced to think about.

Several years ago a young man, named Brian Sternberg, held the world record in the pole vault. He had beaten out John Pennel to represent the U.S. in Moscow, Russia at the World Games, 1963. Brian was a handsome, strong, brawny athlete. He was a proud man and had life by the tail. He was an excellent athlete. During a training session for the World Games Brian was working on a trampoline. It was on this trampoline that this happy, successful, talented athlete met adversity face to face. He landed wrong and broke his neck. Suddenly, very quickly he had to face the fact that he would never vault, run, swim, play games again. He was to be confined to a wheel-chair for the rest of his life. It was at this time that he had to painfully realize that life was indeed very fragile, something all of us take for granted, and that building a trust in sport for all of your happiness and needs was again very fragile. Brian struggled with the question, "Why?" for a long time. He thought more and more about the meaning of life. It was in this helpless state that he reached out for God and touched what he reached for. He said it was the first time that he really had something solid and firm to put his faith in. Before it had been sport. Brian somehow was able to thank God for his condition because it slowed him down enough to open his eyes to what life was really all about. It showed him that life was more than a sport. It showed him that there really was a God who cared when all else failed. Brian believes that paralysis, sick-ness, or disease are not God's will for any-one's life. But he understands that it was through tragedy that he met Christ, and to him meeting Christ and knowing Him is more important than anything else in life. Speaking to an F.C.A. Conference Brian said, "Paralysis is terrible in many ways and I hate it, but it is far better than being healthy and to not know the power of Jesus Christ."

In 1978 at Baylor University a young man, a defensive back for the Bears, hit the practice field face down, never to get up under his own power again. During a tackle Kyle Wood snapped his neck. It shattered the team, the coaches, and most of all, Kyle. Kyle coped by reaching out to a God who took hold of his crippled body. Kyle was diagnosed as a complete quadraplegic. Two years ago, the year of his accident, he

was wheeled out on a stretcher to see his team win the Peach Bowl. One year later he made miraculous recovery in rehabilitation that baffled even the most optimistic doc-tors. He entered the locker room prior to the rival contest with Arkansas in his wheel-chair, pushed himself up, stood on his feet and reached out his arms and received the game ball. He got a standing ovation from 80,000 fans. Kyle attributes the miraculous progress to God's power in his life. Doctors don't understand.

We have talked about the use of two meth-ods that one may use to reach a greater per-formance in athletics and life, or overcome the crisis — sport psychology and Chris-tianity. But if Christianity is only seen as a tool that a coach uses to help an athlete to reach max performance in sport, then I've failed miserably. There have been too many miracles, to many coincidences, and too many *real* experiences down through the years to just to brush off the idea that re-ligion is just a psychological tool.

As a sport psychologist or coach, what are you going to do when you are called into an athlete's hospital room and there they lie with bolts in their neck and head, para-lyzed from the neck down?

Their life of sport shattered, what do we respond with when they ask with tears in their eyes, "Coach, there is a God, isn't there?" He will help me, won't He? Please say yes, coach. He is my only hope." And as a coach or sport psychologist, who holds much confidence in the kids' eyes, we had better have thought through the question (our answers better not just be a tool to help the kid, because he'll see right through it), and our answer better be real.

31

Coach And Athlete Burnout

Sarah Odom and Tom Perrin
University of Virginia

INTRODUCTION

Erin is a coach at a major university. She has had the job for a few years and has learned firsthand about the tremendous pressure to win in women's sports. Erin spends what little "free" time she has alone and wishes she had a more normal social life. She has begun having headaches and just can't get to sleep lately even though she is very tired. This didn't happen when Erin was a high school coach. She wasn't aware that college coaching would be so different from high school coaching. She just was not prepared. Erin would give almost anything to have a family, or even a few close friends. In fact, this is so important to her that she's going to quit coaching as soon as the current season ends. Erin is burned out.

John is a high school basketball coach. He got his job as soon as he finished college. John had always wanted to be a coach and was certainly excited that his first teaching job included coaching basketball as well. At first, John felt sure he could produce a winner, fill the gym with fans and make money for the school. But now, after five mediocre seasons, John doesn't fill the stands and the administration offers no moral or financial support. If John isn't planning practices, he's doing lesson plans for the classes he teaches and many evenings he's not home until 7 or 8 o'clock at the earliest and often it is nearer midnight when he arrives home. At this point of the evening he's ready to just drop into bed and go to sleep. The enthusiasm is gone. The excitement is gone. The fun is gone. John is burned out.

Al coaches a minor sport at a university. Of course, this sport doesn't get the money or the fans that the football team gets, but Al still must spend hours and hours at practice, games, and in recruiting efforts. Seems he's never at home and hardly ever has time to really talk to his wife — and his children seem to be growing up so fast. He wishes he could talk to his wife or even just have some friends to talk to. But no one outside coaching really understands and Al doesn't risk showing too much dissatisfaction to those he works with at the university. Al knows the athletic director doesn't like the minor sports taking money that could be spent on the football team and he feels that all the athletic director needs is a good excuse to get rid of him and the program. Al spends all day with people but he's lonesome and he needs someone to talk to. Al is burned out.

Marge is twelve years old and has already won several state and regional tennis titles. She has lots of potential, a good coach, supportive parents, and practices many long hours every day. Marge began playing tennis almost as soon as she could walk and had logged considerable playing time even at the young age of twelve. Before and after school each day Marge meets her coach to practice and works on homework the rest of the day. During tournaments Marge often misses school for a few days. Seems she really doesn't know anyone there anyway. The kids know she's good and they're proud she's from their school, but they don't understand why she misses so many classes and never seems to go to any parties. Marge has always loved tennis — and it's not that she doesn't still love it — but it's not the only thing she would like to be doing. She wishes she had more friends and might even like to try some other sports when she goes to junior high school. But there just isn't time for all that. Marge knows she has the talent to one day play on

214

the professional tour and dreams of being successful at major tennis tournaments — that is, if she can just stay with tennis that long. Practice makes her tired; school makes her tired; homework makes her tired. Marge is in danger of burning out before she ever has a chance to see how good she can really be.

These four people involved in athletics are suffering from a condition that appears to be on the increase among coaches and athletes. They are victims of *burnout*. Burnout has begun to affect many people in all professions. It is partly caused by a society that has high expectations and it is partly caused by individuals who have high expectations. In either case, burnout victims try too hard to achieve high goals and sacrifice themselves in the process. Family and friends may also suffer but the primary victims are the coaches and athletes themselves. This chapter will explore exactly what burnout is, its symptoms, why it happens, and steps that can be taken to combat it or, better yet, avoid it.

WHAT IS BURNOUT?

The term "burnout" first appeared in the professional literature in 1974 in the writing of Herbert J. Freudenberger. Since that time, numerous authors have attempted to apply this concept to a variety of fields and professions such as teaching, counseling, law enforcement, and coaching (Austin, 1981; Bardo, 1979; Boy & Pine, 1981; Cunningham, 1982; Edelwich & Brodsky, 1980; Ellison & Genz, 1978; Jones and Emmanuel, 1981; Malone and Rotella, 1981; Maslach, 1976; Spaniol and Caputo, 1980).

Burnout is a debilitating physical, psychological, and emotional condition. Although it is not accepted as a specific medical condition, it does exist as a very real response to stress. While it may erupt suddenly, burnout is generally considered to be chronic in nature. Its occurrence, including acute manifestations, is believed to reflect the buildup of stress over an extended period of time (Freudenberger with Richelson, 1980).

Accurately defining burnout is not easy. It exists as both a "process" and a specific "state" or condition. Freudenberger (1974) chooses to consider burnout as defined in a dictionary: "to fail, wear out, or become exhausted by making excessive demands on energy, strength, or resources" (p. 73). Another definition comes from Maslach (1978) who sees burnout as a "loss of concern for people with whom one is working. It is characterized by an emotional exhaustion in which the staff person no longer has any positive feelings, sympathy, or respect for clients" (p. 113). In other words, the professional, be this someone in a "helping profession" or a coach or athlete, just does not care anymore and can find nothing good about his or her job or sport.

Burnout is easily cultivated by contemporary society which entices individuals through financial reward, status and recognition to work hard and get ahead. The pressure to achieve, whether imposed by self or others, can be very stressful. If individuals fail to cope and deal constructively with the stress of hard work and unfulfilled wishes, they can easily feel worn out, depressed and frustrated. If left alone, this condition usually worsens until an individual feels physically, psychologically and emotionally exhausted. Individuals become just too tired to care about anything in their lives (Edelwich & Brodsky, 1980; Freudenberger, 1980).

SYMPTOMS AND STAGES OF BURNOUT

Early recognition of the symptoms of burnout can prevent burnout from occurring or at least lessen its effects. Anyone who is familiar with the work done in the area of stress will quickly recognize burnout symptoms. The symptoms of burnout are actually reactions to stress that have continued for so long they have completely exhausted the victim.

Think for a moment and you may recall coaches you know who are always tired — who even wake up tired. Or coaches who have trouble sleeping or who have ulcers. Or coaches who seem depressed much of the time. Or coaches who have no patience with their athletes, who constantly yell at their athletes, or who just do not care about their athletes. Or coaches who feel they really cannot do their jobs because the school administration controls every move they make.

Perhaps you can recall athletes who never have time for anything but practice. Or athletes who feel like their entire careers and lives are being shaped by their parents and/or their coaches. Or athletes who "fly off the handle" if every little detail of practice does not run smoothly or their performance in practice does not meet their expectations for that particular day.

Some of the symptoms of burnout have been categorized by Cardinell (1980). These symptoms are divided into physical and behavioral aspects in the following manner:

A. Physical
1. Fatigue and physical exhaustion
2. Headaches and gastrointestinal disturbances
3. Weight loss
4. Sleeplessness
5. Depression
6. Shortness of breath

B. Behavioral
1. Changeable mood
2. Increased irritability
3 .Loss of caring for people
4. Lowered tolerance for frustration
5. Suspiciousness of others
6. Feelings of helplessness and lack of control
7. Greater professional risk taking

Burnout seems to occur in stages of severity. The symptoms are essentially the same in first and second degree burnout with the distinction being the length of time the symptoms last. First degree burnout, according to Reed (1979) is "short bouts of irritability, fatigue, worry and frustration" (p. 68). Second degree burnout is similar but lasts for two weeks or more. Symptoms of third degree burnout are more severe and reach more into the realm of actual physical symptoms such as "ulcers, chronic back pain, and migraine headaches" (p. 68). If any of these symptoms are present, it may be time for the affected coaches and athletes to look at their schedules, interactions and themselves to see if the symptoms warrant some constructive action.

WHO IS SUSCEPTIBLE TO BURNOUT?

Burnout has little regard for age, sex, or background. It is not unique to any single profession or stratum of employment. Those most susceptible to experiencing burnout are those individuals who are extremely dedicated, high-achieving and goal-oriented. They are determined individuals who tend to take on more than their share of responsibility and do more than their share of work. They are overachievers and perfectionists. They feel a strong need to succeed, they worry about getting things done, and they find it difficult to relax (Freudenberger with Richelson, 1980).

It is important to note that despite possessing all of these characteristics, some individuals are still able to avoid burnout. For whatever reason, they are able to cope effectively and resist stress. In most cases, however, the combination of several of these personality traits may cause problems for individuals at some point in their lives.

Because these individuals are very competent and self-sufficient, they often refuse to accept the fact that they have problems, limitations or weaknesses. The early signs of burnout are difficult to recognize in these individuals. When faced with recurring failure and frustration, they tend to work harder. They are challenged to push on where others would stop and seek help. In fact, individuals with these types of personal characteristics are either likely to blame others, or blame circumstances beyond their control before they will admit they have a problem. Their self-perception simply does not allow them to consider that what is wrong is a function of factors within themselves (Edelwich & Brodsky, 1980; Freudenberger with Richelson, 1980).

Individuals in the so-called "helping professions" are frequently prone to burnout. In addition to possessing many of the previously noted personal characteristics and values, individuals in these fields must deal with the inherent difficulty involved in working with and attempting to change other people. Doctors, nurses, teachers, coaches, social workers, day care workers and police officers are often very idealistic individuals. They are frequently motivated to enter their field by a strong desire to positively impact society and the world around them in some way. These individuals want to "make a difference" in the lives of others (Edelwich & Brodsky, 1980).

Edelwich & Brodsky (1980), however, consider this type of attitude to be a "built-in

216

frustration" which is characteristic of individuals in the helping professions. For, unfortunately, these professions are filled with suffering, frustration and misery. Teachers are continually faced with overcrowded classrooms and students who do not want to learn. Police officers and social workers battle crime, poverty, and hopelessness on a daily basis. Coaches are faced with limited budgets, poor facilities and lack of support. Doctors and nurses often see their patients suffer and die despite their efforts and the advances of modern medicine.

Individuals in the helping professions can easily become disappointed and disillusioned by what they experience. They are often motivated by such a strong desire to give that they set unrealistic goals and place excessive demands upon themselves. Dramatic discrepancies between the expectations which these individuals hold and reality often exist. This discrepancy is often precipitated by the necessity for these individuals to exhibit different, if not contradictory, skills simultaneously. Because they work with people, individuals in the "helping" fields are often required to interact with and be sensitive to others while, at the same time, maintain distance and detachment (Edelwich & Brodksy, 1980; Ellison & Genz, 1978; Maslach, 1976).

In addition, the act of helping is usually "non-reciprocal" in nature. Individuals tend not to seek nurturing and support from those they help. And those who are receiving support tend not to give it in return. Thus, individuals who are often sacrificing themselves in an attempt to provide for others are often not receiving any support in return, from those whom they seek to assist. This is simply one more cause for the buildup of frustration and discouragement which can lead to burnout by individuals in the helping professions (Spaniol & Caputo, 1980).

Just as there are certain personal characteristics which predispose an individual to burnout, there are also job or work related factors to be considered. Most typically, jobs that are repetitive, routine, unchallenging and controlled by administrative directives are very conducive to causing burnout. The continued presence of such characteristics in one's daily work environment depreciates individual self-worth and self-

esteem. An individual will find work to be unchallenging and will lack the motivation to perform the job well. Frustration, boredom, and depression can easily develop and burnout can result. Listed below are other common situational factors frequently cited as potentially contributing to burnout:

—Long hours
—Low pay
—Isolation
—Time constraints
—Lack of peer support
—Poor supervision
—Limited feedback
—Information overload
—Sexism
—Poor working conditions
—Pressure to be creative
—Lack of professional mobility
—Lack of reward

(Austin, 1981; Cunningham, 1982; Earls, 1981; Edelwich & Brodsky, 1980; Ellison & Genz, 1978, Kohlmaier, 1981; Walsh, 1979).

The Coach. Coaches, just like people in the helping professions, want to "make a difference in someone else's life." This worthy goal can lead them to set unrealistic goals and make unrealistic demands of themselves. They take care of everyone but themselves. They want to help others so much that they give much more to others than they get in return.

For coaches, this means that in addition to actual coaching duties, they may counsel their athletes about personal problems with girlfriends or boyfriends while having marital problems themselves. This also means there are coaches who spend every free moment planning practices and games, giving support and encouragement to players but getting no encouragement or support, either moral or financial, from their own school administration.

Coaches spend a large majority of their time in contact with other people. These other people can provide coaches with many varied challenges during the course of a day. Athletes have different personalities, different problems, possibly the same problems but with different perspectives of them. Coaches, therefore, must constantly be on their toes to handle these problems and perspectives. Working with people presents ever-changing challenges.

The frustrating aspect is that just when a coaches may feel they have resolved an athletic problem on the court or the field, the athlete may have a bad experience at home or school, or someone new may enter their life. These circumstances can drastically change any plans and solutions coaches might have had. For example, a basketball player may have just learned to shoot free throws under pressure when a new boyfriend or girlfriend shows up for the first time during post-season play. An athlete's parent may become ill the day of a state tournament. These situations are unexpected and necessitate coaches giving much of their time and much of themselves to deal with the situation. These demands and others like them are contributors to burnout in coaches.

The Athlete. The attitude our society has concerning being the best and getting ahead filters down to even the youngest athletic competitors. Children begin at a very young age to play sports, to play to be the best, to play to win. From the Little League field to the swimming pool to the tennis court, children are working to be the best they can be at their sports. Much time and effort is being put into getting to the top as an athlete.

Women's tennis is a prime example of young girls competing as professionals. There are numerous teenage professionals including one girl who turned pro at age fourteen. In order to become a professional athlete at age fourteen, there had to have been many hours put into this single pursuit. These athletes who work really hard to improve their performance are subject to burnout. Their dedication to practice is just as demanding and requires the same type of sacrifices in other areas of life as those demanded of coaches.

The athlete will probably not have excessive responsibilities like coaches. The main overload feature for athletes is time demands. An athlete who is putting in long hours of practice while attending school can feel much stress from parents, friends, girlfriends, or boyfriends about the lack of time the athlete has with them. As with coaches or anyone else who has strict time demands, it is difficult to balance out time to do everything that requires the athlete's attention.

An athlete in high school or college may have to contend with teachers, professors or administrators who do not understand or sympathize with time demands. There is school all day, practice several hours in the afternoon or games that may include lengthy travel times. After all of this the athlete is expected to study, rest and, if lucky, have some semblance of a social life. Sometimes it is necessary for athletes to be away from campus and classes for extended periods, so some special considerations must be afforded the athlete. These special considerations are more willingly granted if the team or individual is winning than losing. There is always the pressure to win vs. to be considered a failure. Unfortunately, rewards are not generally given for putting forth effort like they are for achievement of the goal of winning.

Young athletes may begin very early and with much enthusiasm to work hard at their sports. Some find it perfectly acceptable to miss out on other areas of life in their quest for athletic excellence. Others may get tired of sports and decide to enjoy those other areas of life they have been missing. For young athletes, their lives are in rapid transition and they may discover they would like to do more things with their friends or improve their grades, which means that sport may no longer be foremost in their lives. If they must work so hard that they do not have time for these other activities on top of their practice schedule, they may come to resent the long hours of practice that take them away from these other interests.

At first, it may not matter that these aspiring athletes' grades are slipping or that they do not have time to date or go to parties or spend casual time with friends. The initial period of enthusiasm and rapid improvement as they are learning their sport make up for the other areas that are being neglected. But later the improvement may not be quite as rapid or it may be evident to the athletes that they really do not have any close friends. The only other people they have time to see are other athletes who are just as motivated as they are to practice hard. Possibly other athletes on the team do not work as hard and they resent the hard work the dedicated athletes put into their sport.

There is the potential for the group of dedicated athletes to be sources of support for each other. But often, there just is not

218

time to get everything done and develop friendships as well. As long as this is enjoyable to the athletes and they can continue this type of schedule on their own accord, they may continue without ever experiencing burnout. Unfortunately, for the very talented athlete, other people — possibly coaches or parents — may become so involved in the athlete's career that they literally take control of the athlete's life. While these coaches and parents may mean well, they can put the athlete in a position of powerlessness so that once enjoyable sport activities become a chore and become someone else's pursuit. It is much more difficult to continue training if the athlete does not have a sense of control over his/her goals.

Burnout can occur in these young athletes as well as older athletes who have become tired and frustrated from years of practice. The commitment must continue through high school, college and the professional ranks and some athletes will burn out if they must concentrate too heavily on their sports at the exclusion of all other things in their life.

WHAT CAN BE DONE ABOUT BURNOUT?

Burnout affects almost everyone to some degree whether or not they realize it. However, steps can be taken to prevent or overcome the occurrence of burnout. Edelwich and Brodsky (1980) refer to the process of taking specific action in response to or anticipation of burnout as "intervention." Combatting burnout may involve changing jobs within one's field or leaving the field altogether. It may mean restructuring relationships with peers or family members. It may mean modifying one's job description, going back to school or taking a vacation. Whatever the action, intervention involves "doing" something to overcome or prevent burnout.

Reality Therapy. To address the psychological and emotional disturbances which result with the occurrence of burnout, Edelwich and Brodsky (1980) propose a two-part process. The first phase of this process involves the use of Reality Therapy. Although it does not provide any specific answers to the problems that can lead to burnout, Reality Therapy does provide a general framework within which given problems can be confronted and dealt with constructively. In short, Reality Therapy places responsibility on the people who have been victimized by burnout for first recognizing their personal needs and then taking action to bring about a fulfillment of those needs, regardless of the reality of the situation in which they find themselves.

The specifics of Reality Threapy will not be discussed here. These specifics can be found in the work of Glasser (1975) and Ellis & Harper (1975). The information provided here will give a general outline of the important steps necessary for examining one's personal values and beliefs as part of the process of overcoming burnout.

1. TAKE RESPONSIBILITY. The first step in the process simply requires that individuals know exactly what responsibilities they do and do not hold. Specifically, individuals must accept that they are solely responsible for their own actions and behaviors and not those of others. Regardless of how others may act in their personal lives or on the job, individuals must assume control of themselves.

2. HOLD REALISTIC EXPECTATIONS. Individuals must also be sure their expectations are in line with reality. They must be willing to accept the "givens" in their situation, this is, those things which are beyond their control. Interpretation of actions and behaviors is critical. Individuals must be careful not to judge themselves or others by an unrealistic standard of perfection. Unfortunately, people who are very achievement-oriented and dedicated find difficulty in doing this and, consequently, experience the discrepancy between their expectations and reality. This often precipitates burnout.

Setting realistic expectations can be aided by knowing what to expect. This means knowing ahead of time what the requirements of coaching or participating as an athlete entail. Anticipation of potential problems and developing strategies ahead of time to deal with these problems can help prevent burnout. The following are lists of things coaches and athletes should know before totally commiting themselves to athletics.

Things Coaches Wish They Had Known Beforehand:

1. There will be a demand for huge amounts of your time. You'll not only have actual coaching and teaching duties, but you'll probably have administrative duties such as paperwork, equipment management, and uniform management among other things.

2. You will be responsible for many other people. Their health, their safety, their performance and their problems will all become part of your life and your responsibility.

3. Do not expect that anyone — including your athletes — will realize or understand that you have so many time requirements and responsibilities as a coach.

4. It is very unlikely that you will receive as high a salary as you would like or need.

5. Your athletic program may have a ceiling on its growth and development because of lack of funds.

6. You may not have as much time for the special person or persons in your life as you or they would like. They may or may not understand this. Your players, your school, and your community may think you're wonderful while, at the same time, those who are the closest to you think less highly of you because you spend so much time away from them.

7. You may not even have time for the social life to pursue that special person in your life. You may just have to accept the fact that it is necessary for you to be unattached during your coaching career. This, and not your success as a coach, may be a determining factor as to the length of time you are a coach.

8. You may not get to spend holidays with family or friends because of tournaments or practices.

9. If you are a college coach of a major sport, you will be expected to do a lot of entertaining. You may have to be a constant host or hostess.

10. Many times high school sports overlap and there is no break for the coach. You may have to continue to work without any "real" vacations.

11. You may not have time for your friends. In fact, you may not have many friends at all. Your only contact with people may be those in your profession — who have as little time as you have.

12. Your life will be public and therefore subject to public scrutiny by the fans, the families of your players, the media — everyone.

13. Your job will many times require that you make quick decisions and the consequences of the decisions will be evident to the public. Everyone in the stands and in the community may have an opinion on the correctness of your judgements.

14. If there are other coaches at your institution, they may all be having winning seasons while you are not. This may increase the pressure for you to perform well.

15. Your athletes may need to confide in you or seek advice from you. You will therefore need counseling skills. You may receive phone calls from your athletes very late at night or very early in the morning.

16. You will need the interpersonal skills to interact with a wide variety of people.

17. Yours is a public relations occupation. You may be asked to make speeches and public appearances above and beyond your actual coaching duties.

18. You will be required to do much travelling. You better enjoy it or at least accept the fact that you may live many days and nights out of a suitcase and a "normal" home life may be impossible.

19. Your job will probably depend on your success as measured by number of wins and losses. You may be an excellent skills teacher and all of your athletes may be improving and having fun, though they are still losing contests. You may, therefore, be considered by many as a failure as a coach.

20. Your occupation may not be highly

regarded by some people outside of athletics. You may just be considered a "play person" in the eyes of some and may not receive support from the administration and other faculty members.

21. On the other hand, if you are very successful and you are held in high regard by others, you may have to learn to handle the "glory" and publicity and the possible invasion of your private life.

22. Your athletes may have many demands placed upon their time from other sources. You may be working with athletes who do not wish to devote as much time to athletic pursuits as you.

23. You need to know your ultimate goals in coaching. You may have problems if these goals involve making lots of money or furthering your education. There may not be time for a second job or a chance to take more courses. Know and understand the limitations of the goals you set.

24. You may constantly be rearranging schedules for courts, fields, pools, etc. because of lack of facilities, particularly if you are a female coach or a coach of a minor sport.

25. Female and Black coaches should beware. There still seems to be discrimination in terms of facilities and money for your programs. Depending on the sport, it may be very difficult for Black coaches to even be hired.

Things Athletes Wish They Had Known Beforehand:

1. There will be time for almost nothing other than your sport.
2. If you play more than one sport you may not get any breaks from your sport activities.
3. Others — coaches or parents — may decide where you will spend almost every minute of your day.
4. It may be hard to make friends with people outside your sport who do not understand your long hours.
5. You may be too busy to be able to develop a close relationship with that "special person."

6. Some people think athletes are just "dumb jocks" who play all the time — a very negative image.
7. If you are very successful, people may want your friendship just because of "who you are."
8. There may be lots of travel for your contests — home may seem to be only a suitcase at times.
9. Your grades may suffer because you are just too tired to study.
10. You may not get to spend holidays with family or friends because of tournaments or practice.

In order to assist someone in developing realistic expectations and assuming responsibility for actions, more specific steps should be taken. These steps are appropriate for both the coach and athlete in dealing with burnout. The steps are as follows:

1. SET REALISTIC GOALS — Define goals precisely. Understand what you are capable of achieving within the limitations of personal time and energy. Do not try or expect to change the world.
2. FOCUS ON SUCCESS, NOT ON FAILURE — No one can help everybody nor can they accomplish everything they would like to. Failure is part of life. Most people will experience many more failures in their lifetime than successes. Know what proportion of successes makes your job worthwhile.
3. FOCUS ON THE PROCESS, NOT THE PRODUCT — Seek to gain enjoyment through "doing" and through working with others to achieve an end. Focusing on the exercise of skills, the human contact, the emotional involvement and the development of rapport with others can bring tremendous satisfaction.
4. KEEP A TIME PERSPECTIVE — Do not expect results immediately. Do not try to achieve all that you hope to in the first month or year. Create a realistic time frame by which to interpret results.
5. DO NOT INTERPRET RESULTS SELF-REFERENTIALLY — Keep your own efforts in perspective when evaluating both good and bad outcomes. Be objective. Be fair to yourself.

6. DEFINE SUCCESS REALISTICALLY —
Understand how you define success.
Evaluate the criteria used in that definition. Be sure it corresponds accurately with your own abilities as well
as the "reality" of the situation in
which you work.

Problem Solving. The second part of the
plan proposed by Edelwich and Brodsky
(1980) for addressing burnout is that of
problem solving. This phase of the process
involves "actively" confronting a specific
problem whether it be on or off the job. In
this case, an athlete's job is competing at
his or her sport. The following is an outline
of this process.

1. What is the specific problem? Has it
already occurred or is it likely to occur in the future? What does it feel
like physically and emotionally? How
have you tended to respond to it up
to this point?
2. Identify alternative solutions to the
problem. What are barriers to change
which may prevent you from pursuing one of these options? How realistic is change? What are the costs and
benefits of each of these alternatives?
What are the consequences of alternative behaviors?
3. Choose a realistic alternative behavior which can bring about the desired
change.
4. Make a formal commitment to act on
that choice within a given period of
time.
5. Solidify that commitment to change
by avowing it to another person or
persons. Enlist the support of a
helper to provide feedback and encouragement.

Although presented in abbreviated form,
Reality Therapy and Problem Solving are interventions which can be employed at any
stage in the burnout process in an attempt
to alleviate or prevent it. Because most of
the problems which lead to burnout center
around thoughts, feelings, beliefs, and perceptions these techniques can be employed
to restructure cognitions so they are more
closely aligned with reality. In this way, the
likelihood of a person becoming frustrated
is reduced and so, in turn, is the likelihood
of burnout.

Specific Interventions. Many other authors and researchers have presented some
specific behavioral interventions (Austin,
1981; Boy & Pine, 1981; Cunningham, 1982;
Earls, 1981; Edelwich & Brodsky, 1980;
Freudenberger with Richelson, 1980; Kohlmaier, 1981; Malone & Rotella, 1981; Maslach, 1976; Spaniol & Caputo, 1980). The
most common among these interventions
are as follows:

—Take a vacation.
—Take time off — a week, a season, a
year.
—Gain further education. Improve
skills.
—Change jobs or sports.
—Change fields or professions.
—Make on-the-job adjustments in
such things as schedule or rela-
tions with peers and supervisors.
—Attend conferences, clinics, and
workshops with an open mind.
—Occasionally "blow out.' Let off
frustrations to friends and peers.
—Seek family and peer support.
—Seek professional counseling.
—Alter or discontinue certain habits.
—Maintain good nutrition and exer-
cise regularly.
—Learn to relax.
—Learn to say "No!"

If these techniques, or any others like
them, are to work effectively in combatting
burnout, they must be carried out consciously and with a clear purpose in mind. In
making any kind of change, an individual
must be aware that new solutions can bring
about new problems. No matter which intervention techniques are used, there is no absolute guarantee they will prevent or cure
burnout. In many cases, a coach or athlete
may have to try several strategies before
finding the one which best suits his or her
needs and specific problems.

Regardless of the specific intervention
employed in dealing with burnout, it is generally agreed that the first and most important step which can be taken is to increase
self-awareness. People must honestly seek
to examine their own values and behaviors.
They must learn to read and interpret their
personal experiences related to their profession and those not related to their profession (Edelwich & Brodsky, 1980; Freudenberger with Richelson, 1981).

Coaches and athletes must recognize

222

that if they hold high personal needs for achievement along with an enthusiastic commitment, they are potential burnout victims. They must also evaluate their goals and be sure they are in line with reality. It is also necessary to learn to accept the aspects of society and their sports which cannot be changed. If they do nothing else, increasing self-awareness and keeping a proper perspective will go a long way toward effectively coping with or preventing burnout.

There are no easy answers to burnout, to turning a bad situation into a good one. But there are solutions for those who truly care about their own happiness and who are willing to put some effort into getting the most out of their own life as well as helping others. Persistence is important in athletics — it is important in personal lives as well. Coaches or athletes who are not satisfied with their careers because they are "spinning their wheels" and burning out should persist until they can find a means of balancing the important areas of their life. Hard work is good and can produce benefits for the coaches and athletes but it can also drive them from sport if it is not kept in perspective. Coaches and athletes will find they benefit more if they do whatever is necessary to remain enthusiastic and excited about their sports.

REFERENCES

Austin, D. A. The teacher burnout issue. *Journal of Physical Education, Recreation and Dance*, 1981, *52*, 35-36.

Bardo, P. The pain of teacher burnout: A case history. *Phi Delta Kappan*, 1979, *61*(4), 252-254.

Boy, A. V. & Pine, G. J. Avoiding counselor burnout through role renewal. *Education Digest*, 1981, *46*, 50-52.

Cardinell, C. Teacher burnout: An analysis. *Action in Teacher Education*, 1980, *2*(4), 9-15.

Cunningham, W. G. Research-based strategies for fighting teacher burnout. *Education Digest*, 1982, *48*, 20-23.

Earls, N. F. How teachers avoid burnout. *Journal of Physical Education, Recreation and Dance*, 1981, *52*, 41-43.

Edelwich, J. & Brodsky, A. *Burn-out: Stages of disillusionment in the helping profession.* New York: Human Sciences Press, 1980.

Ellis, A. & Harper, R. A. *A new guide to rational living.* Hollywood, CA: Wilshire, 1975.

Ellison, K. W. & Genz, J. L. The police officer as burned-out Samaritan. *FBI Law Enforcement Bullein*, 1978, 1-7.

Freudenberger, H. . Staff burn-out. *Journal of Social Issues*, 1974, *30*(1), 159-165.

Freudenberger, H. J. with Richelson, G. How to survive burnout. *Nation's Business*, 1980, *68*, 53-56.

Glasser, W. *Reality therapy.* New York: Harper Colophon Books, 1975.

Jones, M. A. & Emmanuel, J. The stages and recovery steps of teacher "burnout." *Education Digest*, 1981, *46*, 9-11.

Kohlmaier, J. Organizing to combat burnout. *Journal of Physical Education, Recreation and Dance*, 1981, *52*, 39-40.

Malone, C. J. & Rotella, R. J. Preventing coaching burnout. *Journal of Physical Education, Recreation and Dance*, 1981, *52*, 22.

Maslach, C. *Burned-out.* Human Behavior, September 1976, 16-22.

Maslach, C. The client role in staff burnout. *Journal of Social Issues*, 1978, *34*, 111-123.

Spaniol, L. & Caputo, J. Professional burnout. *Instructional Innovator*, 1980, *25*(9), 18-20.

Walsh, D. Classroom stress and teacher burnout. *Phi Delta Kappan*, 1979, *61*(4), 253.

SECTION VII

The Acquisition And Performance Of Motor Skills

32

Psychological Concepts For Learning And Performance

Linda K. Bunker and DeDe Owens
University of Virginia

All learning and performance requires the interactive responses of a performer and the environment. Peformers must "act" on their environment, whether it is a ball to be shot through a hoop, or a fellow wrestler to be pinned. In order to successfully act on that environment, athletes must have a clear understanding of the goal or skill and a desire to perform it.

The process of acquiring a motor skill has been described by many researchers (Adams, 1971; Gentile, 1972; Schmidt, 1977). Most of these theories agree that individuals acquire skill through three progressive phases (Futts and Posner, 1967): cognitive, associative, and autonomous. Individual learners begin in a very cognitive way, during which time the *requirements* of the task are intellectualized. They must establish a clear understanding of what is to be accomplished. Following this development of the goals and requirements, individual units of movement become linked together to form patterns of motion during the associative phase. Ultimately, most skills move toward a more or less autonomous phase in which motor programs can run off with much less interference. These motor patterns or schemas form the basis for all movement. They can be run off automatically or changed in very subtle ways to produce very different motor skills. They are essentially adaptable templates for movement.

According to this theory, and the model proposed by Gentile (1972) and later modified as a teaching model by Pease (1977), all athletes or learners must first perceive the skill (the goal) and must also wish to accomplish that goal. Next the learner must begin to differentiate between the relevant and irrelevant factors that influence the performance of the particular skills (see Figure 1).

FIGURE 1: LEARNER AND TEACHER / COACH RESPONSIBILITIES IN SKILL ACQUISITION

(MODIFIED FROM PEASE, 1977)

LEARNER NEEDS

1. Perceive The Desired Goal

2. Identify Relevant Stimuli

3. Formulate Motor Plan

4. Emit A Response

5. Attend To The Results
   (internal and external feedback)

6. Revise The Motor Plan And
   Begin Again

1. Provide "Set To Learn;" Provide Description Or Model Of Goal

2. Provide Teaching Cues Or Learning Environment

3. Assist With Motor Plan Formulation

4. Provide Environment And Opportunity For Learners To Emit A Response

5. Provide Internal Feedback And Learning Cues
   Assist Learner In Interpreting Internal And External Feedback

6. Restructure Environment To Allow For Revised Motor Plan

226

Once these preliminary pieces of information are established, the learner must formulate a motor plan, a blueprint or template, for the accomplishment of the desired skill. After this plan has been established, the learner is ready to try the skill, and through successive approximations, with each attempt at the skill, develop a stable yet malleable motor plan.

After the skill has been tried, two types of feedback from the attempt are available and must be compared to the original plan in order to determine if the attempt should be repeated or modified. Internal feedback relates to the actual "feel" of the executed skill. For example, in the initial stages of learning to effectively throw a ball, the individual may create excessive tension in the arm and shoulder. The motion may feel tight, restricted, or forced. This is in contrast to the free, loose, or relaxed feeling of motion in more mature, well-learned throws. The second form of feedback comes from outside the body and is the result or end product of the movement. In the previous example of throwing a ball the external feedback or knowledge of results would tell you if you hit the target, or how fast you threw the ball.

Each time the skill is executed the performer must use the available feedback, compare that feedback and the desired performance results to the existing motor plan, and revise the plan if necessary. This cycle is essential for skill acquisition and continued learning.

This understanding of how skills are learned has direct implications for how we teach skills, or more appropriately, how we create situations in which skills can be learned. The combined models of Gentile (1972) and Pease (1977) provide a useful way to integrate the teaching/coaching and learning process.

There are two critical concepts present in this model. First, students must have a desire to learn and a clear understanding of what is to be learned. Secondly, teachers and coaches must provide carefully designed learning environments and information in order to facilitate performance.

In order to build a desire to learn, learners must be provided with a clear concept of the skill. This may involve not only the specific skill, but also the context in which the skill is to be applied. This helps establish an overall understanding as well as a perception that the skill is indeed worth learning. In addition, the student must believe that the goal is attainable. This is a more difficult responsibility in that coaches must be honest and realistic, discuss the hard work and pain, the plateaus and spurts of progress, but also emphasize that effort and persistence will prevail.

GOAL SETTING

It is critical that target goals be established with all athletes. These goals should be both long range, and short range in nature. For example, assume you are a beginning golfer — to establish shooting par by the end of the summer might be analogous for searching for the pot of gold. But you might realistically shoot for three strokes over, on every hole.

In addition to this global target goal, you might set some short range goals such as increasing the distance and accuracy of your five-iron by five yards. Or next week only hitting seven of ten balls out of bounds from the tee.

It is also critical to remember that an athlete establishes goals and then uses those goals to evaluate their own competence. Highly skilled athletes tend to have very high aspiration levels. If your "minimal" goal is to win the gold medal and you are Bruce Jenner, that provides a very strong motivation. On the other hand, if you are an Olympic calibre diver and do not make the Olympic trials, you feel a failure, whereas less accomplished divers may have as their goal to complete a one and a half off the board.

PROVIDE POSITIVE EARLY EXPERIENCES

Once this enthusiasm for learning has been established it is important to all individuals to try the skill. The long lecture-demonstrated format can have a very stifling effect on performers. Participation in the activity itself is critical to initial learning sets. But beware — this is not an excuse for "throwing out the ball," since the purpose of participation at this point is to get the learner engrossed in the skill and not specifically to assist in the learning process.

This early experience with a new skill should be viewed as a rather short "trying-on" session. It should not be a free play session, but rather a structured experience that enhances enjoyment and does not persist so long that frustration and failure, tarnish the enjoyment. Similarly, the experience must not last to the point of developing inappropriate skills. For if you allow individuals to develop bad habits, you must in essence provide not only new learning experiences but also "unlearning" experiences.

MODELS OF PERFORMANCE

The concept of providing models for skill learning has been incorporated in most teaching and coaching styles. Gentile (1972) and Pease (1977) both suggest that if learners are to accurately perceive the goal, they must have proficient models, either in person or through the use of media. This should, however, be tempered by the notion of what is to be modeled, and by whom.

In choosing a model for proficient performers, it may be helpful to select a role model as well as a performance model. It may also be helpful to select someone of a similar physical size, so that the student may picture himself or herself actually performing as the model does. If you have an Arthur Ashe-sized tennis player, do not choose a Poncho Gonzales model. Similarly, if you want a Tracy Austin or Arthur Ashe disposition, do not choose a John McEnroe . . .

An understanding of any skill must include an understanding of the total sport, the application of the skill and the intricacies of the skill itself. But that does not mean that all things must be initially presented. Choose the most important aspects for the specific students. For example, in teaching open skills, such as tennis, students must at some point see the entire sport, but might also require at another point in time, a more restricted focus when learning the more closed aspects of tennis such as an American twist serve versus a flat serve.

The model presented must be accurate and realistic. A poor model may do more harm than good. Many instructors choose to model in slow motion first, or without an implement — but this does not present an accurate model. If slow motion is used, it should follow up-to-tempo practice, and should be specifically designed to focus the learner's attention on one aspect. Similarly, mimetic drills should be used cautiously since a swing with no implement produces little that resembles the actual performance. Alternating demonstration, speed, and viewing angle will provide many opportunities for learners to focus on important elements of the skill.

ENCOURAGE INDIVIDUALIZATION AND CREATIVITY TO MEET THE DEMANDS

There is one major disadvantage to using the modeling style or approach — it may stifle creativity and force students to imitate on specific style. If we relied only on models, the ali-oop in basketball, the Fosberry Flop, the "system in field hockey," the soccer-style place kick in football, the two-handed backhand, or the dig or bump would probably never have been invented. Most of these skills grew out of a special blend between environmental demands (and rules) and the unique characteristic of specific participants. These unique adaptations provide one of the most intriguing and challenging aspects of coaching.

OPTIMIZING THE PRACTICE ENVIRONMENT

Once the learner has a clear understanding of the skill, and the perceptual elements related to the skill, it is important to organize these elements into an optimal learning environment. Several generalizations about learning environments can be provided.

Perfect Practice Makes Perfect. As previously mentioned, it is important that practice environments foster the development of good and appropriate skills. Practices must therefore be well designed to foster positive skill development. The skills attempted should be of realistic difficulty, and should be structured so as to provide some early successful experiences. Once early success is attained, the skill should be made progressively more difficult in order to keep motivation high.

Practice environments must be systematically changed. Be careful not to fall into the trap of running a practice session "into the ground." One good rule of thumb is to always end practice when the players are enthusiastic and will want to return. The technique of running wind sprints and calisthenics at the end may leave a negative feeling, while if you force players to quit while they are enjoying themselves, they will wish to return.

The perfect practice adage also implies that the end result of the practice session should be the best performance possible. Sometimes it is helpful to end a practice prematurely just to guarantee ending on success.

Practice environments should be as game-like as possible. That is not to say that you should constantly scrimmage, but that as soon as a skill is learned in isolation it should be practiced in the proper context. For example, lay-ups should be executed with defenders, free throws should be practiced while fatigued, soccer kicks should be shot after controlling passes from various angles, etc. Similarly, practices should include experience with "coping" under unusual or adverse conditions (e.g., allow players to experience sudden shifts in defenses, practice under heavy winds, before hostile audiences, etc.).

Coping vs. Mastery Practice. There are two contemporary theories about what should be practiced and when. The mastery practice phase suggests that we should always practice the skill in its perfect form. However, several recent studies (Vedelli and Bunker, 1979) have suggested that students need experiences in error correction and problem solving. One such study showed that if children were to learn to toss a ring five feet, the optimal practice distances would be five, seven, and three feet alternately, rather than merely practicing at five feet. In this variable practice environment it might be hypothesized that learners are establishing a notion of specific constraints and error correction strategies. The percent state of the research seems to suggest that athletes should begin and end practice with the best, targeted behavior, but that they should also have intentional experiences

with its variations. (This is also supported by the implications from the laws of primacy and recency).

Athletes should be encouraged and allowed to practice coping skills. That is, it is silly for you to train a basketball team without anticipating the unknown. The concept of "simulation" which the Russians are purporting merely refers to the positive effects of reducing the unknown. If you can simulate an opponent's defenses (which we have done forever), why not simulate psychology factors as well.

Unfortunately, simulation can work both ways . . . it may be an unconscious form of the self-fulfilling prophecy. For example, do you ever —

1. take out a water ball before you attempt to hit a golf ball over a water hazard?
2. think about double faulting?
3. picture yourself falling on your head?

Practice positive self-talk (not "I've missed seven of ten free throws," but . . . "I hit three really good shots, let's make it four").

Remember, psyche over soma . . .

You may in fact be calling up inappropriate motor patterns or negative images if you talk to yourself about unsuccessful performance. Instead, picture the best performance you can do and rehearse it verbally, visually, and kinesthetically.

Be Realistic about Strengths and Weaknesses. Goal setting allows you to establish important target behaviors and work toward them systematically. In a similar sense, allowing athletes to identify both their strengths and weaknesses will help. As discussed earlier, who wants to practice their weaknesses? On the other hand, if we do, our total efforts will improve.

Set aside some time and practice for everyone to work on their worst skill. It is often a good idea to embed this practice time in the middle of your alotted time. If you place it first or last, you may discover some low achievers trying to avoid it.

Whole-Part-Whole Practices. Practice environments must allow students to formulate total concepts and overall plans for the desired movements. This concept of goal clarification lends support to the whole-part-whole approach to teaching, in which relatively large units are presented initially, and then broken into their subcomponents, and then restructured into progressively larger units.

Another closely related principle is known as the speed-accuracy trade-off, or perhaps more descriptively, the motor pattern-accuracy dilemma. Most performers will report that in skills which require both speed and accuracy (i.e., baseball pitch, hitting a driver off the tee, tennis serve, etc.) if either speed or accuracy is increased the other will be reduced. That is, as performers concentrate or focus on accuracy, their motor pattern is altered, and generally reverts to an earlier, more primitive style of less velocity. There are many arguments about this inverse-relationship or trade-off and its implications for teaching.

In skills that require equal parts of speed or force and accuracy, the general rule is to emphasize speed before accuracy. Beginning students should be encouraged to swing up-to-tempo, and concentrate on the total nature of the movement, rather than focusing on the required accuracy or outcome of the movement. If you do not swing up-to-tempo, you may not even be able to get your body into the appropriate position (a baseball pitcher's arm). Another way to express this would be to emphasize that the pattern or process should be learned and incorporated before the performer's attention is focused on the more subtle aspects imposed by the accuracy requirements.

GENERALIZE LEARNING CUES

During the acquisition of skill, it is easy for competent and personally proficient teachers to over-verbalize the learning cues. When a skill is dissected beyond the learner's level, it may quickly be subject to "paralysis by analysis." A tennis player or golfer who is reminded of everything mechanically wrong with the skill, will concentrate on those parts rather than letting the motor plan run itself off. Cues such as "ready position," "throw that serve," etc. can help trigger off the desired motor pattern or plan by describing rather complex interactions without specifics that often result in cerebral overload.

Once the general pattern of movement has been acquired, then more subtle and specific teaching points should be made during practice. The subtle differences between the speed of forearm rotation on a golf drive can be discussed with someone who has already established that temporal quality concept. That is not to say that you should wait too long, but merely that individuals must not be bombarded with information.

INCORPORATE THE MOVEMENT

Each individual must incorporate each movement pattern into his/her own concept of self. A motor plan is basically a perceptual process, and as such must be perceived by each performer. Performers must have a concept of what they will look like (a visual image) as well as what the movement will feel like. Good teachers and coaches will encourage performers to attend to how the movement feels. Questions such as "Could you feel the full extension in that last jump shot?"; "Feel the stretch in your left side at the top of the backswing?", etc. will help the learner internalize the motor pattern or motor plan.

In attempting to focus on the motor pattern it is often helpful to remove external goals or specific outcome knowledge (KR), which can divert attention. For example, many teachers will teach the tennis serve against the backstop, thus avoiding the accuracy problem. Similarly, golf teachers who begin in driving cages often report that their students develop better and more fluid swings. These approaches seem to reinforce the notion that externally imposed requirements, especially accuracy, often divert the learner's attention away from the process of performance.

FOCUS ATTENTION SELECTIVELY

One of the most difficult tasks of the coach is to aid the learner in not only identifying what is important, but learning to attend to those important elements. If everyone tried to process all of the information available in their environment, there would be a tremendous overload on our perceptual processes. Fortunately, as we become more experienced, we learn to attend to only certain portions of the environment, and discover improved functioning.

The development of good "attending"

skills is based on the recognition of three aspects: alertness and duration of attention, limited channel capacity, and selective attention. The first element is self-explanatory — individuals must keep their eyes and ears open. It is important to realize that only a certain amount of information can be dealt with at any one time. Athletes have limited channel capacities and must therefore be selective about the information to which they attend.

As coaches and teachers, we must help performers learn to attend to the salient elements in the environment. In this way, and as a result of past experience, players learn to pre-select what is likely to occur, and thus be prepared to "read" the situation. Experienced athletes begin to anticipate what will happen, and therefore prime not only their perceptual, but motor systems.

The athlete who is often described as having "great reactions" is quite likely to be more appropriately described as the athlete who anticipates well and therefore can attend to early perceptual cues. (The pure notion of reaction time is almost never observed in sport.) For example, experienced tennis players "read" serves by watching where the opponent tosses the ball, and how the swing progresses. Similarly, basketball players learn that the opponent's head is an unreliable cue to movement, but that by watching the hips, they can see the weight shift much earlier.

Experienced players also learn to predict from initial actions or movements what will occur. In this way, much of the later information becomes redundant. The quarterback who can "read the defense" knows very early what will transpire. These early detections mean that the information processing demands of that element are less, and there is therefore more time and effort available for deciding what to do, or looking for that secondary receiver.

It is therefore critical that performers learn what the elements are and when to attend to their environment. They must actively learn to block out some stimuli while carefully attending to others. (It has always intrigued me that some of our star basketball players, such as John Lucas, can deal so well with rowdy, loud crowds, but when he steps on the tennis court he expects a more quiet environment, and when on the golf links, a laugh two fairways over will distract him.)

PROVIDE USEFUL KNOWLEDGE OF PERFORMANCE

As previously suggested, there are two different aspects that must be considered in evaluating performance: the process of the skill or pattern itself, and the product or result of applying that skill to a specific sport situation. Performers receive information about both of these aspects from internal as well as external sources. The internal kinesthetic feedback helps to shape the motor pattern in a more or less automatic fashion as the learner acquires the ability to feel or sense the movement. The external sources of information about performance include the environment and/or other individuals. These sources can be usefully manipulated in order to provide the best and most appropriate information.

Performers must learn to link the external knowledge of performance with the internal feelings. Teachers and coaches must provide cues which help the learner integrate cause and effect relationships, rather than merely providing qualitative comments such as "nice shot," "what a dive," or "Oh — almost . . ." The key here is to link the KR with the cues provided earlier so that individuals can learn to be self-correcting, active participants. For example, if a tennis player's backhand always goes out of bounds on the backhand side, it should be suggested that this is most often the result of an elbow lead, or a late swing. Similarly if you tend to slice the ball, you may have too much tension in the non-target side arm. This understanding of cause and effect relationships has been well developed in some skills such as golf.

The verbal cues provided by observers during practice should thus focus on elements of the performance or motor pattern itself and not the product. Products of movement should however be thought of as cues to the nature of the motor pattern.

In general then, facilitators, teachers, and coaches should focus on appropriate and rather specific feedback about performance. This information must, however, be matched with the level of the performer and the situation. Appropriate KR for begin-

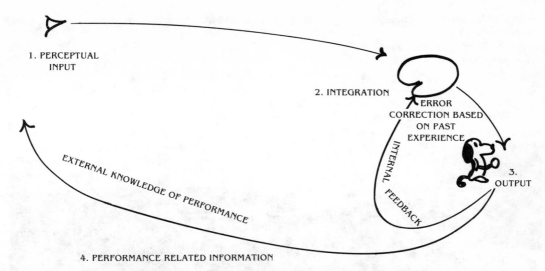

1. PERCEPTUAL
   INPUT

2. INTEGRATION

ERROR
CORRECTION BASED
ON PAST
EXPERIENCE

INTERNAL FEEDBACK

3.
OUTPUT

EXTERNAL KNOWLEDGE OF PERFORMANCE

4. PERFORMANCE RELATED INFORMATION

FIGURE 2. MODEL OF MOTOR SKILL ACQUISITION

ners (or skilled players learning a new technique) would begin in the form of rather general comments, which focus attention on the overall pattern or motor plan. As the pattern is learned the specificity of KR should increase during practice.

The nature of teaching cues and KR during game situations is a very different matter. Performers during competition must not focus their attention on small aspects of performance. They must rely on their motor patterns to automatically "run off." Game time is not the appropriate moment to change a player's technique. It is however the time to utilize their internal perception of the movement. The visual and kinesthetic image or feeling state which was developed during practice should be called upon to guide the movement.

SUMMARY

The nature of motor skill acquisition can be usefully conceived of in terms of a modified closed loop model, in which the teacher and learner have four major elements to evaluate: input, integration, knowledge of performance (internal and external) and output.

This model can provide a very systematic understanding of creating learning environments, and evaluating performance outcomes. For example, let's assume that you have a young tennis player who just cannot seem to pick up "half-volleys." This player's difficulty may stem from any of the four ele-

ments. The perceptual input might not be attended to early enough, or clear enough. On the other hand, the input might be adequate but there could be a major input/output or integration deficiency, or lastly, the image may be perceived, the correct pattern chosen, but just not the correct pattern execution or reception of information about that performance.

The skilled coach must be able to evaluate not only what the problem is, but why it is occurring. You must be a people and task watcher. Be able to analyze what is happening. Develop your observation quotient. Otherwise, the learning environment may be appropriate for remediating a non-existent problem.

REFERENCES

Adams, J. A. A closed-loop theory of motor learning. *Journal of Motor Behavior*, 1971, *3*, 111-150.

Gentile, A. M. A working model of skill acquisition with application to teaching. *Quest*, 1972, *17*, 3-23.

Pease, D. A. A teaching model for motor skill acquisition. *Motor Skills: Theory into Practice*, 1977, *1*(2), 104-112.

Schmidt, R. A. Schema theory: implications for movement education. *Motor Skills: Theory into Practice*, 1977, *2*(1), 36-48.

Vedelli, J., and Bunker, L. Coping strategies for elementary children. Unpublished research, University of Virginia, 1979.

DeDe Owens

33

Teaching For Transfer

Candine E. Johnson
University of Virginia

One of the goals of the primary level teacher (Phase I) is to lay down a basis whereupon the child is given all possible movement experiences (see Fig. 1). In the elementary years (grades 3, 4 & 5) beginning sport skills are introduced (Phase II) and by the middle and high school years it all comes together and the child starts to engage in more organized game-like activities (Phase III). Experience gained in Phase I provides the building blocks for Phase II and Phase III (Gallahue, 1975). The effects that prior experiences have upon the learning of "new" skills is known as TRANSFER.

Some authors say that once the child passes from early childhood "learning" ceases (Schmidt, 1977). How then are "new" skills acquired? Before answering this question it is important to define what is meant by the term "new." It is a completely new movement when a baby takes his or her first steps, or the first time an infant picks up a toy and tries to use it like a bat swatting at objects? If asked to think of a completely "new" skill, most individuals would be hard pressed for an answer. In fact, there would be no answer, because in the early years all the basic movement patterns are acquired. The building blocks are all the same, the way they are put together is what makes a skill "new." By taking past experiences and rearranging them to fit present specifications a child transfers the foundation skills from one situation to another (Schmidt, 1977).

THEORIES OF TRANSFER

The study of the transfer of learning has given rise to three (3) existing theories of how skills or information can be applied in different situations. The first theory, or the

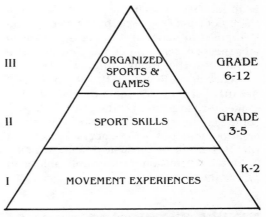

FIGURE 1. DEVELOPMENTAL SEQUENCE OF MOVEMENT SKILLS

concept of FACULTY PSYCHOLOGY (Bunker, 1978) stated that intellectual power was transferred. This concept served as the rationale for why Latin and geometry are studied in school. It was believed that in disciplining oneself to learn Latin grammar or the principles of logic in geometry a student would be able to transfer these abilities to later endeavors, thus assuring success in later academic pursuits.

A second theory was proposed by Judd in 1908. He chose to believe that GENERALIZED ELEMENTS transferred. According to Judd, by understanding the basic principles behind "why" a particular action transferred, performance would increase. By instructing students in basic principles such as the summation of force, or physics principles such as refraction, they could transfer this knowledge to many different and "new" situations in order to improve performance.

Edwin Thorndike, a psychologist, felt that the two (2) existing theories were in error. He felt that to transfer, elements could not be general, they had to be IDENTICAL. In terms of the identical elements theory, when teaching a kindergartener to throw a tennis ball, this ability would transfer to the throwing of a fleece ball because the throwing pattern is virtually IDENTICAL. Therefore, the teacher need only teach the skill or general throwing pattern once, emphasizing the major components and let transfer take over from there.

In recent years there has been a fourth theory that has been proposed as a possible explanation of transfer. This theory is referred to as the SCHEMA THEORY of Richard Schmidt (1977). Schema theory is not a theory of transfer per se, but rather a learning model in general. It addresses itself to all aspects of learning and as a result, it incorporates the many different elements that each of the first three theories proposed. Another aspect of schema theory that makes it so appealing is the way it points to some very practical implications for teachers. However, for the sake of clarity, schema theory will not be discussed here, but held for later discussion of its applicability to physical educators.

NATURE OF THE TASK

The concept of transfer implies that our past experiences affect the future learning of a skill or the retention of a previously learned behavior.

Transfer can therefore have a positive or facilitative effect, or it can have an inhibitory or negative effect. The Skaggs-Robinson hypothesis presents a pictorial display of the circumstances leading to the occurrence of a particular type of transfer (Bunker, 1978). For example, when two items or behaviors are identical or highly similar, positive transfer can be expected (see Fig. 2). Negative transfer is the result of two slightly similar but confusing items such as the forehand shot in badminton and tennis. Both of these sports require tracking skills and the manipulation of an implement, however, these similarities are such that they can both confuse and inhibit responses. On the other hand, when items are completely dissimilar there appears to be little or no transfer.

Aside from the amount of similarity between tasks, the similarity between the stimuli and the response of two tasks is quite important in determining the amount of transfer (see Fig. 3). As the table indicates, a similar stimulus with a dissimilar response will result in negative transfer. A case in point is when a teacher asks a student to switch from right to left. A batter that makes this switch is still perceiving the stimuli in the same manner, however,

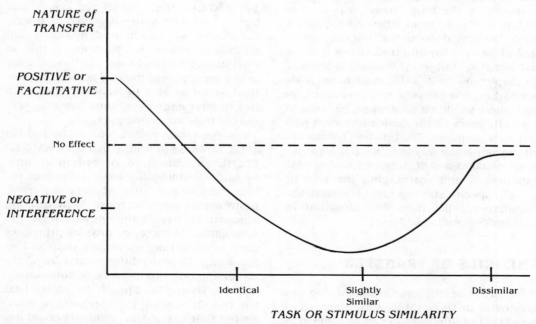

FIGURE 2. SKAGGS-ROBINSON HYPOTHESIS

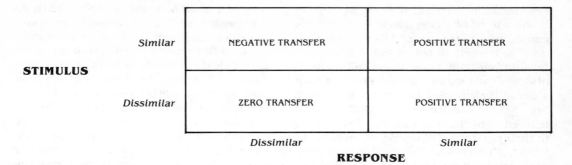

		Dissimilar	**Similar**

	Similar	NEGATIVE TRANSFER	POSITIVE TRANSFER
STIMULUS			
	Dissimilar	ZERO TRANSFER	POSITIVE TRANSFER

Dissimilar   *Similar*

RESPONSE

FIGURE 3. THE INFLUENCE OF S-R SIMILARITY ON TRANSFER

the student must reorganize existing behavior patterns whereupon a dissimilar response is required (Robb, 1972). As stated previously, the building blocks are the same, it's merely a question of organization. When switching from right to left the batter needs to change or reorganize some of the blocks. For instance, the lead foot, the direction of hip rotation and hand placement on the bat are just a few of the changes that need to be made.

Also, when both stimuli and response are similar, positive transfer will probably occur. An example of this would be in tennis with a large prince-sized racket on asphalt and then teaching, using a regulation sized racket on a cement court. The stimuli of perceiving a ball bouncing on the court is similar along with the similar responses or racketwork that is present.

Likewise, when the stimuli and responses are dissimilar there is likely to be no transfer effect. For example, in the case of having a swimming unit followed by an "ultimate frisbee" unit, the expected result would be no transfer. And lastly, all too often students find themselves in situations where they must make a similar response to stimuli that are in fact dissimilar, for instance the handshake and the tennis grip. The teacher is using the similar response hypothesis for two very different stimuli — in one case a human hand while in the other a tennis racket handle. Therefore, teachers need to be able to point out the similarities and dissimilarities that face the learner. Specific cues given by the teacher can aid the student in recalling certain previously learned patterns which are similar to the new skill to be learned. Teachers who emphasize the similarities between move-

ment, such as by pointing out that a movement pattern will "feel" like some other pattern, thus enlarging the learner's point of reference.

BILATERAL TRANSFER

Transfer does not only occur from skill to skill, it can also occur between the two sides of the body. The term used to explain this phenomenon is bilateral transfer or cross-education. In fact, the initial studies in transfer arose from the observation one hand appeared to "teach" the other.

Researchers have concluded that transfer from hand-to-hand will always occur. But why? There are as many reasons to explain bilateral transfer as there are questions about it. A few of the explanations that have been proposed are: cues from verbal self-talk, visual cues, familiarity with the general nature of the task, subliminal practice of the skill by the ostensibly idle limb, subthreshold neural involvement, and past learning of highly similar skills.

When one side of the body is exercised, subthreshold impulses are sent to the non-exercised side. This technique is often used by physicians, physical therapists, and athletic trainers when one limb is immobilized due to injury. By using this technique the injured limb will not be as drastically affected (Bunker, 1978). Cross-education is also useful in counteracting the effects of fatigue on accuracy (Cratty, 1975). Even in gross motor activity some degree of fine neural adjustment is taking place. Therefore, if skill is partially a function of the central nervous system, practice at a cortical level could prove beneficial using the

236

non-dominant hand (Cratty, 1975).

The use of bilateral transfer by athletes can be seen in the switch hitter in baseball and the basketball player that can make a lay-up from both sides. These "all-around" athletes have mastered their skills on both sides of their bodies. However, the secondary skill or the transferred skill was not learned until the first was firmly cemented in their repetoire. Otherwise, attempting to learn both skills simultaneously would probably result in negative transfer, leading to a decrease in motivation, thus counteracting any advantage that it would derive. Motivation also plays a key role when attempting to transfer. Anyone who has tried to use his non-dominant hand to write knows that it is not any easy job for the right hand to tell the left hand what to do!

PRACTICAL IMPLICATIONS

The concept of transfer can be used effectively by practitioners both in the gymnasium and in the classroom. In order to understand relative effectiveness of transfer, the initial level of learning must be considered. It has been found that the greater the overlearning, or the more experience the child has with a task, the greater the transfer possibilities.

By referring back to Figure 1, it can be seen that the base of support and foundation for future movement is labelled Movement Experiences. These experiences are the mainstay of any movement education program. Any teacher that provides developmentally appropriate movement experiences is supplying the student with a foundation which may foster transfer at a later point in the child's world of movement. Underlying most programs of movement education is the assumption that complex movements done throughout life are based upon the assemblage of movement components learned during the early years (Schmidt, 1977). The notion is that students can now piece together what they have learned to produce more efficient motor acts provides the basis for the previously discussed schema theory (Schmidt, 1977).

Schema theory assumes that movement is carried out by a program, but in contrast to other existing learning models, this program is a "generalized" one. A program

may be run off in a variety of ways to fit requirements of the movement (response specifications). Schema theory allows an individual to specify if he wishes to execute a task quickly or slowly, with little force or a great deal of force, or to take a lay-up from 45° or 50°. No other theory affords such flexibility in skill execution (Schmidt, 1977).

Another unique feature of schema theory is the way in which errors are dealt with. They are merely looked upon as another movement in the repetoire that has the same underlying relationship between response specifications and movement outcomes as the intended goal (Schmidt, 1977). An error is viewed as strengthening the schema rather than detracting from it. The schema theory persents a convincing argument for the use of the problem-solving teaching strategy. Students are afforded an opportunity to err, along with gaining invaluable experience about their own capabilities as well as the task requirements. The problem-solving approach, along with movement education increases the amount of variability in the practice and learning environments. This increased variability in experience will result in greater probability for transfer to a novel response of the same class (Schmidt, 1977).

In recent years researchers have attempted to prove these very points and have done so with a high degree of success. Experimental results have substantiated the contention that a variety of movement experiences early in life have increased the child's capacity to transfer this knowledge to move with greater success in novel situations.

SUMMARY

Physical educators and coaches should consciously utilize transfer to facilitate the learning and performance of motor skills. Such techniques will provide students the opportunities to face novel situations with greater success.

In a recent *JOPER* article entitled "Games Teaching: Adaptable Skills, Versatile Players," the author, Kate Barrett (1977), addressed the issue of flexibility as the key to a successful games player. In order to be a success Barrett stated that one needs a large repertoire of movement patterns that can be used in differing ways to fit a situation. But what is a game player? It need not only be the hockey goalie or the basketball forward, it could be a kindergartener attempting to kick a moving ball for the first time or a 2nd grader trying to throw the ball as far as possible using a mature overhand throwing pattern.

Teachers and coaches alike must foster versatility in the games player as well as in the beginner. It is the responsibility of all teachers to enhance transfer by creating experiences that will help children establish a broad base of motor skills, and learn to be adaptable in their movement experiences.

REFERENCES

Barrett, K. Games teaching; adaptable skills, versatile players. *Journal of Physical Education and Recreation*, 1977, 7, 21-23.

Bunker, L. Teaching for transfer and decision making. *Proceedings of Sport Psychology Conference*, Charlottesville, Virginia, 1978.

Cratty, B. *Movement Behavior and motor learning.* Philadelphia: Lea and Febiger, 1975.

Gallahue, D., Werner, P. and Luedke, G. *Conceptual approach to moving and learning.* New York: John Wiley and Sons, Inc., 1975.

Judd, C. H. The relationship of special training to general intelligence. *Educ. Review*, 1908, 26, 28-42.

Robb, M. *The dynamics of motor skill acquisition.* New Jersey: Prentice-Hall, Inc., 1972.

Schmidt, R. *Schema theory: implications for movement education, Motor Skills: Theory into Practice,* 1977, 2, 36-48.

Thorndike, F. K. *Fundamentals of Learning.* New York: New York Teachers College, 1935.

Julie Heyward. Charlottesville, Va.

34

Physiological Prerequisites To Maximal Sport Peformance

John Billing
University of North Carolina
at Chapel Hill

Sport is characterized by physical action: explosive, powerful movements, sustained efforts and intricate combinations of bodily actions. The human machine is capable of remarkable capacities for exhibiting quite varied physical feats. Sport provides evidence of the human ability to lift extremely heavy objects, throw objects great distances, balance in precarious positions, endure prolonged exercise, perform complicated body movements in fractions of a second and manipulate objects with great precision.

Maximal performance in any one physical activity is a complex interplay between a multitude of factors. Among the most important factors influencing sport performances are:

a. genetic endowment
b. physiological development
c. skill attainment
d. psychological qualities
e. environmental conditions
f. luck

Skill attainment and the alteration of psychological qualities are the focus of other sessions of this conference.

The effects of enviromental conditions often go unnoticed or are lightly passed over. Consider for a moment all the environmental variables which could impinge upon a performer. Noteworthy items of the physical environment are heat, humidity, sun, wind, light, and altitude. Less obvious are the existing conditions of play surfaces, equipment, uniforms, etc. Additionally, the social environment includes the actions of others which influence one's performance. The level of play of teammates and opponents, the actions and reactions of the audience, the coaches and the officials all influence the performance. Surely not of least importance is luck, the chance occurrences which often significantly alter the outcome of a sport performance.

Realizing that producing a maximum performance in sport relies on a great number of factors, this paper will concentrate on the importance of two factors which I feel are actually prerequisite to the development of maximum performance. These areas are the genetic influence on physical performance and the physiological development of fitness capacities.

The genetic makeup of an athlete has a profound influence on potential maximal development for a particular sport or position within a sport. Even if we believe (which I personally do not) that all individuals will respond similarly to training we must admit that we all do not begin from an equal base. The obvious differences in height, bone structure, limb proportions and size of hands and feet provide some individuals with superior equipment to perform specific sport tasks. Not so obvious differences are evidenced in the acuity of senses important to sport. The visual clarity and peripheral vision, the threshold for auditory stimulation as well as the richness of kinesthetic sensations and the pain threshold all vary among individuals. Of special importance in many sports is the reaction time of an athlete. Research has demonstrated that this quality is apparently inherited and impervious to training.

Within the last 10 years research in muscle physiology has conclusively demonstrated the existence of large individual differences in the quality of muscle tissue. The terms fast-twitch and slow-twitch muscle fibers are commonly used to describe the proportion of muscle fibers capable of specific functions. Individuals with high percentages of slow-twitch fibers have the innate capacity to sustain work for long periods; those with high percentage of fast-twitch fibers are capable of producing faster and more powerful muscle contractions. The research to date indicated that this slow-twitch fast-twitch ratio is genetically determined and is basically unaltered by training. Of even greater concern is the finding that individuals with strikingly different fiber ratios do not respond similarly when exposed to the same training program. This means an individual will respond most favorably to training of the specific fiber type in which they predominate. Although most of the population approximates a 50-50 distribution of slow and fast-twitch fibers, a few individuals possess quite high ratios of one fiber type over the other. These individuals have the potential to excel in specific activities where these qualities are of major importance. Lucky for most of us is the fact that many of our common sports involve a combination of actions, some requiring quick explosive actions as well as longer sustained efforts and thus a roughly equal ratio of fast to slow-twitch fibers is beneficial.

In addition to the genetic differences which exist in muscle fiber types it is likely that some other organs, important to physical performance, also vary in size due to inheritance. It is logical to believe that heart and lung dimensions could vary just as does head size, limb lengths, and breast development even among individuals of the same stature. In addition to the influence of training on these organs, genetic predisposition to larger and more capable organs would be an obvious advantage in the ultimate sport performance.

Many of the areas noted above as genetic endowment are amenable to change through training, however, inheritance appears to have a strong influence both on the quality of the body and probably upon maximal development possible in any individual.

An apparent application of the knowledge of the differences in inherited physical potential is in the selection, counseling and training of young athletes. It is simply unethical to continue to tell young athletes who do not have the appropriate genetic makeup that if they only work hard enough they can achieve superior levels of success. They should not be eliminated from the opportunity of participating in whatever sport they may select but they should be made aware of the genetic factors which may affect their ultimate achievement in the activity.

To this point the paper has identified those genetic qualities which predispose an athlete to excel in sport. The remainder of the text will focus on those physiological qualities which are responsive to training and which account for a large portion of the differences in physical performance between trained athletes and untrained individuals.

The physiological capacities important to sport are muscle strength, muscle endurance, flexibility and cardiovascular endurance. Each can be substantially altered to provide for significant enhancement of selected sport performances. The literature is replete with reputable techniques for maximizing each of these components. Virtually all legitimate training programs agree on the specific nature of development. That is, we must stress or train to perform under heavy loads. If muscle endurance is sought then lighter loads performed over prolonged periods are appropriate. For flexibility development the joint must be moved through extremes of the range of motion. Cardiovascular development results from sustained large muscle actions which require a substantial and prolonged supply of oxygen to the musculature. Training for any sport activity requires first the identification of the specific physiological capacities important to that sport, followed by adherence to a program designed to progressively maximize these qualities.

It is not necessary to convince most athletes and coaches of the importance of physiological development to achievement in their sport. However, what may be important is an understanding of the value of attention to the physical capacities of students and athletes early in the learning or training process.

The physical fitness components of strength, endurance and flexibility are common to many sport activities. Specific strength in a muscle group may be used advantageously in a large array of movements. Arm extension strength, as an example, is useful in a large number of gymnastic movements as well as in many other sport activities. Improvement in the strength of this one muscle group has potential positive benefit for a great number of activities. Early attention to arm extensor strength could therefore be a valuable asset to learning many skills. High levels of flexibility and endurance can be equally generalizable to many activities.

The correct performance of many sport techniques requires a significant level of the various fitness capacities. Specific strength, endurance and flexibility are, therefore, prerequisites to successful performance of many sport skills. Lack of these prerequisites require the learner to adopt movement patterns which are less than optimal. These must later be relearned when sufficient fitness has been developed.

As a result of possession of the necessary fitness components prior to skill learning, the practical time required to master the skill is reduced. That is of motivational value as well as an efficiency advantage. Rapid improvement can best be assured by possession of the necessary physical capacities essential for the skill being learned.

Elevated levels of the fitness of learners enable them to practice longer with less fatigue. Additionally highly fit athletes can sustain greater amounts of "quality" practice. More, higher quality practice results in rapid learning of skills.

The physiological changes resulting from fitness training occurs quite rapidly. Participants can observe positive changes in their performance and are thus motivated to continue training. Since this motivational value is especially important early in the learning stages, teachers and coaches should select training activities which enable rapid, obvious improvement during the initial phases of training. Physical fitness development offers this possibility.

In addition to the psychological advantages of fitness development as they relate to reduced skill learning time and observable improvement in physical capacity, becoming stronger, more enduring and more flexible appear to produce attitudes of self confidence, assertiveness, and mastery. As they improve in fitness, athletes feel increasingly capable of handling the mental pressures of both training and competition. This attitudinal predisposition is a very positive one for anyone engaging in sport.

Since physical fitness qualities are foundational to learning many sport skills and since there is substantial support for their rapid development and the psychological advantages of enhanced fitness levels, it would appear advantageous to design specific training programs directed at these physiological qualities early in the total sport preparation process.

35

Sex Differences In Motor Performance: Nature Versus Nurture

Linda K. Bunker
University of Virginia

Sport provides an opportunity for children to challenge themselves and to evaluate their individual capabilities. The ongoing debate about sex differences between participants may be a chicken and the egg controversy. The fact that there are observable differences between most performance levels of boys and girls cannot be disputed. Several issues do remain unclear:

a. the reasons behind motor performance differences
b. the impact and importance of these differences to make sport
c. the potential desirability of reducing these differences to make sport a truly fulfilling experience for both sexes.

THE MEANING OF MOVEMENT EXPERIENCE FOR CHILDREN

Children of both sexes participate in and choose experiences through which they attempt to achieve a goal or to meet a standard of excellence (Martens, 1975; Roberts, 1978; Sherif, 1976). These situations provide evaluative experiences for children to judge their own competence in terms of whether they achieve a goal or a standard of excellence. The key to each child's involvement in sport may be threefold: (a) the evaluative judgement or reinforcement provided by others, (b) the attainment of a standard of excellence, and (c) their own self-evaluation of competence.

Children learn to be competitive, based on the rewards and incentives provided by others. Young children demonstrate sport-related movement skills, such as throwing, catching, and running, as a result of interacting with parents or peers. Children under the age of 5 gain enjoyment by pleasing others, or by the pure pleasure of mastering new behaviors. They learn to be truly competitive sometime around 5 years of age.

The onset of this competitive behavior depends upon the environmental (parental, peer, sibling) reinforcement which they receive. For example, we know that a child's social class may influence the development of his/her competitive behaviors. Middle class children, both boys and girls, tend to compete at earlier ages than children whose parents are not in business or education (Sherif, 1976). Thus, the emphasis which a family places on competition and achievement may affect the attitudes and behavior of the children. This same family influence often directs boys toward competitive sport.

The degree to which a child's behavior is rewarded will directly affect the type of activities performed. According to social learning theory, a child will choose to behave according to the response consequences (e.g. reward or punishment) he or she expects (Bandura, 1977; Mischel, 1970; Perry & Bussey, 1979). Parents, peers, and other adults have a very strong influence upon the development of sport skills in children, because of their attitudes toward participation by both boys and girls. For example, active, exploratory, aggressive, and competitive achievement in sport is more strongly stressed in the training of boys. When boys achieve, they are often rewarded

Modified from *The Proceedings of the National Association for Physical Education in Higher Education* — 1980.

with love and affection from parents and social praise and friendship from peers and siblings (Kidd & Woodman, 1975; Murray, 1976; Mussen, Conger & Kagan, 1969; Romer, 1975; DuQuin, Note 1). Girls, on the other hand, are often taught obedience, nurturing, and responsibility (Murray, 1978; Sherif & Rattray, 1976).

Boys learn early that excelling in sport and being physically active are important. They also learn what is not appropriate — how "not to be a sissy, throw like a girl, play with dolls or cry like a baby." Young girls, on the other hand, generally have a wider range of behaviors which are acceptable. But somewhere around school age, both sexes are often forced to conform to sex-role appropriate behaviors. These "appropriate behaviors" provide interactive factors which may combine with biologically predetermined capabilities to impact eventual motor performance.

At least two potential explanations for eventual sex differences in motor performance exist: (a) the actual biological differences, and (b) the environmental or social/experiential differences which may affect the impact of any biological differences. Especially important is to determine whether environment and experience create differences between the sexes, or whether they merely magnify or obscure real biological differences (Wyrick, 1971).

BIOLOGICAL (NATURE) DIFFERENCES BETWEEN THE SEXES IN MOTOR PERFORMANCE

Almost all sports discriminate against those who are smaller, slower, or weaker, regardless of sex (Harris, 1977). Because males in general are stronger and faster, they have an inherent advantage in skills requiring strength, speed, and power.

A discussion of the physiologically based differences in motor performance must be based on real, innate differences between the sexes. Research dealing with real sex differences, which sorts out biological inheritance differences, must meet at least four empirical requirements. The differences must (a) exist across species, (b) exist cross-culturally, (c) be found very early in development, and (d) be related to or subject to hormonal manipulation (DuQuin, Note 1).

Phenotypically, the male is defined as an organism that was subjected in utero to high levels of testosterone, the hormone necessary to stimulate the rudimentary male genitalia. Testosterone is also an important anabolic hormone responsible in adolescence for promoting the development of muscle mass. Male babies are basically females exposed to higher levels of testosterone, and therefore, grow to be slightly larger and stronger at birth. But these high levels of testosterone do not persist after birth (Wakat, 1978). Sex differences based on innate, physiological differences in testosterone levels do not seem to persist between birth and adolescence. In fact, when this is coupled with the increased neuromuscular maturation rate of the female, it appears that the purely innate differencs based on strength should be minimal.

The lack of clearly physiologically related differences in children must be emphasized, especially as contrasted with observable differences in behavior which focus on male children (under 12) who are, on the whole, more active. This increased activity may be the result of social reinforcement, providing boys more real opportunities to develop such things as strength, power, and endurance, through activity.

A review of literature related to physiological characteristics of older male and female athletes suggests some important similarities and differences (Plowman, 1974). Female champion athletes very greatly in body type, are stronger and leaner, and have a higher aerobic capacity than the average female. Generally, female athletes are superior to both untrained males and females. In comparison with champion male athletes, however, females (past pubescence) have less muscle mass, possess less strength, and exhibit lower values of both aerobic and anaerobic variables (Clarke, 1979).

Some physiological equalities between the sexes are the oxygen carrying capacity of the blood per gram of hemoglobin, strength per unit of muscle, and VO_2 max when expressed in ml/LBM/min (Plowman, 1979). A recent study by Jordan, Rhee, Kim, and Low (1980) that corroborates these generalizations found that when cardiovascular differences between male and female marathon runners were indexed for body surface area, no significant differences existed in ejection fraction, end-diastolic volume, or percentage of internal diameter shortening. Thus, women marathon runners have cardiac structural dimensions and adaptations equal to those of men marathon runners (Jordon et al 1980).

Physical Maturation

Girls tend to mature approximately 2 years ahead of boys. A slight difference in bone age exists at birth, and by 10 years, girls are generally 12-18 months ahead of boys the same age. Girls begin their growth spurt between 10.5 and 13.0 years of age and terminate that spurt at the onset of menstruation, when estrogen closes the epiphyses and total growth seems to stop around 16 years (Tanner, 1962). The growth spurt of boys generally occurs between 12.5 and 15.0 years. These extra years of growth, under the influence of growth hormone, account for the 10% greater size difference. (It should be noted that late maturing girls may have longer periods of skeletal growth, and therefore, greater height with longer limbs.)

Muscular Strength

Muscular strength can be assessed quite easily through direct measures such as grip strength. Studies by Espenschade and Eckert (1967). Fleishman (1964), and Montoye and Lamphiear (1977) have shown that males are stronger at ages 10-60. Differences between the sexes appear small at younger ages, but quite dramatic in postpubescent years, up to 50% greater grip strengths for males and higher strength per weight ratios at all ages (Clarke, 1979).

The actual amount of muscle is almost identical in children of either sex in the first decade of life. At maturity however, the muscle mass of women is approximately 50% of men and overall dynamic strength ranges from 59-84%, because of the effect of anabolic hormones, especially the male hormone, testosterone (Laubach, 1976). In girls, the most rapid increase in strength occurs before menarche, as a total growth increases, whereas for males, it is the influence of the increased presence of androgens which allows for greater strength and muscle mass development.

Although women's maximal strength capacity is about half that of men, their efficiency is equal at all ages in skilled work and mild intensity; that is, if males and females are equated in terms of strength (e.g. dynamometer tests), athletic competition might be quite comparable (Clarke 1979).

An analysis of the actual performance for males and females on the AAHPERD Fitness Test (1980) may provide some insight into the potential sex differences (see Table 1). Males and females aged 10 to 12 are able to run the 50-yard dash in essentially the same time (AAHPER, 1976). After ages 13, however, boys continue to improve their speed throughout the teenage years, whereas females seem to regress sometime after 15 years. (Table 1)

This general trend in performance is similar in longer distances, such as the 600-yard run, with males performing better than females throughout school-age years. It should be noted that these differences become more marked after the onset of puberty, probably as a result of the increased strength in males and the relative differences in cardiovascular endurance. If we consider agility and speed, sex differences seem to be reduced; however, significant differences continue to appear in performance after puberty (AAHPERD, 1980).

It thus seems clear that a very significant physical component, namely strength, continues to separate the sexes. This strength component is obviously demonstrated in running skills, but can also be seen in other tasks requiring strength. The ability to perform flexed knee sit-ups illustrates the potential strength advantage for postpubescent males; however, if the young male and female are compared, little difference exists before 12 years of age (AAHPERD, 1980). Power is another physical ability which is obviously related to strength and is sometimes defined as explosive strength. The developmental course of power is essentially parallel to that of strength and looks similar to the sit-up data. Performance on the standing broad jump reflects similar advantages for males, particularly after age 12. (These data may be somewhat misleading, because of the increased height of males; but even if equated for height, males have an advantage in power.)

The most dramatic examples of sex differences appear in sport-related performance, such as the softball throw for distance. The differences at age 10 are observable, but at age 13-17 they are dramatic (see Table 1). Notice that in the pure power measure of the long jump, girls at age 10 scored 95% of boys, and at age 17, 76.4%. In contrast, the softball throw shows female scores of 52.1% at age 10 and of only 39% at age 17; that is, at age 17, females were able to throw the softball only 39% as far as males. If both of these tests are available and valid measures of power, the discrepancy may be due to environment, practice, or reinforcement effects, rather than purely innate (sex) differences.

Flexibility, on the other hand, demonstrates a superiority in favor of the females. Males seem to show a decrease in flexibility, especially hamstring range, around the age of 10. This decrease may appear to be correlated to increases in strength, although these two characteristics are not mutually exclusive (AAHPERD, 1980).

Another area in which performance differences between males and females are highly complex has to do with reaction time and movement time. The speed with which one recognizes, interprets and begins to physically respond to a stimulus is referred to as reaction time. Strength as such, therefore is not a factor. Reaction time does, however, vary both between and within individuals, based on both intrinsic and extrinsic factors. For example, factors such as the nature of the stimulus, complexity of stimulus, age, internal and external body temperature, degree of fatigue, time of day, and limb dominance may all affect reaction time. In general, reaction time gradually improves with age (Takamo & Frijiyoshi, 1965) and it has been found that athletes manifest a faster reaction time than non-athletes (Hodgkins, 1963).

Sex differences in reaction time and movement time have not been consistently demonstrated. For example, females appear to have a slight advantage over males in simple reaction time to a predetermined stimulus, whereas males have an advantage over females in movement time (Fulton & Hubbard, 1975). Movement time (MT) is related to reaction time, but is not dependent on it, because it refers to that period of time between the start of the recordable movement and the completion of that movement. The data on movement time are more confusing, with no general sex difference in

tasks which do not require excessive amounts of speed and power (Ikai, 1966). In those movements, which require speed and power, however, men show a decided advantage, whereas in situations where a dual task of reacting and moving occurs, there may be a trade-off effect, with females choosing to react to the stimulus and males moving faster (Fulton & Hubbard, 1975). This has also been observed in tasks which require both speed and accuracy, or small precise movements, where females tend to be more accurate and males faster.

Training Effects

The case for lifestyle, or experiental, rather than biological differences is particularly significant when we compare the effect of systematic educational and training experiences on performance. For example, when college age females are given an opportunity to build strength over a 10-week period, their improvement is even more dramatic than males. The women improved their leg strength 29.5% compared to a 26.0% increase for men; for arm and shoulder strength, it was more dramatic, with a 28.6% improvement for the women compared to a 16.5% increase for men (Wilmore, 1977). Similarly, Scotland (1976) compared strength, muscular and cardiovascular endurance trainability of males and females 18-25 years of age. On pretests, male strength was nearly twice as great as female strength (104 vs. 57 pounds), while the percentage of gain after 6 weeks was identical (12%). No significant differences between males and females existed for muscular or cardiovascular endurance (Scotland, 1975).

If the figures are equated relative to lean body mass, they show that women may be able to leg press slightly more than men. Unfortunately, these calculations have little significance in discussing athletic performance, since we cannot "remove our fat and leave it at the starting line."

Differences in cardiovascular endurance are obviously related to aerobic capacity which provides an advantage for most men because of such things as increased size of the lungs and chest, and higher hemoglobin levels. Not every woman has a smaller vital capacity than every man, however; the evidence clearly shows that some factors, other than sex, may be more important. A trained female can exceed untrained males; however, given equal training, males will have an advantage. These aerobic advantages are seen clearly in such activities as the mile run or the nine-minute run (AAHPERD, 1980; Table 1).

It would be interesting to speculate on the "Battle of the Sexes" by optimizing each group's strengths. For example, if you take a male and female who run 6 miles in the same time and then hold a 1-mile and a marathon (26 miles) contest, the male will almost always win the mile, but the woman will probably win the marathon (Ullyot, 1977).

Many performance differences appear to be the result of cultural influences. For example, sex differences may occur within one culture but be absent across cultures. Women swimmers in Australia, East Germany, and the United States hold national records which exceed the same year male national records in other countries such as Canada (Dyer, 1976).

Historical Performance Shifts

The performance history of males and females in some sports is particularly intriguing. For example, if we compare the best performance of male and female track and field experts, we find a great deal of improvement from 1954 to 1979 (see Table 2). An examination of track and field records indicates an overall performance difference of 18.4% in 1954, while in 1979 that difference dropped to 12.5%

The performance differences between most males and females are irrefutable — the data exist for what can be observed in almost every sport setting. It is not, however, clear what causes these differences to be as large as they are. Obviously, there are some physiologically-based differences, but these should not be reflected in the data before the onset of puberty.

This is especially true since girls mature earlier than boys, and if pursued to its logical conclusion, girls should, therefore, be performing better than boys prior to the hormonal changes associated with puberty. Thus, not all differences are the result of biology, but may reflect experimental differences and differences in the reinforce-ment provided children for physical prowess.

Although differences do exist, a significant overlap occurs between the curves representing performance. Some girls can throw a ball farther than most boys, and some boys cannot jump as high as most girls. Height, weight, age, and perhaps most significantly, past experience, are often more important predictors of athletic ability than sex. This has particular relevance to those individuals who provide developmental sport experiences for children.

PSYCHO-SOCIAL DIFFERENCES

Many of the apparent sex differences in motor performance may be affected by personality and by the dissimilar achievement values of males and females, which are culturally acquired or learned, and are not biological (Bem, 1974; Fauls & Smith, 1956; Sage, Note 2; Sherif & Rattray, 1976). These attitudes are therefore susceptible to change (Murray, 1976; Orlick & Botterill, 1975).

Sex differences in general personality traits are a major concern for parents and children — both from a cause and effect standpoint. In the past, it was often felt that masculine and feminine traits laid along a single bipolar continuum, such that if you had more masculine traits, such as aggression, achievement motivation, you had to be less feminine (by definition). Fortunately, it is now recognized that each of us has many masculine as well as feminine characteristics (Bem, 1974; Helmreich & Spence, 1977; Harris, 1979). Androgynous individuals possess many of the positive attributes formerly attributed to each sex differentially. For example, athletes, both male and female, who are successful basketball or track participants, have been found to be more alike than different (Harris, 1979). Women who are classified as androgynous have higher self-esteem, are more secure, competitive, independent, and possess a stronger mastery motive. These characteristics are highly valued and acceptable for both boys and girls, especially as contrasted to the more often verbalized characteristics of dependence, passivity and nurturance.

The relationship between athletic prowess and sex-appropriate behavior is a confusing one for young boys and girls. Young athletic girls find that they represent a socially acceptable and mandated reality (Title IX), but simultaneously are a social anomaly. They know that to be successful in sports is a very positive goal for some, yet realize that there may be limits to the desirability of winning, especially in co-educational environments. This creates a serious dissonance between what the female athlete thinks herself to be, and what society, especially the adolescent peer group, expects her to be.

Unfortunately, many young girls resolve this value-laden issues by withdrawing from sport altogether, or by seeking more feminine appropriate sports, such as tennis, golf, gymnastics, swimming, and track and field. These sports, though equally demanding, have come to be perceived as more socially acceptable for females. When females pursue other sports, they often feel compelled to compensate by attaching feminine artifacts to their attire; thus, the popularity of such things as pierced earrings, gold necklaces, and bracelets. These young women seem to be saying, "I am a highly skilled, feminine athlete."

The problem of sex-role stereotyping is equally as detrimental for young boys. As long as the social system continues to define femininity and masculinity in terms of adolescent's physical and/or sexual prowess, both sexes will experience conflict. Males who pursue sports that are considered neutral or nonmasculine have difficulty retaining their sexual self-esteem. Boys who participate in dance, gymnastics, figure skating, and even tennis may feel more social pressure than those in football, basketball, and soccer.

Role Models

Psychological differences, and probably performance differences, between the sexes are, at least in part, perpetuated by the fact that boys and girls as groups are inclined to imitate responses displayed by same-sex models than they are to imitate opposite sex models. Within each sex, individual differences in children's masculinity and femininity are believed to stem in part from the children's tendencies to prefer imitation of one sex model over the other (Perry & Bussey, 1979).

Children acquire, at least cognitively, the potential to perform an extensive repertoire of behaviors that includes behaviors which are deemed appropriate to the child's own sex, but also to the other sex. According to social learning theory, this is accomplished through observational learning strategies such as mentally rehearsing a model's actions, and coding the model's responses into covert imaginal or symbolic representations. It has also been proposed that children code, or organize in memory, the notion that some responses are male-appropriate or female-appropriate on the basis of their having witnessed different proportions of males and females performing the responses (Perry & Bussey 1979). For example if children observe that 75% of all available male tennis players hit winning overheads and poach at the net in tennis, whereas only 10% of female models perform these skills, it is likely that these desirable tennis skills will be coded as male-appropriate or masculine.

An even more serious consequence of the association between sex roles and sport may relate to the impact on boys of coed experiences. If boys are taught to define sport in terms of its relationship to "being a man," than competition with females may be very threatening. The very language of sport has tended to make the female an intruder in a segregated place (Johnson & Cofer, 1974). For example, if a boy "plays like a man," what does a girl play like? If a tough scrimmage for males, "separates the men from the boys" what does that experience do for females? If the terms "jock" athlete or an athletic build suggests admirable male traits, what do they suggest for females — or what are the comparable terms.

Social Influences on Performance

Many social influences are impacting the performance of motor skills. The influences may be dramatic for both boys and girls. For example, it becomes evident, after a literature review, that tasks requiring little or no learning are better performed in coactive groups than alone. This follows the hypotheses proposed by Zajonc (1965) that the presence of others was arousing and might therefore increase the probability of emitting the dominant response. This notion has received limited support by researchers dealing with female performers. Carmen and Latchford (1970) found a faster lever-pulling response with female coactors, although males in same-sex dyads showed no improvement over their individual performances. The relationship between these socially facilitating responses and male-female interaction is less clear.

The important role of developmental experiences for children cannot be overstated. In an attempt to explore one part of this complex issue, Bunker (Note 3) studied children in two local schools which have strong coeducational physical education programs. These children were divided into groups, one which consisted of mandatory coed pairs and one which was allowed to "pick a partner" (PAP). The results were rather dramatic, because the PAP group performed as a typical sample (their data were the same as the AAHPERD norms), whereas the coed group performed quite differently. In the sit-up tests, for example, males performed about the same in both groups, but females significantly improved their scores (p<0.05) when placed in coed groups (see Figure 1).

Coed groups generally did better than PAP groups (these consisted of same-sexed partners), but this was particularly true of the females in the coed groups. This is somewhat perplexing, because some data on college-age students suggests that male subjects perform better under same-sex pairs than either coed or no competition, while females perform better in coed groups than in same-sex groups (Freischlag, 1971). Several possible explanations may be offered for this, but of particular importance is the change in performance levels by simply shifting the composition of the group.

Also interesting is that when the children were asked to pick a partner, all but two children (both females) selected a partner of the same sex. This supports previous research which has shown that males almost always choose male partners and opponents. DuQuinn (1980) found, however, that this selection was based on a bias toward the perceived superiority of males by males. In her study, if boys were asked to select partners from opponents who had previously beaten their own performance, partners were selected on the basis of competence and not sex.

Endurance and Pain Tolerance

In an attempt to investigate the effect of coeducational coaction on an endurance task, Ryan (1977) investigated the performance of 192 high school sophomores tested in coed tetrads, same sex-tetrads, and alone conditions on the performance of a leg extension task (time for holding the position). Martens and Landers (1969) had done a similar study on males only (aged 8, 13 and 18), in groups of ones, twos and fours. They found that boys could endure the most pain and, therefore, hold the position longest in tetrads. Studies dealing with females are much more sparse, although investigators, such as Byrd (1971), have found females also perform better in coaching situations than alone on such tasks as manual dexterity.

The Ryan (1971) study, however, found no difference between the sexes in the leg extension task, although in previous studies males have been shown to perform endurance tasks for longer periods of time. No significant effects for the social situation were observed when males and females were considered together. All groups did better in same-sex tetrads than alone, but females failed to maintain this social facilitation in performance when placed in coed situations.

Competitive Effects

In an attempt to sort out several variables related to sex and social facilitation, Hall and Bunker (1980) undertook a study to investigate the effect of social facilitation tested either alone or in tetrads, with or without competition, on performance of college-age males and females. When the data were analyzed in terms of coaction versus alone, it showed that males performed equally in either situations, but females improved their performance greatly when coacting. Males performed significantly better than females under the competitive situations, whereas females showed better performance in the competitive situation and equalled the score of the males.

One possible explanation is that males have traditionally been socialized to be more competitive under all circumstances, whereas females respond to certain situations differently (Hall & Bunker, 1980). Could it be that females have not learned to be independently (or internally) competitive?

INFLUENCE OF EDUCATIONAL EXPERIENCES

One of the major problems with most reported data on sex-differences in motor performances is that it compounds experiential differences by employing one session testing procedures; that is, all children are tested in one-trial or pretest types of design. The use of repeated measures designs with educational interventions would obviously help differentiate between real biological differences versus past experience and motivational differences.

Clifton (Note 4) recently reported a series of experiments with 2-6 year olds on skills related to interception of objects, object projection (throwing and kicking), body projection (long jump), and body stability. These studies spanned a 9-month period in the mid-seventies and reported initial performance levels, final performance levels, and "gain" scores. Performance levels for interception, stability, and body projection (long jump) skills showed no differences between the sexes at either the initial or post test, although girls had significantly better gain scores on the stability and long jump test (Note 4). Clifton found that at the initial test date, boys ages 2-6 threw a softball and kicked a soccer ball farther, but that after 9 months of educational experiences, no significant differences existed between the sexes.

This reduction of performance differentials between males and females after organized learning corroborated data reported by Bunker (Note 4). A group of first, third, and fifth-graders were taught to perform rugby-style drop kicks and overhand throws. Fifty-four children participated in two weeks of instructional activity. The males and females both benefitted greatly from this experience, with females improving more markedly. During initial test situations, large sex differences were seen in kicking, with boys starting at a much higher level, probably due to transfer from soccer-style or football experience. After two weeks of classes, no sex differences were observable (see Figure 2) (Bunker, Note 5).

Bunker (Note 5), also investigated throwing skills which are often thought to be sex-linked. Boys and girls were initially tested on throwing abilities of both their dominant and nondominant hands. Marked sex differences were found for dominant hands throwing abilities at the initial test. After 2 weeks of instruction and approximately 50 trials, no differences existed between nondominant hand throws of boys and girls. In addition, this benefit of the instructional program for nondominant hand throws transferred to produce significant posttest improvement in dominant hand throws for girls.

RESEARCH PROBLEMS

Differences in motor performance do exist, and they do have significance for participation in physical education and athletics and for other tasks which are physically demanding. At least two causes of sex differences exist that are related to both the degree of participation and the level of performance: biological or genetic causes (nature) and environmental or experiential (nurture) causes. Identifying biological differences is much easier than isolating environmental influences on motor performance. It is difficult to determine whether environmental or experience creates differences between the sexes that may not biologically exist, or whether these influences are obscuring the function of genetically determined differences. Physique type, structure, and composition of mature male and female bodies do eventually cause differences in their ultimate physical or motor capabilities. The magnitude of these differences may, however, be increased or decreased, depending on each individual's past experience and training.

Biologically, the greatest differences between the sexes occur after puberty through maturation. The importance of the nature-nurture issue is thus most obvious at prepubertal ages. During this period, most of the differences in performance levels seem to be due to social learning and experiences provided for the development of skill.

Analysis of previously published research on sex-differences in sport and motor performance is limited in value, because of several major problems:

1. Overrepresentation of certain topical areas (e.g. strength, aggression, and competition are discussed more frequently than stability, nurturance, and cooperation).
2. Overrepresentation of certain age groups and lack of systematic reporting based on ages (e.g. a 9-year-old may be 8-9, 8.5-9.5, or 9-10).
3. Single sex subject utilization (all males or all females) or noncomparison mixed-sexed samples.
4. Task influences on subject performance (lack of novelty, increase in sex-typed tasks).
5. Experimenter influences on subject performance (experimenter-subject interaction social facilitation effects).
6. Experimenter bias (unconscious expectations in qualitative judgements).
7. Single-session test designs which amplify past experiences.
8. Overstatement of mean scores (without SD) and nonpublishability of nonsignificant differences.

IMPLICATIONS FOR THE FUTURE

The question of gender-related motor performance differences and the future of coed youth sport is obviously a very complex one. Male and female youth athletes appear to be perhaps more similar than different, with most prepubescent differences being culturally or experientially induced, rather than genetic in nature.

Our task as professionals involved in youth sport will be to continue to investigate such things as (a) optimal learning strategies (b) optimal motivational techniques, and (c) reduction of cultural and experiential differences. Our focus must be on those things which we can change.

If, as the research suggests, motor competence is related primarily to past motor experiences and the reinforcements received for those experiences, systematic investigations of the effects of androgynous, early motor experiences must continue. As our society continues to provide for more educationally equitable movement experiences for boys and girls, the performance levels of all children should improve.

REFERENCE NOTES

1. DuQuin, M. E. Sex differences in motor development, Audio tape of presentation at AAHPERD Convention, Detroit, MI, April 1980. Washington, D.C. AAHPERD On-the-Spot Tapes.
2. Sage, G. H. Psychological implications of age group sports programs. AAHPER Convention, Anaheim, CA, 1974.
3. Bunker, L. K. Social factors affecting performance on the AAHPER Youth Fitness Test. Unpublished manuscript. Motor Learning Laboratory, University of Virginia, 1975.
4. Clifton, M. Sex differences in motor development. Audio tape of presentation at AAHPERD Convention, Detroit, MI, April 1980. Washington, D.C.: AAHPERD On-the-Spot Tapes.
5. Bunker, L. K. Analysis of social factors on throwing and kicking in children. Unpublished manuscript, Charlottesville, VA 1978.

REFERENCES

AAHPER Youth Fitness Test. Washington, D.C. *AAHPER Publications*, 1976.

AAHPERD Health Related Fitness Test. Washington, D.C.: *AAHPERD Publications*, 1980.

Bandura, A. *Social learning theory.* Englewood Cliffs, NJ: Prentice-Hall, 1977.

Bem, S. L. Sex role adaptability: One consequence of psychological androgyny. *Journal of Personality and Social Psychology*, 1974, *31*, 634-643.

Byrd, A. M. Effects of social facilitation upon females performance of two psychomotor tasks, *Research Quarterly*, 1973, *44*, 322-330.

Carmen, D. W. & Latchford, M. Rate of simple motor responding as a function of coaction, sex of the participants, and the presence or absence of the experimenter. *Psychonomic Science*, 1970, *20*, 253-254.

Clarke, A. H. (Ed). *Physical fitness research digest*, 1979, *9*(4), 1-24.

Dyer, K. F. Social influences on female athletic performance. *Journal of Biosocial Sciences*, 1976, *8*, 123-129.

Espenschade, A., & Eckert, H. M. *Motor*

development, Columbus, OH: Charles E. Merrill Books, 1967.

Fauls, L. B. & Smith, W. Sex role learning of five year olds. *Journal of Genetic Psychology,* 1956.

Fleishman, E. A. *The structure of measurements of physical fitness.* Englewood Cliffs, NJ: Prentice-Hall, 1964.

Freischlag, J. A comparison of the effects of sex, competition, and ability on a perceptual motor task. Unpublished Doctoral Dissertation, Florida State University, 1971.

Fulton, C. D., & Hubbard, A. W. Effect of puberty on reaction and movement times. *Research Quarterly,* 1975, 46, 335-344.

Hall, E. G., & Bunker, L. K. Locus of control as mediator of social facilitation effects during motor skill learning. *Journal of Sport Psychology,* 1980, *1,* 332-335.

Harris, D. V. Physical sex differences: A matter of degree. In M. Adrian & J. Brame (Eds.) *NAGWS research reports (Vol. 3).* Washington, D.C.: AAHPER, 1977.

Harris, D. V. Personality in athletics. In L. K. Bunker & R. J. Rotella (Eds.) sport psychology: *From theory to practice (Vol. 2).* Charlottesville: University of Virginia, 1979.

Helmreich, R., & Spence, J. Sex roles and achievement. In R. W. Christina & D. M. Landers (Eds), *Psychology of motor behavior and sport (Vol. 2).* Champaign, IL: Human Kinetics Publishers, 1977.

Hodgkins, J. Reaction time and speed of movement in males and females of various ages. *Research Quarterly,* 1963, 34(3), 335.

Ikai, M. Work capacity of the Japanese related to age and sex. *Journal of sports medicine and physical fitness,* 1966, 6, 100.

Johnson, W. R., & Cofer, C. N. Personality Dynamics: Psychological implications. In W. R. Johnson & E. R. Buskirk (Eds.), *Science and medicine of exercise and sport.* New York: Harper & Row, 1974.

Jordon, D. B., Rhee, J. J., Kim, J. M., & Low, M. Echocardiographic analysis of men and women marathon runners. *Medicine and Science in Sports and Exercise,* 1980, 12(2), 136.

Kidd, K. R., & Woodman, W. F. Sex and orientation toward winning in sport. *Research Quarterly,* 1975, 46, 476-483.

Laubach, L. L. Comparative muscular strength of men and women: A review of the literature. *Aviation, Space and Environmental Medicine,* 1976, 47(5), 534.

Martens, R. *Social Psychology in physical activity.* New York: Harper & Row, 1975.

Martens, R. & Landers, D. M. Coaction effects on a muscular endurance task. *Research Quarterly,* 1969, 40, 733-737.

Mischel, W. Sex-typing and socialization. In P. H. Mussen (Ed.), Carmichael's *Manual of child psychology,* New York: Wiley, 1970.

Montoye, H. J. & Lamphiear, D. E. Grip and strength in males and females, ages 10-69. *Research Quarterly,* 1977, 48(1), 109.

Murray, M. C. The relationship of attitudes toward achievement of elementary school girls and participation in educational sport. Unpublished Doctoral Dissertation, University of Connecticut, 1976.

Murray, M. C. Organized sport for children: Growth and development. Proceedings of the NAPECW/NCPEAM National Conference. Chicago: University of Illinois Publications, 1978.

Mussen, P. H., Conger, J. & Kagan, J. *Child development and personality.* New York: Harper & Row, 1969.

Orlick, T. & Botterill, C. *Every kid can win.* Chicago: Nelson-Hall 1975.

Perry, D. G. & Bussey, K. The social learning theory of sex differences: Imitation is alive and well. *Journal of Personality and Social Psychology,* 1979, 37(10), 1699-1712.

Plowman, S. Physiological characteristics of female athletes. *Research Quarterly,* 1974, 45(4), 349.

Roberts, G. C. Children's assignment of responsibility for winning and losing. In R. Smith & S. Small (Eds.). *Psychological perspectives of youth sports.* New York: Hemisphere Publishing, 1978.

Romer, N. The motive to avoid success and its effect of performance in school-age males and females. *Developmental Psychology,* 1975, *11,* 689-699.

Ryan, D. A. The effects of coaction groups and sex on the performance of a physical endurance task by high school-aged students. Unpublished master's thesis, University of Virginia, Charlottesville, VA, 1977.

Scotland, B. M. Strength, muscular endurance, and cardiorespiratory endurance changes in college males and females as a function of training. Unpublished master's thesis. SUNY: Brockport, 1976.

Sherif, C. The social context of competition. In D. Landers (Ed.), *Social problems in athletics.* Urbana, IL: University of Illinois Press, 1976.

Sherif, C. W., & Rattray, G. D. Psychosocial development and activity in middle childhood (5-12 years). In G. Albinson & G. M. Andrews (Eds.) *Child in sport and physical activity.* Baltimore: University Park Press, 1976.

Takamo, K., & Frijiyoshi, J. A study of timing in sensory motor performance viewed from the developmental stages. *Journal of Sports Medicine and Physical Fitness,* 1965, 5, 50.

Tanner, J. M. *Growth at adolescence.* Springfield, IL: Charles C. Thomas, 1962.

Ullyot, J. *Record-breaking women.* Science News, 1977, *112,* 172-174.

Wakat, D. K. Physiological factors of race and sex in sport. In L. K. Bunker & R. J. Rotella (eds.), *Sport Psychology: From theory to practice.* Charlottesville: University of Virginia, 1978.

Wilmore, J. H. The female athlete. *Journal of School Health,* 1977, 47, 227-233.

Wilmore, J. H. The female athlete. *Journal of School Health,* 1977, 47, 227-233.

Wyrick, W. How sex differences affect research in physical education. In D. V. Harris (Ed.), *DGWS research report: Women in sports.* Washington: AAHPER, 1971.

Zajonc, R. B. Social facilitation. *Science,* 1965, *149,* 269-274.

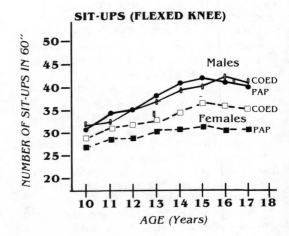

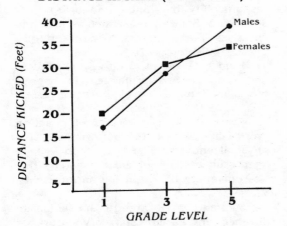

Rugby-Style Drop Kick Performance of First, Third, and Fifth Grade Males and Females (Bunker, 1978).

Table 1
Physical Fitness Data for Children

	Age												
	5	6	7	8	9	10	11	12	13	14	15	16	17
50-Yard Run (secs.)[a]													
Boys						8.2	8.0	7.8	7.5	7.2	6.9	6.7	6.6
Girls						8.6	8.3	8.1	8.0	7.8	7.8	7.9	7.9
600-Yard Run (mins. and secs.)[a]													
Boys						2: 3	2:27	2:19	2:10	2: 3	1:56	1:52	1:52
Girls						2:56	2:53	2:47	2:41	2:40	2:37	2:43	2:41
Shuttle Run (mins. and secs.)[a]													
Boys						11.2	10.9	10.7	10.4	10.1	9.9	9.9	9.8
Girls						11.8	11.5	11.4	11.2	11.0	11.0	11.2	11.1
Sit-Ups (number of)[b]													
Boys	18	20	26	30	32	34	37	39	41	42	44	45	46
Girls	19	22	25	29	29	32	34	36	35	35	37	33	37
Standing Broad Jump (ft. and ins.)[a]													
Boys						4'11"	5'2"	5'5"	5'9"	6'2"	6'8"	7'0"	7'2"
Girls						4'8"	4'11"	5'0"	5'3"	5'4"	5'5"	5'3"	5'3"
Softball Throw (ft.)[a]													
Boys						96	111	120	140	155	171	180	190
Girls						50	59	64	70	75	78	75	75
9 Minute Run (yds.)[b]													
Boys	1170	1280	1440	1595	1660	1690	1725	1760	1885	1956	2027	2098	2169
Girls	1140	1208	1344	1358	1425	1460	1480	1590	1577	1615	1653	1691	1729
Mile Run (mins. and secs.)[b]													
Boys	13:46	12:29	11:25	11:00	9:56	9:19	9:06	8:20	7:27	7:10	7:14	7:11	7:25
Girls	15:08	13:48	12:30	12:00	11:12	11:06	10:27	9:47	9:27	9:35	10:05	10:45	9:47
Hamstring Flexibility Sit and Reach (cms)[b]													
Boys	25	26	25	25	25	25	25	26	26	28	30	30	34
Girls	27	27	27	28	28	28	29	30	31	33	36	34	35

□ *Note.* Data represents norms at the 50th percentile
a AAHPER Physical Fitness Scores, 1976
b AAHPERD Health Related Fitness Scores, 1980

Table 2
World Track Records for Men and Women — 1954-1979

Event	1954			1975			1979		
	Men	Women	% Diff	Men	Women	% Diff	Men	Women	% Diff
100 Meters	10.2	11.4	11.8	9.9	10.8	9.1	9.9	11.0	11.1
200 Meters	20.2	23.4	15.8	19.5	22.2	13.9	19.5	22.2	13.85
400 Meters	45.2	57.0	26.1	43.9	49.9	13.7	43.9	49.29	12.28
800 Meters	1:46.6	2:07.2	19.4	1:43.7	1:57.5	13.3	1:43.5	1:54.9	11.0
1500 Meters	3:35.6	4:17.3[b]	19.1	3:32.2	4:01.4	13.8	3:32.2	3:56.0	11.2
3000 Meters	7:58.8			7:35.2	8:46.6	15.7	7:35.2	8:45.4	15.42
Mean Differences			18.4			13.2			12.5

[a] 1957
[b] 1967

Julie Heyward, Charlottesville, Va.

36

Mental Rehearsal In Sport

Joel Vedelli
James Madison University

Great advances are being made in understanding the means by which individuals learn to move, and the means by which these movements are combined and incorporated into meaningful patterns of movement known as motor skills. In order to refine and increase the performance of these motor skills an element of practice is necessary. Practice has traditionally been viewed in terms of the overt or physical performance. The amount of practice and learning that occurred was assumed to be a function of the period of time the individual participated and the number of repetitions that were successfully completed. However, physical educators, coaches and researchers are coming to realize the function of the brain in planning and controlling motor skills.

It has now been recognized, and in fact well documented, that mental practice will facilitate the improvement of learning and performance. This facilitation occurs as the individual "thinks" about the skill between active practice trials. This mental practice, or "thinking" about a skill, is more specifically stated as a symbolic or mental rehearsal as opposed to overt rehearsal, which is the actual physical performance of the skill. Though mental practice has been the term most frequently used, a variety of other terms have been, or are continuing to be used to refer to mental practice. Some of these terms are: symbolic rehearsal, conceptualizing practice, introspection and mental imagery. Barrow (1971) states that mental practice and mental imagery are not the same. Mental imagery, according to him, is the retaining of images from previous performances and may in fact, be a result of one's actions and an image of the image itself. Mental practice on the other hand, is the actual mental rehearsal or the review-ing of previous cues for performance. Concentration is on the movement and not its outcome such as direction, accuracy or distance.

Various experimental designs have been employed to study the effects mental practice has on skill acquisition and performance. Experiments on the acquisition of skill have usually employed three basic groups of subjects drawn randomly from a homogeneous population or equated on the basis of initial performance levels. Most studies compare initial performance with final physical performance. The number of subjects has varied considerably, along with the amount of time spent in actual covert rehearsal. Experiments in most instances possess three types of practice conditions (1) a physical practice group, (2) a mental practice group, and (3) a group that uses a combination of physical and mental practice and/or a control group that does not practice at all.

All mental practice involves some kind of imagery, employing various techniques. These methods include: (1) reading descriptions of the skill, (2) listening to descriptions, (3) verbalizing about the skill and (4) employing various audio-visual techniques. With regard to these methods of directing practice, some studies have compared one or more of these various methods, while other studies have attempted to find out how these methods compare with actual physical practice or undirected mental practice. Relationships between covert rehearsal and the variables of intelligence, verbal ability and kinesthesis and the ability to practice mentally as measured by physical performance have also been conducted.

Different skills have also been examined regarding mental practice and its effect on performance. Novel skills studied include finger mazes, ring tossing, toy paddle ball bouncing and juggling tasks to name a few. Sports skills studied include basketball shooting, tennis serving, forehand and backhand tennis drives and gymnastics stunts and many more.

Mental practice may also occur at different times in relation to performance. It may occur just before performance, just after performance or between performances, where a quick mental review is made by the performer(s) with attention given to appropriate cues.

Various aspects of mental practice have been investigated. Different experimental designs have been devised, different skills ranging from novel to complex have been studied, and different methods of undirected and directed mental practice have been used and compared. In most instances, mental practice has been shown to positively facilitate physical performance. This is not to discount the fact however, that various studies have shown, that mental practice did not positively affect performance. It is generally agreed however, that mental practice may be used effectively to positively influence the learning and performance of a motor skill.

As previously stated, mental practice involves the conceptualization or the formation of a mental image by the individual practicing in that manner. Warren defines this mental image as "an experience which reproduces or copies in part, and with some degree of sensory realism, a previous perceptual experience in the absence of the original sensory stimulation." What this kinesthetic image is, where it is and what is required for its induction are not known. Evidence suggests that in the synthesis of the kinesthetic image, many parts of the brain are referred to for information. These parts could include the frontal areas, temporal lobe, plus various association areas. Previous research indicates that:

> impulses from different receptors are fed into different parts of the brain, these different areas being involved in audition, vision and proprioception. Previous experiences may be drawn from memory and also used as part of the construct (Jones, 1965).

It is not known precisely how these memory traces are drawn upon. However, informa-

tion accumulated from various receptors is used along with proprioceptive feedback to enhance the completion of the image. It is believed that there is an integrating center in the central nervous system whose function is to receive all sensory stimuli, evaluate and alter them and project them to appropriate brain areas for responses.

The mental image that is formed during mental practice causes certain physiological responses within the body. Washburn wrote in 1916 on the phenomenon of imagining a movement. He suggested, "tentative movements" or movements of slight magnitude that actually occurs during imagining. He also stated that these centrally excited sensations are much less steady and enduring than peripherally excited sensations. Because of these statements, implications were made regarding mental practice as not being as valuable for practicing as real peripheral experiences. Studies of mental imagery became concerned with the interaction of the mind and body. Thus, experimentation led to the conclusion that thought processes produced measurable muscular contractions particularly in muscle groups used to produce the imagined movement. Assumptions that were made suggested that in physical performance, there is some degree of related mental activity, just as in mental practice there are certain neural and muscular responses.

Following these assumptions, research was conducted in which these muscular responses were actually substantiated and ultimately recorded. In 1930, Freeman investigaged the neuromuscular spread during exercise and the actual implicit muscular activity that occurred during mental activity. Jacobson (1932) and Shaw (1938) also reported that covert rehearsal excited the nervous system and that actual muscular contractions did occur. This first related study was conducted by Jacobson in 1932. He thoroughly studied this muscular phenomenon, by using electromyographical measurements to provide evidence of these nervous and muscular changes that resulted in regard to this increased action potential during mental activity. It was reported that Jacobson's subjects, trained to relax, demonstrated action potentials only in the muscles involved in the particularly imagined activity. Muscles in the eyes also contracted as though the individual was looking at something. When practicing "inner speech," the muscles in the tongue and lips also contracted as if to say words. Jacobson stated that "evidence is thus afforded that the physiology of mental activity is not confined to closed circuits in the brain, but that muscular regions also participate.

Elaborate experiments have been conducted employing electrical, chemical and surgical techniques that have revealed pertinent facts that will foster better understanding of the role of the central nervous system to learning. The importance of these studies relates to the emphasis placed on sensory control of motor response and the role of perception in motor response.

Various theories have been presented regarding the process by which mental practice contributes to learning. The following eight points serve to summarize the present theoretical views regarding neurophysiological approaches to learning and the relationship of the approaches to mental practice:

1. Learning is a unified process involving both mind and body.
2. Learning begins in experience and is affected by past experience, emotion and motivation.
3. The central nervous system is a plastic, dynamic, highly integrated, and constantly active system.
4. Activity seems to take place in the nervous system that prepares higher centers for action.
5. Some structural change seems to take place with continued usage or reverberation of circuits.
6. The nervous system seems to function on the basis of patterns of impulses.
7. Learning appears to be closely related to improving with practice through facilitation of synaptic transmission.
8. Learning and behavior seem to result from the interplay of the afferent and efferent pathways, the reticular or nonspecific ascending pathway, and the limbic-mid-brain circuit, providing the informational alerting and motivating components.

The effectiveness of mental practice may possibly relate to the ability of the nervous system to register sensory and motor patterns, and by its ability to recall (memory) and rearrange memory images (imagination). It may therefore be concluded that mental practice might lead to the same changes in the central nervous system as those produced by actual physical work. However, there is no exact answer to what actually does occur. Answers are highly theoretical in nature and more time is necessary to investigate these theoretical approaches to nervous system function and the relation of mental practice and learning.

Historically studies regarding mental activity and physical performance date back to the 1980's. Most of these early studies however, did not clearly isolate and attempt to control mental rehearsal. They were more speculative in nature than anything else. As early as 1892, psychologists were interested in the relationship between thought and motor movement. During the time period between 1900 and 1940, the majority of investigations on mental practice applied to motor skills were conducted by psychologists. They were primarily concerned with the nature of mental imagery, neuromuscular action during mental activity and mental practice as it affected such skills as maze learning, lighting a sequence of lights and piano playing. Investigations during this time were primarily interested in the "pure mental" practice approach to learning.

The first truly significant study related to mental practice and performance was conducted by Vandell, Davis and Clugston (1943). They attempted to isolate the effects of mental practice in the learning of a motor skill. They took a group of 12 senior high school boys that practiced 35 standard basketball free throws under one of three conditions: (1) practiced physically on day one and day 20, (2) practiced physically on each of 20 days, (3) practiced physically on day one and day 20, with 15 minutes of mental practice from the second to the nineteenth day. The high school boys improved 2% under condition one, 41% under condition two, and 43% under condition three. The junior high school boys improved − 2% under condition one, 7% under condition two, and 4% under condition three. The absence of statistical analysis independent of verification of findings seemed to be necessary before a reliable evaluation could be made. These results indicated positive improvements were made by physical practice and mental practice groups. The greatest implication of this study related to the fact that it was the earliest of its type, and it provided the groundwork upon which most current studies were based.

For all intents and purposes, mental practice has been found to be statistically significant in favorably influencing motor learning tasks. Mental practice in combination with actual physical practice is in many instances as effective or almost as effective as pure physical practice. A learner may also develop proficiency in a skill more quickly, thoroughly and possibly with greater retention using mental practice. However, pure mental practice alone has not been shown to be superior to physical practice. Mental practice also seems to be governed by the length of practice bouts, and the massing and distribution of these bouts. Some research implies that the optimum amount of time for concentrated mental practice is five minutes. However, this fact has not been substantiated as of yet. Intelligence of the learner also does not appear to possess any bearing on the amount of learning. Most of all however, it is now realized that motor learning is not purely physical in nature. It is quite evident that people do some degree of thinking when they go through the motions of an activity.

Sage (1971) has presented four theories that highly relate to the effectiveness of mental practice. Highly general in nature, they are most applicable to explaining much of the underlying emphasis for positive mental practice. Initially, it is found that motivation is in part responsible for effectiveness of mental practice. Mental practice groups may become more motivated than a non-practice group because of "ego-involvement" associated with the thinking about a task. Secondly, it was found that a symbolic perceptual hypothesis of mental practice allows the individual to gain perceptual "insights" into the movement pattern. This results in a reduction of errors and a subsequently improved performance. A third, very popular theory relates to neuromuscular units that are used while carrying out the task. Therefore, actual practice is occurring in a reduced degree. These "action currents" occur when a muscle is actually used or when a particular action is imagined. The final concept mentioned by Sage related to the neurophysiological theory. This theory states mental practice activates neural components in the brain which are responsible for directing movements. The neural component which is activated in mental practice is the motor component which actually sends signals to the muscles during movement execution. This therefore implies that the effect of neural activity modifies the "circuitry" so as to bring about more effective performance when the task is performed again. In essence, these four concepts serve to broadly incorporate most of the thought regarding mental practice.

Oxendine (1968) suggests some practical techniques for mental practice. He suggests mental rehearsal may be used immediately preceding, following, or coinciding with the performance. The pre-performance review is illustrated by a bowler or a high jumper focusing his attention on the task at hand and rehearsing his way through the movement pattern. The after-performance rehearsal is illustrated by a golfer replaying a shot without a ball or a basketball player determining why he missed his first free throw. The during-performance rehearsal is exemplified by a player reminding himself to concentrate on the important aspects of the performance. The second technique emphasized by Oxendine involves mental rehearsal between practice sessions. This has great potential, as demonstrated by a variety of studies that have been done on this topic, but it is rarely used by physical educators and coaches. A third mental rehearsal technique might involve rehearsing game strategy between contests or even during lulls in a contest. This technique might be used to rehearse the various situations that arise in a game and mentally working out how to respond to these situations before they occur.

REFERENCES

Barrow, Harold, M. *Man and His Movement: Principles of His Physical Education.* (Philadelphia; Lea and Febiger, 1971).

Jacobson, Edmond, "Electrophysiology of Mental Activities," *American Journal of Psychology* 44 (1932): 677-94.

Jones, John Gerald. "Motor Learning Without Demonstration of Physical Practice, Under Two Conditions of Mental Practice, *Research Quarterly*, 36 (October). 270-6, 1965.

Oxendine, Joseph B. *Psychology of Motor Learning.* (New York: Appleton-Century-Crofts, 1968.)

Sage, George H. *Introduction to Motor Behavior, A Neuropsychological Approach,* (Reading: Addison-Wesley Publishing Company, 1971), 328-31.

Shaw, W. A. "The Distribution of Muscular Action Potentials During Imagining." *Psychol. Rec.* 1938, 2:195-216.

Vandell, R. A., R. A. Davis, and H. A. Clungston, "The Function of Mental Practice in the Acquisition of Motor Skills." *Journal of General Psychology,* 29, 243-50, 1943.

Warren in Laura Lee Luebke's "A Comparison of the Effects of Varying Schedules of Mental and Physical Practice Trials on the Performance of the Overarm Softball Throw." Masters thesis, University of Wisconsin, 1967.

Washburn in Charles B. Corbin's "The Effects of Mental Practice on Skill Development After Controlled Practice," *Research Quarterly,* 38 (December 1967): 534-8.

37

Coaching Applications Of Mental Rehearsal

Laura Siebold Caudill
Ball State University

Mental rehearsal, as we use it in competitive athletics, refers to how one systematically thinks about his or her performance in a past or present athletic endeavor (Nideffer, 1976). Many athletes use mental rehearsal to prepare for what they are about to do or to analyze what they have already done. By mentally rehearsing, the athletes try to get a mental picture and/or sequence of skills. Many athletes use the idea of mental rehearsal as a means of increasing their learning speed and improving their performance (Nideffer, 1976).

Probably the question which comes to mind most often when speaking of mental practice is "How effective is mental practice in learning or performing a motor skill?" The following are two studies done specifically to find an answer to this question.

The first study (Stebbins, 1963) compared the effects of physical and mental practice in learning a motor skill. In the study, Stebbins found a positive relationship between mental practice and the acquisition of motor skills. In other words, mental practice seemed to be a useful tool in learning a skill.

His experiment was composed of five different groups. The groups were as follows:

1. Control group: no practice sessions.
2. Mental practice group: mental practiced by watching the physical practice group.
3. Physical practice group: practiced throwing.
4. Mental-physical practice group: mental practiced first through tenth session and then physical practiced the eleventh through the eighteenth sessions.
5. Physical-mental practice group: physical practiced first through the tenth session and mental practiced the eleventh through the eighteenth sessions.

The skill being taught was that of throwing a rubber ball at a target. Results of the study showed that combination groups such as groups No. 4 and No. 5 were superior to the mental practice and control groups, while group No. 3 (physical practice) was not significantly different from any other group. Thus, Stebbins concluded that mental practice was effective when combined with physical practice, but mental practice alone did not produce an improvement in learning simple hand-eye coordination skills (Stebbins, 1968).

The second study was done by Stephen Phipps (1969) who found that mental practice was effective for simple skills, but not complex motor skills. He did this by testing subjects in three different skills — each skill at a different level of difficulty. The three skills listed in order of difficulty were the hock swing, jump foot and soccer hitch kick. There were two groups — a mental practice group and a control group. The mental practice group was instructed to relax, close their eyes, imagine the skill, then practice it ten times. The control group was asked to do the actual physical practice. The skill was considered learned after performing it successfully two consecutive times. The results showed that the only significant score between the control group and the mental practice group was in learning the hock swing (they learned the skill in fewer number of times). Yet there was no significant difference in learning the more difficult skills. Therefore, Phipps hypothesized that mental practice was effective in learning most simple tasks, but not necessarily the more difficult ones.

Mental practice can also be effective in

preventing excess muscle tension. It has been found that many athletes who are in a "slump" seem to have their mind dominated by negative thoughts. This adds to muscle tension which results in a decrease in skill performance and prevents athletes from reaching their peak level. This positive mental rehearsal can be a very effective relaxation technique and this will aid in improving performance.

There are different types of mental practice which can affect learning, acquisition, and performance in different ways. One aspect of mental practice which has been studied is that of negative versus positive mental practice. In positive mental rehearsal, subjects form mental images of a good performance, whereas in negative mental practice they form images of a poor performance. Graham E. Powell (1975) conducted an experiment in which he compared negative and positive mental practice. In it he divided eighteen subjects into two groups ($G+$ and $G-$). The motor skill for this experiment was dart throwing. $G+$ mental practiced by imagining the darts landing in the center of the target, while $G-$ imagined the darts landing away from the center. When comparing the first trial from the last trial, data showed that $G+$ subjects improved by 28%, while $G-$ subjects deteriorated by 3%. This finding was rather surprising since subjects participating in physical practice not only showed no improvement, but actually decreased in skill level. Results showed that what subjects imagine during mental practice does affect performance. Positive mental practice proved to be a more effective learning procedure than negative mental practice (Powell, 1973).

There are several other ways of using mental rehearsal in sports. It can be up to the coach to decide the best method for each individual athlete. The following is a list of different ways to mentally practice:

1. Rehearse performing skill perfectly or rehearse performing skill with mistakes and then coping with these mistakes.
2. Rehearse skill in a relaxed situation.
3. Rehearse performance in slow motion. If anxiety or tension is felt, relax, breathe deep and slow, concentrate and rehearse performing skill perfectly again.

4. Rehearse performing skill at normal speed.
5. Rehearse performing against upcoming opponent, possibly even rehearse numbers of players on the other team.
6. Rehearse strategy for upcoming game.
7. Rehearse offense and defense with all possible options and how to react to them.
8. Rehearse in the most anxiety-filled situation imaginable. Be very specific — imagine arriving at a championship game site, picture game site, screaming fans, experience having been there many times before.

MENTAL PRACTICE AND COACHING IMPLICATIONS

As a swimming and diving coach I have gathered a great deal of information about mental practice, both from my own personal experience as a diver and from interviews and talks with other divers. For example, as a coach, I talk to each diver prior to and following each diving meet, as well as countless other times throughout the school year. It is important to find out precisely what the athlete was thinking and how these thoughts and cognitions influenced his or her performance. Therefore, I would ask questions such as "What were your thoughts prior to competition, during competition, and following competition?" "Did you get any type of mental image or mental feeling for the dive before actually doing it? If so, what and describe." For most of my divers, many of these thoughts were in the form of a "mental image or mental kinesthetic feeling." Some divers have been taught how to use these techniques by past coaches and others have taught themselves. However, for a few divers, mental rehearsal was a new and unfamiliar concept. Therefore, I would have to teach these divers how to use mental practice and explain the advantage of using it.

As a coach, it is important to me that all divers have a clear understanding of what mental rehearsal is and how it can be used effectively in athletics. Mental rehearsal is basically practicing a specific skill or sequence of skills in one's head through mental images and/or body feelings (kinesthetic cues). These mental images and feelings can be of themselves, someone else, or of a dark image performing the task. To get a mental image of themselves practicing the skill is thought to be the best way, but some people have a difficult time imagining themselves. Then the person should work on developing an image of someone else or of an unidentified image or person performing the skill. This idea of trying to get a mental picture or mental image of someone performing the skill is called external mental rehearsal. When the person mentally rehearses by getting bodily feelings or kinesthetic cues for the skill, then this is called internal mental rehearsal. These are just two types of mental rehearsal, which can be further expanded into other types of techniques, which I will further explain. We will see that both of these aspects of mental rehearsal and many others are very important to how an athlete mentally prepares himself to perform a specific task.

Many athletes are able to use mental rehearsal as if they were mentally imagining themselves doing the skill. Some of the more fortunate are able to imagine themselves as clear and as vivid as if they were watching a movie of themselves in their head. Some people might be able to do this quite easily with all skills, and some people can only use this technique on certain skills, which are usually simple. For example, in my own personal career as a diver I was able to clearly imagine myself performing some of my dives as if I were watching a movie. Again these were the easier dives or the ones in which I felt particularly confident. For example, it was, and still is, very easy for me to visualize myself doing a front dive layout, which is one of the easier dives required by all competitors. As I am able to visualize myself, I am able to get a clear picture of myself walking down the diving board, swinging my arms naturally at my sides as I press down into the board with my last step. The mental picture continues as I see myself pushing up into the hurdle with my arms extended straight overhead in a "y" position. I can then visualize myself landing down on the very end of the board as my arms swing by my hips and up in front and over my head to set for the front dive. At this point I am able to continue visualizing myself as I push off the board into the front

dive layout position in the air. From here I picture myself preparing for the entry as I begin to close up with the arms and reach for the water. From beginning to end I am able to get a clear and detailed mental picture of this. In talking with some of my varsity divers, they too have had similar experiences in using mental rehearsal.

As a coach at the University of Virginia, I had one of my female varsity divers use mental practice for all of her dives and in all competitive or practice sessions. She was able to get a clear and vivid mental image of herself as if she were watching a moving picture of herself in her head. She was able to do this for nearly all of her dives. The only dives that she was not able to use this type of mental practice for were new dives that she had just learned. For these dives the mental image was harder to form and when there was a mental image, it was usually less vivid and not as clear. After she developed more confidence in the new dives and they were easier for her, then she was able to get a better mental image for the dive.

Throughout the season this diver was continually encouraged to use mental practice before each diving meet as well as before each practice. She would spend time each day before practice and then time between each dive at practice to mentally rehearse and prepare for the next workout, meet, or the next dive. She would also do the same for each diving meet she competed in. The night before each meet she would go through each dive in her head as if she were at the pool and the meet was going on. Then she would do the same thing before her actual diving event started. In a college swimming and diving meet there are usually several events before the first diving event. So, she would use this time during the swimming to find a place to lie down, relax, and mentally rehearse each dive she was going to do that day. In addition to the actual physical benefits of mental rehearsal it also kept her relaxed and her arousal level at an ideal level to compete at. However, this would be a typical meet preparation for a dual meet or for a small championship meet that didn't have any competition for her at all.

She had a more difficult time preparing herself for championship meets such as nationals. Rather than relax and concentrate

264

on herself and her mental practice, she would make herself more nervous by worrying about the meet, her competition, the audience, and all of the girls who were better divers than she was. Instead, she needed to relax and prepare herself for this situation and concentrate on her mental practice. This is all very crucial in meets like this that put a lot of pressure on the diver.

Some athletes cannot mentally practice by mentally seeing an entire moving picture of themselves. Instead, some of these people mentally rehearse by mentally imagining certain parts of the movie. These specific parts of the movie are usually the more crucial and important parts. People can imagine these parts of the movie as moving or still. For example, some divers can get a clear mental image of specific required dives as they are in the pike or layout position in the air. These are quite often still images or images much like a snapshot picture. However on some of the more difficult dives, such as a forward three and one-half somersault, it may only be possible to get a mental picture of my legs and feet on the board as they go through the hurdle and then push off the board.

To supplement a mental image, most athletes are able to get a mental feeling of the activity. In other words, they are able to mentally rehearse the kinesthetic cues or body feelings which accompany the sport. By developing this mental and bodily feeling for the activity, it becomes even more realistic for the athlete as he can recall the sensation of sound and smell. For instance, in trying to get both the image and feeling for a dive the athlete will be able to attend to and concentrate more on the correct feeling and correct picture and be able to make corrections as they are needed. This will hopefully improve the divers performance on that specific dive and make it a consistent improvement.

One excellent example of this technique is that of a male varsity diver who was able to get both an excellent mental picture and a mental or body feeling for most of his dives. Again, the only dives he had difficulty with were the new and more difficult dives. He would work to get this picture and feeling for every dive he did in a meet and in practice. Another would always work to get a mental feeling or body feeling for each dive. However, he would never get a mental

picture to accompany the feeling. He would only get a body feeling for the dive, which was all that he thought was important for him. To learn new dives that he had never done before he would prepare himself by watching someone else perform the dive and from that he would develop his own body or mental feeling for the dive. This appeared to be very successful for him since he learned quickly and improved a considerable amount over the season. However, most of the divers performed best and felt better about their performance when they were able to get a mental picture with a mental or body feeling for their dives.

Some athletes are unable to see themselves in their mental picture, but instead may visualize someone else or some unidentified figure perform the skill. This is particularly true when athletes are trying to get a mental picture of one of their more difficult dives. As the dive gets easier for the athlete to do, then the mental picture is easier to form and possibly the athlete will be able to mentally imagine themselves performing the dive. However, many people have found a considerable amount of success mentally rehearsing someone else performing the dive.

An example of this type of mental rehearsal is when I started learning how to dive on a ten meter tower. The reverse dive pike is one of the first dives I learned. Before I started diving ten meter I would always imagine what it would be like to be a tower diver. I used to get a great mental picture of a particular diver performing the reverse dive pike and other dives on ten meter. She was nationally ranked and an Olympic champion. She became my diving idol and someone like whom I wanted to learn how to dive. By mentally imagining this Olympic champion perform the reverse dive pike, I developed a great desire to learn the dive. Once I learned the dive I was then able to develop a mental image of myself performing the dive in addition to the Olympic champion performing the dive. This all developed great motivation and confidence inside myself to learn how to dive ten meter.

Many divers have similar experiences where they mentally imagined someone else performing the dive. This is a good technique to use in learning new dives when the diver finds it difficult or impossible to imagine himself doing the dive. However, it is best to mentally picture yourself performing the dive.

Mental rehearsal can also be used in preparation for every practice and for every meet. In practice, the importance of using mental practice to make corrections and to get the most out of every dive and every practice session must be emphasized. Divers must be encouraged to start preparing for practice before they come to the pool. For example, take time to mentally go through some of, or all of the dives that they wanted to work on that afternoon at practice. Encourage them to mentally practice and prepare for any new dive that they would be doing that day. This would help to make the most of every practice session.

Mental rehearsal is even more beneficial when used to prepare for competition. Divers should mentally practice each dive, just as if they were at the pool and in the meet. Try to mentally imagine themselves at the meet with their competition and with the audience watching them. This is all rehearsed over and over in their heads the night before the meet or even days before the meet. As they imagine themselves at the meet they should be able to experience nervous and anxious feelings much like they will actually experience in real life. This way they can learn how to mentally prepare themselves for this and learn how to control and cope with these anxious feelings.

In addition to preparing days before and the night before a meet, mental practice should be employed during the entire diving meet. For example, before each dive the diver should go over the dive in his or her head by mentally picturing and mentally feeling the dive. This not only helps the diver feel more confident about that particular dive but it also helps him to relax and attend to only the dive and not to distracting thoughts such as the audience.

SUMMARY

There are many types of mental rehearsal and there are many different ways that each athlete can use it to fit his or her own style of diving and mental preparation. Coaches must teach their athletes how to use mental practice, but to also open up and share with them their own experiences in using it. If these personal experiences include having mental images of winning the nationals or of winning the Olympics, then a coach shouldn't hesitate to share these experiences with his or her athletes. This way we can use mental practice as both a motivational technique as well as a way to learn and improve one's performance.

REFERENCES

Nideffer, R. M. *The Inner Athlete: Mind Plus Muscle for Winning.* New York: Thomas Y. Crowell Company, 1976.

Phipps, J. J. and Morehouse, C. S. "Effects of Mental Practice on the Acquisition of Motor Skills of Varied Difficulty." *The Research Quarterly,* 1969, 40, 777-788.

Powell, G. E. "Negative and Positive Mental Practice in Motor Skill Acquisition." *Perceptual and Motor Skills,* 1973, 37, 423-425.

Stebbins, R. J. "A Comparison of the Effects of Physical and Mental Practice in Learning a Motor Skill." *Research Quarterly,* 1968, 39, 714-720.

University of Virginia photo services

38

Practice And Competitive Schedules

Richard K. Stratton
Virginia Polytechnic Institute

Any discussion of the scheduling of practice sessions is best begun with a review of the concepts of massed and distributed practice. These two concepts specify the allotment of time to skill learning within practice sessions. Massed practice can be defined as the continuous practice of a skill to be learned without any intermittant pauses (Singer, 1975). Distributed practice refers to practice periods which are divided by rest periods or intervals of alternate skill learning (Singer, 1975). The critical issue for all teachers and coaches is to establish the best relationship between work (practice) and rest in order to achieve maximum levels of learning.

In order to analyze the effects of these schedules experimentally, a paradigm which equates the actual time spent teaching a skill must be employed. A field setting analogy to this paradigm might have the instructor teaching a skill for 50 minutes in one session (massed) or for 10 minutes on five successive days (distributed). The research generally tends to support the effectiveness of the distributed practice methodology. The major problem with distributed practice can be the extensive use of rest periods which may not be economical when applied to a field setting.

These findings primarily reflect immediate test results. In terms of skill retention, the difference between massed practice and distributed practice is not as clear cut. In fact, there is evidence that the two methods, when appropriately applied, are equally effective in terms of the degree of learning achieved (Stelmach, 1969; Whitely, 1970).

Cratty (1973) has suggested that the complexity of the question is in part due to the large numbers of potential variations of distributed and massed practice. In addition to the three forms cited earlier, Cratty includes:

1. initial massing of practice and gradually increasing the length of the rest intervals
2. initial spacing and progressive massing or decreasing the length of the rest intervals
3. initial massing with irregularly introduced rests (p. 364).

Additional problems in terms of effectiveness relate to the types of skills being taught, i.e. fine motor or gross motor. In addition, the degree to which fatigue is produced by a specific task may result in differential practice designs. That is, athletes involved in an activity which produces higher levels of fatigue will not be able to withstand as intense massed practice sessions as those in a less fatiguing activity.

CHANGES IN LEARNING SCHEDULE

The concept of initial massing of practice with subsequent increases in rest intervals has received support in the literature. Cratty (1973) suggests that this schedule, in essence, creates a warm-up effect. Others have found the opposite, initial spacing with increased massing, to be more effective. Lashley (Cratty, 1973) attributed this to achieving initial success in the activity thus reducing fatigue or boredom. The hypothesis proposed is that once initial levels of success in an activity are experienced, the learner is more apt to be motivated to continue practicing, even under more intense practice schedules.

LENGTH OF REST PERIODS

Ideally we would like to be able to specify the optimal length of a rest period. That is, how long does one need to rest in order to achieve maximum learning with minimal loss of practice time? Cratty (1973) cites studies which report a variety of optimal times including 10 minutes, 20 minutes, and 24 hours. Since all of these results were reported from studies using the pursuit rotor, generalizability is extremely limited. Travis (Cratty) did report that gross motor skill performance was benefitted by rest periods which were approximately twice as long as those used for fine motor skills. Thus, the nature of the task appears to be a relevant factor in establishing the length of rest periods.

REMINISCENCE

Reminiscence refers to the concept that after a rest period, performance levels on a learning curve are higher than they were in the trials immediately preceding the rest period. This phenomenon has been interpreted as evidence that learning has occurred during the final few trials prior to rest even though it was not evident in the performance on those trials. This effect seems to be especially prominent in early learning of a skill. Others have interpreted this effect differently, some suggesting that mental practice during the rest period is the factor causing the learning. Hull (1943) has suggested that the spacing of practices resulting in the reminiscence effect reduces the build-up of inhibitory processes which would otherwise disrupt learning in a massed practice situation.

In any case, the decision to mass practice or distribute practice is not an easy one. The existent research does little to provide answers as to the best choice. How does one decide?

FACTORS TO CONSIDER IN DESIGNING PRACTICE SESSIONS

Lawther (1977) suggests that we consider six factors in designing practice sessions. The six are:
1. the age of the learner

2. the complexity and strenuousness of the skill
3. the specific purpose of the particular practice
4. the level of learning already attained
5. the experiential background of the learner
6. total environmental conditions, including other demands and distractions, activity between practices, and other factors (p. 139).

These six factors point heavily to the potential problems of fatigue. A discussion of the role of fatigue in learning situations is probably not warranted here. Suffice it to say that typically, low to moderate levels of fatigue may well enhance learning or performance but high levels of fatigue are usually disruptive of the learning process. The desirability of practicing while fatigued to enhance the ability to perform in a fatigued state is a question still open to debate. The ultimate decision on scheduling practice sessions must be made in light of the six factors listed above and other considerations unique to the particular setting.

COMPETITIVE SCHEDULING

There is little available research which directly approaches the problem of competitive scheduling. One factor is that the question of how to schedule competition is an incredibly complex and interactive one. So many variables play a role in this situation.

Based in part on the research on attribution, confidence development, and risk taking, it is suggested that the coach ask himself and the staff (and possibly even the athletes) the following types of questions:
1. Do you want to build from easy competition to more difficult competition?
2. Do you want to find out how good the team really is? If so, you might schedule a difficult opponent early in the season.
3. Is each contest as important as the others? In some sports, such as ski-racing or stockcar racing, championship or cup points accumulate constantly during the season with points earned early in the season worth the same as points earned late in the season.

4. Are you trying to train or peak for a particular event, especially championship meets at the end of the season?
5. How much risk are you and the team willing to take?
6. How much confidence do you have in your team and their abilities?
7. How much confidence do the athletes have in their abilities?
8. Do you have any choice in scheduling? In many cases, team sport schedules are relatively rigid and you are forced to take on your opponents as they come.

Whether or not the coach is able to manipulate the schedule, there must be an attempt to provide an adequate and realistic attributional analysis prior to the contest (and season) and an appropriate analysis after the competition. It may be very helpful to future performances if the athlete can understand the causes of successes or failures in previous competition.

REFERENCES

Cratty, B. J. *Movement Behavior and Motor Learning,* 3rd Edition, Philadelphia: Lea and Febiger, 1973.

Hull, C. *Principles of Behavior.* New York: Appleton-Century-Crofts, 1943.

Lawther, J. *The Learning and Performance of Physical Skills,* 2nd Edition, Englewood Cliffs, New Jersey: Prentice-Hall, Inc., 1977.

Singer, R. N. *Motor Learning and Human Performance,* 2nd Edition. New York: Macmillan, 1975.

Stelmach, G. Efficiency of Motor Learning as a Function of Intertrial Rest. *Research Quarterly, 40,* 198-202, 1969.

Whitely, J. Effects of Practice Distribution on Learning a Fine Motor Task. *Research Quarterly, 41,* 576-583, 1970.

SECTION VIII

Coping With Changing Athlete Status

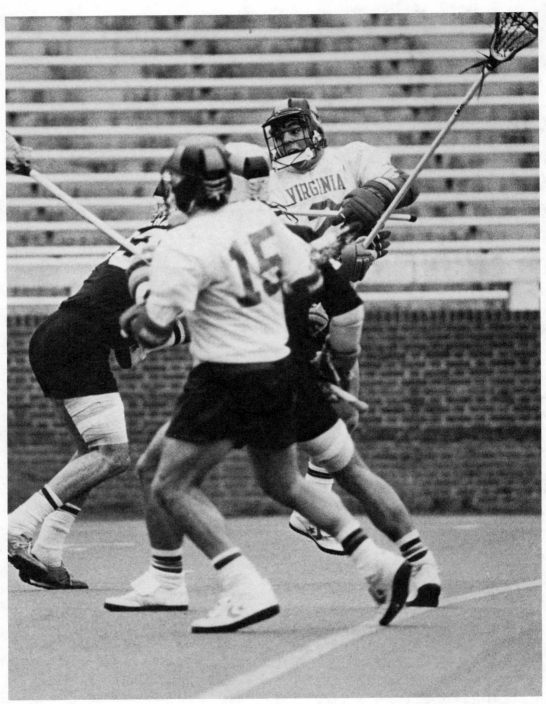

Julie Heyward, Charlottesfille, Va.

39

The Psychological Care Of The Injured Athlete

Robert J. Rotella
University of Virginia

In recent years it has become obvious that closer attention must be given to the psychological rehabilitation of injured athletes. For too long it has been assumed that when the body is ready to return to competition the mind would also be prepared. For many athletes this has not proven to be the case.

Unfortunately, this reality was realized the hard way. Athletes had to suffer. Sometimes anxiety related to an injury led to: (1) reinjury, (2) injury to another body part due to favoring the recently injured limb, (3) a temporary performance decrement due to lowered confidence, and (4) permanent loss of confidence and ability to perform.

The future demands careful consideration to the mental and emotional aspects of injury. Numerous cognitive — behavioral strategies are now available to aid in this process.

Clinical studies have closely followed the coping processes utilized by individuals faced with various injuries. Researchers such as Arnold Lazarus (1974) emphasized the need to study and understand not only the true nature of the injury but more importantly the *perceived severity* of the injury. With this orientation in mind research began to explore the cognitive appraisal of an injury, the perceived threat of an injury, the process of self-control and regulation, and the role of mental skills which are capable of being learned in the coping process. The result today is a greater understanding and appreciation of the manner in which psychological and physiological factors interact with one another.

An abundance of knowledge of potential benefit to sport psychologists, team physicians, trainers, and injured athletes has been developed out of *crisis theory* which is concerned with the manner in which people cope with important life crises.

According to Moss and Tsu (1976) crisis theory has been influenced by four major intellectual developments:

1. Evolution and its pertinence for communal and individual adaptation
2. Growth theories of human motivation
3. A life-cycle approach to human development
4. The study of coping behavior under extreme stress.

A crisis is self-limiting because an individual is incapable of remaining in an extreme state of disequilibrium. Injured athletes will search for balance both cognitively and physically. The equilibrium achieved will either be positive and growth oriented or negative and self-defeating. Athletic injuries may become an important transitional period in the lives of injured athletes. It is crucial that this experience is managed in an efficient manner beneficial to life inside and outside of the athletic arena.

Athletes, like other people, are likely to respond to injury with fear and/or guilt. Past experiences with injury may greatly modify these responses. But for the most part these emotions and thoughts will occur. Thus, the crucial factor becomes one of how to cope with the crisis of injury and the related thoughts and emotions.

How athletes cope with the "loss of identity" will be vitally important. Loss of identity may be temporary as the result of a "minor" injury, or long term from a more permanently debilitating injury. In either case successful coping will influence physical and psychological rehabilitation.

Attacks on self-image and self-esteem, the loss of an opportunity to display prowess, the feelings of helplessness, and the uncertain future that lies ahead will be challenges encountered on the road to successful rehabilitation. Coping may be influenced by a wide variety of situational factors. To one athlete an injury may be perceived as disastrous, to another an opportunity to display courage, and to another a welcome relief from the embarrassment of poor performance, lack of playing time, or a losing season. Professionals involved in the rehabilitation of injured athletes must maximize the possibility of successful *physical* and *psychological* rehabilitation. Without both rehabilitation is incomplete.

Rudolph Moss and Vivian Tsu (1979) have developed a conceptual framework for understanding the life crisis of individuals facing serious illness or injury which has application to aiding injured athletes. This framework, although particularly valuable to seriously injured athletes, is useful in the treatment of all injured athletes with some modification.

Their framework implies that injured athletes' cognitive appraisal of the significance of injury establishes basic adaptive tasks to which various coping skills can be applied. Factors such as background and personal characteristics, illness-related factors, and features of the physical and sociocultural environment significantly influence athletes' cognitive appraisal of the injury, the perception of the tasks required, and the selection of the relevant coping skills. The author's experience with injured athletes suggests that these coping factors are also influenced by the array of coping skills available and the emotional control and self-discipline possessed by athletes. These three factors are learned and should, therefore, be taught to all injured athletes. This does not imply that *all* athletes will necessarily need the skills taught. However, it does provide all athletes with the opportunity to gain self-control over the phases of rehabilitation which they are capable of controlling.

Successful rehabilitation will require healthy adaptation by family members, therapeutic personnel, coaches, teammates, and other significant individuals in the athlete's socio-cultural environment. These individuals must understand and utilize coping skills similar to those being used by the injured athlete. They will often serve as powerful models.

Moss and Tsu have argued that the major adaptive tasks can generally be divided into seven categories. The first task requires the seriously injured athlete to effectively respond to the discomfort, incapacitation, pain, weakness, loss of perceived control, and the permanent disfigurement which may occur with some injuries. A second task includes coping with the stresses of special treatment procedures and of certain conditions of the hospital and training room. Most athletes are not comfortable around hospital equipment, surgical operating rooms, and orthopedic devices. They have always been associated with experience contrary to the health and vigor characteristics of athletic success. They also suggest a great amount of therapeutic activity which will require effort not usually perceived as enjoyable.

When these environmental factors are combined with a "separation from their normal circle of friends a routine injury can indeed be stressful." But the individual must adapt.

The third task "requires athletes (and in many cases their family) to establish communication and rapport with the hospital and training room staff." This indeed can often be a difficult challenge. But the anxieties and questions on one's mind must be answered or the athlete will be troubled. An athlete cannot be positive and relaxed if he is left wondering. How should I question the doctor's decisions? How can I make the doctor realize how important a quick and complete recovery is to my life? How can I get more attention? Is there something wrong with me for feeling so much pain? How can I keep the people in the training room from thinking I'm a malingerer? What will I do if I can never play sports again? How can I still compete? How can I possibly get better when I have someone different treating me each day?

The fourth task "entails maintaining a reasonable emotional balance." With few exceptions, if any, there will be many emotional upsets that will arise and must be controlled. It is impressive how well many athletes who have learned to handle their emotions during competition have controlled themselves while injured, but even the best patients have their moments. "Often, regrets of having been in the wrong place at the wrong time or having made a dumb play can add to the problem. Athletes have good reason for concern. They have often dedicated their lives to an endeavor which requires a healthy and responsive body and mind. An injury which leaves the athlete uncertain about complete recovery is, indeed, cause for "alarm." The consequences could be hazardous to their future playing career. In some cases, the injury may alter or end their life. Such a situation leads to the fifth task which involves "maintaining a healthy self-image." This includes sustaining a sense of competence and mastery. When athletes are injured in a manner which causes a loss of physical functioning the potential for an "identity crisis" is present. Due to the emphasis placed on sport in our society, sport performance plays a dominant role in the formation of an identity for many athletes. When the athlete's skills are tarnished or totally eliminated a difficult, but important, adjustment is required. This adaptation process "may include a change in expectancies and perceptions." "The athlete will have to learn how to remain positive despite lowering his own expectations as well as those of others." The athlete who may have set high goals will have to learn to reset these goals. In most cases, the goals remain high but are channeled in a new direction. The injured athlete and his family will often have to devaluate the importance of athletics and their feelings that such abilities are necessary to a happy and successful life. Their perceptions will have to change.

In a similar manner athletes must learn to cope with the sudden need for dependence upon others for physical and emotional support. This can be a very successful challenge for athletes who have always valued independence, both physically and emotionally. Fortunately, most athletes have well established friendships as a result of their participation in sport with people who can understand this problem. An equally, if not more, difficult challenge may involve finding a healthy balance between accepting help from others and regarding self-control and direction at the appropriate time.

A sixth task "requires injured athletes to maintain relationships with family, friends, teammates and coaches. Injured athletes often feel alienated and left out. Often their perception causes them to stay away from practice or games which adds to their isolation." In some cases such behavior by an injured athlete causes teammates to question their loyalty to the team because they are not showing up and supporting the team. When this occurs the athlete's sense of isolation is further complicated.

If an athlete is injured during an important stage of the season, during a tournament, or on the road, the athlete may receive little or no support or communication from teammates. This can be difficult for the athlete to understand.

Oftentimes the task of preserving relationships is more difficult for the athlete with a non-serious, yet debilitating, injury. The athlete cannot go to visit teammates and teammates are not as concerned about the injured athlete's health and thus there is little communication. When rehabilitation takes place at home and the family is present, alienation is less than when an athlete is left alone in a dormitory or empty house.

Athletes must frequently learn to cope with the guilt associated with disrupting the normal family activity patterns. A supportive and loving family can greatly diminish the difficulty of this adjustment.

The seventh task "entails preparing for an uncertain future." Ironically, this challenge has been made more difficult by advances in surgery and training room therapy. The athlete must be prepared for the end of participation in sport and yet remain positive and enthusiastic about a total recovery.

J. R. Richards, a pitcher for the Houston Astros, must be prepared to never play professional baseball while at the same time remain hopeful that medical advancement and a strong body and mind will allow him to recover completely. Unfortunately, his rehabilitation may be further hampered by his awareness that team physicians and perhaps some teammates and fans questioned his desire when he first reported that he didn't feel well. The experience may deter rehabilitation or become a challenge which will increase motivation and his chances for future health and happiness. He might have been as thrilled if the physician were to have found a cause for his tired arm. Perhaps he was relaxed and thrilled to have proof that there was a real reason for his problem.

The second example is the case of Phil Mahre, the talented United States Ski Team star. Near the end of 1977-78 racing season he broke a number of bones in his ankle. The injury was so serious that hardly anyone expected him to ski successfully in competition again, let alone in a year or less in time for the 1980 Olympics at Lake Placid, New York. However, through the will power and determination of Mahre and Dr. Richard Stedman who operated, directed the rehabilitation and honestly told Mahre his status and what he would have to do to recover, rehabilitation was complete. Mahre went on to win a medal in the 1980 Olympics on the same mountain he had originally been injured. Medical advancement gave him the hope and the ability to return in spite of nearly impossible odds.

The eighth task for injured athletes involves the process of accepting the restriction of the injury and adjusting goals and lifestyles accordingly. Athletes who must spend the remainder of life in a wheelchair may have a much greater life adjustment to make than individuals who have been used to a sedentary lifestyle. But today even handicapped athletes can find active competition in the variety of sport competition presently growing in popularity.

Athletes who recover physically must be certain that they are also mentally ready to return. This process will be discussed in more detail later in this chapter. But athletes may have to overcome fears associated with the return to competition and the struggle of winning back a position on the team that was earned once and now has been lost.

TYPICAL RESPONSES TO INJURY

The tasks which have just been detailed demand a response. It is well documented that athletes do find ways to adapt. Sometimes the responses are adaptive and other times maladaptive. Since the acceptance of the research of Elizabeth Kubler-Ross (1969) on the stages of death and dying, it has become evident that injured athletes typically progress through very similar and predictable stages.

Athletes normally respond to injury with (1) disbelief, denial, and isolation, and as they are made more aware of the extent of their injury, advance through the states of (2) anger, (3) bargaining; (4) depression; and (5) acceptance and resignation while continuing to remain hopeful.

It is common for athletes to respond to an injury by stating that there is no damage, it is less extensive than originally thought, or it will probably be better tomorrow. When tomorrow comes and the injury persists, momentary isolation and loneliness may follow. But, once the athletes attend to injury, it is common for them to become irritated with themselves and others. The soccer goalie may blame the opponent for aggressively mis-kicking the ball and hitting his face, or blame the fullback on his team for letting the opponent get by. The lacrosse player may blame her opponent for checking out of control and hitting her on the head. The football quarterback who learns that he has suffered a broken leg may initially blame himself for running out of the pocket, condemn his lineman for ineffective blocking, or blame the opponent for a late hit.

Soon, the athlete begins to bargain. "OK, I'm injured, but I must be able to play in time for the playoffs. I'll come for treatments, but we'll do it at my pace and at my time." This stage is typically followed by a true sense of loss. The athlete observes a leg in a cast, an arm in a sling with a lack of the ordinary comfort and freedom. The athlete is well aware that the injured limb is the difference between observing action from the sidelines and performing in the competition. Identity has been lost. A perception is formed that the loss may also be the team's loss.

If the athlete is depressed and guilt-ridden, it may help if the team wins despite his absence. If the team loses, the burden may grow. On the other hand, if the athlete is depressed and uncertain of his role on the team, depression and anxiety may increase when the team wins without him and decrease when his loss is felt. When the latter occurs, depression often subsides, as the athlete gets much publicity recognizing his importance to the success of the team. This can help the athlete through the period of depression and into the acceptance stage with the intent of helping the team. Unfortunately, in some cases, it can also cause the athlete to revel in his injured role. Athletes should be made aware of these potentially conflicting and self-defeating motives.

"Today, we are well aware that there can

be many positive advantages accrued from honestly telling the athlete the details of the injury. Often, athletes left in ignorance, particularly after sustaining severe injury, have difficulty overcoming the feelings of denial and isolation associated with this initial stage. Honest and accurate information can help athletes move more readily into acceptance. This is similar to the findings of counselors working in the area of death and dying" (Kavanaugh, 1972). Disclosure of details should, however, always be padded with hope. Too often physicians, trainers and psychologists have erred and underestimated the potential of athletes to cope with and recover from injury. The mind uses a filtering system in conjunction with the process of perception, which will sort out any information the mind is not ready to know. Often in our daily lives, this process causes us to have perceptual blindspots as to our weaknesses. In dealing with information presented to athletes concerning an injury, it can have an important protective function. The information will be accepted and absorbed when the mind is ready. The rate and degree of acceptance will vary from athlete to athlete.

COGNITIVE — BEHAVIORAL METHODS

In recent years a variety of specific strategies have been devised to help athletes cope with the mental and emotional challenge of injury. These new strategies focus on providing athletes with the ability to self-regulate their own behavior so that they can maximize their mental and physical effectiveness in responding to injury.

Cognitive Restructuring

In general, the techniques involve a process known as *cognitive restructuring*. Cognitive restructuring is a simple and useful strategy designed to help athletes become more aware of their own thinking patterns which often lead to ineffective behaviors. A goal will be to change these thought processes to more productive ones. A wide variety of cognitive and behavioral methods have been developed to facilitate this change.

Far too often in the stress-filled world of sport, athletes react to situations in an emotional-irrational manner. Frequently, such a response leads to behaviors which are self-defeating rather than self-enhancing. Examples are abundant.

How often have we seen athletes badly sprain an ankle and decide to "tough" it out for the rest of practice with the result that they sit out for two weeks instead of two days? How often have we prescribed treatment for an athlete and had them fail to show up because they couldn't stand the thought or feeling of putting their leg or arm in ice? How often have athletes failed to get to the training room for their rehabilitation exercises following a perfectly executed surgical operation despite emphasis on its importance? How often has surgery and rehabilitation been executed perfectly only to have the athlete return to the playing field mentally unprepared. And how often have athletes been so eager to return to competition following an injury that they came back too fast and ended up hurting themselves?

Most trainers and physicians have experienced these problems on numerous occasions. Usually there is a great amount of emotional involvement which interfaces with effective thinking. When emotions are further influenced by the coaches' desire to see the athlete return quickly the problem is exaggerated. This is especially true if the injured athlete is a star player and there is a "big" game coming up.

But the problem may go deeper than this. The athlete has put in years of time and effort to prepare for success. The result is many *self-imposed* pressures. An athlete may perceive that he/she must live up to the expectations of *others*, including teammates, parents, friends, and peers. Certainly the love of competition and the desire to return and take part in such enjoyable experience can be an important emotional influence. Likewise, when an athlete has been playing poorly, has been benched, or the team has been losing, all of the above-mentioned factors may pull the athlete in the opposite direction and delay the return to competition.

Athletic trainers and team physicians are human also. Like highly motivated athletes they have pride in what they do. Sometimes this pride can interfere with their ability to think rationally. As a result they can make decisions which are emotionally based and possibly to the detriment of athletes. So recognize that although self-control techniques outlined are provided to give the athlete self-control, they may also benefit the trainer, physician, or sport psychologist.

Rational Thinking

Perception is often inaccurate when our responses are emotionally based. These emotionally-based responses are usually influenced by conscious assumptions, evaluations and interpretations of situations. Athletes often feel anxious, guilty, and depressed when they are injured or think that they are injured because they feel that it is "awful" or "catastrophic" that they have been injured and may not be able to reach a goal of great importance to them. Their emotional reaction may intensify if they begin to fear that they will be rejected by their coach and teammates. Soon they may think that they are unimportant and useless if injured. The emotional reactions to these thoughts *may* be hazardous to their rehabilitation.

The A-B-C Approach

The developer of rational emotive therapy, Albert Ellis, argues that the relationship among thinking, feeling, and behaving follows an A-B-C paradigm. Athletes can begin to control their emotional reactions to injury, pain, or other performance situations likely to engender an emotional response by conceptualizing their thoughts along the A-B-C steps instead of dichotomizing their thoughts and feelings as is the inclination.

Point A represents a *situation* or experience which an athlete finds upsetting, e.g. spraining an ankle two days before a major contest or tearing a ligament in your knee. At point B the athlete may irrationally believe: "If I tell coach I turned my ankle, he will think I'm less than 100% healthy and won't play me," or in the second example, "I've torn ligaments in my knee. I will never be able to perform effectively again. I have ruined everything. I'm competent and a failure to myself and my teammates. I can't stand myself or this injury. This is intoler-

able." At point C the athlete *consequently* feels anxious, guilty, depressed and therefore might avoid telling the coach or trainer about the potentially sprained ankle or avoid having knee surgery or doing the rehabilitation exercise prescribed for a speedy recovery if surgery is performed.

Emotional and irrational thinking has now taken over. The athlete is now most likely to continue thinking, feeling, and behaving in an illogical and self-defeating manner. Point D consists of the intervention strategies which an athlete can use to overcome irrational thoughts. At point D the athlete attempts to *determine* the irrational beliefs connected to their inappropriate injury-related behaviors. To do so the athlete must understand that when he/she is faced with an injury that can block their attainment of important goals, it is: (1) Rational and appropriate to think it is unfortunate, untimely, and inconvenient and to feel frustrated, sad, or irritated; (2) Irrational to catastrophize by convincing oneself that it is awful and terrible and to think absolutely that you must hide your injury from the coach or trainer or that your season or career is ended or that you will never be able to perform effectively again. So at point D the athlete's irrational beliefs are *disputed* and challenged. What would be so awful about telling the coach or trainer that I might have sprained my ankle? Why would they keep me out of competition because I tried to take care of my health? Why is knee surgery so terrible? How could this destroy my career? Do I have reason for excessive guilt? Perhaps it is appropriate to add that it may be important to discuss the differences between tearing knee ligaments or spraining an ankle two days before an important contest during a drill in practice versus doing so while raising hell in a drunken stupor at a party. Perhaps there is a place for guilt in the latter situation which should be discussed and used to help the athlete understand responsibility to the team and hopefully lead to a change in behavior in the future. But in general, the emphasis at point D is to dispute and challenge irrational behaviors.

At point E the athlete learns to substitute rational ideas for the previously held irrational beliefs. The athlete who has just torn knee ligaments might think: "O.K. I tore my ligaments. Gosh, I'm disappointed, I hope

Table 1
Rational and Irrational Responses of Injury

Irrational Thoughts Self-Defeating	Rational Thoughts Self-Enhancing
1. "I'll never be able to perform effectively again. I've ruined everything."	1. "This is a momentary setback. I'll have surgery if the team physician says it's needed and do the rehabilitation exercises prescribed by the trainer, and I'll be back in no time."
2. "I've let my coaches, teammates and friends down by getting injured."	2. "I'm disappointed about my injury. I'll show the team how much I care for them by getting my treatments on a regular basis and attending practice and games and being enthusiastic and helpful in any way possible."
3 "This is a very serious injury. I'll have to be very lucky to ever come back to full strength. Many athletes never do."	3. "This is a very serious injury, but, with the quality physician and trainers I have available, I will do fine, as long as I do what they tell me to do. This is what athletes who successfully recover do. I must make sure that I do my part."

the team will do alright without me. The best way I can show my appreciation to my coach, teammates, and friends who have helped me is to have surgery, do what the physician and trainer tell me to do and get back to competition."

"If I do I'll be back in a short time period. Many other athletes with the same injury or a worse injury have come back with no problems at all. Some feel they are even stronger and perform better." Such thinking shows the athlete's concern for the injury but initiates a well thought out plan for returning. If after making a rational plan and sticking with it rehabilitation is not perfect, the athlete can rationally think: "I did everything that I could do. I have no reason to feel guilty. This injury sure is inconvenient but I can handle it." This line of thinking and planning will reduce the athlete's anxiety when coaches, teammates, and friends are encountered. Such thoughts will also begin to prepare the athlete for the subsequent treatment and/or rehabilitation.

If the athlete were to respond irrationally he might think: "This is awful. Why does this have to happen to me? This is totally unfair." Reactions such as these are likely

to enrage the athlete, cause the athlete to become defensive and blame others (coach and us doing a stupid and dangerous drill, teammate made a dirty play, trainer failed to prepare our knees for the sport properly), excuse his own mistakes and responsibilities, become lost in "the work of worry" associated with the injury, or become overwhelmed with feelings of helplessness and hopelessness. When the athlete becomes preoccupied with these or similar irrational dichotomized thoughts and feelings he/she is likely to do little if anything about improving their condition.

Athletes who respond with such irrational thoughts are likely to feel insecure. The result will be self-doubt and depression. It is tremendously important that athletes realize that these self-defeating thoughts are based on the irrational belief that things ought to be different, instead of more rational understanding that things would be better if they were different and injury had not occurred.

Individuals responsible for the mental and physical wellbeing of athletes should attempt to anticipate the possibility of these irrational, self-defeating thoughts entering athletes' consciousness prior to the occurrence of injuries and arm them with an effective and rational view of their injury when it does occur. Then when injury occurs athletes will only have to be reminded to view their injury in a self-enhancing rather than a self-defeating perspective. Trainers, physicians, and psychologists could greatly help athletes by developing a list of irrational responses to injury and an opposite list of rational responses to injury. (Table 1). This list could be continually updated and made available to athletes when appropriate.

Modification of Self-Statements

The last decade of research in the area of cognitive-behavioral psychology has seen a growth of interventions designed to identify faulty or self-defeating "internal dialogues" and to develop coping skills which could aid in the process of self-control. Much of the work in this area has been influenced by the writings of Aaron Beck, Donald Meichenbaum, and Michael Mahoney (1970; 1977; 1974).

In general, their research suggests that what athletes say to themselves (e.g., self-talk, self-thoughts, images, evaluations, etc.), prior to, during and following an injury or rehabilitation will be an important determinant of their behavior. Likewise, what athletes fail to say to themselves can influence how they act.

It logically follows, then, that athletes ought to learn how to control what they say to themselves, so that their self-thoughts will be more useful. Whereas Ellis' Rational Emotive Therapy might focus on the importance of irrational versus rational thinking, Meichenbaum's approach would argue that it is the presence or absence of coping skills that is important. The first approach placed major emphasis on responding rationally, the later in preparing productive self-statements. Both strategies are useful and should not be considered necessarily different or incompatible.

My experiences with injured athletes support the value in considering this viewpoint. Many athletes who have successfully rehabilitated themselves initially had irrational beliefs but eventually learned to cope with them. Possibly, by preventing irrational thoughts and providing coping skills, the rehabilitation process can be hastened.

INCREASING AWARENESS

The first step involved in the modification of internal dialogue is to help athletes increase their awareness of their inner speech and become increasingly sensitive to faulty dialogue.

One useful way to help athletes in this process is to ask athletes to close their eyes and recall their troubles, feelings and images immediately following getting injured until the subsequent start of rehabilitation and/or surgery. This process may often lean to the expression of dialogue which may progress as follows: "I can't believe this has happened to me. It's probably not serious. I'll be all right tomorrow" to "This really makes me mad. I hate being laid up like this." To eventually "I'm really down about this. I think I'll just stay in my room. I'm of no value when I'm injured like this." to the gradual acceptance that "I'm injured and I'm going to have to live with this."

Notice that this is the reaction to injury outlined earlier which discussed athletes progressing from disbelief, to anger, to depression, to acceptance. Certainly one of the aims of teaching athletes coping skills is to either eliminate or shorten the amount of time it takes to move from disbelief to acceptance. But, of equal, if not more importance, is the need to help athletes progress from acceptance to productivity moving to rehabilitate the injured body part and return to competition.

The more efficiently this process is undertaken, the more likely other confidence- and discouragement-related problems can be prevented. So, it is important that athletes not only become increasingly aware of their faculty thinking styles, but that they also begin to understand why they thought this way (perhaps to feel sorry for themselves, to get sympathy, to protect themselves in case they don't make it back) and to gain confidence that they can learn to change how they think and behave, which can help make their rehabilitation more successful. When athletes are gaining an understanding of why they thought the way they did, it is best to anticipate these thoughts and provide examples where such thinking worked to the disadvantage of complete and rapid recovery from injury for other athletes. This approach is usually much more effective than waiting until you suspect the athletes of thinking in this self-defeating manner because they are missing therapy and then accusing them. Far too often there will be an emotional reaction to such accusations, which will often make them quite useless.

Aaron Beck has been able to identify several examples of faulty cognitions which can be detrimental to athletes: 1) *drawing conclusions when evidence is lacking or even contradictory.* For example, a "minor sport" athlete believes that the trainer or physician gives preferential treatment to "major sport" athletes, because someone told him so. In fact, the person who told him didn't get quality treatment because, in the past, the athlete did not follow the rehabilitation procedures outlined by the trainer or physician, and, as a result; they have lost some interest in this athlete. In fact, the trainer or physician was once a minor sport athlete and is very sensitive to this issue. Athletes often perceive situations inaccurately. You should try to anticipate these and make sure they are accurate. Athletes often hold similar perceptions towards the treatment given to "star" athletes versus "bench-warmers," and male versus female athletes; 2) *exaggerating the meaning of an event* (e.g., thinking your athletic career is ended when you are injured); 3) *disregarding important aspects of a situation* (e.g., an athlete getting terribly discouraged after 10 days of therapy when the trainer and physician told her that it would take at least two to three weeks; 4) *oversimplifying events as good/bad, right/wrong;* 5) *overgeneralizing from a single event.* For example, an athlete knows a fellow athlete who had a similar injury and, despite intensive rehabilitation, didn't recover, so assumes nothing can help him/her recover. Sometimes, athletes get injured once and decide that they are injury-prone and become increasingly anxious and, as a result, do start getting injured more.

UTILIZING COPING SKILLS

Eventually, awareness of faulty dialogues serve as a cue to cope and change the athlete's thinking. Often, when the faulty thinking is recognized, a process known as *Thought Stoppage* is utilized. This process involves having the athlete repeat the word "STOP" when he recognizes self-defeating thoughts and then begins to repeat self-enhancing thoughts.

The following (Tables 3 & 4) should serve to clarify how coping skills training and thought stoppage could be utilized in the rehabilitation process with injured athletes.

The examples provided in the above tables should give you a clearer understanding of how self-statements and coping skills training can influence success in injury rehabilitation. These are examples provided by athletes with whom the author has worked. But, every athlete is different. All team physicians and trainers should either include a sport psychologist in rehabilitation or become more adept themselves at understanding faulty thinking patterns in athletes.

The better the understanding, the more thoroughly you will be able to anticipate the occurrence of these destructive thoughts and *innoculate* athletes against them. You may wish to develop tapes of athletes who are successful in rehabilitation. Simply ask them to talk aloud as they go through the different stages of injury. You may also make copies of tables 3 & 4 and hand them out to athletes or have them made into cassette tapes that they can listen to. It is important that athletes have models that they can imitate who have been successful in rehabilitation. It is also important that they understand that the way in which they think to themselves and cope with the emotional responses to injury will be important determinants of their success in injury rehabilitation.

Visual Imagery As A Coping Skill

Self-statements are not the only way in which we think. Often, when we think, we make sure of our vivid imaginations. Because our vivid imaginations or visual imagery can also greatly influence the manner in which the mind and body respond to injury, it should also be included in the process of injury rehabilitation.

Oftentimes, like self-statements, imagination, if left uncontrolled, will work to the disadvantage of injured athletes. The imagination often "runs wild" and imagines the worst that could happen. The result is

282

Table 3

Coping Skills Training: Preparing And Coping With Rehabilitation

Anticipation And Preparation For Stress Of Injury Rehabilitation

Rehabilitation is going to be long and demanding.
It's going to challenge my self-discipline and my will power.
If I want to attain the goals that I have outlined for myself,
I can't let this injury stand in my way.
What must I do?
I'll work out a plan that will set me up for successful rehabilitation.
I must have confidence in my ability to overcome this challenge.
I must keep my cool and respond intellectually rather than emotionally.
If I find myself responding emotionally, I'll relax and become more aware of
  my self-statements. If I'm thinking self-defeating thoughts, I'll "STOP" them
  and repeat helpful thoughts to myself.
Many athletes have their careers ruined by injuries like mine. But, the
  successful ones realize that successful management of injury and
  rehabilitation is part of becoming a successful athlete.
If I get discouraged, I will think of athletes or others with far worse injuries
  that have been overcome.
I must realize that I may get lazy and make up excuses for missing
  treatments. I'll be aware of this, especially when progress is slow and be
  certain to talk myself into going to treatment.
There will be many excuses ("I can't find time," "I'm too busy," "I have a test
  tomorrow," "The training room hours are ridiculous").
I will make sure that I'm ready for these excuses and realize that they will only
  work against me. I will always find a way to get my treatments.
Remember now. Stay calm. Keep my sense of humor. Think about how good
I'll feel when rehabilitation is successful.

Using Coping Skills During Treatments

Thought Control:
  Remember to listen to what the trainer wants me to do and then do it.
  If I have questions, ask them, but do so in a positive rather than critical
    manner. When treatment is finished, be sure to thank anyone who helped me.
  This hurts, and I don't feel like it. I must think of how good I will feel shortly.
  The trainer is hurting me, but it's for my own good.
  Stay calm and relaxed. Think of something enjoyable. Do not think of the
    negatives.
  I feel really good. Most of the thoughts and feelings I anticipated have crossed
    my mind. I was prepared for them and dealt with them really well.

Body Control:
  Stay relaxed. I'm making my entire body tight and tension-filled.
  Getting tense will only increase the pain.
  Take a deep breath. "Let go" all of your body tension.
  There I go again, I'm biting down on my jaw. I'm clenching my fist.
  "Let go."
  Good, I feel better already.
  Now stay calm.

Post Treatment Self-Evaluation

Fantastic! I had a great day.
I was prepared, and I controlled myself really well.
If I can do this everyday, I will be better soon.
Remember to remain patient. I will not get better overnight.

Table 3 (continued

    I am headed toward a successful rehabilitation. I should be really pleased with
       myself.
    This will be an important step in my development as an athlete.
    Now I know that I can come back even from a serious injury.
    I must make sure I continue my discipline until I am ready to return.
    The trainer will probably tell the coach how well I'm doing.
    The coach will be impressed. I will be impressed with myself.

Table 4
Controlling Inner Dialogue With Thought Stoppage

Injury Related Situation (Potential Sourse of Stress	Self-Defeating Inner Dialogue	Self-Enhancing Inner Dialogue
1. The extent of the injury is explained to the athlete, and a rehabilitation program is outlined.	Athlete worries about injury and feels sorry for self. "I'll never play again this year, if ever." There's no sense listening to this, it will heal itself eventually anyway. I know others who went to therapy and it didn't help them anyway." The athlete is so preoccupied with self-defeating thoughts that he doesn't even hear the rationale for rehabilitation or the program outlined. Gives himself excuses for missing treatments.	Athlete recognizes worrying and feeling sorry for self is of no value. So, athlete stops negative thoughts and redirects thoughts to listening closely to rehabilitation program outline. Asks questions about exercise he is not sure of. Directs thoughts to preparation for tomorrows first treatment session. Plans schedule for tomorrow and look forward to realization in a positive manner.
7:30 A.M.		
Athlete gets up and limps to training room for rehabilitation exercises and training room is locked with no trainer in sight.	Athlete gets mad at trainer for not showing up for therapy session planned yesterday. "This is typical. He never shows up. He gives me a big talk on importance of rehabilitation, and then doesn't show up. To hell with him. I won't show up anymore either until he comes and apologizes to me." The athlete sees only the negative side of this. Accepts no responsibility for himself. Fails to realize that he will be the one who will suffer by not getting therapy.	Athlete gets mad but then recognizes that this is self-defeating. Relaxes and takes deep breath. Stops thoughts and thinks: "I wonder what happened. He never misses a treatment. Something important must have happened. I know he wants me to get better. If I'm going to get better, I will need my treatments. If I don't, I'll be the loser. I'll stop by later to find another meeting time for my treatment." The athlete attempts to understand why the trainer didn't show up. He recognizes importance of taking responsibility for therapy and makes sure he gets it so he can return to action sooner.

284

Table 4 (continued)
Controlling Inner Dialogue With Thought Stoppage

10:30 A.M.		
In class getting constant attention from classmates concerning injury.	Athlete enjoys the attention. "This is nice. I enjoy the attention. I feel like someone special. Gosh, many peers who never recognized me before now know who I am." The athlete begins to enjoy the attention of others that comes from being injured. May begin consciously or subconsciously to like being injured and questions the value of a speedy rehabilitation.	Athlete enjoys the attention but recognizes that this may work to his disadvantage by decreasing motivation to get better. Athlete thinks: "It's nice to know that others care, but I don't want their sympathy: I want their respect as an athlete. The best way to get it is to rehabilitate this injury and get back to competition." The athlete feels good that others care about him and uses these pleasant thoughts to motivate himself to get back to competition quickly.
2:30 P.M.		
Athlete is in training room receiving treatment and going through rehabilitation exercises while experiencing a great amount of pain and little apparent improvement to injured body part.	Athlete worries and questions the benefit of treatment and exercises. "This is awful. This hurts too much to be of benefit. These exercises will probably cause me more harm. Besides, I've been doing this for three days now, and I can't see any progress being made. It would be a lot easier to just let it heal on its own. I don't think I'll come in tomorrow. If it's really important, the trainer will call me. If he doesn't, it will mean I was right. It really doesn't matter if I get treatment." The athlete doesn't get as much out of today's treatment and begins to develop excuses for not continuing therapy.	Athlete worries and questions the benefits of treatment and exercises. Thinks "STOP." These exercises hurt, but it's OK — they will pay off. I'll be competing soon because I'm doing these exercises. I must not let the pain bother me. If the pain gets too severe I'll be competing soon because I'm doing these exercises. I must not let the pain bother me. If the pain gets too severe, I'll speak up and tell the trainer. He'll want to know. Otherwise, I'll live with it and think about how happy I'll be to be competing again." The athlete has a quality treatment session and prepares himself to continue for as long as necessary. Develops rapport with the trainer who feels good about the athlete.
4:00 P.M.		
Athlete watches practice session.	Athlete observes other athletes practicing and feels sorry for self. "Why am I the one who has to be injured? I was in better shape than anyone. I'll probably lose my position	Athlete observes others. Starts to feel sorry for self, recognizes these inappropriate thoughts and "STOP"s and redirects them. "I wish I hadn't been injured. The fact that I'm in really good shape will help

285

Table 4 (continued)

on the team by the time I'm healthy again. I hope the team doesn't play too well without me. I hope I'm missed. The athlete gets more discouraged with self. Seen by teammates in a negative light. Obviously more concerned with self than team.	me get back in the field a lot faster. I hope everyone plays well without me so we can still go on the tournament. I'm going to do everything I can to help. I'll go to practice and help out and cheer for others. I'll make sure I know what's going on so that when I'm healthy again I'll be ready to return. The athlete feels good as a result of enthusiasm during practice. Teammates happy to see him and encourage him to stick with treatments, and get back soon. the team needs him.

increased fear and anxiety.

But, fortunately, it is possible to teach athletes to control their visual images in a manner similar to the way in which they can control their self-statements. When athletes control their imaginations and direct them productively, the imagination can reduce anxiety and aid in the rehabilitation process.

A technique known as *emotive imagery*, developed by Arnold Lazarus and Arnold Abramovite in 1965, is a useful way to therapeutically help athletes gain confidence and feel good about themselves. The technique works because athletes are more likely to follow the prescribed treatment and do their rehabilitation exercises when they are emotionally in control and are feeling positively about themselves. The procedure includes certain kinds of imaginary scenes which produce positive, self-enhancing feelings, like enthusiasm, self-pride and confidence.

An athlete would be instructed to think of other athletes similar to herself who had successfully overcome the same injury being experienced by the presently injured athlete. The recalled scene helps the athlete feel secure and confident that rehabilitation will be successful. As a result, the athlete will be more relaxed and motivated to continue rehabilitation.

The goal of emotive imagery is not to fool the athlete into a state of false confidence. Rather, emotive imagery makes use of imagery which in the past generated anxiety to elicit calm and helpful feelings in the athlete.

The thearapist should help the injured athlete discuss and generate other scenes which could produce positive feelings. For some athletes, recalling the success they have had in the past recovering from injuries and returning to competition is productive. For others, thinking of the admiraration that coaches, teammates and friends will have for them when they overcome their injury works.

A second technique which utilizes mental rehearsal is called *body rehearsal*. In this procedure, the injury is explained in detail to the athlete. Whenever possible, pictures are used to help the athlete develop a mental picture of the injury. Next, the purpose and intent of rehabilitation is explained so that the athlete can visually imagine what exactly is happening internally to the injured body part throughout the rehabilitation process. Finally, after the athlete has developed a clear picture of the healing process, he is asked to visually imagine the healing process. Whenever possible, the athlete is asked to imagine in color. The intent is to facilitate the healing and rehabilitation.

There are two additional visualization strategies that are useful in the rehabilitation process. They are *mastery rehearsal* and *coping rehearsal*. In general, when these strategies are utilized, their purpose is to prepare injured athletes for difficult situations that might be encountered. The situations rehearsed might include: 1) setbacks in rehabilitation, 2) anxieties associated with returning to competition, 3) preparing for complex medical and rehabilitation procedures, 4) showing up for practice in front of your teammates for the first time, or 5) imagining the accomplishment of each goal outlined in the rehabilitation plan. In each case, imagery is employed to help athletes successfully achieve an important task.

Mastery rehearsal is a positive kind of imagery technique in which only the successful completion of tasks is imagined. Surgery, rehabilitation and return to competition are all managed perfectly. There are no problems. Coping rehearsal is quite different. In this strategy, problems that might occur are actively anticipated. The imagination is used to anticipate problems and inappropriate responses to the problems, and to plan effective and appropriate approaches to coping with the difficulty.

An example might clarify the difference between mastery and coping rehearsal. Recently, a young rock climber was about to have surgery for cartilage damage in his right knee. A mastery rehearsal approach might sound like this:

"I'm looking forward to surgery. I'm glad I will no longer be bothered by my knee. I have a well-qualified surgeon who will assure me of a successful operation. I will begin rehabilitation shortly afterwards with a caring and talented athletic trainer. Rehabilitation will be short and successful. Each day I will make progress. I will feel good and I will be excited. In a few weeks, I will be starting to climb again. I feel great about the upcoming operation and rehabilitation. I know I will be successful."

A coping rehearsal program for the same athlete might sound quite different:

"I'm looking forward to surgery, but I am somewhat anxious. I'm likely to get even more anxious as the date for surgery approaches. I'm likely to get nervous and uptight. My mind is likely to get lost in the "work of worry." If I allow these things to happen, they will work to my disadvantage. Whenever I feel myself getting tense, I will "let go" and relax. Whenever I realize that my mind is running wild with anxiety, I will "STOP" and replace it with helpful thoughts.

I will probably experience pain which is likely to cause me to get tense and irritable. I may use this as an excuse for not going for treatment and therapy. I must recognize these signs and make certain that they can't work to my disadvantage. I must anticipate that there will be days in therapy on which I may see little or no progress. When they occur, I may get frustrated and uptight. I must remember to stay calm and positive. If I do, the trainer will enjoy helping me more, and I will feel better about myself . . ."

Both of these techniques have their advantages and disadvantages. Coping rehearsal is more realistic and in this author's experience does a better job of preparing the athlete for the difficulties that will realistically occur. But, in the process of preparation, it does induce a degree of anxiety that may overwhelm some injured athletes. Mastery rehearsal is very confidence-inducing, and, in this respect, is very useful, but it isn't as useful for preparing athletes for what is to come. It does, however, provide a motivational framework that can be very important.

Mastery rehearsal is, however, commonly utilized to aid in the process of physical rehabilitation. The team physician and/or trainer must explain in detail to the injured athlete what must occur inside the body if healing of the injury is to take place. The athlete must be able to conceptualize the inner workings of the body. When this is accomplished, the athlete is asked to visualize healing taking place inside the body. There is little experimental research supporting this approach, but research in this area appears to be growing with the National Institute on Health beginning to support such ventures.

Typically, visualization exercises are facilitated by the use of relaxation training. Relaxation allows athletes to develop more vivid and productive visual images.

CONCLUSION

Injury is a very real and uncomfortable experience that is a part of sport. Success in sport demands the ability to effectively respond to injury. The advancement of knowledge and understanding of the crucial role of the mind and emotions in successful rehabilitation should take us a step closer to assuring athletes of a positive sport experience. Sport psychologists, coaches, trainers, and team physicians need to be aware of self-control strategies which can aid their athletes to a safe and positive return from injury.

REFERENCES

Averill, J. Personal control over aversive stimuli and its relationship to stress. *Psychological Bulletin, 80,* 286-303, 1973.

Bean, K. L. Desensitization, behavioral rehearsal, the reality: A preliminary report on a new procedure. *Behavior Therapy, 1,* 525-545, 1970.

Beck, A. Cognitive therapy: Nature and relation to behavior therapy. *Behavior Therapy, 2,* 194-200, 1970.

Blitz, B., & Dinnerstein, A. The role of attentional focus in pain perception: Manipulation of response to noxious stimulation by instruction. *Journal of Abnormal Psychology, 77,* 42-45, 1971.

Chavers, J., & Barber, T. Cognitive stratgies, experimental modeling and expectation in the attention of pain. *Journal of Abnormal Psychology, 83,* 356-363, 1974.

Evans, M., & Paul, G. Effects of hypnotically suggested analgesia on physiological and subjective responses to cold stress. *Journal of Consulting Clinical Psychology, 35,* 362-371, 1970.

Foreyt, J. P., & Rathjen, D. P. (Eds.): *Cognitive behavior therapy: Research and application.* New York: Plenum Pess, 1978.

Greene, R., & Reyher, J. Pain tolerance in hypnotic analgesia and imagination states. *Journal of Abnormal Psychology, 77,* 42-45, 1977.

Hamburg, D., & Adams, J. E. A perspective on coping behavior. *Archives of General Psychiatry, 17,* 277-284, 1967.

Jacobson, E. *You Must Relax.* New York: McGraw-Hill, 1934.

Jacobson, E. *Progressive relaxation.* Chicago, IL: University of Chicago Press, 1938.

Jacobson, E. *Anxiety and tension control.* Philadelphia, PA: J. B. Lippincott, 1964.

Janis, I. L. *Psychological Stress: Psychoanalytic and behavioral studies of surgical patients.* New York: John Wiley & Sons, 1958.

Johnson, R. Suggestions for pain reduction and response to cold-induced pain. *Psychological Reports, 18,* 79-85, 1966.

Kavanaugh, R. E. *Facing death.* Los Angeles, CA: Nash Publishing, 1972.

Kubler-Ross, E. *On death and dying.* New York: Macmillan, 1969.

Lazarus, R. S. Psychological stress and coping in adaptation and illness. *International Journal of Psychiatry and Medicine, 5,* 321-333, 1974.

Lindmann, B. Symptomatology and management of acute grief. *American Journal of Psychiatry, 101,* 1-11, September 1944.

Lipowski, Z. J. Physical illness, the individual and the coping processes. *Psychiatry and Medicine, 1,* 91-102, 1970.

Mahoney, M. *Cognitive and behavior modification,* Cambridge, MA: Ballinger, 1974.

Meichenbaum, D. *Cognitive behavior modification: An integrative approach.* New York: Plenum Press, 1977.

Meichenbaum, D. *Cognitive behavior modification.* Morristown, NJ: General Learning Press, 1978.

Melzack, R., & Casey, K. Sensory motivational and central control determinants of pain. A new conceptual model. In D. Kenshado (Ed.): *The skin senses.* Springfield, IL: Charles C. Thomas, 1968.

Melzack, R., & Wall, P. Pain mechanisms: *Science, 150,* 197, 1965.

Moss, R. H. *The crises of physical illness: An overview in coping with physical illness.* New York: Plenum Medical Book Co., 1979.

Reeves, J. EMG-biofeedback reduction of tension headache: A cognitive skills training approach. *Biofeedback Self Regulation, 1,* 217-225, 1976.

Rotella, R. J. Systematic desensitization. Psychological rehabilitation of injured athletes. In L. Bunker & R. Rotella (Eds.), *Sport Psychology: From theory to practice.* Charlottesville, VA: Department of Health & Physical Education, University of Virginia, 1978.

Selye, H. *The stress of life.* New York: McGraw-Hill, 1956.

Sternback, R. *Pain: Psychophysiological Analysis.* New York: Academic Press, 1968.

40

Psycho-Social Adjustment Of Athletes To Retirement

Frank J. Gorbett

The purpose of this paper is to explore the socio-psychological adjustment of athletes who have had to give up participation in sports. This termination can take place in different ways. It could come about through injury or being cut from a team. Whatever the rationale, this experience may be devastating to an individual who has devoted 25 to 30 years to a particular sport or a young college athlete who finds himself lacking direction without sports.

LIFE TRANSITIONS / PRERETIREMENT COUNSELING

Over the last few years the use of preretirement counseling programs for people about to retire has emerged. Usually these programs are company-based and often times they are an adjunct service of a community counseling program. This type of counseling is geared toward helping the individual prepare for retirement. The preparation may entail developing new skills such as poblem-solving or resource development within a group counseling model (Manion, 1976). It may also involve individual personal counseling, resource identification, and planning (Kleiber and Thompson, 1980).

The philosophy of the preretirement counseling approach is based on the fact that positive actions taken before retirement will prevent or minimize social and emotional deprivations in retirement and old age. Business leaders see this service as good for business because it shows a concern for the worker. In their view the recognition and help given to loyal, long-term employees is a way to exercise a proper social responsibility by easing out older workers in a positive manner (Manion,

1976). Although this type of counseling has a thin research base, there is some evidence (Lumsden, 1978) that this type of counseling can be one of the best ways to insure positive adjustment after retirement.

One can see the applicability of this approach for an athlete who is leaving sports either voluntarily or involuntarily. The athlete and the 65-year-old retiree have something in common. They are both making a transition. The job situation though is different. The athlete is facing a job market where his peers may have had a five to ten year jump on him in experience and job skill development. This presents unique problems for the athlete. The adult transition literature does not speak directly to the athlete, but it does point out variables in adjustment which have universal application. So let us now take a look at the characteristics involved in a successful transition and different counseling approaches used in preretirement counseling.

Schlossberg (1981) has theorized that there are three factors that influence adaptation to a transition. They are the characteristics of the transition, the characteristics of the pre- and post-transition period, and, lately, the characteristics of the individual. These factors all interact with each other to bring about the successful/unsuccessful adaptation.

The first factor, the characteristics of the transition, involves whether the emotion exhibited is positive or negative, whether change is voluntary or involuntary, whether transition comes gradually or suddenly, and the degree of stress associated with these variables. There is sparse research done on these factors, but one can see the relevance to the ex-athlete's situation. For example, often times when an athlete retires he/she undergoes a role change which they perceive as a loss instead of a gain, and as a result they experience emotion of a negative type. This may be compounded by the fact that the transition is of an involuntary nature. These conditions may interact to increase the athlete's degree of stress.

The second factor, the characteristics of the pre- and post-transition, involves the environment providing the interpersonal and the institutional support needed for the transition. The interpersonal support may come from intimate relationships, the family unit, or a network of friends. Dimsdale (1976) cited group affiliation as one necessary behavior that survivors of the Nazi concentration camps shared. This affiliation provided the support to overcome the physical and emotional obstacles provided by this oppressive environment. Institutional support is the second critical environmental variable. Schlossberg and Leibowitz (1980) studied a job counseling and training program that N.A.S.A. instituted for those people whose jobs had been terminated. They found that those men responded favorably to this program because it gave them the support they were looking for. They were able to express their feelings of anger and resentment at being laid off while in counseling. Job-seeking and problem-solving skills were also taught. Those individuals reported that they had a stable adjustment process because of this program.

The third factor involved in successful adjustment are the characteristics of the individual. This includes one's sense of psycho-social competence, one's sex, age, state of health, race, socioeconomic status, value orientation, and previous experience with a transition. One's sense of confidence or competency is an important variable in any discussion of adaptation. The maintenance of a positive self-image is important if one is to adjust to any transition that may elicit stress. This fact is supported by research (Dimsdale, 1976; Peppers, 1976; Hopson and Adams, 1977) that has looked into one's personal worth during times of crises, stress, or transition. Heddesheimer (1976) also talks about the importance of self-confidence in making a career change. "If one lacks confidence there may be feelings of fear, uncertainty, and anxiousness." "These feelings arise as an individual realizes that new skills will need to be mastered since a temporary change will occur in oc-

cupational status. The individual will move from a position of being consulted because of his experience to one where he is once again a novice and will have to compete with individuals who are probably younger than oneself" (p. 111). This statement seems exactly the position a lot of ex-athletes may find themselves in. The importance of having confidence in one's abilities and competencies seems paramount.

Other characteristics of an individual that are worth noting are the individual's socioeconomic status and the individual's state of health. These may be more directly related to an athlete's situation. Hill (1965) found that lower socioeconomic families have more difficulty adjusting to transitions than middle-class families. Although state of health is a crucial dimension, especially for athletes to date, no research has been conducted on this variable.

Another way of viewing adjustments to transitions is provided by Hopson. Hopson (1981) has proposed seven stages that an individual goes through during a transition period. The seven stages are immobilization, minimization, self-doubt, letting go, testing out, searching for meaning, and internalization. The immobilization period is followed by the minimizing stage which is the minimizing of the negative feelings engendered by the loss of something. A period of self-doubt follows that may be accompanied by feelings of depression. A person will not emerge out of this until he or she has successfully dealt with his or her feelings of loss, anger, and disappointment. Letting go of these feelings through counseling or cartharsis leads to an upward swing. Stage five, the testing out period, is when the preparation for a new career is contemplated. This leads to the sixth stage. the search for meaning, where one gets a perspective on the earlier stages of immobilization, minimization, and self-doubt. After this insight is obtained, it is then internalized. The person is thus renewed and accepts the fact that the transition is complete.

Several different approaches to preretirement counseling has been proposed. In the following section the goals and methodologies employed in some of those approaches will be didcussed.

Manion (1976) describes four approaches to preretirement counseling. Briefly they are coping, prescriptive, educational, and involvement in a group. The coping approach suggests how one might cope with the problems of more time and less money while the prescriptive approach is geared to a set formula to follow when retirement occurs. The third category is an educational approach dealing with possible retirement cases and situations. The idea is that the individual can objectively learn by objectively discussing retirement cases and situations. The fourth approach uses a T-group model that includes the spouse and is designed to generate and resolve questions about the individual's life in retirement and his/her resources, relationships, and personal needs. This takes place with one's peer group in a group setting. Manion (1976) feels that the group process integrated with an educational approach is the most facilitative of all approaches. The individuals can learn skills in life planning and action-taking didactically while also experientially learning and practicing communication and interpersonal skills within the group process. Group support for learning these skills is strongly provided by the process itself.

Kleiber and Thompson (1980) propose a Rogerian non-directive approach to preretirement counseling. "Such an approach allows the individual to explore interests, potentials, and values in a nonjudgmental atmosphere while at the same time promoting a greater sense of personal control" (p. 12). They also recommend the counseling technique of fantasy. Since preretirement counseling is future oriented, it is important to be able to fantasize about the future. By projecting oneself into the future one can then evaluate that future view and its implications for current plans.

In summary, preretirement counseling programs consist of some individual counseling, but the bulk of their work takes place in groups (Manion, 1976; Kleiber and Thompson, 1980; Brammer and Abrego, 1981). When discussing before the adaptation to a transition (Schlossberg, 1981), the importance of interpersonal support was mentioned. The group process can provide this support for people ready to make a transition.

In the present section, the factors involved in making a career transition or adjustment have been ascertained, and counseling strategies utilized to facilitate that transi-

tion were presented briefly. Much of the current knowledge in this area is theoretical and needs empirical testing. Nevertheless, the present section sets the stage for a more specific discussion of the psycho-social adjustment of the athlete to retirement.

PSYCHOSOCIAL ADJUSTMENT OF ATHLETE TO RETIREMENT

The athlete who has to retire may face a number of problems that can impede his adaptation to a non-active status. The discussion in our previous section (Schlossberg, 1981) about the characteristics of a transition aptly describes the situation of many ex-athletes. Their decision to retire is often involuntary, they often lack institutional support from their school or professional organization, and their change in roles can be dramatic. As a result, the athlete may experience a loss of self-respect. McPherson (1980) points out that the problem of adjustment is more critical with the athlete because they have been accustomed to living in the public eye and because retirement at an early stage is not normally socially sanctioned.

The role of status loss for the athlete is another issue. Sheldon (1975) found that people who experienced the most anxiety were those who felt they would experience the loss of the sense of being important to others. Certainly the loss of the athletic role engenders in some athletes a loss of being important to others. This is true if their self-esteem is shaped by the role "athlete."

Of course, not all athletes have difficulty making a transition. McPherson (1977) suggests that there is a wide variance in adjustment to the retired state. "The psychological reaction or adjustment to this state can range from satisfaction, if the process is voluntary or planned far in advance, to traumatic if the process is involuntary. In many cases the reaction depends on age, the options or alternative lifestyles available, the degree of sport involvement, and the amount of preplanning for alternative roles" (p. 135). While this theorizing makes sense, it is important to look at the available data to prove or disapprove currently held theories on psychosocial adjustment. Studies that describe the psychosocial adjustments that an athlete goes through in making the transition from athlete to ex-athlete will be reviewed.

Mihovilovic (1969) studied 44 former soccer players in Yugoslavia. Mihovilovic divided his study into three parts: (1) the end of the sport career; (2) the attitude of the environment toward the athlete after retirement; and (3) how to make the retirement from active sports easier.

Results showed that 95 percent of the athletes sampled reported that the process of retirement was imposed on them, thereby suggesting that there is a conscious attempt to extend the playing career as long as possible. Fifty-three percent missed the popularity that being a team member gave them. It was concluded that retirement and subsequent loss of popularity causes in former athletes a feeling of neglect and regret due to the loss of the fame associated with sport. Retirement for those who had no profession to move into was a traumatic experience characterized by personal conflict, frustration, increased smoking, drinking, neglect of physical exercise, and loss of friends on the team. Mihovilovic found that 39 percent took up smoking after retirement and 16 percent began drinking more. One of the reasons for these adverse effects was that "retirement is perceived negatively since it represents a devaluation in status, a reduction in income, and necessitates the need to acquire other roles in a new social world" (p. 83).

The former athletes thought their retirement from sports could be made easier by entrusting them with various functions while they were still active by continuing to work with the same club after their playing careers were over, or by using their knowledge and experience in future work with the team.

This study was of an "ex post facto" variety. It was a very simply designed study involving the percentage ranking of yes-no answers from a questionnaire. There was no statistical analysis involved. Nevertheless, it uncovered some variables that seem to be involved in an unsuccessful transition to retirement. These variables include: (1) a lack of interpersonal and institutional supports, (2) sudden loss of job, (3) loss of role, and (4) the involuntary nature of the retirement. These were all factors that were included in previous discussions (Schlossberg, 1981).

In a more extensive analysis, Haerle (1975) examined the social, psychological, and occupational dimensions of adjustment to retirement in former professional baseball players. Haerle used a path diagram and path coefficients to sketch the path of background and baseball career factors influencing baseball fame and occupational achievement. He found that players with more education tended to sign their contracts at a later age, thereby retaining their amateur status for longer. There was a strong tendency for those individuals to enter the baseball leagues at higher levels. He found a significant correlation coefficient of .34 between those who had more education and the fact the entered at higher levels (i.e. AAA or majors). Thus, the more educated, the faster you would advance occupationally. He also computed path coefficients from a path diagram of background and baseball career factors influencing post-playing occupational achievement. Once again, education was a critical variable in adjustment. Being a well-known player opened doors to all sorts of business opportunities. Over the long haul though, the players' level of post-playing occupational achievement was more related to the traditional factor of education ($r = .41$).

Haerle (1975) also found that 75 percent of the 312 respondents did not begin to consider their post-career life until they were in their early or mid-thirties; that approximately 50 percent reported that they were oriented more toward the past than to the future at the time of their retirement and that the forced decision led to feelings of regret, sadness, and shock at the reality of the aging process. Only 25 percent were future oriented in that they were confident and accepted the inevitable fact of retirement. When asked to comment about the most difficult adjustments they had to make upon retirement, one-third of the respondents stated that they missed the friendships and personal contact they experienced which were lacking in their lives since retirement.

Haerle (1975) also found that those who remained inside baseball as coaches, managers, or scouts had a less stable career pattern in the postplaying years than those who moved into an occupation outside baseball immediately at the conclusion of their playing careers. Additionally, he reported that those who retired as a player at a later

292

age, often ending their career in a lower minor league, were more likely to remain in baseball as a scout, coach, or manager. Thus, for those employed outside baseball, the playing career may have been a stepping stone to a more secure white-collar occupation. McPherson (1980) speculates that those people who have no advanced college education or any non-athletic skills may choose to stay in the sport sub-culture so they do not have to face an identity crisis in the non-athletic world. This is plausible since there has been data (Haerle, 1975) that shows a relationship between advanced college education and postplaying occupational achievement. It is not known though how that affects the athletes' identity.

The previous two studies (Mihovilovic, 1968; Haerle, 1975) are the most widely quoted studies on athletic socio-psychological adjustment to retirement. These studies have confirmed some of the characteristics of an unsuccessful adaptation to retirement mentioned previously. They have also brought another critical variable into the picture. That variable is education. Education is crucial for occupational adjustment, as well as the socio-psychological areas.

Two other studies deem mentioning. Hallden (1965) studied the adjustment of Swedish athletes to retirement. His sample was made up of amateur athletes. They were asked to fill out a Likert-type attitude scale. Each subject was also interviewed individually. Statistical comparisons and conclusions were then made. Out of 61 athletes, 45 athletes were critical of their emotional adjustment. This study did not include statistical analysis (i.e. tests of significance) and no conclusions were drawn.

In an occupational adjustment study (Weinberg and Arond, 1969) done with professional boxers, it was found that the general pattern for boxers after retirement was rapid economic and status descent, often accompanied by severe emotional problems in adjusting to the world outside the boxing subculture. These findings were obtained from data collected in anecdotal interviews with former professional boxers. What was left unstated in this study was specifying the types of emotional problems that boxers experienced and the fact that most professional boxers lack the education that may give them economic stability after re-

tirement. Perhaps just as with baseball players (Haerle, 1975), there is a relationship between education and post-boxing occupational achievement. This may be a research question that deserves further investigation. A future study may investigate the relationship between loss of status and post-boxing career. It seems boxing more than any other sport is subject to adjustment problems. A current example is Muhammed Ali and Joe Frazier coming out of retirement to fight. It may be that, besides the money, boxers miss the status associated with being a champ. An interesting study would be to investigate the relationship between loss of status and adjustment.

In reviewing the previously mentioned studies, the key factors to successful adjustment seem to be education, voluntarily retiring, planning for retirement, acceptance of the loss of the role "athlete," and having institutional and interpersonal supports. Future studies may want to study the relationship between state of health (i.e. disabling injuries), athlete's self-concept, and socioeconomic status as it relates to psychosocial adjustment. With the burgeoning salary structure in professional sports becoming commonplace, a study relating socioeconomic status with positive adjustment might prove or disprove the adage that money cannot buy happiness. Also, study of the adjustment factors present in the high school and college amateur athlete when they have to leave sports is needed. Research on the female athlete, of which there is none at the present time, becomes more important as female athletes become more integrated into American sport.

In conclusion, there seems to be evidence (Haerle, 1975) that many athletes are recognizing the importance of an education, the need to invest earnings, and developing off-season careers. Also, many professional sports now have pension and disability programs to protect the retiree in later life. Thus, in the future, the economic and occupational adjustment of athletes may not be as severe as it was in the past. On the other hand, the loss of status and prestige may continue to be psychologically traumatic to those athletes whose self-concepts and self-identities are built from their role as an athlete.

A PROPOSED SOLUTION TO ATHLETES ADAPTATION TO RETIREMENT

As can be seen from the information presented, the athlete is often put in a situation of making the adjustments to the end of his career isolated from other people. He may have to deal with it by himself. The interpersonal support system of his family and close friends may be present, but often times the athlete does not have the support of his professional team or university in making this transition. In the previous discussion (Schlossberg, 1981), the importance of this institutional support was highlighted.

What follows is a proposal for a preretirement counseling program for athletes. It seems the sport industry should provide this service as other professions do. This program needs to start at the university or possibly the high school level. This is where a lot of athletes who have devoted eight to ten years to an athletic career may see it terminated due to injury or by the fact that they are not good enough to continue onward in their career. This may be a stunning revelation for the athlete, but one which has to be confronted so they can get on with their life. Recent evidence (Sowa and Gressard, 1981) has pointed out a lack of vocational maturity regarding career-decision tasks among college athletes as compared to non-athletes. If an athlete lacks adequate career decision-making skills, then it may be predicted that some athletes will have career adjustment problems after their collegiate careers are over. Perhaps these career adjustment problems will precipitate socio-psychological problems. This is conjecture, but it points out the need for some type of preretirement counseling for athletes to prepare them for the transition.

Let me briefly sketch what a preretirement counseling program might consist of for athletes. It could be jointly programmed with the academic advisor's office, and the university's counseling department would provide the counseling services. Who would be referred for counseling? It seems ideal candidates would be those athletes with injuries that are career threatening or ending, and third and fourth year athletes facing the end of their careers. Of course, the program must be flexible enough to include any athlete irregardless of year. The referrals specifically would include those athletes whose grades may be deficient and whose career plans are not clear. Specific behaviors the counselor would look for would be verbalizations of self-doubt, isolative behaviors indicating lack of interpersonal support, and the lack of integrating one's education with some definite career goals. Any of these behaviors may indicate potential adjustment problems.

The goals of the counseling would be to develop problem-solving, decision-making, and self-assessment skills for the purpose of developing internal support systems (i.e. more positive self-image) and external support systems (i.e. increased positive family or peer relationships). These can be developed through self-strategies of reinforcement, self-relaxation, and cognitive restructuring of negative self-statements.

It would seem that to be facilitative the program should also work out of a group model. As has been discussed beforehand (Schlossberg, 1980; Manion, 1976), the importance of interpersonal support during a transitional stage has been seen. The goals of the group would be to be supportive and nurturant of each other, but also learn problem-solving, decision-making, and self-diagnostic skills within the group process. These skills can be taught didactically and experientially in the group (Manion, 1976). As trust develops in the group, the athlete's feeling of isolation dissipates as he/she finds that other fellow athletes share the same types of feelings (i.e. anger, resentment) and experiences.

Specific counseling strategies that would help the athlete need to be elucidated upon further. The purpose of the present paper has not been geared to specificity but in presenting some general ideas needed in a counseling program. Sport industries and institutions need to support their athletes. While people may scoff at that idea because they perceive today's athletes as pampered, it still remains the sports establishment's responsibility to provide help for athletes who are undergoing a transition to the ex-athlete role.

294

REFERENCES

Brammer, L. and Abrego, P. Intervention strategies for coping with transitions. *The Counseling Psychologist.* 1981, *9*(2), 19-32.

Coddington, R. D. and Troxell, J. The effect of emotional factors on football injury rates — A pilot study. *Journal of Human Stress,* 1980, *6*(4), 3-5.

Dimsdale, J. E. The coping behavior of Nazi concentration camp survivors. In R. Moss (Ed), *Human Adaptation: Coping with Life Crises,* Lexington, Mass: Heath, 1976, 182-210.

Haerle, R. Career patterns and career contingencies of Professional Baseball players: An occupational analysis. In D. Ball and J. Loy (Eds) *Sport and Social Order.* Reading Mass: Addison-Wesley, 1975, 457-511.

Hallden, D. Adjustment of athletes after retiring from sports. *Proceedings: International Congress of Psychology and Sports,* 1965.

Heddesheimer, J. Multiple motivations for mid-career changes. *Personnel and Guidance Journal,* 1976, *55*(2), 109-111.

Hill, R. Generic features of families under stress. In H. J. Parad (Ed.) *Crisis Intervention: Selected Readings.* New York: Family Services Association, 1965, 110-124.

Hopson, B. Response to the papers by Schlossberg, Brammer and Abrego. *The Counseling Psychologist,* 1981, *9*(2), 36-39.

Kleiber, D. and Thompson, S. Leisure behavior and adjustment to retirement: Implications for pre-retirement education. *Therapeutic Recreation Journal,* 1980, *14*(2), 5-17.

Leclair, S. Path analysis: An informal introduction. *Personnel and Guidance Journal,* 1981, *59*(10), 643-646.

Lumsden, B. Educational implications of research on retirement. *Educational Gerontology,* 1978, *3,* 375-386.

Manion, U. V. Preretirement counseling: The need for a new approach. *Personnel and Guidance Journal,* 1976, *55*(2), 119-121.

McPherson, B. P. Former professional athletes adjustment to retirement. *The Physician and Sportsmedicine,* 1978, *6*(8), 53-58.

McPherson, B. P. Retirement from professional sport: The process and problems of occupational and psychological adjustment. *Sociology of Sport,* 1980, 126-143.

Mihovilovic, M. The status of former sportsmen. *International Review of Sport Sociology,* 1968, *3,* 73-93.

Peppers, L. Patterns of leisure and adjustment to retirement. *The Gerontologist,* 1976, *16*(5), 441-445.

Schlossberg, N. and Liebowitz. Organizational support systems as buffers to job loss. *Journal of Vocational Behavior,* 1981, *7*(3), 8-16.

Schlossberg, N. A model for analyzing human adaptation to transition. *The Counseling Psychologist,* 1981, *9*(2), 2-18.

Sheldon, R. Self-confidence in preparing for retirement. *The Gerontologist,* 1977, *17*(3), 28-38.

Sowa, C. and Gressard, C. Dimensions of Vocational Maturity and Personal Adjustment among Athletes and Non-Athletes. Unpublished manuscript, 1981.

Weinberg, S. K. and Arond, H. The occupational culture of the boxer. In J. W. Loy and G. S. Kenyon (eds) *Sport, Culture, and Society.* New York: Tte Macmillan Co., 1969.